D0984461

THE LIBYAN OIL INDUSTRY

The Libyan Oil Industry

FRANK C. WADDAMS

The Johns Hopkins University Press
Baltimore and London

First published in the United States of America, 1980, by
The Johns Hopkins University Press, Baltimore, Maryland 21218
First published in Great Britain, 1980, by
Croom Helm Ltd, 2-10 St John's Road, London SW11

Library of Congress Cataloging in Publication Data

Waddams, Frank C
   The Libyan oil industry.

   Bibliography: p. 331
   Includes index.
   1. Petroleum industry and trade — Libya. 2. Petroleum
law and legislation — Libya.   I. Title.
   HD9577.L52W32 1980   338.2'7282'09612 80-13939
   ISBN 0-8018-2431-1

Printed in Great Britain

CONTENTS

ABBREVIATIONS AND ACRONYMS

AFRA, Afra	Average Freight Rate Assessment
AGIP, Agip	Agenzia Generale Italiana Petroliche, SA (subsidiary of ENI)
API°, °	American Petroleum Institute, degrees of gravity
ARCO	Atlantic Richfield Company
B, b, bl, bbl	barrel, barrels
b	billion (one thousand million)
BMA; BMA lira	British Military Administration; BMA currency
BP	British Petroleum Company
btu	British thermal unit (of gas)
c, ¢, US¢	US dollar cent
cf, f³, cf/d	cubic foot: cubic feet daily
cf.	compare
c.i.f.	cost of insurance and freight; the delivered price of cargo at port of destination after sea voyage
CFP	Compagnie Française des Pétroles
d	day
EIU	*Economist Intelligence Unit*
ENI, Eni	Ente Nazionale Idrocarburi
ERAP, Erap	Entreprise de Recherches et d'Activités Petrolières
f, ff	following page, pages
f	foot, feet (see cf. above)
f.o.b.	free on board; the price or cost of cargo delivered on board ship at export point
GDP, GNP	Gross Domestic Product; Gross National Product
INJAZ, Injaz	Arabian Gulf Exploration Company (subsidiary of Libyan National Oil Company)
km, km²	kilometre, square kilometre
£	Pound Sterling
£L	Libyan Pound
LAR	Libyan Arab Republic
LD	Libyan Dinar
LARC	Libyan American Reconstruction Commission
Linoco	The Libyan National Oil Company (1970 and after)
Lipetco	The Libyan General (National) Oil Company (1968-70)

LNG	Liquid Natural Gas (ethane, methane, etc.)
LPDSA	Libyan Public Development and Stabilization Agency
LPG	Liquid Petroleum Gas (butane, propane, etc.)
LRI, LRII	Large Range I, Large Range II: sizes of tanker to which Afra applied
lt	litre
m, mb/d	million, million barrels daily
MEES	*Middle East Economic Survey* (weekly)
n.a.	not available
NGL	Natural Gas Liquids (naphtha)
NOC	The National Oil Company (see Linoco)
OAPEC	Organization of Arab Petroleum Exporting Countries
OPEC	Organization of Petroleum Exporting Countries
passim	in many places
RCC	Revolutionary Command Council
p., pp.	page, pages
p.a.	per annum
PIW	*Petroleum Intelligence Weekly*
PPS	*Petroleum Press Service*, subsequently *Petroleum Economist* (monthly)
sc.	scirelicet: that is to say
sic	quoted as said or printed
Socal	Standard Oil Company of California
T, t, t/d	ton, tons daily, tonnes, tonnes daily
TFP	Temporary Freight Premium
WS	Worldscale

TABLES

FIGURES

Charts and Diagrams

Maps

PREFACE

In 1950 Libya had no known commercial oil. The country became an independent sovereign nation in 1951, and four years later the Government introduced petroleum legislation. Subsequently all the major international oil companies and many others were granted oil concessions. Most concession-holders carried out vigorous exploration programmes and by 1959 several oil accumulations had been discovered, some of which were thereafter rapidly developed.

Production of crude oil began in 1961, and by the end of the decade Libya had become one of the leading oil producers and exporters of the world. For a few months in 1969 and 1970 exports reached an average of 3½ million barrels a day. From this high level there was a decline of production to a low point of 800,000 barrels a day in early 1975, since when it has recovered to 2 million barrels a day.

This book describes the growth and progress of the Libyan Oil industry, and in particular three aspects of it:

(1) relations between the Libyan governments and the concessionary oil companies;
(2) the impact of Libyan oil and events in Libya on the petroleum markets of Europe and the world;
(3) the response of the Libyan economy to the development of its oil industry.

It comprises three clearly defined and separate periods. The first, from 1950 to the first export of oil in September 1961, is the subject of Parts I and II. The second, from 1961 to the revolution of 1 September 1969, is dealt with in Parts III and IV. Finally, events after the revolution are covered in the last part, Part V, which brings the story to the end of 1976.

The work was originally prepared as a doctoral thesis. It bears the imprint of such in its lengthy notes and many references which, although perhaps welcome to a scholar, may be tedious to the reader of less academic interest. The latter − indeed any reader − passing by these details of no significance to him may even so from time to time be glad of confirmatory references.

The sketch of the world petroleum industry in the 1950s, inserted as Chapter 2 by way of background to the Libyan narrative, may give enlightenment to some, but annoyance to others who have observed or learned about the same complex facts from a different viewpoint. My view was from the central offices of a major international oil company. Later, in the operations of the oil consortium in Iran, and then as gamekeeper (in oil matters) to the Libyan Government, I saw other facets of the industry. These observations have led me, if not 'to see life steadily and see it whole', at least to some comprehension of the many different aspects of oil, its economics and politics, its causes and events, and their unfolding to the present time. I hope I may pass on some of this experience to the reader.

It behoves me above all to acknowledge a debt to Prof. Edith Penrose, who supervised my studies and helped them with her counsel, great learning and deep understanding of the subject; to Mr Ken Miller, Eastern Hemisphere Editor of *Petroleum Intelligence Weekly*, whose unsurpassed knowledge of events of the oil industry and of Libya has been continuously at my disposal; and to Mr J.E. Hartshorn, who made valuable comments on the text leading to its improvement. Needless to say, all statements of fact or opinion are my own. I wish also to express my gratitude to Sue Lloyd-Evelyn, who accomplished single-handed all the secretarial and typing work involved, and to Siân Cardy, for her assistance with the diagrams and maps. Finally, the Polytechnic of Central London, and particularly its School of Management Studies, afforded me some abatement of my normal duties to enable me to complete the work; for this relief much thanks.

F.C. Waddams
London

Part I:
THE BACKGROUND — LIBYA AND THE
INTERNATIONAL PETROLEUM INDUSTRY IN
THE 1950s

1 THE POLITICAL AND ECONOMIC STRUCTURE OF LIBYA

1.1 The Political Background

Libya became an independent sovereign state on 24 December 1951. The gathering together of a vast area of 1,760,000 square kilometres into one state owed more to history than to the rationale of geographical or economic unity. The new country, with an Arabic-speaking Muslim population of around one million, comprised two areas of agricultural and pastoral development — the Gefara or coastal plain of Tripolitania and the plateau region of Cyrenaica, Jebel Akhdar, the latter together with its coastal strip (see Map 1.1). These are separated from each other by 400 miles of desert. The whole of the hinterland is desert, with scattered oases; the caravan routes between them, before the advent of the aeroplane, formed the sole internal communication. The southern frontiers, bounded by the former French colonial territories of Niger and Chad, are defined but not demarcated, as is also the boundary with Sudan in the south-east. The same applies to much of the eastern boundary with Egypt, and the western with Algeria and Tunisia.

The new 'United Kingdom of Libya' was established as a federal state with three constituent provinces of Tripolitania, Cyrenaica and the Fezzan, this last comprising the desert oases south of Tripolitania. In ancient times the two coastal provinces had different histories. Tripolitania was first colonised by the Phoenicians centred on what is now Tunisia, Cyrenaica by the Greeks. They both subsequently became part of the Roman Empire during the first century BC but continued to live separate existences throughout the Roman period.

It was not until the middle of the nineteenth century that some sort of political unity of Cyrenaica and Tripolitania, including the Fezzan, was established under Turkish hegemony. This was maintained during the Italian colonial period, which began with the invasions of 1911 and 1912, and lasted until the second world war. The Italian administration formally unified the different territories in 1934 into the colony of Libya.

After the war Tripolitania and Cyrenaica were for a time under British military administration, and the Fezzan under French. The United Kingdom of Libya came into being in accordance with a decision taken by the General Assembly of the United Nations in 1949. On

21

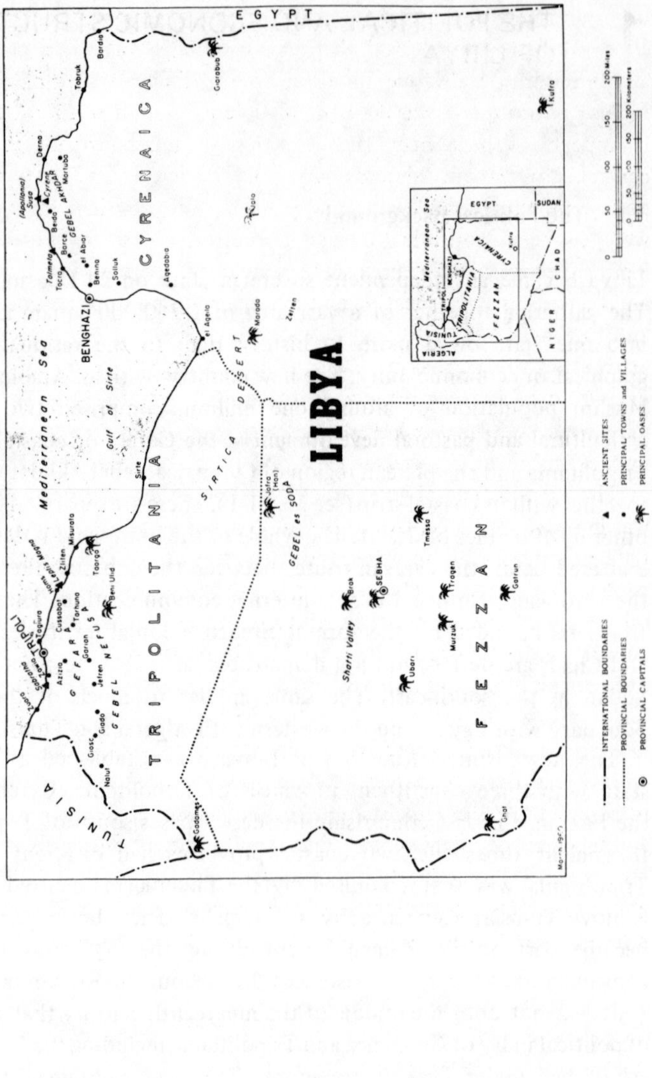

Map 1.1: Libya : Political

its establishment Libya was endowed with a constitutional monarchy, Emir Mohammed Idris al Senussi becoming King. The constitution attributed the legislative function to the federal authority, and the federal government was to control defence and foreign affairs. While it appears to have been the intention of the constitution that the central government should have sole responsibility in determining policy in fiscal and economic matters, the provincial governments were to be responsible for their execution. These federal authorities included control of banks and companies, income tax, monopolies and concessions, prospecting and mining, shipping and navigation, ports and civil aviation.[1] Residual powers were vested in the Provinces. The attribution of law-making and policy-making to one authority and its execution to another resulted in some administrative confusion, which may well have impaired the efficacy of early development and had its impact on the administration of the petroleum law and regulations.

The Libyan federal government, under the leadership of King Idris, was in every way receptive to the approaches by western concerns to initiate a search for oil, more especially by European and American oil companies. The benefits to be gained from the discovery and development of oil were likely to be on a scale hitherto outside the reach of such a poor country. Nationalism in the early 1950s, in the form of antagonism to overseas undertakings in industry and commerce, had not yet developed. So, at a time when in other countries, such as Iran, Indonesia, Venezuela, Mexico and Brazil, there had already been antipathy to and conflict with overseas oil companies, to the point of expropriation and exclusion in some cases, the Government of Libya was ready to give every encouragement to them to come, explore for and obtain oil from Libya on terms highly attractive to the companies. The Minerals Law of 1953, granting survey and exploration facilities, was passed less than two years after independence, and the Petroleum Law of 1955 within four years.

1.2 The Economy

A census taken in 1954 with the help of the United Nations gave a total population of 1,100,000, of whom 738,000 were living in Tripolitania, 291,000 in Cyrenaica and 59,000 in the Fezzan. Three-quarters of the population were classified as settled and the remainder as nomadic or semi-nomadic. One-quarter of the settled population was concentrated in the two main cities of Tripoli (130,000) and Benghazi (70,000). The proportion of nomads was highest in Cyrenaica (45 per cent of the total population) and lowest in the Fezzan (10 per cent).

Of the whole area of the country not more than 10 per cent could be put to productive use owing to lack of water; and only 1 per cent was suitable for settled cultivation. Even so, on the basis of the existing population this provided about 4 acres of cultivable land per inhabitant, which is high in relation to land being cultivated in most Middle East countries.

Agriculture and animal husbandry always have been and must clearly continue to be one of the mainstays of the Libyan economy, and there is enough land and water, if properly conserved, to supply a considerably larger farming population than at present at a higher standard of living.[2]

At the time of independence there were a number of small factory industries clustered for the most part around Tripoli, established and managed by Italians. They included flour-milling, olive-oil-refining, tobacco and salt manufacture (both state monopolies), textiles, footwear and clothing, vehicle repairs, printing, fish processing, soap manufacture, the canning of fruit and vegetables and the manufacture of beer, wine and soft drinks. Factory industries employed 15,000-20,000 people and contributed one-tenth of the GDP.

Early in 1952 a national currency – the Libyan pound – was created to replace previous moneys – the Egyptian pound in Cyrenaica, BMA lire in Tripolitania and Algerian francs in the Fezzan. This pound was fixed at par with sterling and the initial issue was provided with 100 per cent sterling backing by the British Government. The Libyan pound maintained its parity with sterling until the latter's devaluation in 1967. This arrangement, besides providing a comparatively stable money for Libya, which was of great value in its early years of development, greatly facilitated the financing and payment of oil company operations, since foreign payments were easily made through London, which provided ample transfer facilities to and from most parts of the world, and more particularly afforded a channel for the transfer of funds by the US oil companies as their activities in Libya grew. Foreign concerns, including oil companies, were not permitted to borrow money in Libya.

The National Bank of Libya was established in 1956 to replace the Libyan Currency Commission, and maintained close relations with the Bank of England, Libya being a member of the Sterling Area. In the 1950s all commercial banks in Libya were branches of foreign banking institutions; three had their head offices in Italy, two in Great Britain, and one each in Egypt, Jordan and France.

Figures for the national income are available for the first time for 1957, when the GDP was estimated at £L45 million – approximately

Table 1.1: Expenditures on Gross Domestic Product and Imports, 1957/8 (£L millions)

(1)	Private consumption expenditure (1957)	28.3
(2)	Government consumption expenditure (1957/8)	12.0
(3)	Fixed capital formation in public sector (1957/8)	5.0
(4)	Private fixed capital formation (1958)	3.5
(5)	Exports and re-exports of goods (1957)	5.2
(6)	Exports of services (1957)	
	(a) foreign government expenditure in Libya	10.7
	(b) oil company expenditure in Libya	4.1
	(c) other	1.7
(7)	Total expenditure on gross domestic product and imports	70.5
(8)	Less imports of goods and services (1957)	25.5
(9)	Gross domestic product at factor cost	45.0

Source: World Bank Mission, *The Economic Development of Libya* (Johns Hopkins University Press, Baltimore, 1960).

£L41 *per capita* (Table 1.1).

In public finance, the first year for which reliable data are available is the financial year from April 1954 to March 1955 (Table 1.2). They indicate total revenues of some £L11 million, of which half came from external assistance. Expenditures of under £L9 million left a substantial surplus, which was repeated in each of the next five years except 1956/7. Less than half the domestic revenues of £L5.5m accrued to the federal government, the source of which was almost entirely customs duties, with a small amount from posts and telecommunications and other stamp taxes. The main sources of the provincial revenues were income taxes, tobacco and salt monopolies and sugar-trading. In the five years subsequent to 1954/5 public revenues doubled in a steady progression; these increases were attributable in almost equal proportion to domestic sources and overseas assistance.

In overseas payments Libya showed a favourable balance on current account during the five years 1954-58 (Table 1.3). The balance of trade was substantially adverse, but this was offset throughout the period by military expenditures and official donations from overseas. During these years the widening gap between exports, which increased by only a small amount, and imports, which doubled, was made good by increasing foreign contributions and, from 1957 onwards, by rising expenditures of oil companies on exploration. The result was that the foreign exchange holdings of the National Bank of Libya rose from

Table 1.2: Public Revenues and Expenditure in Libya, 1954/5—1958/9
(£L'000: fiscal year beginning April)

	1954/5	1955/6	1956/7	1957/8	1958/9
Domestic Revenues					
Federal Government	2,561	3,565	4,100	5,090	6,532
Tripolitania	1,784	2,243	2,605	2,986	3,709
Cyrenaica	726	774	932	943	1,189
Fezzan	40	51	64	94	119
Municipalities	438	428	446	482	500
Total domestic	5,549	7,061	8,147	9,595	12,049
External Assistance					
Grants from United					
Kingdom	3,750	3,750	4,000	4,250	3,250
Grants from United States	1,786	2,500	3,214	6,099	6,785
Loans from United States	—	—	—	1,250	—
Other	105	20	20	470	1,010
Total external	5,641	6,270	7,234	12,069	11,045
Total Revenues	11,190	13,331	15,381	21,664	23,094
Expenditures					
Federal government	1,501	2,120	2,719	3,589	4,948
Tripolitania	3,652	3,805	3,992	4,614	5,008
Cyrenaica	2,062	2,340	2,646	2,751	3,178
Fezzan	398	404	504	635	892
Municipalities	431	408	452	464	500
LARC	—	2,485	4,038	3,851	3,938
LPDSA	753	1,416	1,082	1,127	715
Total Expenditures	8,797	12,978	15,433	17,031	19,179
Surplus or deficit of revenues over expenditure	+2,393	+353	−52	+4,633	+3,915

Source: World Bank Mission, *Economic Development of Libya.*

£L11.5 million in its first years of operation to £L25.4 million at the beginning of 1960 (Table 1.4).

In summary, in its early days, Libya afforded a milieu favourable to oil operations by overseas companies, both politically and economically. The country itself and the regime owed their existence to the Western Allies. After independence, overseas advisers, mostly British — a corollary of the previous British military administration — assisted the Government and the development of the Civil Service at the levels both of policy and administration. A substantial British and American military presence remained, which provided a significant spin-off of consumption expenditures, stimulating the civilian economy. Financial arrangements and the currency tied to sterling, smoothed out the problems of

Table 1.3: Libya's Balance of Payments, 1954-8 (£L million)

	1954	1955	1956	1957	1958
Current Account					
Exports and re-exports, f.o.b.	3.5	4.3	4.0	5.2	4.8
Imports, c.i.f.	11.3	14.3	16.5	22.8	23.9
Trade balance	−7.8	−10.0	−12.5	−17.6	−19.1
Imports of non-monetary gold	n.a.	n.a.	n.a.	−0.5	−0.7
Foreign military expenditures	+5.6	+6.2	+10.8	+9.8	+6.9
Other services (net)[a]	−2.1	−1.3	−4.6	+4.4	+9.7
Balance of goods and services	−4.3	−5.1	−6.3	−3.9	−3.2
Private donations and transfers (net)[b]	−0.5	−0.6	−0.6	−0.8	−1.2
Official donations	+5.1	+8.4	+10.1	+7.5	+9.4
Current account balance	+0.3	+2.7	+3.2	+2.8	+5.0
Capital Account					
Private capital receipts (net)	+1.2	+0.6	+1.3	+1.0	+0.3
Change in net foreign assets of official and banking institutions (increase −)	−2.6	−3.9	−4.5	−4.6	−5.1
Capital account balance (improvement −)	−1.4	−3.3	−3.2	−3.6	−4.8
Errors and omissions	1.1	0.6	−	0.8	0.2

Notes: a. Including oil company expenditures in Libya, which explain the marked
improvement in this item in 1957 and 1958.
b. Mainly outward remittances by Italians resident in Libya.
For continuation after 1958, see Table 11.2.
Source: Government of Libya, Central Statistics Office, quoted by World Bank,
Economic Development of Libya.

international payments. Libya's ties, political and economic, were
entirely with the west, subject only to a qualification in respect of
Egypt, whence came, in the later 1950s, the first indications of nationalism and anti-western sentiment.

1.3 The Beginning of the Search for Oil

So far as geology is concerned, the scattered pieces of direct evidence of
the existence of oil in Libya before the middle 1950s gave little indication of locations where the substantial oil pools were subsequently to
be found. In the nineteenth century several geographical expeditions had
recorded the sedimentary nature of the more accessible parts. The first
known indication of the existence of subsoil hydrocarbons was of a
trace of methane gas in the neighbourhood of Tripoli, obtained during
the drilling of a water well in 1914.

Table 1.4: Foreign Exchange Holdings of the National Bank, 1957-60
(£L'000, end of March)

	1957	1958	1959	1960[b]
Issue Department				
Foreign government securities	4,622	5,587	7,497	7,848
Deposits with foreign banks	1,495	1,500	545	1,944
Total (equivalent to currency in circulation)	6,117	7,187	8,042	9,792
Banking Department				
Foreign currency notes	3	14	9	19
Balances with overseas banks[a]	724	2,176	5,223	8,165
Foreign government and other securities	4,614	7,947	6,400	7,393
Total	5,341	10,137	11,632	15,577
Total holdings of National Bank	11,458	17,324	19,674	25,369

Notes: a. Including net claims on National Bank of Egypt under the bilateral
trade and payments agreement — £756,887 at the end of March 1959
and £2,117,395 at the end of January 1960.
b. End of January 1960.
Source: National Bank of Libya, quoted by World Bank, *Economic Development of Libya.*

More indications of both gas and crude oil were found in the same area of the Tripolitania gefara during the 1920s and 1930s. The principal figure in examining the possibilities of oil during this period was Professor Ardito Desio of Turin University. He published a geographical map of the country in 1933,[3] and by 1934 a surface geological survey was completed under his direction. In 1937 the Italian State oil concern AGIP[4] sent out a survey team. In conjunction with Desio a map of the country was drawn up, dividing it into 12 zones, the Sirtica basin being considered the most favourable area for the existence of oil in the ground.

The events of the second world war delayed further progress in these matters, and this delay was prolonged during the period of military administration which followed the war. The British in Cyrenaica and Tripolitania, and the French in the Fezzan, administered the country on a 'care and maintenance' basis, in accordance with the Hague rules established in 1907. This precluded the grant to any overseas interest of survey facilities or concession rights. Indeed, in 1947, a three-man survey team sent by Standard Oil of New Jersey, after study of the Italian documents on the subject, was required to leave the country by the British military administration.

By the early 1950s it was known that much of the country was underlain by sedimentary rocks. The tertiary cover in the north of the country was pierced by cretaceous windows, and the whole area was expected to be underlain by older mezozoic and palaeozoic formations.[5] All the major international oil companies,[6] with the exception of Gulf and five independents, had embarked on survey work under a law of 1953[7] which legitimised reconnaissance for minerals to be carried out under permit. Their reconnaissance studies showed large anticlinal structures thought to be particularly promising in two areas — the extreme north of Cyrenaica and north-western Tripolitania (see Map 1.1). The former area was subsequently acquired by Libyan-American and the latter by Compagnie des Pétroles Total (Libye), a subsidiary of CFP, which was already operating in adjacent Tunisia.

At the end of 1955 substantial oil was found at Edjele, in Algeria, contiguous to the Libyan border. This directed attention to the area of Libya next to this border, and Concession No. 1 was granted to Esso Standard Libya covering this part. The first drilling operations, begun in 1956, were carried out by Libyan-American in northern Cyrenaica and by Esso in Western Libya. The former drilled three dry holes, and the latter, though finding some oil, adjudged it far too insignificant to justify commercial development in view of the logistics of this far-away place of difficult terrain even for the Libyan desert.

This account of early exploration activities confirms — if confirmation were needed — that the oil companies have no prescience of where ultimately they are going to find substantial oil resources. The search for oil is conducted anywhere in the world where geology, terrain and political climate are favourable. The only way to establish the existence of commercial oil is to drill for it in hopeful locations. To set up drilling activities, especially in remote places, is immensely costly. In 1956 oil company expenditures for Libya amounted to £L4.5m., although only one well had yet been drilled. By 1959 they had increased to £L35m. In none of the areas orginally considered most promising had exploration been successful, and it was not until 1958 that attention was to be concentrated on the Sirtica basin, culminating in Esso's Zelten discovery in June 1959. Before this over 50 exploration wells had been drilled and found to be dry or to contain hydrorcabons inadequate for commercial development, at a total exploration and drilling cost of some £L50 million.[8]

In summary, the causes of the progress made in prospecting for oil after independence in 1951 are not difficult to identify. Large untested areas with a favourable geology; a hospitable and encouraging regime which quickly afforded overseas oil interests facilities to survey in the Minerals Law of 1953, and followed this by the Petroleum Law of

1955; granting favourable terms for exploration and production; and a wealth of international technical talent backed by firms bent on securing and improving their future supplies of oil to meet the requirements of an expanding market, or, as was the case with new-comers, to undertake overseas expansion.

In addition to these factors, there were many technical advances in transportation, logistics and communications made during the war years. The application of these methods materially improved the efficiency and effectiveness of field operations in the Libyan desert, and enabled them to be conducted in remote areas hitherto inaccessible, as well as to give hope that, if oil were discovered in distant parts, the possibilities of successful commercial development would be greater than before. New and improved geophysical techniques, such as common-depth-point seismic mapping and controlled seismic energy input, substantially increased geophysical resolving power. With such favourable political, economic, technical and commercial circumstances, if oil were there, it was only a matter of time before it was discovered, developed and used.

Notes

1. Articles 36-39 of the Libyan Constitution.
2. World Bank Mission, *The Economic Development of Libya* (Johns Hopkins University Press, Baltimore, 1960), p. 28.
3. No further geological map was published until 1964, when the US Geological Survey did so with the aid of contributions from oil companies.
4. Agenzia Generale Italiana Petroliche.
5. D.B. Eiches, 'Libya' in *A History of Exploration for Petroleum* (American Association of Petroleum Geologists, 1975), p. 1438.
6. The following companies obtained reconnaissance permits:

Mobil	CFP	Continental
Esso	Amoseas (Socal & Texaco)	Bunker Hunt
Shell	Oasis (Marathon)	Libyan American
BP	Amerada	(Texas Gulf Producing Co.)

For a more detailed description of the majors, see Chapter 2, section 2.2.

7. Mineral Law No. 9 of 1953 (published in *Official Gazette*, 18 Sept. 1953).
8. Ministry of Petroleum Affairs, *Petroleum Development in Libya, 1954-1964* (Tripoli, 1965), which gives the following figures of annual expenditures of oil companies for their Libyan operations.

	£L millions	US$ millions
1956	4.5	12.6
1957	13.5	37.8
1958	24	67.2
1959	35	98.0
1960	61	170.8
1961	72	201.6
1962	87	243.6
1963	106	296.8

2 THE WORLD PETROLEUM INDUSTRY AND THE MARKETS FOR OIL IN THE POST-WAR PERIOD UNTIL 1960

2.1 Introduction

For this study a description of the state of the world petroleum industry is germane to the extent that it throws light on petroleum development in Libya, and particularly on the decisions of the oil companies and others to take concessions, spend money on exploration and, when successful, to undertake the development of commercial oil.

The main features of the scene as it was in 1950 are well known. Outside North America and the Communist sphere of influence, the large discovered oil resources, mostly in the Middle East countries bordering on the Arabian Gulf, were owned and operated, through concession contracts with host governments, by a handful of major international oil companies.[1] The markets for oil products in most of the consuming countries were dominated by these same companies. They were fully integrated in the sense that they searched for and produced their own crude oil, transported it by pipeline and tanker from producing to consuming centres, refined it and marketed the refined products. Integration of the oil companies, developed over a long period, reflected overwhelmingly an urge to obtain secure and low-cost supplies of crude oil for markets or, conversely, assured market outlets for supplies of crude oil.

2.2 The Ownership and Corporate Structure of the International Oil Industry after the Second World War

The principal groups of companies operating in the international oil industry after the second world war, identified by the name of the parent organisation, were as follows:

Standard Oil Company of New Jersey: This USA company was the largest of the progeny of the Standard Oil Company, dismantled in 1911, and also the world's largest oil group in size of production, assets, sales and profits. It was the parent company of the Esso

31

organisations throughout the world and was normally called 'Esso', by which name it will generally be referred to here. The parent company changed its name to 'Exxon' in 1972.

Shell Transport and Trading Company/Royal Dutch Petroleum Company: The merger of these two groups in 1907 gave rise to the Royal Dutch/Shell Group, normally known as Shell. Neither the Royal Dutch/Shell Group, nor 'Shell', are juridical entities. The shareholdings of the subsidiary and operating companies are owned by the two parent holding companies, one British and the other Dutch, in such a manner as to ensure Royal Dutch a 60 per cent interest and Shell Transport a 40 per cent interest in all the operations of the Shell companies throughout the world. In size of operations world-wide this group was at the time, and still is, a close second to Esso; if North American operations are excluded, on many counts it was the equal of Esso.

Socony Vacuum Oil Company: Another USA offshoot of the old Standard Oil Company. It has changed its name to Mobil Oil Corporation and is referred to as 'Mobil'.

The Texas Company: A US company which subsequently changed its name to Texaco Inc. and is normally referred to as 'Texaco'.

Standard Oil Company of California: A US company, also, as its name implies, a successor to part of the old Standard Oil Company; abbreviated as 'Socal', and also, more recently, called 'Chevron'.

Gulf Oil Corporation: A US company, referred to as 'Gulf'.

Anglo-Iranian Oil Company: A British company, in which the UK Government has usually held a majority interest. Its name has been changed to British Petroleum, and it is normally referred to as BP.

Compagnie Française des Pétroles (CFP): A French company, with a minority shareholding of the French Government. Its subsidiary companies usually incorporate the word 'Total' in their title. This company is not normally classified with the previous seven as a 'major', but cannot be omitted from the list because of its interests in Iraq, Iran, Qatar and, later, Abu Dhabi.

In 1950 these eight groups of companies between them held title to 99.4 per cent of the crude oil produced in the major oil exporting countries of the world outside North America and the Communist sphere.

The production operations in the Middle Eastern countries were joint ventures of two or more of these companies, and from these countries came more than half of the total crude oil production of the world outside North America and the Soviet sphere, Venezuela accounting for most of the rest.

The shares of the companies in the oil production of the Middle East, Venezuela and Indonesia in 1950 are given in Table 2.2. In four out of five of the Middle Eastern oil producing countries of the time — Iraq, Qatar, Kuwait and Saudi Arabia — there was an operating company or companies set up jointly by the concession-holders, who were the sole shareholders, to work the concessions (see Table 2.1 below). In the fifth — Iran — Anglo-Iranian was the sole concessionaire in 1950, but in 1951 was expelled. In 1954 its place was taken by the Iranian Consortium, whose participants are also given in Table 2.1. The shareholders financed the operations and owned the oil produced in proportion to their shareholdings.

Table 2.1: Ownership of Principal Middle Eastern Concessions, 1950

Country: Operating Company:	Iraq and Qatar Iraq Petroleum Company Basra, Mosul & Qatar Petro- leum Com- panies		Saudi Arabia Arabian Ameri- can Oil Com- pany (Aramco)		Kuwait Kuwait Oil Company		Iran (1954) Iranian Oil Operating Companies	
Shareholding Companies:	Shell	23¾%	Esso	30%	Gulf	50%	BP	40%
	BP	23¾%	Texaco	30%	BP	50%	Shell	14%
	CFP	23¾%	Socal	30%			Socal	7%
	Esso	11⅞%	Mobil	10%			Esso	7%
	Mobil	11⅞%					Gulf	7%
	Gulben- kian	5%					Mobil	7%
							Texaco	7%
							CFP	6%
							US-Inde- pendents	5%

Independents[2] made their appearance in Iran in 1955 and in the

Arabian Gulf at about the same time (the American Independent Oil Company (Aminoil) obtained the Kuwaiti interest in the Kuwaiti-Saudi Neutral Zone in 1948, Getty the Saudi interest in 1949 and the (Japanese) Arabian Oil Company the off-shore Neutral Zone interest in 1957).

Gulbenkian's 5 per cent interest in Iraq and Qatar is not normally classified as an independent interest, since he was a 'sleeping participant': the major shareholders were obligated to buy his share of oil at full price and dispose of it in their own downstream operations.

In Indonesia there were two joint production operations — Caltex (50 per cent Socal, 50 per cent Texaco) and Stanvac (50 per cent Esso, 50 per cent Mobil). Shell operated on its own.

In Venezuela, although virtually all oil production was then in the hands of the majors, they each had separate production operations. The ownership of the crude oil produced in the world outside North America and the Soviet sphere in the years 1950 and 1957 was as shown in Table 2.2. These figures show that in 1950 all Middle East production (excluding Gulbenkian in Iraq and Qatar), and virtually all the remainder of the crude oil produced in the world excluding North America, Eastern Europe and Russia, were controlled and owned by the eight major internationals. By 1957 the proportion owned by others than the majors had risen to 8 per cent. This was accounted for by growing production of independents in Iran, the Saudi Arabia/Kuwait Neutral Zone and Venezuela.

2.3   The System and Methods of Operation

In order to judge the extent to which the markets for oil were influenced by the behaviour expected of such an industry structure, a description in broad outline of the companies' methods of operating their integrated business, of their pricing practices and of their actions in pursuit of the goal common to all business activity of profit-making will be given below.

Exploration for, development and production of crude oil was conducted by an operating company or companies under the control of the participant shareholding companies, who authorised these activities by agreement between themselves. In effect, the participant oil companies obtained their equity shares of crude oil at cost from the operating companies, whatever the accounting procedures involved. They funded the operating companies for their capital and operating

Table 2.2: Major Oil Company Crude Oil Production outside North America 1950 and 1957 thousands of barrels daily

Country	Esso	Mobil	Socal	Texaco	BP	Gulf	Shell	CFP	Others	Total
1950										
Iran	–	16	–	–	665	–	–	–	–	665
Iraq	16	16	–	–	32	–	32	32	8	136
Qatar	4	4	–	–	8	–	8	8	2	34
Kuwait	–	–	–	–	172	172	–	–	–	345
Saudi Arabia	174	58	174	174	–	–	–	–	–	579
Sub-total	194	78	174	174	877	172	40	40	10	1,759
Indonesia, etc.	3	3	16	16	–	–	41	–	–	79
Venezuela	818	48	15	–	–	231	378	–	10	1,500
Total	1,015	129	205	190	877	403	459	40	20	3,338
1957										
Iran	50	50	50	50	289	50	101	43	36	720
Iraq	54	54	–	–	108	–	108	108	22	452
Qatar	16	16	–	–	33	–	33	33	7	138
Kuwait	–	–	–	–	570	570	–	–	–	1,140
Saudi Arabia	297	99	297	297	–	–	–	–	–	990
Others	–	–	–	–	–	–	–	–	230	230
Sub-total	417	219	347	347	1,000	620	241	184	295	3,670
Indonesia, etc.	16	16	87	87	–	–	223	–	–	429
Venezuela	1,150	115	92	45	–	405	751	–	285	2,843
Total	1,583	350	526	479	1,000	1,025	1,215	184	580	6,942

Source: M.A. Adelman: *The World Petroleum Market* (Johns Hopkins University Press, Baltimore, 1972), p. 80.

expenditures and, in the case of all countries but Saudi Arabia, lifted their shares of oil at cost (which had already been advanced to the operating company by the parent organisations) plus a small commission per ton (usually one old shilling). Only in Saudi Arabia they bought the oil from Aramco at posted prices (less discounts), but the difference between this price and cost (including tax cost) returned to the shareholders in the form of dividends. Elsewhere the arrangements with the host government were such that the participant companies were responsible, either through their trading subsidiaries or their operating companies, for paying taxes.[3] Early in the 1950s profits taxes[4] were introduced and came to be defined as the amount which would make total payments to government, including royalties, equal to 50 per cent of the accounting profits of the production operations, revenues for this purpose being based on posted prices less allowable discounts.

The oil lifted from the producing countries by the oil companies was transported by sea, either as crude or refined products, mostly in their own tanker fleets, to the consuming countries. About four-fifths of total supplies were passed on to their refining and/or marketing affiliates in the integrated operations of these companies.[5] The crude refined in or near the country of origin in export refineries – more particularly at the great refinery at Abadan in Iran and, for Venezuela, at the refineries in both the country itself and the off-shore installations of Aruba and Curaçao – was disposed of in a similar manner.

The individual oil companies were at no time in exact balance between their supplies of crude oil and their refining and market requirements for oil products. Some had crude production in excess of their market capacity (as BP), while for others market capacity was in excess of their crude availability (as Shell). There were thus company imbalances between crude oil production and product markets, and in addition there were imbalances of supply in geographical areas and of qualities of oil required by markets. Crude oil from different sources, and even from the same country, varied widely in gravity, waxiness and sulphur content, all of which had to be tailored by each company to suit the requirements of its markets. There was thus a substantial business of exchange between the oil companies, as well as of sales and purchases of crude oil, and these transactions were conducted in accordance with contractual agreements of long-term or short-term duration as between principals acting in a commercial manner. The companies nevertheless sold their products in the final markets in competition with each other, except in the case of the joint marketing operations mentioned below.

The tanker fleets in which the oil was transported were for the most part controlled and managed by the oil companies. The companies varied widely in their policies of percentage ownership of their tanker fleets, which could be as low as 20 per cent and as high as 50 per cent. The remainder was chartered, some on a 'bare-bottom' basis, the rest on long-term or medium-term charters. The companies strove to cover all their transport requirements in this way, leaving only a 1 or 2 per cent margin, in normal times, to be covered by short-term charter. The costs of owned tankers, and of charters of ships of different sizes and at different times, all varied from each other. The costs, both fixed and incremental, attributable to individual cargoes of oil, or even on the same journeys, varied according to whether the journey was one which included a return trip in ballast, a partial or full back-haul cargo, a dog-leg freight, partial loads or multiple-port unloading, or were part of a complex journey involving a number of freights from different origins and to different destinations. Thus, though the cost of freight was an integral and important part of the pricing of crude oil and oil products at destination, it made no commercial sense to attempt to calculate the true costs per barrel for each individual shipment to use in the price build-up. Fluctuating freight prices for each shipment, moreover, would be embarrassing and even unacceptable to the buyer, whether a refining affiliate of the seller or a third party.

At the refineries in consuming countries oil of different gravities and qualities and from different origins was blended in order to provide the mix most suitable for the product requirements of the markets which the refinery served, whether these were domestic or export. In many countries the refineries were jointly owned by more than one oil company, and many more had contractual processing arrangements with other oil companies. As with the crude oil production operations already described, in the former cases each participant contributed his share of refining costs, and took the same share of the refined products, imbalances being compensated between the companies concerned by contractual arrangements incorporating, for accounting purposes, bench-mark values for the products.[6] Since crude oil when refined yields joint products – principally gasolines, kerosenes, gas oil and fuel oil – in proportions which cannot be varied greatly from a barrel of crude charge, it is not possible to calculate a 'true' cost for an individual product, or to price it on a cost, or cost plus, basis.[7] Some of the refinery products were passed on to the company's chemical operations or sold to others as feedstock; the former did not involve a market price, but only a transfer price within the company itself. As in the case of crude oil, there were many exchange arrangements involving oil products 'at refinery gates' between the major oil companies and in different geographical areas, as well as inter-company sales and purchases.

The refined products were for the most part passed to the marketing organisations for sale to consumers in the company's markets. It was at this point of sale, and only at this point, that the bulk of a company's revenues were earned. In the 1950s there were still, in many parts of the world, joint marketing companies formed by two or more oil companies, and it was in these that cartel selling arrangements were manifested. The most notable joint marketing companies were Shell-Mex and BP in the United Kingdom, in which Shell, BP and originally Mexican Eagle Oil Company (by then Eagle Oil and Shipping, later absorbed by Shell) participated in the ratio approximately of 40:40:20. Throughout much of Africa, Shell and BP conducted 50:50 marketing operations under the aegis of the Consolidated Petroleum Company and its subsidiaries. In Pakistan and India there were joint marketing companies of Shell and Burmah Oil Company (Burmah-Shell). Throughout most of the Eastern Hemisphere Socal and Texaco conducted both joint refinery and joint marketing operations under the name of Caltex.

The joint marketing operations normally specified a percentage supply right for each participant, although the selling, particularly through the petrol pumps, was frequently done by one of the companies in its own name. For instance, in the UK, where Shell pumps and BP pumps have for long been segregated, the pumps might be supplied with either Shell-refined or BP-refined products according to the logistics and economics of refinery availabilities and locations, and transportation from refinery to distribution depot and selling point. But whatever the proportion in which the two companies' oil products were bought by consumers, the supply and proceeds of sale were attributed to each company according to the contractual percentage share rights to supply of the companies. Imbalances in the actual supply proportions of the companies were compensated between the companies by internal accounting payments and exchanges. Such arrangements implied a uniform selling price as between the joint companies, which would eliminate any competition in the markets between them, but might be subject to pressure from other oil companies, with whom they were in competition. Most of these joint marketing operations have now broken up.[8]

2.4   Costing and Pricing of Crude Oil and Oil Products

For the oil companies it was neither practicable nor commercially expedient to establish prices for crude oil on a cost or cost-plus basis. The expression of cost most frequently used by oil company decision-makers at that time was an accounting measurement of the full cost of the crude, usually on an annual basis. However, the cost per barrel in a single country during the period of a year, calculated in this manner, can vary by a factor of three or four in accordance with, on the one hand, allocation of sunk and on-going costs of exploration, drilling and development in a heavily front-end loaded investment situation; and on the other with the amount of oil produced during the period. Both the numerator and the denominator of this expression are subject to such wide variation that it can give little indication of the long-run economic cost of crude oil.[9] The problems of dealing with unrequited exploration expenditure and overheads in other parts of the world, and of inflation, baffle any attempt by a company to identify the current or replacement cost of a barrel of crude produced in an individual country, at least for pricing purposes.

The oil companies, being few in number and operating jointly in the production of oil, were able to establish a stable pricing system for crude oil without overt collaboration (which would have attracted unwelcome attention for some companies under the US anti-trust laws). This was accomplished by posting prices, i.e. publishing prices at which the posting company was willing to sell crude oil to third-party buyers at point of export from the producing country. The prices chosen were not related to production costs, but loosely to the cost to a buyer of alternative supplies delivered in a principal market.

The level of posted prices in the Middle East, at the time of their initiation in the early 1950s, was derived from a 'net-back formula'[10] — a phrase used to describe the calculation which intended to equate the price of Middle East oil delivered to New York or North-West Europe with that of Gulf of Mexico or Caribbean oil at the same point of delivery. If New York were used as delivery point, the delivered price of Gulf of Mexico/Caribbean oil c.i.f. New York was taken, and from it was deducted a freight from Middle East export point to New York in order to establish a price f.o.b. export terminal in the Arabian Gulf.[11]

In this calculation, the freight rate chosen was critical in the calculation of the Middle East export price, and freight rates were prone to substantial fluctuation. The oil company interest, at the time of initiating Middle East postings, was to maintain as high a price as could be defended, for reasons which are described below. The prices established were clearly far above the costs of production, whatever method might be used in their estimation.

The first Arabian Gulf posting was $1.71 per barrel, by Mobil, for 34° Arabian oil ex Ras al Tanura in 1950. The freight rates used in the calculation leading to this posting and the values of quality differentials are not publicly known. But having once published an Arabian Gulf price the other oil companies with Saudi Arabian oil followed suit and those concerned with exports from other Middle East export points (including the Mediterranean terminals of oil from Iraq and Saudi Arabia) used this price as a bench-mark for posting their own prices, making allowance for different points of export and differences in gravity and quality.

In the markets for oil products, the major oil companies' control was less complete because of independent refiners,[12] and of growing supplies from the Communist countries to Western Europe.[13] Nevertheless they retained a predominant influence, since the independent refiners purchased the bulk of their supplies of crude oil from the majors, most on long-term contract. The companies posted prices for products, beginning in the Caribbean in 1950, and extending the practice to the Far East in 1955 and the Middle East in 1957. The Caribbean postings followed closely those of the USA. Product postings closely reflected the changes in crude postings in the same localities up to 1960, after which the latter stabilised[14] as a result of pressure from the newly formed Organisation of Petroleum Exporting Countries.

The list prices for bulk products in consuming countries were based – in the integrated oil companies – on the charges made by the company to its affiliates in the receiving country for the crude oil delivered, to which were added the costs of refining. At the beginning of the period the value of the oil as invoiced by the oil company to its refining affiliate in the countries of Western Europe was normally, in the case of crude, posted price plus freight from export point to destination; and in the case of products to marketing organisations 'Low of Platts'[15] plus freight from Netherlands West Indies to destination, before postings were inaugurated in the Arabian Gulf; afterwards, posted price plus freight to destination.

The pricing of freight based on costs of individual shipments also presented problems, and a system was evolved by which the oil companies charged their affiliates in consuming countries a calculated average freight rate set, at that time every six months, by an independent London Tanker Brokers' Panel. This rate, known as AFRA

(Average Freight Rate Assessment) in and after 1954, was intended, as its name implies, to be a statement of the average prices of new charters, of different size ships and varying lengths of time, made in the preceding period.[16] It thus avoided the wild fluctuations of the spot market which sometimes occurred. AFRA itself was subject to significant fluctuations over the years, and was particularly affected by the closing of the Suez Canal toward the end of 1956 (see Chart 2.1) and again in 1967. The fluctuations had a profound influence on oil prices in consuming countries which, in the case of crude, consisted of two elements — a price for the oil itself and a price for the transportation of the oil to destination. The freight element not only had great significance in the final prices of oil, but also in oil company profits, since AFRA fluctuated within wide limits, while a company's own transportation costs in normal times changed more slowly (consisting as they did of the costs of its owned fleet plus substantially long-term chartered tankers).[17]

Chart 2.1: Tanker Freight Rates, 1954-9

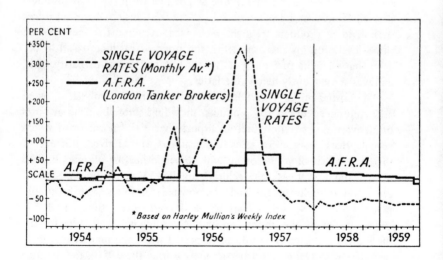

Source: *Petroleum Press Service* (August 1959).
For an explanation of 'Scale' see note 16.

Thus the final list prices of oil products in the markets (before modi-

fication by discount etc. imposed by market conditions) were built
up from:

(1) a posted price for crude which, in the Arabian Gulf, was many
    times higher than cost of production;
(2) a freight charge, which bore only a tenuous relationship to the
    oil companies' real shipping costs (but could be, and was at
    times, below these costs in periods of low freight rates, as well
    as far above them when freights were high);
(3) refining costs which for pricing purposes were calculated by
    accounting methods as so much per barrel of crude input or
    composite products output;
(4) marketing and distribution costs.

It was at the final point of sale that market influences made themselves
felt. If, for instance, the demand for middle distillates was strong, the
pattern of products turned out by the refinery would result in a surplus
of gasoline, the price of which would have to be lowered to dispose of
excess supplies; at the same time the price of gas oil would harden.
Similarly with kerosenes and fuel oils, the objective of the companies
being to achieve as much revenue as possible from the joint products
derived from a barrel of crude oil.[18] The relationships between prices
of individual products frequently changed. At export refinery posted
price level, for instance, in 1952 the price of gasoline was 130 per
cent that of light fuel oil, but by 1961 it had fallen to parity with,
and was subsequently below, the latter.

   The posted prices for crude and products, and the published, listed
and announced prices for products, including ships' bunkers at ports
of delivery and aviation fuel at airports, were the norm from which
actual prices charged for sales to consumers were derived. But except
in the retail gasoline, kerosene and domestic heating oil markets, the
posted and list prices were seldom equalled by actual prices. Sales of
crude oil to independent and state-owned refineries were invariably
made in bulk by period contract, and even during the early 1950s
those of which the terms are publicly known showed substantial
discounts on posted prices during a period when the market was firm.
As sales of crude to third parties grew during the 1950s, the practice
spread of giving hidden discounts in the form of freight rebates, and
even absorption of freight over long hauls by the seller in sales of
crude to third parties. In the product markets all bulk purchases by
customers, whether for bunkers, aviation, power production, industrial

use or transport, were by period contract in which reductions from list prices, large-quantity discounts, tapering prices and other forms of price abatement were normal. They were influenced primarily by the state of the market as regards both supply and demand and by intense competition between the oil companies. In a functional analysis of oil company profits, during most of the 1950s virtually the whole of the consolidated profits of a company from operations was attributable to the production function. This was because the prices at which the crude oil was transferred to the refining function were far above the costs of its production plus tax payments to producing country governments. Indeed during the less profitable years, the downstream functions of refining and marketing suffered considerable losses on this basis, and the investment in them was regarded as a cost of bringing the oil to market in the form of saleable products derived from the crude, to the production of which the bulk of the profit was attributed.

Thus the large profits in the production function, with its revenues based on posted prices, do not give a reliable picture of oil company total profitability. The companies earned their revenue from sales, not of crude to affiliates, but of oil products to third parties in the markets. To achieve these sales huge investments and unrecovered costs in the downstream functions were required, and these as a rule substantially eroded the high profitability apparent in the production function. Note 28 gives a brief survey of profitability of oil companies' integrated operations in the 1950s.

2.5 The Nature and Structure of the Petroleum Markets

From this analysis we can derive some conclusions about the nature of oil markets at the beginning of the 1950s. The first step in the international oil industry operations was the winning of crude oil by the oil companies. The concessions — the contracts by which the oil was secured by the companies — covered generally the whole country (or at least that part of it containing known oil resources). They lasted for a long time (50-75 years) without escape clauses, and in each producing country were shared by a number of oil companies operating together as a unit. All these factors excluded the possibility of any new entrant bidding for other supplies yet undiscovered in the conceded territory.[19]

The levels of Middle East posted prices for crude oils, begun in 1950, were established (see note 10) by selecting a balancing figure which, taken in conjunction with an ephemeral freight rate, equated the price of Middle East oil with US Gulf oil, both delivered (at that time) at New York. The prices posted signified a price at which the posting company offered to supply the oil to all comers. Since each company needed most of its planned production for its own downstream operations, it would be unlikely to pitch the price at so low a level as to cause embarrassment to its own supply arrangements and invite damaging competition in its product markets by attracting third party customers. Moreover, its ability to provide extra oil by producing more was inhibited, in the short run at least, by its off-take agreements with its partners in the producing concession, as well as by the physical limitations to the capacity of the producing oilfields.

Another reason for the pitching of initial posted prices high is to be found in the US tax system. This effectively made the level of income tax paid in overseas producing countries (calculated as 50 per cent of revenue at posted prices less allowable costs), if not a matter of indifference, certainly of less importance in the US consolidation of accounts than it might have been. US companies were liable to US taxation on the profits of their overseas subsidiaries, but received a tax credit for similar taxes paid, in this case, by the producing subsidiary to the host country government overseas. The US fiscal accounts of the overseas subsidiary (on which US tax was levied) allowed an option to take a 'depletion allowance', at that time 27½ per cent of gross income from a concession, with a ceiling of 50 per cent of net income. The inclusion of such tax allowables in the US accounts was likely to result in a much smaller tax liability than that in the overseas producing country subject to 50/50 profit-sharing on a posted price basis. Thus the credit in the USA for foreign tax paid covered the whole of the US tax liability and left a substantial sum unused against the US tax. This 'unused foreign tax credit' could then be offset against liability of the same group of companies to US tax of any of their overseas operations (of any sort) throughout the world.[20]

Thus the level of the first Middle East posting reflected the major oil companies' control of supplies outside North America and the Communist sphere. The choice of price was made by a price leader with the considerations and under the pressures described above. The other companies followed, thus demonstrating the conventional characteristics of an oligopolistic market.

It was not until after 1957 that posted prices became unrealistically high in relation to actual 'realisations' from sales of crude oil to third parties, and to the 'net-back to crude' (that is, the proceeds of sales of products derived from a barrel of crude in the integrated business, after deducting all the downstream costs of transportation, refining and marketing, including the cost of capital employed in the integrated downstream operations). Thus the companies had forged a weapon for use by host country governments, since posted prices became the yardstick by which the latter calculated royalties and taxes, which came to be levied, after 1950, in accordance with the 50/50 profit-sharing principle.[21] Before long the oil-producing country governments started exerting strong resistance to decreases in posted prices and pressure to increase them. The oil companies, who had originally pitched them high in their own best interest, strove to reduce them – in order to lower their tax payments – and succeeded in doing so in 1959 and 1960. When the time came to make the first Libyan posting – by Esso in 1961 – the oil company interest was to keep it as low as possible. How this was done, and resisted by the Libyan Government as being explicitly contrary to the provisions of the concession agreements, will be told later.

Sales of crude oil to independent refineries throughout the world were usually made on a c.i.f. basis, and in this case the price included the posted price of the oil and the freight charged for its transportation. The norm for the freight charge was the going AFRA rate. The oil companies also used AFRA in their own price build-up for charges to affiliates in consuming countries. Indeed the AFRA awards were made largely for oil company use in this connection, and enabled them to argue that a fair independently assessed freight rate was being charged, in the event of price criticism or price control by consuming country governments. It also enabled the oil companies to harmonise their price build-ups in consuming countries without overt collaboration.

But the use of posted prices and AFRA freight rates as the norm did not mean that all sales of crude to third parties were made at these prices. On the contrary, the evidence available of actual prices of contracts in the first half of the 1950s[22] makes it clear that throughout this period of general firmness of oil prices there was widespread rebating and discounting of both the posted price of the oil and freight rates in sales of crude oil by the major oil companies to independent refineries. In some cases the majors adopted similar practices for sales to affiliated refineries, if only as a cosmetic to avoid showing refining losses which might be unacceptable to fiscal authorities, as well as objectionable to the refining and marketing managers.

The prices published and listed for oil companies in consuming countries were established in an analogous manner. The crude oil (or products) was normally invoiced by the oil companies to their affiliates in consuming countries at posted price (f.o.b. export terminal) plus AFRA; the refining and marketing affiliates added to the prices they paid to the parent for the crude oil intake into the refinery and for products imported into distribution depots, the refining and marketing costs, building up their wholesale, bulk and retail prices accordingly. This left scope for variation of price for individual products and between different products, as already described. After the early 1950s in Western Europe it was seldom possible to recover the whole of the prices charged for the delivered crude, plus refining and marketing costs, from the market, and it became the rule rather than the exception in most countries for the subsidiaries conducting these downstream operations to show losses in their fiscal accounts, or to have them made good with rebates on crude supplies given by the parents, which would impinge in reality on the large paper profits of the crude function.

In summary, the eight major oil companies had undisputed control of crude oil supplies at the outset of the 1950s, which was somewhat impaired during the course of the decade by the arrival of the independents in the Arabian Gulf, and by increasing Russian exports. The prices at which the major oil companies strove to conduct business with third parties and final consumers were derived from the benchmarks of posted prices and freights plus downstream costs. These yardsticks indicated tacit understanding, if not overt collusion, between the companies. Within this framework of oligopoly there was fierce competition in securing sales of crude, bulk contracts for products, ships' bunkers, sales to airlines and other business.

This competitive environment resulted in wide and ubiquitous differences between actual 'realisations' and prices built up on the basis described. The sales prices were determined by market conditions to the extent that might be expected in such an integrated industrial and operational structure. The prime criteria by which oil companies judged their own and others' performance were share of market and return on investment. It was on the whole integrated business of the company that they assessed the margins of their sales prices over costs and their net income in relation to their investment; and this could only be done by reviewing financial performance after the event.

2.6   An Outline of the Course of Oil Prices, 1950-60

After the period 1947-9, when prices charged by the oil companies for Middle East crudes fell by about 25 cents per barrel, there followed, until 1957, a period of general firmness of crude oil prices. There were two increases in posted prices – one in the middle of 1953, averaging on Middle East posting 12 cents a barrel; the second, in the early summer of 1957, averaged 13.5 cents. Thereafter, in 1959 and 1960 postings were reduced by 18 cents and 8 cents respectively. After the last change the posted price for 34° API gravity oil in the Arabian Gulf was around $1.80 a barrel with minor variation due primarily to differing points of origin and difference of quality.[23]

In the Middle East, the rises in posted prices between 1951 and 1957 of about 15 per cent[24] were smaller than increases in the Caribbean and the USA of over 25 per cent. The divergence may be ascribed to the fact that the influence of higher US costs and prices had less of an impact in the Middle East, as the latter's supplies, particularly to Europe, were, with exceptions mentioned below, plentiful, and rapidly replacing supplies from the Western Hemisphere. It is significant that the greater posted price rises in Venezuela and the USA, both in 1952 and 1957, took place when there was a constraint on Middle East supplies to Europe – the first because of the drying up of the stream of crude oil from Iran, the second when the Suez Canal was closed. At these times supplies of crude oil, from Venezuela particularly, and to some extent from the USA necessarily made good the short-term deficits caused by shortfalls from the Middle East.[25] The large rises in freight rates in 1956 and 1957, making the shorter haul from the Caribbean to Western Europe comparatively less costly, also reacted on the relative rises in posted prices of crude oil in the two areas.

Within this context of generally firm crude oil posted prices, substantial discounts were developing in crude oil sales to third parties. Contract sales of crude to independent refineries in Argentina, Japan, Brazil, Italy and elsewhere in Europe are recorded with discounts of up to 15 cents a barrel in 1953, 34 cents in 1954, 40 cents in 1955, 60 cents in 1956, and in Japan in 1957, 33 cents.[26] During this period there were also reported a number of hidden discounts in the form of freight rebates and absorption of freights by the seller, technical and money contributions to refinery improvements, long-term credits, acceptance of soft currencies, buy-back of products at uncompetitive prices and the provision of more costly 'spiked' crudes at the same price as untreated crude.

Movements in prices of oil products during this period may be briefly summarised. Prices of main products were posted at the great export refineries, in the Caribbean from 1950, Indonesia in 1955 and the Arabian Gulf in 1957. They followed the crude oil postings upwards, rising during the period to 1957 and falling thereafter along-side the reductions in crude postings. Within this composite picture, the relationship between the products varied as one or another came to be in a deficit or surplus position.

Actual realisations from sales of products are not easy to identify before 1960, except in the Western Hemisphere. Here the Venezuelan 'realised' prices, and the import prices for fuel oils into the USA and Canada, are reported in the official statistics published in these countries, and in addition the New York harbour prices for fuel oils and other products were regularly published in *Platt's Oilgram* and elsewhere. So far as Europe is concerned there are some figures pro-vided, for 1956 and later, in the *Annual Reports* of the European Coal and Steel Community. All the records point to firm prices in 1951, lower prices in late 1952 and early 1953. There was an improvement in the following years, culminating in very high prices in 1957, at the time of the closing of Suez.[27]

Thereafter they fell back rapidly to their previous levels. But in addition to these falls, substantial rebating in Europe took place from 1957 onwards. At this time, because of cylical and seasonal factors working on demand, changes in the product pattern of consumption, the removal of all politically induced constraints on supply and the increase of extraneous supplies, there emerged a large surplus of fuel oil. The weakness of the fuel oil price in Europe was accelerated by a collapse in freight rates which followed the re-opening of the Suez Canal in June 1957. Realisations fell to about 50 per cent of their pre-1957 levels by 1959. Fuel oil comprises between 30 and 50 per cent of the yield from a barrel of crude oil. The prices obtained for sales of fuel oil are thus of importance in the profitability of oil company operations, and its price movements indicative of the degree of oil company control, or lack of it, over market prices of oil products generally.

2.7   Summary of the Influence of Eastern Hemisphere Oil Market Conditions on Decisions to Embark on Oil Operation in Libya

(1) Demand for oil products was strong and increasing, particularly in Western Europe, throughout the 1950s. Consumption in the non-Communist world outside North America rose during this period at an

average compound rate of over 10 per cent a year.

(2) Crude oil supplies rose *pari passu* to meet rising demand. Most of the increases came from the production of the major oil companies in the Middle East, and during the same period there was a marked substitution of Middle East oil for Western Hemisphere oil in the markets of Western Europe. At the same time exports of oil and products from the USSR and its satellites were rising rapidly, providing 8 per cent of consumption in Western Europe by the end of the decade. After the middle of the 1950s small quantities started to come from independents with oil from Iran and the Arabian Gulf area. The remainder came from the major international companies.

(3) After the re-opening of the Suez Canal in 1957, posted prices of crude, which were many times the cost of production of the crude, ceased to give a reliable indication either of oil company returns from their market sales of crude and products, or of the profitability of oil industry operations. After 1960, being maintained by pressure from OPEC, they became primarily reference prices for calculation of royalties and taxes paid to oil-producing country governments. Profits taxes thus virtually took on the nature of a fixed per barrel levy, like royalties. The profitability of oil companies had always been dependent, not upon the level of posted prices, but on the revenues obtained in the markets for sales to third parties — predominantly of oil products sold by their own downstream organisations — prices of which were more often than not set in highly competitive conditions.

(4) The profitability of the major oil companies, which at the beginning of the decade was historically high, fell up to 1954, was thereafter fairly steady up to 1957, after which it dropped drastically, more particularly in the Eastern Hemisphere.[28]

(5) The dramatic fall in product realisations and profitability during the latter part of 1957, which continued low thereafter for a decade, occurred within a year of the start of exploration drilling in Libya, four years before the first production. Production in Libya did not initiate the secular fall in oil prices, although the Libyan independents, it will be argued later, significantly affected the movement.

(6) The decisions of oil companies to embark on costly and risky investment in an unproved area were based, not on prospective short-run profitability, but on long-term considerations of a fast-expanding market for a primary energy source. There was no substitute for oil in transportation, and it had a built-in superiority over alternative sources in most other uses. The open-door policy of the Libyan Government allowed both major internationals and new-comers equal opportunity

to participate. The majors were anxious to the point of obsession to obtain secure additions to their future supplies. Independents took the opportunity to embark on new ventures in the context of a great burgeoning of transnational activities of US companies, particularly in Western Europe. The small costs of securing concessions lowered the threshold of entry. The large front-end loaded investments in exploration and development which would be required were, for most of the entrants, less of a deterrent because of the knowledge that, if the prospects of commercial oil were good in their concessions, financial, technical and operating co-operation could be obtained from the giants in return for participation in the enterprise.[29] In the event, only one major (Esso) and much later on, in the late 1960s, one independent (Occidental) developed and operated on its own, without participation by others, a major oilfield in Libya, including pipelines to marine terminal.

Notes

1. The word 'company' is applied to the whole of each group's world-wide management and operations. Each group in fact consisted of hundreds of different companies, established in many countries to accord with legal requirements and to optimise their operations in respect of fiscal and currency laws and regulations.

2. 'Independents' usually refers to all oil companies other than the majors; they are normally considered to include companies of the private sector, mostly of US parentage, and State-owned oil companies of oil-consuming countries (but not of oil-producing countries).

3. Before 1950 taxes on profits were little imposed, payments by the oil companies being, for the most part, in the form of royalties.

4. The words 'income tax', 'profits tax', 'surtax', 'supertax' and 'corporation tax' are variously used to describe the tax payable to the host country government on the profits of the oil companies as defined by law and the concession contracts. They do have different shades of meaning; here the words 'profits tax' will normally be used for the total tax levied on the profits of the concessionaires in the crude oil production operations. In Libya the terms adopted in the Petroleum Law were 'Income Tax and Surtax'.

5. Most of the remainder was sold to other majors and to independent refineries under long-term and medium-term contracts: transportation of oil to independent refineries was generally provided by the seller.

6. In the processing deals, the normal procedure was for the oil company customer to supply the crude, pay a per barrel fee for refining and lift or sell the products deemed to have been yielded from the crude supplied.

7. It is true that some attempt could be made to calculate marginal costs of varying the product pattern to produce, for instance, more gasoline or to upgrade octane ratings, or for de-sulphurisation of gas oil and (more recently) fuel oil. The practical application in oil company operations of such incremental analysis would generally be for specialist investment decisions of the longer

term. The capital-intensive nature of the operations, the predominance in operating costs of overheads and the hypothetical nature of opportunity costs in such
appraisals, as well as imperative market requirements, precluded the use of
marginal costing of this type in day-to-day decisions on refining and product
yield.

8. Caltex disbanded in Europe, beginning 1967; Shell-BP in UK in 1971.
A few Consolidated and also Caltex marketing companies remain elsewhere.

9. The long-run economic cost of crude oil should theoretically be calculated on a replacement cost basis world-wide, as is argued by M.A. Adelman,
The World Petroleum Market (Johns Hopkins University Press, Baltimore, 1972),
p. 45ff). The application of these concepts was not practicable in the pricing
decisions of the oil companies, nor was it detectable in short-run price behaviour
in the markets for oil. The concepts may be considered relevant for the longer
term, however, in that at that time the major oil companies generated some 95
per cent of the funds they needed for new investment from depletion, depreciation and amortisation provisions and retained earnings. Thus in effect they
strove to charge in the price of oil an element necessary to cover the bulk of their
replacement and expansion capital costs, as well as world-wide exploration and
research.

10. The historical background to the development of Middle East crude oil
price levels is narrated in H. Frank, *Crude Oil Prices in the Middle East* (Praeger,
New York, 1966). This book describes their evolution from their equalisation
with Gulf of Mexico prices (the base point) before and during the second world
war, to a second phase of 'dual basing points' (i.e. Arabian Gulf and Gulf of
Mexico). The third stage was the application of the 'net-back formula' with the
origin of the bench-mark oil first the Gulf of Mexico and subsequently the
Caribbean, and the equalisation point first a port in North-West Europe and
subsequently New York.

11. Since the US ocean terminals for Texan oil were situated in the Gulf of
Mexico, it is sometimes referred to as the US Gulf. The Persian or Arabian Gulf
is called throughout this work the Arabian Gulf.

12. The majors owned about 70 per cent of total refining capacity outside
North America (see N.H. Jacoby, *Multinational Oil: A Study in Industrial
Dynamics* (Macmillan, London, 1974), p. 187ff, and Adelman, *World Petroleum
Market*, p. 95).

13. See C. Tugendhat and A. Hamilton, *Oil — The Biggest Business* (Eyre
Methuen, London, 1975), p. 235. Net Eastern bloc exports to the West at the
end of the 1950s were *c*.450,000 b/d; total crude oil production outside North
America and the Communist sphere was *c*.7 million b/d: see also Ch. 6, note 12.

14. There were falls in Middle East crude postings of 18 cents/b in February
1959, and of 8 cents/b in August 1960; in Venezuela of 25 cents/b in spring
1959; and in Indonesia of 17 cents/b in March 1959, and 11 cents/b in September
1960.

15. Prices published in *Platt's Oilgram*, later *Platt's Oilgram Price Service*,
for prices posted and prices of transactions notified in the US Gulf area. There
was a range of prices and the 'Low' is self-explanatory.

16. The AFRA award was expressed in terms of 'scale' plus or minus so much
per cent.

'Scale' was the London Market Tanker Nominal Freight Scale. It was a list of
notional freight rates between each significant loading and discharging terminal in
the world, issued by the London Tanker Brokers' Panel.

It did not represent either an actual or normal level of rates but a base rate
against which an actual market rate can be measured. Thus, Chart 2.1 shows the
level of AFRA in relation to the base rates during the 1950s. AFRA was the actual

rate used by oil companies in their charges to affiliates in consuming countries and to third-party buyers of c.i.f. cargoes.

Scale was later termed 'Intascale' and is now referred to as 'Worldscale'. The base rates are altered from time to time to take account of changing economic, cost and inflation elements in tanker operations.

17.   To give an example of the weight of the freight element in the price of crude oil, the average freight at 'Scale flat' (i.e. the base rate, with no percentage added or subtracted) from Arabian Gulf ports to North-West European ports through Suez was $1.04/b (including 12 cents/b Suez Canal dues). If crude was posted at $1.71/b the total delivered charge for this oil, with AFRA at 'Scale flat', would be $2.75/b. The freight thus would comprise nearly 40 per cent of the total charge. A one-cent variation in freight charged, if recovered in prices to final consumers, with freight costs to the company unchanged, would thus alter pre-tax profits by $1 million for every 100 million barrels sold.

As can be seen from Chart 2.1, AFRA was above Scale flat for the whole period from its inception in 1954, up to late 1959; this being so, the freight would comprise a larger proportion of the delivered price than indicated above. In the first half of 1957, when the Suez Canal was closed, AFRA rose to Scale +70 per cent, giving a freight of about $2.50/b from the Arabian Gulf to Rotterdam round the Cape of Good Hope. At this level the freight charge would comprise nearly 60 per cent of the total delivered cost of the oil in the consuming country, exceeding that of the oil itself.

18.   An analogy can be made with a butcher pricing the different cuts of meat to cover the cost of the animal slaughtered plus his own operating costs.

19.   This point is significant for Libya, since it was the latter's open-door policy which enabled newcomers to dent, if not break, the majors' hold on supplies of crude oil; other developments in the same direction in the 1950s were the participation by a group of US independent companies in the Iranian Consortium (under pressure from the US Government) and the entry of Aminoil, Getty and the (Japanese) Arabian Oil Company in the Kuwaiti-Saudi Neutral Zone, all of which started producing in the 1950s.

20.   It may be observed in passing that the operation of the percentage depletion allowance in the USA was a strong influence in keeping US postings of crude oil high. Tax relief available in the production function was a powerful incentive to channelling profits into this function and away from the downstream operations. This influence existed even though postings were made by independent buyers of crude as well as affiliates of the integrated producers. See M.G. de Chazeau and A.E. Kahn, *Integration and Competition in the Petroleum Industry* (Yale University Press, New Haven, 1959), p. 222, where it is calculated that for a fully integrated US producer a price rise in crude, even if not recovered at all in product prices, would increase after tax consolidated net income.

Since the USA postings supplied the start-point for the original Caribbean and Middle East postings, the latter were also high because of their derivation from USA postings.

21.   The 50/50 profit-sharing principle was introduced in Venezuela in 1948, Saudi Arabia in 1950, Iraq in 1951, Qatar and Kuwait in 1952 and Iran in 1954. It was only after much dispute that posted prices were accepted by the companies operating in the Middle East as the yardstick for calculating taxable profits, and applied retroactively to the date of their initiation.

22.   See Frank, *Crude Oil Prices*, and Adelman, *World Petroleum Market*, p. 37, for prices of known contracts.

23.   *Petroleum Press Service* and *Platt's Oilgram* regularly reported posted prices and price changes during this period.

24.   During the same period, consumer price indices rose some 17 per cent in

the USA and about 40 per cent in the remainder of the OECD countries according to the cost-of-living indices reported in the UN *Monthly Bulletin of Statistics*. Thus in real terms (price movement in oil compared with general price
movement) Middle East oil prices were more or less constant during the period.
As these prices were expressed in dollars, comparison with the USA rate of
inflation is the more appropriate measure.

25. See Royal Dutch Annual Report for 1956: 'Shortages of Middle East
crudes were made good by increased supplies from the Western Hemisphere,
particularly from Compãnia Shell de Venezuela'.

26. Information on actual prices of contracts is fragmentary and derived
most frequently from *Platt's Oilgram*. In the case of Japan, a price analysis
is contained in M. Suzuki, *Competition and Monopoly in the World Oil Markets*
(Institute of Energy Economics, Tokyo, Feb. 1968).

27. Comments in oil companies' Annual Reports (*passim*) confirm these
general price movements.

28. Profitability of operations may be realistically assessed only after the
event and by a review of earnings in relation to investment. The application of
financial analysis to international oil industry operations was in its infancy in
the early 1950s. Because of the complexity of the international operations
already described and the inextricable intertwining of their myriad strands, the
intricate problems of consolidation of accounts and economic analysis of the
accounting records were only then being developed. The information available,
nevertheless, can give valid indications of trends, even though the absolute figures
for any one year or an individual aspect of operations may not do so.

The trend in profitability at the beginning of the period may be summarised
in the following quotation from an article by the writer in the UK *Institute of
Petroleum Review* of November 1955:

> If there is a consistency over a large part of the industry in return on capital
> employed at the present time, there is another and less comforting consis-
> tency in the movement of this return over the past four years. That is to say,
> the return has been falling, and if the return on the whole investment has been
> falling, it may be deduced without difficulty that the return on the new invest-
> ment for new trade has been falling much faster. In fact, to take a representa-
> tive selection of the 20 largest companies, in the past four years ending with
> 1954 the return on capital invested has been, in round figures, 15, 14, 13 and
> 12%. The return on new investment, though more difficult to gauge owing to
> annual fluctuations both in trade increases and investment expenditures, was
> clearly much lower in the past three years − perhaps on average lower than
> 5% − than in the previous two, when it was over 20%.

These figures refer to the oil industry operating both in the United States and in the
rest of the world. It was only in 1956 that there was some evidence to segregate
results in the Eastern Hemisphere, as will be shown below. The 20 companies,
however, include all the major internationals except CFP, and their world-wide
operations.

In its annual *Financial Analysis of a Group of Petroleum Companies* published
in 1965, the Chase Manhattan Bank asserts that for several years before 1958 the
rate of return on average invested capital for the group of companies was fairly
consistent at around 14 per cent a year. In 1958 this dropped sharply to less than
9.5 per cent and thereafter made only a slow recovery to 1964, when it was 11.1
per cent.

The records of the two largest international companies during the period −
Esso and Shell − shed further light on trends in profitability during the decade.

These two groups between them accounted for about 50 per cent of the international operations of the majors and their results may be regarded as a representative sample of those of the whole international industry. They are shown in Table 2.3.

Table 2.3: Profitability of Esso and Shell, 1954-60

	Esso Net Income as Percentage of Shareholders' Equity	*Shell* Net Income as Percentage of Average Net Assets (i.e. Share- holders' Equity)
1954	13.6	14.0
1955	15.1	14.3
1956	15.9	14.7
1957	13.9	15.3
1958	8.6	9.4
1959	9.4	9.2
1960	10.1	8.5

Source: Annual Reports and Accounts of Standard Oil Company of New Jersey and of Royal Dutch Petroleum Company.

Figures for Eastern Hemisphere earnings and return on investment are available for these two groups from 1956 onwards, since from that time they were reported in the parent companies' Annual Returns to the New York Securities and Exchange Commission.

It would be inadvisable to draw direct conclusions about absolute profitability from these figures, since the Shell figures of Eastern Hemisphere assets are heavily loaded with all their home assets, including Head Office and liquid funds, which were centralised in Europe, while Esso's were centralised in the USA. This has the effect of increasing the denominator of the ratio in the case of Shell, and hence reducing the apparent return on investment, and vice versa in the case of Esso. Nevertheless, the figures give a valid indication of trends. They are shown in Table 2.4.

Table 2.4: Eastern Hemisphere Profitability of Oil Company Operations, 1956-60

	Esso Net Income as Percentage of Net Assets	*Shell* Net Income as Percentage of Net Assets
1956	27.1	9.7
1957	20.7	7.7
1958	18.9	5.2
1959	19.9	6.9
1960	18.2	7.8

Source: Annual Returns of Standard Oil Company of New Jersey and of Royal Dutch Petroleum Company to the New York Stock Exchange Securities and Exchange Commission.

29. The three independents (Continental, Marathon and Amerada) forming the Oasis Group, substantial in themselves, together had combined resources equal to most of the majors.

Part II

THE DEVELOPMENT OF THE LIBYAN OIL INDUSTRY,
1955-1961

3 THE LIBYAN PETROLEUM LAW OF 1955

3.1 The Formulation of the Law

The Minerals Law of 1953 had enabled survey work to be carried out in any area for which a permit was obtained, but did not allow any drilling operations, nor the exclusive allocation of specific areas to individual prospectors. This was done by the 1955 Petroleum Law, which provided the legal basis for the development of the Libyan oil industry and still remains to this day on the Statute Book in an amended form.

The events preceding the promulgation of the Law which might shed light on the influences at work and the hopes and intentions of those concerned are not well documented. In the period leading up to its enactment, oil affairs were under the jurisdiction of the Ministry of Finance and Economics, which was advised and assisted in this matter by Ess. Anis Qassim, who held the position of legal adviser in the Ministry of Justice, and later became Chairman of the Petroleum Commission.[1] In 1954 a draft law was circulated among oil companies interested in obtaining concessions in Libya, and representatives of these companies were invited to participate in a committee under Ess. Qassim to discuss the draft. At these discussions Ess. Qassim was assisted by Mr A. Hogenhuis, who on retirement from Royal/Dutch Shell had taken a post with the Libyan Government to assist in oil affairs, and Mr C. Andrews, a British adviser in the Ministry of Justice.[2]

Another source[3] states that the new Libyan Government requested oil industry assistance in the formulation of petroleum legislation and that Messrs Hogenhuis, Dale and Pitt-Hardacre (who was British adviser to the Government) helped in the drafting on the Government side. This source adds that a first draft of the Law granted priority to British companies, but that this was protested by the Americans and French, who insisted on an 'open-door' policy – in a manner reminiscent of the Iraqi negotiations of the early 1920s – and in the event these views prevailed.

The Law comprised 25 Articles and two Schedules. The First Schedule gave the wording for a preliminary reconnaissance permit for petroleum, and was thus transferring the provisions of the Minerals

Law of 1953 to the Petroleum Law. The fee for a reconnaissance permit was fixed by this Schedule as £L500 for a year, renewable annually.

The Second Schedule gave the wording of the actual concession deed granted to each successful applicant, consisting of 30 Clauses. Article 9 of the Law stated that 'The Commission[4] may grant concessions in the form set out in the Second Schedule to this Law and not otherwise, provided that they may contain such minor non-discriminatory variations as may be required to meet the circumstances of any particular case.' This provision ensured that the Libyan authorities had no latitude to favour any applicant in concession terms, which were absolutely rigid. Moreover the same Article required the Commission to grant a concession to the first eligible application received in the case of overlapping.[5] Only when conflicting applications were received simultaneously (defined as on the same day) did the Commission have discretion, after every attempt at mediation, including encouragement of pooling or division of the area overlapping, 'to adopt such objective solution as it deems appropriate'.[6]

3.2   The Petroleum Commission

In order to adapt the Petroleum Law to the then federal political structure of the country, Article 2 established, as an autonomous public agency, the Petroleum Commission. This body, to which were appointed by the Government a representative of each of the Provinces under a federal Chairman, was to be responsible for the implementation of the provisions of the Law under the supervision of the federal Minister responsible, at that time the Minister of National Economy. The tasks of this Commission included decisions on grant, assignment, renewal, surrender and revocation of concessions, which were then approved or rejected by the Minister. The Commission was to appoint a Director of Petroleum Affairs who was to be in charge of the administration of the Law and the execution of matters arising from it in relation to concessionaires. The Commission was also charged with the responsibility of preparing Regulations for the implementation of the Law, which were then to be approved by the Minister.

During the early stages of exploration these provisions worked fairly well. The cumbersome nature of the Petroleum Commission machinery — requiring the co-operation of the representatives of all three Provinces to make decisions, and a subsequent referral to the competent Minister

— undoubtedly caused delays in dealing with applications for concessions. Such delays may have been irritating at the time to the impatient applicants, but in retrospect do not appear to have been significant in their effects on development. Within a year of the enactment of the Law, 51 concessions had been granted, and this number had risen to 84 by the end of 1959. The successful applicants, having been granted concessions, were not encumbered by interferences in their operations other than by the delays inherent in an inexperienced and slow-reacting bureaucracy.

When the time for petroleum production approached, the increasing complexity of the problems and administration of the industry showed the Commission to be quite inadequate for its task. A Ministry of Petroleum Affairs was created in 1960, and in 1962 the Minister was given authority to supervise the Commission,[7] including the power to make his own decisions under the Law if the Commission did not respond to his wishes within 15 days. Finally, under a further Law of 1963,[8] the Commission was abolished and all its powers and responsibilities transferred to the Ministry of Petroleum Affairs.

Though the Petroleum Commission may be criticised for its inadequacy in dealing with matters effectively and expeditiously, it may be said in its favour that, being bound by the provision of the Law and its own majority vote, it ensured an impartial allocation of concessions, since it was obligated by the terms of the Law to grant concessions on a first-come-first-served basis, subject only to the maximum areas and the requirements of competence defined in Article 5 of the Law.

3.3 The Grid System of Concessions and the Objectives of the Law-makers

The Petroleum Law divided the country, for the purpose of allocating concessions, into four zones, corresponding in area to the three provinces of Tripolitania (Zone I), Cyrenaica (North — Zone II, and south of the 28° parallel — Zone III) and the Fezzan (Zone IV)[9] (see Map 4.1). There was no significance in this zoning other than to achieve a correspondence with the three Provinces, and the fact that the remoter Zones III and IV carried lower rents and lower minimum working obligations. Applications for concessions were to conform as far as possible to the grid lines of the official map,[10] and each concessionaire was to be limited to a maximum of three concessions in each of the first and second zones and four in the third and fourth zones. Total area allocated to any one concessionaire should be limited to 30,000 square kilometres in each of Zones I and II and to 80,000 square kilometres in each of Zones III and IV.[11]

Since the total area of the country was 1.76 million square kilometres, these limitations, together with the surrender provisions mentioned later, make it clear that the compilers of the Law intended an open-door policy of inviting many concessionaires to undertake oil operations in Libya in competition with each other. This policy contrasted with the practice hitherto adopted in other Middle East countries, where very large concessions — in the case of Iraq, Saudi Arabia and Kuwait covering effectively the whole land area of the country — had been given to one major oil company or, more commonly, to a joint exploration and production subsidiary of two or more of the major international companies. The Libyan Law did not, however, preclude two or more oil companies mounting joint operations in Libya in one or more concessions, and this was done extensively, both by the majors and the independents.

'The intention behind the issue of the Petroleum Law of 1955 was to induce the largest number of oil companies to come to Libya and carry out oil operations therein.'[12] It has been reported that those responsible for compiling the Law and those subsequently concerned in granting concessions decided not only to depart from Middle East practice in pursuit of these objectives, but also to take other measures to try to ensure that major international oil companies did not obtain control, either jointly or severally, over the whole of any Libyan oil resources there might be. A commentator states that the Government decided that the best interests of the country would be served by giving to independent oil companies concessions in what were then assumed to be the most favoured areas; and that major international companies should not be allowed to hold contiguous applications for areas in sought-after sections. 'By separating the majors each would have to make greater exploratory efforts, having regard to Middle East concession arrangements.'[13] Although this result was achieved in the event, it worked out in a manner very different from the alleged intentions of the Government in their allocation of the early concessions. In the most favoured areas — north-west Tripolitania and north Cyrenaica, granted to a CFP subsidiary and to Libyan American respectively — no commercial oil was found; and it was only in 1959 that Esso's discovery at Zelten on Concession No. 6 pointed to the probability of large deposits in the Sirtica desert — an area which had not been considered the most promising in the early 1950s.

Nor did this reported policy of encouraging independents *vis-à-vis* the majors appear materially to have influenced the aggregate outcome. There resulted an allocation of concessions between majors and independents such as might reasonably have been expected in consideration of the qualification requirements and time priority of application laid down in the Law. Thirty-one out of the 51 concessions granted within a year of the promulgation of the law were to the majors;[14] and of the 12 oil strikes recorded in 1958 and 1959 eight were by the majors, and these included three out of the five subsequently to be developed commercially.[15]

There were two Articles in the Petroleum Law designed to stimulate concession-holders to vigorous exploration activity. Article 10 required them to surrender 25 per cent of the area of a concession within five years from the date of the original grant, 50 per cent within eight years and $66^{2}/_{3}$ per cent in the first and second zones within ten years, 75 per cent in the third and fourth zones. This provision, which had become normal practice in the granting of concessions by other countries (though varying in percentages and periods), proved to be an effective encouragement to industrious exploration. The oil companies, being concerned not to surrender an area subsequently found fruitful, strove to cover the whole of their concession by survey at least, and the more promising parts by wild-cat drilling before being called upon to choose areas for surrender.[16]

Article 10 of the Law contained provisions for minimum working obligations, designed to ensure that a company did not obtain a concession and leave it idle. This might occur even in the case of a major enterprise, if it suited the company's world-wide development and supply planning to leave an acquisition for examination and development to a future date; but there was also a danger that unscrupulous operators, having surmounted the competence test for award of concessions, might obtain them for speculative purposes, hoping to assign or sell out at a gain subsequently, without themselves having performed, or having the capability to perform, exploration and development work. To forestall such actions, Article 17 required the Commission's consent to assignment of concessions other than to affiliates of the concession-holder. The minimum working obligations are shown in Table 3.1.

These obligations referred to expenditure in Libya, or elsewhere in connection with the Libyan operations. As an example of their effectiveness, they ensured minimum expenditure, during the first five years, of £L22,500 a year for 15,000 square kilometres (the average

Table 3.1: Minimum Working Obligations

	Zones I & II £L per square kilometre per annum	Zones III & IV £L per square kilometre per annum
During the first five years	1½	1½
During the next three years	3½	1½
Subsequently	6	3½

size of concession during these years was about 14,000 square kilometres). This sum, even if it had been entirely spent in Libya, would not have amounted in five years to the cost of drilling one wild-cat well.[17] With the inclusion of unauditable expenditure outside Libya it was a nugatory sum in relation to the costs of effective exploration in Libya. There was a further easement in that over-expenditure in any one year could be carried forward against obligations in the following year or years. This provision, in short, was quite ineffective to achieve rapid exploration and development effort on the part of the concessionaires.

Article 9 required a bond or banker's guarantee of £L50,000 throughout the life of a concession to secure the 'due performance of the concession-holder's obligations under all concessions held by him in Libya'. This may have had some effect in deterring applications of a purely speculative nature. In fact nearly all the early concessions were granted to bona fide operating oil companies, and it was not until the 1966 round of concessions that a number of 'wheeler-dealers' appeared on the scene.

3.4   Fees, Rents and Royalties

Fees and rents were pitched in the Law at a low level, the effect being not to deter any bona fide applicant from acquiring a concession by reason of an unacceptable initial cost. The fee payable on grant of a concession was £L500, and the rents are shown in Table 3.2.

These provisions contained an ambiguity, which was corrected in the 1961 amendment to the Law. It was intended that the high rent of £2,500 should apply immediately on the discovery of petroleum in commercial quantities, whenever that took place, but the wording of the original Law applies this only to the period after the eighth year. The object of this greatly increased rent was to stimulate a concessionaire

Table 3.2: Libyan Concession Rents

	Zones I & II £L per 100 sq. kilometres per annum	Zones III & IV £L per 100 sq. kilometres per annum
For the first 8 years	10	5
For the next 7 years or until petroleum is found in commercial quantities	20	10
Thereafter	2,500	2,500

into fast development of discovered oil and not to leave it undeveloped, as might well be the case, particularly with the major companies, in order to fit in with their long-term world-wide oil development plans and also with their allocation of capital for development programmes. In fact it turned out to be ineffective, since there was no objective criterion or definition of 'commercial quantities'. Fields discovered were declared commercial *ex post facto*, after the companies concerned had actually begun development, and the decisions to develop were the only objective measure of their commerciality acceptable by a company.

The higher rent was thus charged only after a company had begun development. It played no part in decisions to develop – indeed it could have held back such activity on the part of a company unwilling greatly to enhance rent payments. Several disputes arose between the Government and concessionaires over this point, but were invariably left unsettled in the concessionaire's favour, since the Government was not willing to go to arbitration in such a matter. Moreover, in the case of concessionaires who had already begun production from one field, the payment of the higher rent on a second concession deemed commercial was of no consequence, since any money paid under this heading was an offset against royalties paid on production, and income and surtax paid on profits, from the producing field.

Concessions were granted for a period of 50 years, and were renewable for a further period of 10 years, making 60 years the maximum period for which they might be held.[18] During this period the concession could not be revoked except for the following reasons:

(1) The concessionaire company had failed to begin operations within eight months from the date of grant of the concession or failed to meet its expenditure obligations within each of two consecutive periods.

(2) Rents or royalties due were more than six months in arrears.
(3) The company went into involuntary liquidation or a receiver was appointed.
(4) The company defaulted on its surrender obligations or assigned the concession improperly without the Commission's assent.
(5) The company failed to pay any sums awarded against it in arbitration within 90 days of the award.[19]

A royalty of 12½ per cent of its value 'on the field' was to be paid on crude oil 'won and saved into field storage', and on natural gasoline, both after deduction of those quantities used by the company in its operations of producing the oil and transporting it to seaboard terminal. A similar royalty was to be charged on natural gas sold in Libya or exported.

The value of the oil for calculating the royalty was to be based on the 'free competitive market price' f.o.b. at seaboard, from which were to be deducted the handling charges and costs of transportation from field storage; if there was no such price, then its value was to be derived from the free competitive market price published for similar quality and gravity oils at the nearest seaboard terminal outside Libya.

For natural gasoline the value was to be calculated in a manner to be agreed upon from time to time between the Director and the company. For natural gas the value for calculating royalty was to be the sale price less costs of transportation from well-head if sold in Libya, and in addition other relevant costs for handling and deliveries when sold outside Libya.

In the definition of the value of royalty there was no reference to posted price, nor is there any such reference throughout the 1955 Law. The Law attempted to define royalty as a percentage of income received by the producer from selling the petroleum. Since in fact there was to be no free competitive market price for crude oil at seaboard terminal — virtually all the oil to be produced in Libya being transferred to the producer's affiliated companies at a price decided by the companies themselves — nor any published market price which was free and competitive[20] at any seaboard terminal outside Libya, either 'nearest' or elsewhere in the world, these royalty definitions in respect of crude oil were, to say the least, imprecise.

They also give an impression that royalty is a tax related to income, and in this they are similar to the royalty provisions in other concession agreements of that time in the Eastern Hemisphere. It is true that royalty forms part of the government's 'take' in all countries except in North America and Eire. It is, nevertheless, a payment to the owner of the subsoil rights (in the case of mineral extraction) by the extractor of the minerals for winning and possessing these resources. In the early Middle East concessions the royalty was a fixed sum per ton or barrel of oil extracted.[21] It came to be associated with profits taxes when governments of oil-producing countries were dissatisfied with a fixed sum royalty payment, which was in many cases pitched at a low level, particularly if the value of the oil on which it was levied was expected to rise and the profits made from it were believed to be large. More so, when the profit-sharing principle became more widely accepted, royalty came to be regarded, whatever its level, as a contribution to the Government's share of the profits of the concessionaire, and hence was confused with taxes on profits.

This was the prevalent attitude of the time in the Middle East concessions, and was incorporated in the 1955 Libyan Law, with the result that royalty paid was treated as an advance payment towards the 50 per cent of the 'profits' which comprised the Government's share of the concessionary company's revenues from its oil operations in Libya. It was not until 1964 that the major oil companies conceded to OPEC that royalty should be 'expensed', and not treated as a tax credit, thereby acknowledging that it was an operating cost and not a tax on income. The change was not made in Libya until 1965, when it was incorporated in the amendment to the Petroleum Law.

3.5   Taxation and Division of Profits

Article 14 of the Law and Clause 8 of the concession dealt with taxation and the division of profits. In brief, they provided that the concession-holder would pay income taxes and other taxes and imposts payable under the laws of Libya, and in addition a surtax which would make the total of his payments equal to 50 per cent of his profits. Fees, rents and royalties paid were regarded as advance payments of the profits to which the Government was entitled.

The fees, rents, royalties and surtax were to be paid to the Petroleum Commission. The other taxes and imposts — mostly customs duties, stamp taxes and vehicle licence levies — would be paid, as they were incurred, to the appropriate government authority. If all these payments combined exceeded the company's liabilities to the Commission (for rents, fees, royalties and surtax) the excess was to be carried forward and deducted from payments to the Commission due in the following year or years. Thus if there were no profits — and as will be shown below there were unlikely to be any under the provisions of this Law for many years, if at all – the general taxes payable in Libya were to be recovered by the concession-holder offsetting them against the fees, rents and royalty payments to which the concession-holder was liable in that year or in future years.

In Article 14 of the Law 'profits' were defined as 'the income of the concession holder obtained from all his petroleum exploration, prospecting, mining and producing activities in Libya after deducting allowable costs and expenses'. These latter included all expenses and losses attributable to his petroleum operations in Libya, irrespective of where incurred. Exploration and prospecting expenses and intangible drilling costs might be deducted in the year in which they were incurred, or capitalised and amortised at a rate of 20 per cent p.a., at the option of the concession-holder – an option which could be exercised annually. The costs of physical assets for exploration incurred before production were amortisable at the rate of 20 per cent a year, and of those acquired after production had begun at 10 per cent p.a.

There was also a depletion allowance introduced into the 1955 Law, following North American practice but contrary to the trend in Middle East concessions. This allowed a deduction from taxable income of 25 per cent of gross income derived from operations up to a maximum of 50 per cent of net income. In lieu of depletion allowance the concession-holder might amortise his intangible pre-production exploration expenditure at 20 per cent p.a. Since such expenses were also allowed to be deducted in the year in which they were incurred, the last provision was of no effect, as 100 per cent expensing, which could be carried forward in the case of losses, was clearly more beneficial to the company than a 20 per cent amortisation, and could be taken in addition to the depletion allowance.

The definitions contained in the 1955 Law of 'profits', which were to be shared equally between Government and company, have been described in some detail so that an evaluation of their aptness can be made both from the point of view of equity, and in comparison with the arrangements existing at the time in other oil-producing countries. In this period the 'conventional' concession containing the 50/50 profit-sharing principle was predominant outside North America. It had been introduced in 1948 in Venezuela, and spread to Saudi Arabia, Kuwait, Iraq and Iran before 1955. Since all the major international oil companies had been involved in the recently consummated Consortium Agreement in Iran, and since most of them were consulted and exerted considerable influence in the formulation of the Libyan

Law of 1955, a comparative appraisal may be made in evaluation of the Libyan provisions.

The calculation of the profits which are to be equally divided between Government and company is crucial. In this respect, the Libyan Law was imprecise in the definition of income and permissive in that of costs and expenses allowed to be set against income in order to identify the taxable profit. The definition of income indeed confines itself to a statement of principle — 'the income of the concession-holder obtained from all his petroleum . . . activities in Libya'. It pays no heed to the fact that such an income from exports of crude oil, by the majors at least, is never identifiable. The oil exported by the major international oil companies is transferred to affiliates, who transport it overseas and sell it to other affiliates in consuming countries where, mixed with crudes from other sources, it is refined, distributed and sold as oil products and chemical and other feedstocks. The oil company, even by the most sophisticated accounting methods, is unable to identify the profits attributable to operations in Libya contained in sales of final products jointly refined from blended crudes from many sources. But there is no profit realised at all until the cash register rings at the service station, or the kerosene, gas oil and fuel oil is delivered and invoiced to the final consumer. The interpretation of the definition of income in the 1955 Law was never put to the test, since it had been replaced by what was intended to be a more precise identification in terms of posted prices in the 1961 Amendment, before exports had begun. The 1961 Amendment, however, proved to be equally imprecise, as will be described below, and it was not until 1965 that a tightly worded definition of the value of crude oil exported in unequivocal terms of posted prices was to be effective.

The generous provisions for allowable expenses have already been mentioned — 20 per cent a year amortisation of pre-production expenditure on physical assets and 10 per cent on such post-production expenditure; and 20 per cent amortisation of pre-production expenditure other than on physical assets, this being optional in lieu of depletion allowance. But the wording of the paragraph of the Law which followed allowed losses to be carried forward and set against profits for a maximum period of ten years. This would effectively have nullified the provisions for amortisation of exploration expenses, since these could be charged 100 per cent in the year in which they were incurred, and carried forward as losses to be set against taxable income until they were extinguished up to a maximum of ten years. Thus, while the Law clearly intended one thing, its wording allowed a procedure much more favourable to the concession-holders, which would have delayed their liability to surtax for some years after they had begun exports of oil. This, again, was never put to the test, since the 1961 Amendment allowed only exploration expenses incurred after production had begun to be charged 100 per cent, and if necessary carried forward and set against profits of subsequent years; pre-production intangible expenditure was to be capitalised and amortised at 5 per cent a year.

The further provision of the 1955 Law that expenses and losses 'irrespective of where incurred' were allowable against taxable profits also gave potential scope for a concession-holder to raise excessive charges against his Libyan income, by including many overseas expenses — such as, for instance, time of home office staff and facilities deemed to have been devoted to Libyan matters — which by nature would not be satisfactorily auditable. This provision, though changed subsequently to 'the cost of services rendered by third parties or affiliates to the concession-holder',[22] was to give rise to many disputes between the Government and the companies. In general, the major companies, who had much experience of the charging of home office expenses in other countries, interpreted this clause with discretion; the newcomers, with no such experience, not unnaturally tended to regard it as an opportunity to off-load large sums on to their Libyan accounts, thereby giving rise to disagreements, and impairing the confidence established between government and company.[23]

3.6   Favourable Terms for the Oil Companies

It has frequently been suggested that these generous terms, so far as taxation was concerned, were of importance in attracting oil companies to Libya. It has also been represented, particularly by oil company interests, that the subsequent amendment of the terms was unfair, and even fraudulent — 'changing the rules of the game during play' — by unilateral violation of a solemn contract. At the time that the 1955 Libyan Law was passed, the major oil companies had had experience of practice in a number of other countries, and since they were influential in proposing the terms of the Libyan Law, this experience could have been applied to Libya. Of these other arrangements, one example only suffices for comparison — Iran, where the Consortium Agreement had recently been completed, in October 1954. All the major internationals participated in the Iranian Consortium, and the provisions of the agreement, hammered out over a period of about two years, may be regarded as a model of contemporary oil concession contracts. It unequivocally established posted prices for calculation of income and of the 'Stated Payment' (equivalent to royalty), with only those discounts (if any) approved by the Iranian authorities; and while allowing 10 per cent depreciation of fixed assets, it limited charges of individual consortium members from outside Iran to services actually rendered in connection with the operations in Iran, which had to be specifically negotiated at arm's length by the Iranian Operating Company with an individual Consortium member.

Why were similar arrangements not applied in Libya? Had this been done, fiscal equity, as between Iran and Libya, would still (as it turned out) have left Libyan oil with a substantial cost advantage over Iran, because of its nearness to Western Europe and the higher gravity and low-sulphur quality of its oil.

It is open to question whether the permissive nature of the tax provisions of the Libyan 1955 Law were a *sine qua non* for oil companies to come to Libya, explore for and develop oil; it is equally questionable whether, had the companies known that the rules were going to be changed later, they would not have undertaken the operations in the first place. When oil production was a far-away speculative prospect, the taxation details were hypothetical and, provided they were not worse than elsewhere, of little practical significance in decisions to apply for concessions. At the time of drafting the 1955 Law the Government side had no experience of oil taxation, nor specialist knowledge of practice elsewhere. This knowledge was all on the side of the major internationals, who advised the Government, and who succeeded in obtaining an ideal contract from their own viewpoint. It must have appeared unlikely to the companies, even at that time, that, in the event of Libya proving to be a major oil province, they would be allowed to enjoy such favourable tax treatment.[24]

These favourable terms for the concession-holder in the Libyan Law were secured for the whole period of the concession, since Clause 16 of the Second Schedule states that 'the contractual rights expressly created by this concession shall not be altered except by mutual consent of the parties.' This clause implied that, in the event of future legislation which changed the tax and other provisions, such legislation would not apply to the existing concession-holder without his consent. In subsequent amendments, this provision was not omitted but strengthened, to state explicitly that no amendment or repeal of the Petroleum Regulations would affect the contractual rights of the company without its consent.

The inclusion of this provision was an understandable ambition on the part of the companies, since they sought as much protection as possible against arbitrary action and unilateral legislation which might, at a stroke, damage or destroy their operations and the profitability of their large and irreversible investments in the country. A similar undertaking was incorporated also in the Iranian Consortium Agreement relating to the tax clauses only. It has persisted to the present day in Libya — even through the revolution — in the letter if not in the spirit, and has profoundly influenced company-Government relations at all times. It has raised fundamental questions of the compatibility of the sanctity of contract with the principle of sovereignty, when one party to the contract is a commerical entity, and the other a sovereign power dealing with matters within its jurisdiction.

But in the Libyan Law there was no most-favoured-nation clause, as existed in Iran, Iraq and Saudi Arabian agreements. The Iranian Consortium Agreement, in supplementary letters, guarantees most-favoured-nation treatment in respect of payments to the Government if two or more members of the Consortium reach a new agreement with any other country bordering on the Persian Gulf whereby that country's percentage share of profits is higher than Iran's.[25] This undertaking offset the rigidity of the guarantee of performance of the concession terms by admitting their adaptability to changed circumstances.

The favourable terms of the Libyan Law of 1955 and the concessions were a foretaste of paradise for the oil companies. It is facile to assert, with hindsight, that they were doomed not to last in the event of a large oil industry developing in Libya. They were not even comparable with other agreements of the time, the details of which were known to the oil companies — and only to them, since they were confidential and unpublished — who played an influential role in the formulation of the Libyan Law.

Notes

1. Abdul Amir Q. Kubbah, *Libya — Its Oil Industry and Economic System* (Rihani Press, Beirut, 1964). Mr Kubbah was Petroleum Economist in the Libyan Ministry of Petroleum Affairs from 1962 to 1964.

2. Mr Anis Qassim, writing in Ministry of Petroleum Affairs, *Petroleum Development in Libya, 1954 through 1958* (Tripoli, 1965), p. 6.

3. D.B. Eiches in his article on Libya in *Trek of the Oil Finders — A History of Exploration for Petroleum* (published for the American Association of Petroleum Geologists, 1975), p. 1438.

4. See following paragraphs for description of the Petroleum Commission.

5. 'If more than one person submit applications for concessions over areas which overlap in whole or in part, preference shall be given to the first person to apply to the Commission'; Article 9 (1).

6. 'If an agreement by mediation cannot be reached, the Commission may either require the applicants to pool the overlapping area . . . or may adopt such objective solution as it deems appropriate'; Article 9 (2) (d).

7. Law No. 6 of 1962.

8. Law No. 6 of 1963.

9. The Libyan Petroleum Law, 1955, Article 3. See Map 4.1.

10. Ibid, Article 7.

11. Ibid, Article 9.

12. Ibrahim Hangari, *The Libyan Petroleum Law, 1955, as Amended up to 1965* (Tripoli, 1966). Mr Hangari was subsequently Director of Petroleum Affairs, and then Under-Secretary at the Ministry of Petroleum Affairs.

13. Eiches in *Trek of the Oil Finders*; it is difficult to reconcile this report of allocation rationale with the provisions of the Law to ensure impartiality of allocation as between applicants.

14. Ministry of Petroleum Affairs, Kingdom of Libya, *Libyan Oil 1954-1967* (Tripoli, 1968).

15. Zelten, Concession 6, by Esso on 13 June 1959; Beida Concession 47, by Amoseas on 26 Sept. 1959; Amal, Concession 12, by Mobil on 1 Nov. 1959. The other two were Daḥra, Concession 32, and Waha, Concession 59, both by Oasis on 30 Apr. 1959 and 27 Dec. 1959 respectively.

16. The major discovery by Occidental of the Idris field (later renamed 'Intissar') in 1967 was in an area surrendered previously by Mobil; it was reported that the discovery well of Occidental was at the location where formerly Mobil had an exploration camp.

17. Estimated to be between $500,000 and $1,000,000 at that time, according to depth, location and penetrability.

18. Article 9 (4).

19. Second Schedule, Clause 27.

20. Posted prices were not free and competitive, although they purported to be, being posted by oil companies for sale of oil available to all comers. This point is discussed in Chapter 2.

21. Cf. Iraq, where the 1925 Agreement stipulated a royalty of 4 shillings (gold) per ton.

22. Petroleum Regulation No. 6, Article 8 (3).

23. At about this time, Venezuela had refused to accept Head Office charges in concession-holders' Venezuelan oil accounts. The UK 1975 Oil Taxation Act expressly forbids any such charges except interest on loans. But there were − and still are − devices available for raising charges by the home office against the overseas subsidiary; for instance, the sale of second-hand equipment at inflated prices, interest payments on current and loan account debit balances with the parent company, and the concoction of a variety of services for which fees are charged. The difficulty of auditing such charges satisfactorily and of providing and paying an organisation to do so were doubtless an element in the Venezuelan decision to disallow them totally.

24. A similar situation arose in the UK in the 1970s, although the UK Government might then be expected to have more experience and sophistication than the Libyan in the 1950s. In the UK the royalty and tax provisions were equally favourable to the concessionaires as were the Libyan in the 1950s; it was only when major production in the North Sea became imminent that, by the passing of th Oil Taxation and the Petroleum and Submarine Pipelines Acts of 1975, a

'Government take' was ensured comparable with the 'old' concessions elsewhere in the world.

25. Letter dated 20 September 1954, to the Iranian Minister of Finance from the Members of the Consortium.

4 THE COURSE OF DEVELOPMENT FROM 1955 TO 1961

4.1 The Award of Concessions

The first two concessions were awarded, one to Esso and the other to Nelson Bunker Hunt, on 20 November 1955. These awards were followed in December and January by many others, and by the end of January 1956, 47 concessions had been allocated. Thereafter others followed at irregular intervals, until the eighty-ninth concession, awarded on 18 June 1960 (see Appendix 4.1 and Map 4.1).

By this time the whole of Zone II and Zone I had been allocated, including sea areas off-shore in the Gulf of Sirte, from approximately Misurata in the West to Benghazi in the East and also off Cyrenaica. Including Zones III and IV, the greater part of the country north of 'latitude 24° 15' had been awarded. After this time, areas of the early concessions began to become available for reallocation under the provision of the Law stipulating 25 per cent surrender within five years of grant. Six more concessions were granted in April 1961 of areas surrendered by other concessionaires before further action was suspended — as it turned out for five years — pending legal measures altering conditions of award. By then 95 concessions had been given.

The gross area covered by the concessions amounted, at its maximum, before revocations, surrenders and reallocations, to 1.28 million square kilometres. Excluding off-shore concessions of $37,000km^2$, the concession areas comprised 70 per cent of the whole of the land area of the country. The non-conceded areas were in the far south where, even if oil existed, it would almost certainly be commercially unexploitable because of logistic and transportation difficulties.

4.2 Exploration Activities

In the notes to Chapter I some figures of oil company expenditures for operations in Libya in the early years of development are given. They show that, beginning with the year 1956, the cumulative expenditures up to the end of the discovery year of 1959 amounted to £L77 millions; in terms of US dollars,[1] in which much of the expenditure was

73

Map 4.1: Petroleum Concessions in Libya

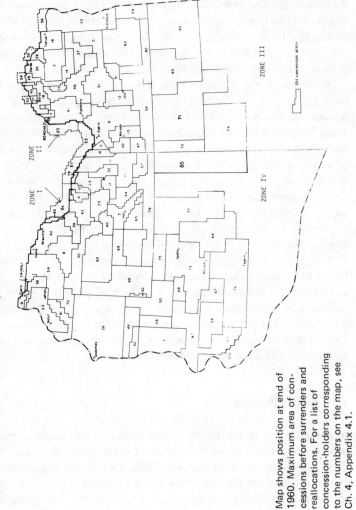

Map shows position at end of 1960. Maximum area of concessions before surrenders and reallocations. For a list of concession-holders corresponding to the numbers on the map, see Ch. 4, Appendix 4.1.

incurred, $216 millions. At this time very little had yet been spent on development of oilfields. By the end of 1961 total expenditure had risen to £L210 millions ($588m).

These expenditures give some indication of the quickly growing intensity of exploration activities even before the discovery of commercial oil had given expectation that, for some at least, there would be a return of and on the money being spent. Translated into identifiable works on the ground, the record is as shown in Table 4.1.

Table 4.1: Survey Work, Drilling and Employment in the Libyan Oil Industry, 1956-61

	1956	1957	1958	1959	1960	1961
Surveys — Party/Months						
Topographical survey	51	155	100	84	58	76
Geographical survey	81	155	224	200	355	356
Magnetometric survey	14	28	47	3	19	8
Gravimetric survey	45	110	138	38	60	27
Seismic survey	27	115	215	310	473	439
Drilling Activity						
Number of rigs	1	4	9	28	36	36
Rig-months	9	24	90	203	388	410
Footage drilled (thousands of feet)	9	34	144	314	937	1,332
Wells completed —						
exploration	1	4	26	32	71	97
development	—	—	1	9	68	130
Percentage of exploration wells in which oil/gas found	—	—	15%	32%	10%	19%
Persons Employed — Year-end						
Libyan	1,150	2,900	4,600	5,000	7,600	7,950
Expatriate	350	850	1,300	1,800	2,650	2,700
Expenditures of Oil companies on Libya, £L millions	4.5	13.5	24	35	61	72

Source: Ministry of Petroleum Affairs, Tripoli, Libya.

4.3 The Oil Companies' Organisation and Success

A review of the corporate arrangements of the oil companies in the early years of their operations in Libya will shed some light on their capabilities and fortunes. The account given below deals first with the majors and then with the independents.[2]

All the majors, including CFP, obtained concessions near the beginning. Of these, Esso, Shell, Mobil, Gulf, BP and CFP began by operating on their own, while Texaco and Socal formed a joint operating company (Amoseas), in which they each had a 50 per cent undivided interest.

Esso discovered oil in large quantities at Zelten on Concession No. 6 in June 1959, and rapidly developed the field for commercial production, beginning exports in 1961. In addition, in 1959 Esso entered into a partnership with Libyan American and Grace in which it obtained a 50 per cent interest, and was operator, in Concessions Nos. 16, 17 and 20. In all these concessions oil was discovered, but developed only in Concession No. 20.

Of the other majors, Shell, Gulf and CFP, although discovering some oil, did not develop it commercially, and (with the exception of Shell who in 1965 acquired a half interest in Amerada's share of Oasis' production) did not succeed in obtaining from their operations in Libya any oil for export.

Texaco and Socal, with their subsidiary Amoseas as operator, discovered commercial oil in September 1959, which they subsequently developed slowly to make their first exports in 1964.

Mobil also discovered oil in 1959. Previous to this, in July 1958, it had accepted in all its concessions as a partner the West German firm of Gelsenkircher Bergswerk (Gelsenberg).[3] Gelsenberg took an undivided 25 per cent interest in Mobil's concessions, later raised to 35 per cent. Mobil remained operator, shipping their first oil in 1963.

BP did not succeed during these years in discovering commercial oil in the concessions it obtained in the years 1957, 1958 and 1959. In 1960, however, it took a half interest, and became operator, in Nelson Bunker Hunt's Concession No. 65, where commercial oil was discovered in 1961 but, being far from the coast, not exported until 1967.

In summary, four of the eight majors found and developed their own oil resources. Of these, Esso was the only one who went the whole way alone with a major oilfield; doing this, it gained the advantage of freeing itself from the constraints of joint decision-making with others on development, production levels and other operations. Esso also bought into concessions held by independents, where commercial oil was quickly discovered and developed under Esso's operation. Mobil, Texaco and Socal worked in partnerships. BP bought its way into promising concessions and was itself an operator responsible for discovering and developing commercial oil. Shell bought at a later date an interest in an existing commercial operation, but did not actively participate in the operations.

Of the independents the most notable was the partnership of three sizeable US companies in the operation carried out by the Oasis Oil Company of Libya. The parents of Oasis were Amerada, Continental and Marathon (formerly Ohio Oil Co.). With the exception of small interests in the Iranian Consortium these companies were newcomers in overseas oil, although each of them had substantial operations and resources in the United States. They originally took concessions independently of each other, but subsequently pooled them and their own resources in the joint venture which was to become the largest single operation in Libya, exports beginning in 1962.

Libyan American Oil Co. (a subsidiary of Texas Gulf Producing Co. − a company with small resources later acquired by Sinclair Oil Co. and then by Atlantic Richfield (Arco)) acquired seven concessions at the beginning and led the way at first in exploration drilling. After failure to discover oil, it soon began to feel the strain on its capabilities; two concessions were revoked early in 1957 because the company had failed to commence operations within eight months.[4] It invited W.R. Grace, altogether a newcomer in the oil industry, to take a 49 per cent share in the remaining concessions, and subsequently this joint operation invited Esso to take an undivided 50 per cent interest in three concessions out of the five remaining which appeared promising, and to become operator in these. Oil was shortly afterwards discovered and developed on Concession No. 20, exports commencing early in 1965.

Nelson Bunker Hunt, a US oilman conducting his own operations, obtained Concession No. 2 in 1955 and No. 65 in 1957. Little active exploration was attempted and, when oil was discovered in the concession adjacent to No. 65, BP took a 50 per cent interest in the latter, became operator and soon discovered a major field.

Other independents appeared on the scene between 1958 and the spring of 1961, at which time the grant of concessions ceased in anticipation of a new Law which would alter conditions of award. Of these, Gelsenberg has already been mentioned. Three more West German companies − Deutsche Erdoel AG, Wintershall AG and Elwerath; two Italian companies − Compagnia Ricerche Idrocarburi (CORI) and Ausonia Mineraria; and the French company, Société Nationale des Pétroles d'Aquitaine (SNPA) also took concessions in various partnership combinations.[5] Two further substantial American independents − Phillips and Standard Oil of Indiana (Pan American, later Amoco) − also took concessions on surrendered areas and each succeeded in developing a minor operation with the aid of pipelines constructed by the Oasis Group, exports beginning in 1966 and 1967 respectively. Finally, Libya Atlantic (a subsidiary of Atlantic Refining Co. – sizeable in the American market, but with no production experience) took four off-shore concessions, but was obliged to invite Phillips to take a 50 per cent interest shortly afterwards, although continuing to be operators. Gas was subsequently discovered, but no commercial operation developed.

The above summary points to a conclusion that very few oil companies had the resources of their own, or access to the resources, to finance single-handed exploration and production operations leading to the development of a major oilfield, including pipeline transportation to sea, in Libya. The sole exception to this generality in Libya in the early days was Esso[6] which, because of the size of its operation and speed of development, became the 'leader' of the concessionaires in matters of co-ordination of oil company views *vis-à-vis* the Government, and particularly in the posted price issue. Other majors might have developed operations alone if they had had better fortune in discoveries. Gulf discovered substantial oil in Concession No. 66, but it was far from the sea and would have required a long and difficult pipeline of its own; in spite of pressure from the Government, Gulf declined to develop and subsequently abandoned it. The larger independents, acting jointly as the Oasis Group, did, for the first time in the Eastern Hemisphere, mount a major operation. The smaller independents, in the case of successful discovery, either invited the larger companies to talk half shares and conduct operations, as in the case of Nelson Bunker Hunt and Libyan American/Grace, or mounted a small operation, relying on the use of pipelines financed and constructed by others, as with Phillips and Pan American.

4.4   Waivers and Benefits Offered by New Concession Applicants and Assignees

Within a short time of the enactment of the Petroleum Law, and well before commercial oil had been discovered, there is evidence of some realisation in government quarters that, in the event of an oil industry developing, its fiscal terms were in some respects inordinately generous. Beginning with the 73rd concession awarded on 10 November 1957, undertakings were given by new concessionaires which waived the claiming of depletion allowance and/or undertook to increase royalty;

in addition there were offers of bonuses and of government participation in the event of commercial development. A list of the recorded
agreements is given in Table 4.2.

Table 4.2: Undertakings of Conditions Outside the Terms of the Law
by Oil Companies Obtaining New Concessions and Assignments

Date of Concession	Concession No.	Concessionaire	Condition Undertaken by Concessionaire
10 Nov. 1957	73	Texaco/Socal	Depletion allowance limited to actual amount spent on exploration in concessions.
17 Mar. 1958	74, 5, 6	Panam	Ditto plus bonus of $5m by instalments (1/24 of value of oil production) if and when production of oil occurs.
14 Aug. 1958	77	DEA/WIAG	$1 million expenditure on exploration in first two years; extra 2 per cent royalty up to $1m.
19 Nov. 1959	82	CORI	Royalty 17½ per cent. Depletion allowance waived. Government 30 per cent participation option.
9 Apr. 1961	90-92	Phillips	Royalty 19 per cent. Depletion allowance waived.
5 Sept. 1959	80, 81	BP	Depletion allowance waived.
2 June 1959	78	Elwerath-DEA-WIAG	Extra 2½ per cent royalty not credited against tax. Half depletion must be actually spent on exploration to be deductible.

Assignments		Assignee/Assignor	
Date of Assignment			
17 Apr. 1959	16, 17, 20	Esso Sirte — 50 per cent of Liamco/Grace concessions	Minimum expenditure of $6m by all partners. Esso to dispose of partners' share downstream at same prices as its own (at their option). Esso Sirte to construct refinery in Libya.
Sept. 1960	65	BP — 50 per cent of NB Hunt Concession	Surrender of depletion allowance on all Libyan acreage plus unspecified drilling obligations.

Sources: A.A.Q. Kubbah, *Libya — Its Oil Industry and Economic System*
(Rihani Press, Beirut, 1964); Ministry of Petroleum Affairs; *Petroleum Times*. For
fuller description of companies see Appendix 4.1.

None of the waivers and undertakings by the concession-bidders had any immediate effect on payments to the Government, and some of them would not have done so even in the event of commercial development under the terms of the Law as it then was. The first point conceded was the percentage depletion allowance, which, it will be remembered, through oil company influence in drafting, was incorporated in the 1955 Law after the US pattern and contrary to that of major Middle East concessions. The waiver of this by concession-seekers could scarcely be represented as a sacrifice since, even without it, they could deduct from income tax for tax purposes 100 per cent of all intangible exploration and drilling costs in the year in which they were incurred (and carry them forward in the event of losses for ten years). In addition, all concessions in Libya were to be treated as a single operation for accounting purposes, thus ensuring 100 per cent charging against income, when achieved, of all exploration expenses (except on physical assets) anywhere in Libya. It was unreasonably generous to allow percentage depletion as well, seeing that, if granted, it could be used, at the company's discretion, for further exploration anywhere in the world.

Another benefit offered by concession-seekers was increase in royalty payments. Under the terms of the Law royalty was to be treated as a pre-payment of tax, and was credited against the income and surtax liability of that and future years' operations. Thus no extra payment was involved in such an offer, provided that surtax liability was sufficient to absorb the royalty. There may have been some major benefit to the Government by virtue of earlier receipt of moneys in respect of royalties, which were paid quarterly within two months of the period concerned irrespective of whether there were taxable profits or not, while surtax was paid annually within four months of the end of each year. Only in the case of Concession No. 78, where Elwerath, in conjunction with DEA and WIAG, offered an extra 2½ per cent royalty to be treated as an expense and not credited against tax liability, was there real extra payment, albeit contingent, offered to the Government.

Other agreements included CORI's offer, in respect of Concession No. 82, to the Government of a 30 per cent participation option in the event of discovery of commercial oil. If this had been taken up, the Government would have been obliged to reimburse the company for all exploration and development expenditure, as well for the pre-production as for the commercial period, up to the percentage of participation. Another concession-seeker — Panam — offered, in respect of

Concessions 74, 75 and 76, a bonus to the Government of one-twenty-fourth of the value of its oil production, if and when it occurred, up to a maximum of $5 million. There is no evidence whether sums paid would have been treated as a tax deductible in Panam's accounts (and therefore 50 per cent recovered in lower tax payments); nor whether such payments were undertaken and made in respect of the later Concessions 93-95, where commercial oil was developed (operations in Concessions 74-6 not having been successful).

These agreements were not officially published. The Petroleum Law stipulated[7] that 'the Commission may grant concessions in the form set out in the Second Schedule to this Law and not otherwise.' It also provided that in the event of conflicting applications 'preference shall be given (sc. among qualified applicants) to the first person to apply.'[8] It can only be assumed that the Commission, in granting concessions to those who offered waivers and extra benefits outside the terms of the Law, was exercising discretion by virtue of the word 'may', which presumably exempted it from an absolute obligation to grant a concession to the first qualified applicant.

There were no such considerations in the case of assignment of concessions. Article 17 of the Law stated: 'a concession may not be assigned except with the consent of the Commission subject to such conditions as it may deem appropriate.' By virtue of this provision Esso, in order to buy into the promising concessions of Liamco/ Grace (Nos. 16, 17 and 20), undertook to construct a refinery, and BP, in order to acquire a 50 per cent interest in Nelson Bunker Hunt's Concession No. 65, agreed to surrender percentage depletion on all its Libyan acreage and to undertake certain drilling obligations, which were not divulged, but were in excess of the minimum expenditure obligations stipulated in Article 11 of the Law.

4.5　The Watershed of 1961

The year 1961 marks the end of the first stage and the beginning of the second in the development of the Libyan oil industry. In April the last concessions were awarded under the unamended 1955 Law. In anticipation of changes in the award procedures and conditions, new awards were thereafter suspended — as it turned out for five years. In July a major amendment to the 1955 Law was introduced; and in September Esso began exporting oil from its Zelten concession, thus placing Libya among the oil-producing and -exporting countries. The changes and developments are described in Part III of this book.

Notes

1. The Libyan pound (£L) was at that time tied at par to the £ sterling, and each pound was equal at par to US $2.80.

2. A chronological list of concessions granted and of the concession-holders is given in Appendix 4.1. A record of oil and gas discoveries is contained in Appendix 4.2.

3. *Petroleum Times*, 18 July 1958.

4. *Petroleum Times*, 29 Aug. 1957. Clause 4 of the Concession Deed required the Company 'to commence operations to explore for petroleum within the concession area within eight months from the date of grant of the concession'; Clause 27 stipulated that the concession may be revoked for failure to do this.

5. No oil development took place in any of these concessions.

6. Occidental Petroleum was to provide a second notable exception in the late 1960s.

7. Article 9.

8. Article 6.

Appendix 4.1: Chronological List of Concessions Awards from November 1955 to April 1961

Concession Number	Date of Grant	Parent Company of Original Concessionaire	Libyan Subsidiary of Parent Company	Operating Company	Zone	Area of Concession		Subsequently Recorded Changes and Other Comments (For nationalisations see also Appendix 4.2)
						Original ('000 sq. kilometres)	As at 31.12.64	
1	20.11.55	Standard Oil Company (New Jersey) (Name later changed to Exxon)	Esso Standard (Libya) Inc.	Esso Standard (Libya)	IV	20.8	10.4	Surrendered, 1971
2	20.11.55	Nelson Bunker Hunt	N.B. Hunt	N.B. Hunt	II	11.7	5.8	Surrendered, 1971
3	12.12.55	Standard Oil Co. (New Jersey)	Esso Standard (Libya) Inc.	Esso Standard	I	10.9	4.9	
4	12.12.55	"	"	"	I	3.1	1.6	
5	12.12.55	"	"	"	I	1.7	0.9	
6	12.12.55	"	"	"	II	25.7	12.8	
7	12.12.55	"	"	"	II	1.3	0.7	
8	12.12.55	"	"	"	I	11.9	5.9	Surrendered, 1971
9	31.12.55	Socony Mobil Oil Co. (Name later changed to Mobil Oil Corp.)	Mobil Oil Libya Ltd	Mobil (Libya)	I	2.0	1.0	25% undivided interest in all Mobil concessions assigned to Gelsenberg Benzin AG (parent co. — Gelsenkirchener Bergwerk AG) in July 1958 — raised to 35% in 1967
10	31.12.55	"	"	"	I	2.3	1.2	"
11	31.12.55	"	"	"	I	19.0	9.4	"
12	31.12.55	"	"	"	II	8.0	4.0	"
13	31.12.55	"	"	"	II	6.9	3.0	"
14	31.12.55	"	"	"	II	7.8	3.9	"
15	31.12.55	"	"	"	II	0.8	0.4	"

Appendix 1 *(continued)*

Concession Number	Date of Grant	Parent Company of Original Concessionaire	Libyan Subsidiary of Parent Company	Operating Company	Zone	Area of Concession Original ('000 sq. kilometres)	As at 31.12.64	Subsequently Recorded Changes and Other Comments (For nationalisations see also Appendix 4.2)
16	12.12.55	Texas Gulf Producing Co. (acquired by Sinclair Oil Corp. and later by Atlantic Richfield (Arco))	Libyan American Oil Co. (Liamco) (Arco)	Esso Sirte Inc. (from 1957)	I	3.7	1.9	49% interest assigned to W.R. Grace, and 50% of the combined interest assigned to Esso Sirte Inc. (parent company Standard Oil, New Jersey) in 1957. Interests then were — Esso: 50%, Liamco: 25.5%, Grace: 24.5%
17	12.12.55	"	"	Liamco	I	4.5	2.2	49% interest assigned to W.R. Grace
18	12.12.55	"	"	"	II	7.2	3.5	Surrendered, 1970
19	12.12.55	"	"	"	II	7.4	3.7	As Concessions 16 and 17 above
20	12.12.55	"	"	Esso Sirte Inc. (from 1957)	II	4.7	2.4	"
21	12.12.55	"	"	Liamco	IV	33.5	—	Concession revoked in 1957
22	12.12.55	"	"	"	IV	39.6	—	"
23	31.12.55	Compagnie Française des Pétroles	Compagnie des Pétroles Total (Libye)	CPTL (Total)	I	14.9	7.4	Surrendered, 1970
24	31.12.55	Amerada Petroleum Corp.	Amerada Petroleum Co. of Libya	Oasis Oil Co. of Libya	I	6.2	3.0	Concessions 25-33, 59, 60 and 71, were pooled by the concessionaires — Amerada, Continental and Marathon — each taking a 33⅓% undivided interest. Oasis Oil Co. of Libya
25	12.12.55	"	"	"	I	8.4	4.2	
26	12.12.55	"	"	"	IV	53.6	26.8	
27	12.12.55	"	"	"	II	0.9	0.5	
28	12.12.55	"	"	"	II	1.8	0.9	

Appendix 1 *(continued)*

No.	Date	Original company	Current company				Notes
29	12.12.55	"	"	II	2.5	1.3	was operator. Subsequently, in 1966, Amerada assigned 50% interest in its share to Shell
30	12.12.55	Continental Oil Co. (Delaware)	Continental Oil Co. of Libya	I	16.4	8.2	"
31	12.12.55	"	Oasis Oil Co. of Libya "	II	26.3	13.1	"
32	12.12.55	Ohio Oil Co. (later Marathon Oil Co.)	Marathon Petroleum Libya Ltd (previously Oasis Oil Co.)	Oasis Oil Co.	I	5.1	2.6	26 and 30 surrendered, 1970 Concessions 25-33, 59, 60 and 71 were pooled by the concessionaires — Amerada, Continental and Marathon — each taking a $33\frac{1}{3}$% undivided interest. Oasis Oil Co. of Libya was operator. Subsequently, in 1966, Amerada assigned 50% interest in its share to Shell
33	12.12.55	"	"	II	26.1	13.0	
34	28.1.56	British Petroleum Co. Ltd.	British Petroleum Exploration (Libya) Ltd (originally D'Arcy Exploration Africa)	British Petroleum Exploration (Libya) Ltd (BP)	I	20.1	10.0	Surrendered, 1971
35	28.1.56	"	"	II	1.8	—	Surrendered, 1960s
36	28.1.56	"	"	II	5.6	3.0	Surrendered, 1971
37	28.1.56	"	"	II	8.8	4.4	Surrendered, 1971
38	11.1.56	Royal Dutch/Shell	Libya Shell NV	Libya Shell NV (Shell)	I	6.1	3.0	Surrendered, 1970
39	11.1.56	"	"	I	6.2	3.0	Surrendered, 1960s
40	11.1.56	"	"	I	4.8	2.5	Surrendered, 1960s

Appendix 1 *(continued)*

Concession Number	Date of Grant	Parent Company of Original Concessionaire	Libyan Subsidiary of Parent Company	Operating Company	Zone	Area of Concession ('000 sq. kilometres) Original	As at 31.12.64	Subsequently Recorded Changes and Other Comments (For nationalisations see also Appendix 4.2)
41	11. 1.56	Royal Dutch/Shell	Libya Shell NV	Libya Shell	II	16.1	3.1	Surrendered, 1970
42	31.12.55	Texaco Inc. Standard Oil Co. of California	Texaco Overseas California Asiatic	American Overseas Petroleum Ltd (Amoseas)	I	13.7	6.8	
43	31.12.55	"	"	"	I	8.3	4.1	
44	31.12.55	"	"	"	I	6.9	3.4	
45	31.12.55	"	"	"	II	1.8	0.9	
46	31.12.55	"	"	"	II	18.6	9.3	
47	31.12.55	"	"	"	II	4.1	2.1	100% nationalised, 1974
48	2. 5.56	Standard Oil Co. (New Jersey) (Exxon)	Esso Standard (Libya) Inc.	Esso	IV	6.8	3.4	Surrendered, 1971
49	2. 5.56	Compagnie Française des Pétroles	Compagnie des Pétroles Total (Libye)	CPTL (Total)	IV	9.7	5.0	Surrendered, 1970
50	2. 5.56	Socony Mobil Oil Co. (Mobil)	Mobil Oil Libya Ltd	Mobil (Libya)	IV	19.7	9.8	Gelsenberg 25%, later 35% participation as under Concession No. 9
51	2. 5.56	Texaco Inc. Standard Oil of California	Texaco Overseas California Asialic	Amoseas	II	5.4	3.0	100% nationalised, 1974
52	15.12.56	Royal Dutch/Shell	Libya Shell NV	Shell	IV	4.3	2.2	Surrendered, 1970
53	22.12.56	Continental Oil Co.	Continental Oil Co. of Libya	—	II	1.0	—	Surrendered, 1960s

Appendix 1 *(continued)*

No.	Date	Company	Operating company				Remarks
54	22.12.56	Continental Oil Co.	Continental Oil Co. of Libya (later Marathon)	—	II	1.4	—	Surrendered, 1960s
55	22.12.56	Ohio Oil Co. (later Marathon)	Oasis Oil Co.	—	II	1.7	—	"
56	22.12.56	"	"		II	3.5	—	"
57	26. 1.57	Socony Mobil Oil Co. (Mobil)	Mobil Oil Co. Libya	Mobil (Libya)	II	5.8	3.0	Gelsenberg participation as in Concession 9, etc.
58	11.12.56	Standard Oil Co. (New Jersey) (later Exxon)	Esso Standard Libya	Esso	IV	16.8	8.3	Surrendered, 1971
59	22.12.56	Amerada Petroleum Corp.	Amerada Petroleum Co. of Libya	Oasis	II	24.4	12.1	Pooled with partners in Oasis as for Concessions 25-33
60	26. 1.57	Ohio Oil Co. (Marathon)	Oasis Oil Co. (later Marathon)	Oasis (Libya)	I	24.9	18.6	Surrendered, 1970
61	4. 3.57	Compagnie Française des Pétroles	Compagnie des Pétroles Total (Libye)	CPTL (Total)	I	8.6	6.4	Surrendered, 1970
62	20. 2.57	Socony Mobil Oil Co. (Mobil)	Mobil Oil Co. Libya	Mobil (Libya)	I	1.1	0.9	Gelsenberg participation as in Concession 9, etc.
63	14. 7.57	British Petroleum Co. Ltd	BP Exploration Libya (originally D'Arcy Exploration Africa)	BP Exploration (Libya)	I	7.0	5.2	Surrendered, 1960s
64	14. 7.57	"	"	"	IV	29.1	21.8	Surrendered, 1971
65	18.12.57	Nelson Bunker Hunt	N.B. Hunt	BP Exploration (Libya)	III	32.9	24.6	50% interest assigned to BP, who became operator. BP nationalised 1971: Hunt, 1973
66	8. 4.57	Gulf Oil Corporation	Gulf Oil Co. of Libya	Gulf	I	29.1	14.5	Surrendered, 1970

Appendix 1 (continued)

Concession Number	Date of Grant	Parent Company of Original Concessionaire	Libyan Subsidiary of Parent Company	Operating Company	Zone	Area of Concession As at 31.12.64 ('000 sq. kilometres)		Subsequently Recorded Changes and Other Comments (For nationalisations see Appendix 4.2)
						Original	As at 31.12.64	
67	8. 4.57	Gulf Oil Corporation	Gulf Oil Co. of Libya	Gulf	IV	45.6	28.2	Surrendered, 1970
68	8. 4.57	"	"	"	IV	21.6	5.0	"
69	10.12.57	Royal Dutch/Shell Group	Libya Shell NV	Libya Shell	I	7.8	5.8	Surrendered, 1965
70	10.12.57	"	"		I	5.0	3.7	Surrendered, 1970
71	10.12.57	Amerada Petroleum Corp.	Amerada Petroleum Co. of Libya	Oasis (Libya)	III	60.6	45.4	
72	18.12.57	Socony Mobil Oil 75% Gelsenkirchener Bergwerk AG 25%	Mobil Oil Libya Gelsenberg Benzin AG	Mobil (Libya)	III	11.0	8.2	Changed to 65/35 in 1967
73	10.11.57	Texaco Inc. 50% Standard Oil Co. of California 50%	Texaco Overseas California Asiatic	Amoseas	IV	40.4	30.3	
74	17. 3.58	Standard Oil Co. of Indiana (later American Oil Co. — Amoco)	Pan American Libya Oil Co. (later Amoco Libya Oil Co.)	Pan American Libya (later Amoco Libya)	III	37.2	27.9	Surrendered, 1970
75	17. 3.58	"	"		IV	11.0	—	Surrendered, 1960s
76	17. 3.58	"	"		IV	44.7	33.5	Surrendered, 1972
77	14. 8.58	Deutsche Erdoel AG 50% Wintershall AG 50%	DEA Libya WIAG Libya	DEA Libya	IV	39.9	10.1	Originally granted to DEA; 50% assigned to WIAG Surrendered, 1971
78	2. 6.59	Gewerkschaft Elwerath 33⅓%	Elwerath Oil Co. Libya	Elwerath Libya	I	21.8	15.8	Originally granted to Elwerath; ⅓ assigned to DEA

Appendix I *(continued)*

No.	Date	Concession holder	%	Operating company	Operator		%	%	Remarks
78 (cont.)		Deutsche Erdoel Wintershall	33⅓% 33⅓%	DEA Libya WIAG Libya					and WIAG each
79	22. 5.59	Gulf Oil Corp.		Gulf Oil Co. of Libya	Gulf	I	0.8	—	Surrendered, 1960s
80	5. 9.59	British Petroleum Co. Ltd.		BP Exploration (Libya) Ltd	BP Explora- tion	II	13.6	10.2	
81	5. 9.59	"		"	"	III	49.5	37.1	
82	5. 9.59	Compagnia Ricerche Idrocarburi		CORI	CORI	II	30.0	18.9	
83	6.12.59	Texaco Inc. Standard Oil Co. of California	50% 50%	Texaco Overseas California Asiatic	Amoseas	II	8.3	6.2	Surrendered, 1974
84	10.12.59	Standard Oil Co. Indiana (later Amoco)		Pan American Libya Oil Co.	Pan American Libya	II	8.3	6.2	Surrendered, 1971
85	30. 3.60	Ausonia Mineraria Deutsche Erdoel AG Société Nationale des Pétroles d'Aquitaine	60% 20% 20%	Ausonia Mineraria DEA SNPA	Ausonia Mineraria	IV	30.5	30.5	Originally granted to Ausonia Mineraria; 20% each assigned to DEA and SNPA 16.12.62; surrendered, 1971
86	18. 6.60	Atlantic Refining Co.		Libyan Atlantic Co.	Libyan Atlantic	I	8.8	8.8	Off-shore concessions, half- share assigned to Phillips Petroleum Co.; surrendered 1971
87	18. 6.60	"		"	"	I	8.3	8.3	Surrendered, 1970
88	18. 6.60	"		"	"	II	4.9	4.9	
89	18. 6.60	"		"	"	II	5.0	5.0	

Appendix 1 *(continued)*

Concession Number	Date of Grant	Parent Company of Original Concessionaire	Libyan Subsidiary of Parent Company	Operating Company	Zone	Area of Concession ('000 sq. kilometres)		Subsequently Recorded Changes and Other Comments (For nationalisations see also Appendix 4.2)
						Original	As at 31.12.64	
90	9. 4.61	Phillips Petroleum Co.	Phillips Petroleum (Libya)	Phillips (Libya)	I	6.6	6.6	Surrendered, 1970
91	9. 4.61	"	"	"	I —		2.1	Surrendered, 1970
92	9. 4.61	"	"	"	I —		1.6	Surrendered, 1970
93	9. 4.61	Standard Oil Co. Indiana (later Amoco)	Pan American Libya Oil Co. (later Amoco)	Pan American Libya (later Amoco)	II	2.3	2.3	Standard Oil Co. Indiana changed its name to American Oil Co. and is usually called Amoco — both parent and Libyan subsidiary; surrendered, 1976
94	9. 4.61	"	"	"	II	1.8	1.8	" " "
95	9. 4.61	"	"	"	II	4.3	4.3	" " "

Appendix 4.2: Record of Oil and Gas Discoveries in Concessions 1-95

Concession Number	Oil/Gas Discovered Date	Production Rate b/d	API° Gravity	Depth '000 Feet	Whether Developed or Not	
1	20. 1.58	508	44.5	2.2	No development	
2						
3						
4						
5						
6	13. 6.59	17,500	37	5.5	Production and exports	51% nationalised, 1973
	30. 8.62	2,550	37.3	8.0		
	3. 6.64	280	32.5	5.9		
	3. 7.64	3,072	45.1	7.8		
	13. 9.64	1,968	31.7	6.1		
	16. 3.65	353	32.8	5.9		
	21. 4.65	86	52.3	9.0		
	30.10.65	2,184	36.5	8.2		
	2. 7.66	3,200	46.7	10.0		
7						
8						
9						
10						
11	19. 2.63	725	26.8	3.1	Production and exports	51% nationalised, 1973
	18. 6.63	438	34.8	4.8		
	2. 5.64	115	41	8.9		
	3.10.64	292	34.3	3.7		
	15. 7.71	6,210	51	3.8		
	29.10.64	216	43.5	3.3		

Appendix II *(continued)*

Concession Number	Oil/Gas Discovered Date	Production Rate b/d	API° Gravity	Depth '000 Feet	Whether Developed or Not	
11 (cont.)	27. 2.65	420	31.3	6.1	Production and exports	51% nationalised, 1973
	28. 5.65	402	32	2.0		
12	1.11.59	990	34	9.9	Production and exports	51% nationalised, 1973
	18. 4.62	1,077	36.2	9.5		
	16. 7.62	1,324	36.8	9.8		
	26.12.64	1,080	35.4	10.2		
	14. 5.66	882	36.4	10.2		
	30. 5.67	620	38.3	2.6		
	13. 6.68	1,225	38.5	11.5		
	2. 2.69	750	37.2	11.8		
	2. 2.69	31	40.7	11.8		
	5. 2.69	953	43.1	12.4		
13	24. 3.70	1,366	37.2	9.8	Production and exports	51% nationalised, 1973
	13. 3.62	70	35.8	7.7		
	26. 5.62	600	36.8	5.3		
	30. 8.62	760	35	7.6		
	28. 4.64	1,344	39.2	9.0		
	10. 8.67	303	51.1	9.1		
14						
15						
16	8. 9.65	480	45.7	6.8	No development	
17	30. 7.59	500	40	5.7	No development	
18						
19						
20	4. 1.61	3,000	40	5.5	Production and exports	63.5% nationalised, 1973/74

Appendix II *(continued)*

21						
22						
23	1. 6.61	1,932	38	8.0		
	31.10.61	1,187	40	4.0		
	2. 4.62	63	46	4.0		
	23. 7.62	300	34	4.7		
	21. 5.63	1,440	38	9.6	No development	
	22.12.63	1,231	41	8.5		
	19. 2.64	2,264	37	9.0		
24						
25						
26	1. 3.61	144	33	4.3		
	6. 8.64	211	22.1	3.2		
	29. 7.65	424	45.4	7.3	No development	
27						
28						
29						
30						
31	17. 1.65	2,340	37	8.5	No development	
32	27. 7.58	500	39	5.8	Production and exports	59.2% nationalised, 1973/4
	30. 4.59	1,061	41	3.2		
	14.11.59	36	43.5	2.8		
33						
34	26. 5.61	160	37.5	7.7	No development	
35						
36						
37						
38						
39						

Appendix II *(continued)*

Concession Number	Oil/Gas Discovered Date	Production Rate b/d	API° Gravity	Depth '000 Feet	Whether Developed or Not	
40						
41	1.12.60	150	32	6.1	No development	
42						
43						
44						
45						
46						
47	26. 9.59	3,650	36.6	4.0	Production and exports	100% nationalised, 1973/4
	2. 4.62	342	37.2	3.2		"
	28. 6.63	850	31.5	5.4		
	16.11.63	1,200	34.2	5.5		
	26. 6.64	351	32.2	5.9		
	20.10.64	850	27.1	4.8		
	29.12.64	336	32.8	6.4		
	6. 6.67	900	36.2	3.0		
48						
49	26.12.58	100	45	4.6	No development	100% nationalised, 1973/4
50						
51	3. 4.62	430	35.7	9.7	Production and exports	100% nationalised, 1973/4
	19. 8.65	420	30.4	2.4		
	28.10.71	42		12.0		
52						
53						
54						
55						

Appendix II *(continued)*

	Date				Production and exports
56					
57					
58					
59	27.12.59	226	21.6	1.5	59.2% nationalised, 1973
	14. 2.60	766	33	5.5	
	12. 8.61	1,188	34.5	5.7	
	16. 9.61	1,093	43.6	8.7	
	9.12.61	420	37	2.7	
	2. 1.62	1,200	33.8	4.5	
	1. 4.62	2,009	37.2	7.4	
	5. 5.62	1,565	36.2	7.0	
	31. 7.62	1,224	36.1	7.3	
	12. 8.62	1,866	32.1	6.3	
	10.10.62	240	32	3.6	
	11.12.62	768	34.3	5.5	
	16.12.62	670	28.6	5.2	
	13. 6.63	1,812	37.6	9.9	
	6.11.63	2,740	37.0	6.7	
	22.11.63	1,960	39.2	10.1	
	19. 2.64	584	36	5.2	
	1.11.64	2,500	36	7.7	
	14. 4.67	2,540	40	10.2	
60					
61					
62					
63					
64					Production and exports
65	28.11.61	3,910	37	8.7	BP 100% nationalised, 1971
	9. 4.66	800	38.8	8.9	Hunt 100% nationalised, 1973

Appendix II *(continued)*

Concession Number	Oil/Gas Discovered Date	Production Rate b/d	API° Gravity	Depth '000 Feet	Whether Developed or Not
65 (cont.)	16. 9.71	10,000		9.2	
	26.12.71	720		10.0	
66	7. 9.59	888	37.9	4.1	No development
	21. 1.66	176	39	5.1	
	28. 4.60	1,200	39.2	5.2	
	15.12.60	650	40	5.2	
	27. 1.61	3,000	40	5.5	
	11. 3.61	1,104	37.6	4.6	
	5. 9.61	400	42.5	5.0	
	1.10.61	600	40.3	5.1	
	22.12.61	1.139	40.6	9.1	
	30.12.61	850	41.4	4.5	
	28. 2.62	684	34.1	4.8	
	29. 4.62	800	42	4.5	
	26. 9.62	665	41.8	3.4	
67					
68					
69					
70	30.10.59	700	49	8.9	No development
	14. 5.61	50	36	7.9	
	14. 5.62	50	36	7.9	
71	27. 3.63	500	31	6.6	No development
	14.12.63	576	53.5	5.3	
72	12. 1.64	303	36	5.4	

Appendix II *(continued)*

73						
74						
75						
76						
77						
78	21.12.61	138	41	6.1	No development	
79						
80	13. 8.67	4,150	37.8	9.7	No development	
81						
82	23. 4.62	345	45	11.1	No development	50% State participation, 1972
	18. 9.65	279	40.4	14.0		
83						
84						
85						
86						
87						
88						
89						
90	1.11.64	1,730	48	4.5	No development	
91						
92	25.11.62	1,100	45	3.1	Production and exports	Surrendered field to State, 1970
	23.11.63	528	84.9	3.8		" " "
93	30. 6.64	4,020	36.4	5.6	Production and exports	" " " 1976
	9. 9.65	480	27	5.5		
94						
95	19. 8.66	820	34.8	11.1	Production and exports	" " " 1976
	27. 1.68	868	40.3	10.3		

Part III

REVISIONS TO LEGISLATION, 1961 AND 1965

5 THE 1961 AMENDMENTS TO THE PETROLEUM LAW AND REGULATION NO. 6

5.1 Introduction

In Chapter 4 it was mentioned that, as early as 1957, there had been some doubts on the Government side about the terms given to concessionaires in the Petroleum Law, and these manifested themselves in a series of understandings with applicants for new concessions and assignments that they would waive one or more of the contractual terms or give an undertaking to provide an extra benefit over and above the terms of the concession contract.

The known undertakings of this nature are listed in Table 4.2. In 1957 no oil of any sort had yet been discovered. It may be inferred from these that, even without the near prospect of oil production and exports, attention was given to the anomalies of the Libyan Law in comparison with prevailing practice elsewhere in the Eastern Hemisphere. From the middle of 1959, when Esso discovered and began to develop the Zelten field, these problems became more urgent. In addition to the Zelten discovery, in 1959 there were others by Oasis at Dahra, Bahi and Waha (32 and 59), Mobil at Hofra and Amal (11 and 12) and Amoseas at Beda (47), which were to be developed commercially.

In 1960 steps were taken to prepare an amendment to the Petroleum Law in order to correct some of the anomalies, as well as errors and ambiguities of wording, in the 1955 Law, and also to make it more comparable with contemporary concession conditions elsewhere.

To assist in achieving these ends the Government employed in 1960 the services of Dr Nadim Pachachi as consultant, an Iraqi who had had a great deal of experience of relationships with the oil concessionaire in his own country, including that of Minister for Oil and of the negotiations which culminated in the agreements of the early 1950s on posted prices and 50/50 division of profits.

5.2 Royal Decree of 3 July 1961

The Royal Decree amending the Law was promulgated on 3 July 1961 and published in the *Official Gazette* on 15 July 1961. It took the form mainly of deletions, amendments and additions to 11 of the 25 Articles of the 1955 Law and 8 of the 29 Clauses of the Concession Deed attached to the Law as its Second Schedule.

Of the many changes to the 1955 Law in the amending Decree, the most significant were (1) the provisions completely altering the procedure for grant of concessions and (2) those altering the definition of taxable profits of the concession-holders, in an attempt to bring Libyan practice in this respect into line with that prevailing in most Middle East oil-exporting countries at the time. The first of these two objectives was attained in a manner satisfactory to the Government, but on the problem of fiscal comparability with concessions in other countries the Amendment floundered. This was because of the opposition of the independents, primarily the Oasis Group who, on the basis of the Clause in the existing concession deeds safeguarding the concessionaire's contractual rights, successfully bargained for wording in the implementing regulation which nullified the intent of the new Law as the price of their consent to it.[1]

The granting of concessions on a time priority basis was replaced by a sealed bid system, tenders to be made in response to invitations by the Petroleum Commission in respect of specified areas. In the event of conflicting applications for the same area the Commission would have 'absolute discretion' as to which application to accept. And in making its decision the Commission 'shall take into account such additional economic and financial benefits and advantages and other things which the applicant is willing and able to offer in addition to those stated' (in the Law).[2]

This Amendment freed the Petroleum Commission from the obligation to grant concessions at any time to any qualified applicant – an unprecedented self-imposed constraint on a sovereign power. At the same time it opened the door to the possibilities of favouritism, intrigue, graft and corruption which were not in fact to manifest themselves until 1966, for it was not until then that further concessions were awarded.

The definition of profits on which the concessionaire was to be charged to tax at the rate of 50 per cent was altered in the following manner: so far as allowable costs and expenses were concerned, the percentage depletion provisions of the 1955 Law were cancelled. Amortisation of pre-production intangible exploration expenses was changed from 20 per cent to 5 per cent p.a., and depreciation of pre-production expenditure of physical assets from 20 per cent to

10 per cent p.a. Exploration expenditure incurred after the 'effective date'[3] anywhere in Libya could be expensed in the year in which it was incurred, and expenditure on physical assets after the effective date continued to be depreciated at 10 per cent p.a.[4]

On the sales revenue side, the income resulting from the operations of the concession-holder in Libya, on which he was to be chargeable to tax, was defined as:

(a) in relation to the export by the concession-holder of crude oil from Libya, the posted price per ton of such crude oil less marketing expenses as defined by Regulations multiplied by the number of tons of crude oil so exported and

(b) in relation to other operations of the concession-holder in Libya the income to be ascertained in a manner to be agreed between the concession-holder and the Commission.[5]

Thus the principle of posted prices for the assessment of taxable income and of royalty was introduced for the first time into the Libyan legislation. The Regulation, however, which defined the marketing expenses, when it was published in December of 1961, did so in such a way as effectively to nullify the intentions of the legislation to establish posted prices as the unequivocal 'tax reference' price. How this came about and its results, leading up to the further Amendment of 1965, will be described in Chapter 6 below.

Other minor matters which the Amendment strove to improve included the following:

(1) A provision to ensure that the areas surrendered after 5, 8 and 10 years should be in one compact block (two in the case of concession areas of more than 12,000 square kilometres). This was to ensure that viable areas would be available to new applicants for concessions from the land tracts surrendered.

(2) Fees payable on the grant of a concession were altered to £100 per 100 square kilometres and *pro rata* for part thereof. This raised the nugatory initial stake of £L500 per concession whatever its size, and may have discouraged reckless bids by applicants of insubstantial backing from applying for very large areas. The new fees were still minute in relation to the large sums involved, even in pre-drilling exploratory activities, of a substantial operator.

(3) The rental provisions of the 1955 Law were also changed, primarily to remove the anomaly of the wording of the Law which resulted in the higher rent of £L2,500 per 100 square kilometres on the finding of commercial petroleum being chargeable only if this event occurred after the eighth year from the granting of the concession. The concession-holder now became liable to the higher rent on commercial discovery whenever that occurred. At the same time rents after the fifteenth year were raised from £2,500 per 100 square kilometres to £3,500, and after the twentieth year to £5,000.

(4) The Amendment changed the valuation for royalty purposes of crude oil production 'won and saved into field storage' to a calculation 'on the basis of the posted price'. Hitherto (although no oil had yet been won and saved) it had been defined as the 'free competitive market price' of the crude oil f.o.b. at seaboard terminal, less handling charges and costs of transportation from field storage.[6] The valuation of natural gasoline and natural gas for royalty remained unchanged.

(5) The royalty rate continued at 12½ per cent of the value of the oil produced, but the Amendment introduced an option for the Commission to take royalty in kind. In the event this was of little significance in the early years, since the payment of royalty in money at posted prices always — until 1970 and occasionally thereafter — provided a larger sum than that which could have been obtained by taking it in oil and selling the oil.

(6) Of greater signficance, however, was an added Clause which provided that rents on concessions declared commercial would be deducted from royalty payments. The result was that once a concessionaire was producing and paying substantial royalty, he effectively paid no more rents on his oil-producing concession since they were offset against his royalty payments. It may be surmised that in negotiations the oil companies obtained this concession in return for those which they gave, in order to avoid paying the high rent of £2,500 per 100 square kilometres on commercial concessions in addition to the royalty.

(7) The Amendment attempted to remove the anomaly of the 1955 Law which allowed all 'taxes and imposts' to which a concession-holder was liable in Libya to be treated as part of the Government's 50 per cent share of profits. The Amendment restricted such allowables against

surtax (the word used to describe the tax payment making the total Government take up to 50 per cent to 'fees, rents and royalties . . . and income tax[7] and other direct taxes'. This Amendment was largely frustrated in its intent since the concessionaires claimed that virtually all their payments of taxes and imposts were 'direct' taxes, and continued to treat them as tax credits against surtax. The whole matter gave rise to prolonged controversy, particularly concerning customs duties, stamp taxes and vehicle licences. Regulation No. 6, to be published in the following December, while attempting to give a ruling on these matters, did little to clear up the problems (see section 5.5.1 below).

(8) At the same time another anomaly was rectified in that, under the 1955 Law, if the payments described in (7) above exceeded the 50 per cent total liability, the excess could be carried forward and deducted from *all* payments due to the Petroleum Commission in subsequent years (which would include fees, rents and royalties); the Amendment changed this to allow the offsetting against income tax and surtax only, thus excluding royalties. However, in the November 1961 Decree, which might be described as an 'Amendment to the Amendment', direct taxes were added back to income and surtax for offsetting purposes (see section 5.4, below).

(9) A small change with big consequences slipped into the 1961 Decree almost unnoticed, although it must have been objectionable to the oil companies. To the 1955 provision (Article 14(5)) that 'in computing profits as herein defined sound accounting practices usual in the petroleum industry shall be employed' there was added 'where more than one such accounting practice prevails the Commission shall decide which practice is to be applied by the concession-holder'. This addition had far-reaching effects, as it deprived concession-holders of the choice of applying in their fiscal accounts the accounting practice most advantageous to themselves in cases of more than one possibility. It may be surmised that in such cases the Government would insist on the practice which led to results most favourable to itself, and this in fact happened on more than one occasion.

(10) The 1955 Law, while not allowing assignment of concessions to third parties without the consent of the Commission, exempted from this consent assignment to affiliates. The Amendment removed this exception and required all assignments to have the written consent of

the Commission 'which may impose any conditions which it may deem appropriate in the public interest'. The object of this measure is not altogether clear, unless it was intended by the Government to stop a loophole for contrived assignments, or to give it a stronger position in persuading concession-holders to amend their concessions to the new Decree. In effect, it gave another reason for demurring concessionaires to resist voluntary amendment. So far as is known the Amendment did not give rise to any significant practical problems.

(11) There was also a change in arbitration procedure introduced in the 1961 Amendment. The 1955 Law required this to be 'governed by and interpreted in accordance with the Laws of Libya and such principles and rules of international law as may be relevant'. The 1961 Amendment added, 'but only to the extent that such rules and principles are not inconsistent with and do not conflict with the laws of Libya'.

It will be described later how the 1965 Amendment to the terms of the OPEC formula changed the arbitration clause to make the principles of international law predominant over those of Libya. In 1961 Libya had not yet joined OPEC. The 1961 Amendment to the arbitration provisions was later described by the Ministry of Petroleum Affairs as 'bringing the Law into line with comparable provisions in agreements concluded between some Arab governments and the oil companies.'[8] The oil companies certainly did not like the change, and it gave them another reason for hesitation over accepting the Amendments. In the event, there was no arbitration during the following 10 years.

5.3   The Seeking of Concession-Holders' Assent

Since the 1955 Law stipulated that the contractual rights expressly created by a concession should not be altered except by mutual consent of the parties, the Government was unwilling unilaterally to impose the 1961 Amendment on existing concessionaires, and sought the agreement of each one to amend its own concession deeds to the new terms. To this end, the 1961 Decree provided for those companies that accepted the revision within six months to extend the tenure of their existing concessions for a period equal to that from the date of grant of the concession to the date on which the new Law took effect.[9] Thus the first concessions granted, at the end of 1955 and early in 1956, would receive an extension of between five and six years. On the other hand, those who did not amend within the six months were debarred, under the same Article of the Amendment, from obtaining any further concessions.

It was to be expected that the concession-holders, whose contractual rights were safeguarded under the 1955 Law, would demur when called upon voluntarily to amend their concessions; and to do so in a manner involving major sacrifices for no consideration except the extension of the concession and exemption from being debarred from applying for new concessions, if and when the opportunity occurred.[10]

There had been extensive talks with the oil companies on the draft terms of the Amendments over a long period before the Decree of 1961 was promulgated, in order to try to reduce them to a form acceptable to existing concession-holders. Different attitudes were adopted by different companies. The majors had few grounds for resisting the Amendments, since they were aware that they did no more than bring the Libyan situation some way towards parity with their other concession agreements in the Eastern Hemisphere. The independents, without other Eastern Hemisphere production operations, had no such inhibitions. The sole incentive for them to amend — apart from the extension of existing and eligibility for new concessions — was the consideration of their relations with the host government of the country from which they hoped to gain considerable wealth. They had had little experience at that time of these delicate relationships, which involved a sovereign power in contractual agreement with them to exploit the most important natural resource of the country.

Esso and the Oasis companies — Amerada, Continental and Marathon — were the concession-holders whose acceptance was the key to the success of the Amendments. In the middle of 1961 Esso was about to begin production (their effective date was at the beginning of September 1961) to be followed by the Oasis companies in the middle of 1962. Before any of them gave their final acceptance, they brought pressure on the Government to issue a further Decree — of 9 November 1961 — modifying the previous Decree on two points to make it more palatable to the companies; and in addition to promulgate Petroleum Regulation No. 6, published in the *Official Gazette* on 23 December 1961, which was the definitive Regulation giving the details of implementation of most aspects of the Law.

Esso signalled its acceptance first but, in accordance with its firm policy of not tolerating more favourable fiscal treatment of others than itself, strove to make it conditional on other producing concessionaires doing the same. The Oasis companies demurred for a long time – well after Regulation 6 had conceded to them a definition of marketing expenses to be deducted from posted prices in calculating taxable income to include rebates, i.e. price-cuts to meet competition (see section 5.5.3 below). This inclusion effectively destroyed the whole posted price edifice which it was the principal object of the 1961 Amendment to establish.

5.4   Royal Decree of 9 November 1961

The principal object of this short Decree was to give some points to the concession-holders on which they were sticking before agreeing to amend to the terms as revised in July. Perhaps the most important matter, in the eyes of the concession-holders, was the demand of as firm a guarantee as possible that they would not subsequently be called upon yet again by the Government to sacrifice their contractual rights which already, under the 1955 Law, could 'not be altered except by mutual consent of the parties'. It appeared that this phrase in the 1955 Law did not altogether satisfy them, and in order to consolidate it a second paragraph was added in the November 1961 Decree, Article 2, to the effect that the concession should

> throughout the period of its validity be construed in accordance with the Petroleum Law and the Regulations in force at the time of granting the concession. Any amendment to or repeal of these Regulations shall not affect the contractual rights of the Company without its consent.

The new Decree added, in Article 3, that, for those concession-holders who amended, the valid Law and Regulations would be those in force at the time of 'amending' the concession. Since the terms of Petroleum Regulation No. 6 were essential to the concession-holders, none of them consented to amend till after its publication on 23 December 1961.

In the second sentence of the passage from Article 2 quoted above, there was mention only of the Regulations and not of the Law. Most oil concessions of the time protected concessionaires from tax changes, substituting the 50/50 profit-sharing principle instead. But a general exemption from changes in the Petroleum Law, which the companies would have preferred, was too much to expect a sovereign government to concede to a private overseas interest. Even without this additional paragraph the concessionaires had as water-tight a guarantee as it was possible for a State to give to an individual. It is difficult to see in what way it could be improved upon for them even in the terms of the 1955 Law. The principle of sovereignty in international law would in the last resort inevitably over-ride that of sanctity of contract between the State and an individual at this stage of the twentieth century, when capitulations were a thing of the past. In fact, the Libyan Government made no overt use of its sovereign powers to over-ride contractual concessionary rights until some time after the 1969 revolution.

The other points conceded to concession-holders in the November 1961 Decree were: (1) for those who amended an exemption from the July 1961 provision that they should surrender areas required under the Law in one compact block; and (2) the addition of 'other direct taxes' to the income tax and surtax against which they could offset balances of direct taxes paid (in addition to fees, rents and royalties) in previous years and brought forward because then there had not been sufficient 50/50 tax liability to absorb them. Neither the rationale of this, nor its application,[11] are easy to comprehend, particularly in the light of the subsequent squabbles about the nature of 'other direct taxes' (see section 5.5.1 below). It seemed at that time to be a point of small significance and was conceded by the Government as such, but in fact the definition of direct taxes had significant consequences, both in terms of money and of fiscal principles.

5.5 Petroleum Regulation No. 6

Regulations Nos. 1-5, issued between mid-1955 and early 1956, dealt for the most part with procedural matters connected with applications for concessions and their consideration by the Commission (Reg. No. 1) and the clarification of obscure or ambiguous passages in the Law itself (Regs. 2-5). They need not detain us. Regulation No. 6, however, was most important. In its 17 Articles it dealt with many facets of the implementation of the Law, and was required in order to clarify beyond doubt the procedures required — particularly in the field of fiscal accounts — at the time when production and exports of oil had already begun, and were expected to increase rapidly in the coming years.

The Regulation was by and large fair to the concession-holders and to the Government. It protected the former against arbitrary Government rulings, and the latter against interpretation by concession-holders of inadequate, ambiguous or ill-defined provisions of the Law in their own favour, contrary to the Government's interest and the Law's intentions.

The draft regulation was submitted to the oil companies, who had the opportunity to comment, propose alterations and submit revisions. Inevitably it was associated with the July 1961 Amendment to the Law and became the vehicle for tempering its provisions to an interpretation on the basis of which the important concession-holders would be, sooner or later, willing to accept the amendments.[12]

There were three provisions of the Regulation which gave rise to major controversy. These were: (1) the definition in Article 6 of 'direct taxes', which were treated as an advance payment of the Government's 50 per cent share of profits ('duties, levies and taxes' which were not direct were to be treated as operating expenses); (2) the procedure for posting prices (Article 14); and (3) the definition of 'marketing expenses' which were to be deducted from posted prices in calculating the taxable income of the concession-holder (Article 15). Of these three, the second and third not only had far-reaching effects on the relationship between Government and oil producers, but also an impact on the cost of Libyan oil in international petroleum markets and on the relationships between the different Libyan oil producers in competition with each other in these markets. The points at issue are described below in greater detail.

5.5.1 Direct Taxes. The definition of 'Direct Taxes' contained in Article 6 of the Regulation was the cause of confusion because in its final form it defined such taxes in terms largely the opposite of the generally accepted meaning of the words and the intention of the 1961 Amendment of the Law. This was because the oil companies were obsessed with their experience in other countries, where devices had been employed by governments to circumvent the fifty-fifty principle by imposing taxes and other duties on the concessionaires in a manner which did not directly violate the wording of the concession agreement. Thus in Venezuela the generally applicable income tax law had been changed in 1958 to raise the tax rate on a progressive scale on profits of very large corporations (which in effect comprised the oil companies only), with the result that the Government's take in 1958 was 65 per cent of oil profits, and 69 per cent in 1959.[13] In Iraq in 1960 higher port dues had been imposed on oil exports[14] in such a way as to evade the concessionaires' contractual exemption from new taxes, so that they had to be treated by the companies as operational expenses, and this treatment violated the 50/50 principle of the Agreement.

In Libya the concession-holders — led on this occasion by Esso, whose parent organisation was concerned with both the Venezuelan and Iraqi events — engineered the wording of Article 6 of Regulation 6 as follows, in order to safeguard themselves against the imposition of further taxation, before they agreed to amend:

> 'Direct Taxes' shall mean any duty, levy or tax imposed by the Federal Government or any Provincial or Municipal authority or Government Agency in respect of the income, properties or the operations[15] of the concession-holder, which exaction or levy is payable by the person bearing the ultimate burden of such exaction or levy.

This definition was interpreted by the concession-holders as embracing, among other things, customs duties, stamp taxes and vehicle licences — the principal sources of Government revenue before the advent of oil revenue — which are normally considered archetypal examples of indirect taxes. The concession-holders were exempted by Article 16 of the Law from customs duties on most of their imports for operations, but there was a grey area in which the Customs Organisation charged duties, usually on the grounds that the items could be used for employees' benefit, passenger vehicles being a notable example. The companies did not make much of a show of disputing the Customs decisions, since it was easy enough to recover by withholding the amounts so paid from their surtax payments under the wording of the Regulation quoted above. This state of affairs gave rise to many disputes and remain unresolved until 1968.

Article 6 stipulated that any duty, levy or tax payable in return for services rendered to the public generally was to be deemed to be a Direct Tax if it 'exceeds a fair and reasonable sum having regard to the purpose for which payment is made'. The Article went on to mention port dues and water rates specifically in this connection. On the other hand, consumer taxes on any petroleum products sold by concession-holders in Libya were classified as not Direct Taxes.

5.5.2 Posted Prices. The July 1961 Amendment, in relating income of the oil companies to their exports of oil valued at posted prices, defined the latter as follows:

> 'Posted price' means the price f.o.b. Seaboard Terminal for Libyan crude oil of the gravity and quality concerned arrived at by reference

to free market prices for individual commercial sales of full cargoes
and in accordance with the procedure to be agreed between the Company and the Commission; or if there is no free market for commercial sales of full cargoes of Libyan crude oil then posted prices shall
mean a fair price fixed by Agreement between the Company and the
Commission or in default of agreement by arbitration having regard
to the posted prices of crude oil of similar quality and gravity in other
free markets with necessary adjustments for freight and insurance.

This passage followed verbatim the wording already adopted in the
Iraqi February 1952 revised concession agreement with the Iraq
Petroleum Company and its affiliates. Leaving aside for the present
the question of whether there was a free market price for individual
commercial sales of full cargoes of Libyan crude oil either at that time
or any other time, or whether there were 'other free markets' from
which prices could be derived (to be dealt with in Chapter 8), the above
passage makes it clear that the Libyan posted prices should be arrived
at 'in accordance with the procedure to be agreed between the Company and the Commission'; and in the second eventuality should be
'a fair price fixed by Agreement between the Company and the
Commission'.

Regulation No. 6, Article 14, stipulated that 'the concession-holder
or its affiliates shall from time to time establish and publish its posted
price for Libyan crude oil . . .' This passage could be considered to
mean — and was so interpreted by the oil companies — that the
concession-holder may post these prices unilaterally, and there is no
mention in the Regulation about agreement by the Government. It
was maintained by the companies that the Regulation by its very
wording gave the Commission's agreement to their unilateral posting
of prices, but this was disputed by the Government, which at one
time took the view that, if the Regulation dispensed with Government
agreement, it was *ultra vires*, since the law explicitly required it. As will
be described later (Chapter 8, section 8.1), prices were posted by Esso
in 1961 which were too low by any reasonable interpretation of the
wording of the Law. The other concessionaires, as they began exports,
all followed Esso's lead in this matter. They did not obtain the agreement of the Government required by the Law. The dispute with the
Government continued until well into the 1970s, when finally in Libya
and elsewhere, oil-producing country governments were able to dictate
to the concessionaires the posted prices which the latter had hitherto
controlled.

5.5.3 *Marketing Expenses*. The July 1961 Amendment defined the taxable income of the companies as their 'exports of crude oil valued at posted price less marketing expenses as defined by Regulations'. Regulation No. 6, Article 15, defined Marketing Expenses as 'the sum of expenses, wherever incurred, of each concession-holder which are fairly, properly and necessarily attributable to the selling, servicing, co-ordinating and arranging for the lifting of crude petroleum for export from Libya'. They include

> the sum total of rebates if any from the posted price which the concession-holder is obliged to grant for the purpose of meeting competition, in order to sell Libyan crude petroleum to affiliated or non-affiliated customers, provided that the concession-holder may be called upon from time to time to demonstrate to the reasonable satisfaction of the Commission, that any such rebates are commercially reasonable and fair in relation to market circumstances at the time they were granted having regard to the buyer's competitive position, the volume and period of sale and all other relevant circumstances.

This passage, which was exacted by the Oasis companies as their price for consenting to accept the 1961 Amendment, destroyed the intention of the Amendment to align the provisions of the Libyan Law with practice in the big Middle Eastern concessions. The latter allowed strictly limited marketing expenses (formerly 2 per cent, then 1 per cent, and by 1963 reduced to ½ US cent a barrel in Iraq, Saudi Arabia and Iran[16]) and few other discounts or rebates on posted prices for calculating taxable income (until new arrangements in the 1964 OPEC formula Agreement). The wording of the Libyan Regulation enabled the oil exporters to charge large rebates against posted price, and to reduce the taxable income from exports of crude, in some cases to less than 60 per cent of the level it would be if valued at posted prices. At no time did such concession-holders demonstrate that these rebates were reasonable and fair, nor did they allow the Government access to the contracts which purported to prove that the rebates were obligatorily granted in order to sell Libyan crude petroleum to affiliated or non-affiliated customers.[17] This issue was finally put to rest by the further Amendment of 1965, which applied the OPEC formula to Libya, and the subsequent quittance for previous years' accounts and tax payments.

5.6   The Establishment of the Ministry of Petroleum Affairs and the Disbandment of the Petroleum Commission

Chapter 3, section 3.2 described the Petroleum Commission, its powers, functions and membership, consisting of one representative of each of the three Provinces under a federal Chairman. After the setting up of a Ministry of Petroleum Affairs in 1960, the Minister took over tutelary responsibility for the Commission's work, and his powers over the Commission were much strengthened in Law No. 6 of 1962.

On 25 April 1963, the federal system of government was abolished, and the word 'United' dropped from the title 'Kingdom of Libya'; henceforth the country became a unitary State. Law No. 6 of 1963 abolished the Petroleum Commission and tranferred all its rights and responsibilities to the Ministry of Petroleum Affairs. The same Law altered the text of the Petroleum Law of 1955, as amended in 1961, to accord with these changes.

The Minister had appointed the Director of Petroleum Affairs to the Commission under the 1962 Law. This post was now transferred to the Ministry. In 1964 the Ministry was organised into five Departments — Technical, Legal, Companies' Accounts, Research and Economics, and Administrative. This organisation was in substance retained throughout the next decade.

Law No. 6 of 1963 also established a 'High Council of Petroleum Affairs', consisting of the Ministers of Petroleum Affairs, Finance, National Economy, Planning and Development, and Industry, and the Governor of the Bank of Libya, together with three members with experience in the fields of petroleum affairs, finance, economy, industry or law appointed by the Council of Ministers. The Council's functions were concerned with 'studying' and 'expressing views' on a wide variety of subjects connected with petroleum policy, but did not include any executive or other decision-making authority without reference to the Council of Ministers.[18] In fact, little was heard of this Council, though its individual members were active in the field of petroleum policy, especially in the events leading up to the 1965 Amendments to the Law.

Notes

1. A.A.Q. Kubbah, *Libya — Its Oil Industry and Economic System* (Rihani Press, Beirut, 1964), p. 197ff.

2. Amendment to Articles 7 and 8 of the 1955 Law, incorporated in Article 1 of the 1961 Decree. All references to the Petroleum Commission were subsequently changed to 'Ministry of Petroleum Affairs' (see section 5.6).

3. ' "Effective Date" means the date on which the concession-holder first commences regular exports in commercial quantities or regular sales in commercial quantities of petroleum derived from any of his concessions in Libya.' Article 14 of the Petroleum Law as amended.

4. At the same time, setting-up expenses, foreign taxation, interest on finance and penalties imposed under the Law, all in respect of Libyan operations, were disallowed in the fiscal accounts.

5. Amended Article 14 of the 1955 Law, incorporated in Article 1 of the July 1961 Decree.

6. This change of valuation of royalty appeared *prima facie* to be disadvantageous to the inner concessions, compared with those nearer the sea. The disadvantage, however, was largely illusory, so long as royalty was treated as an advance payment against surtax, since the higher royalty would be offset by lower net surtax payments.

7. i.e. income tax at rates payable generally by corporations in Libya.

8. Ministry of Petroleum Affairs, Kingdom of Libya, *Libyan Oil 1954-1967*, p.36.

9. Article 5, Royal Decree of 3 July 1961; the six months was from the date of publication in the *Official Gazette* – 15 July 1961.

10. In the event, not all the concessionaires who amended were awarded new concessions in the next (1966) round. Those who were not successful in 1966 included Esso and the Oasis partners (see note 12 below).

11. Since other direct taxes, however defined, were payable to other government departments at the time of incurring them (e.g. customs duties, stamp taxes and road taxes to the Ministry of Finance or other departments), it is difficult to envisage brought-forward 'direct' taxes being deducted from similar payments as though these were made to the Ministry of Petroleum Affairs. So far as is known, the matter was not put to the test, as there were normally sufficient payments due to the Ministry of Petroleum Affairs against which to offset the direct taxes already paid to other departments.

12. Esso was the first to amend, followed by Marathon in late 1962, and Continental and Amerada in 1963. All the majors, whether producing or not, subsequently accepted the amendments, and all but one of the small producers followed suit. Non-producers were not pressed, and the problem ceased to exist with the implementation of the 1965 legislation, which gave a quittance for the years up to 1964 and was eventually accepted by all concession-holders.

13. J.E. Hartshorn, *Oil Companies and Governments* (Faber, London, 1967), p. 303.

14. G. Stocking, *Middle East Oil* (Vanderbilt University Press, Nashville, Tennessee, 1970), p. 218; also S. Longrigg, *Oil in the Middle East*, 3rd edn. (Oxford University Press, Oxford, 1968), p. 263.

15. The wording *'in respect of . . . operations* of the Concession Holder' is significant. The Iraqi Government had been able to impose the greatly increased port dues without violating the concession agreement because the tankers which lifted the oil for export were not owned by the concession-holder, although the oil lifted was 'in respect of its operations'. The 1952 Iraqi Agreement had guaranteed only the concession-holder (and not operations conducted by other companies) from the imposition of further taxes over and above the 50/50 profit-sharing agreement.

16. Stocking, *Middle East Oil*, p. 332 ff.

17. Since any price to 'affiliated' customers was an internally contrived transfer price, it is difficult to see how it could be demonstrated to be obligatory,

except in the sense that the newcomers, breaking into fast-expanding products markets, deemed it obligatory to undercut existing marketers. In doing so they were passing back, to the extent they arbitrarily chose, to be borne by the Libyan Government in lower tax receipts, part of the costs of undercutting the majors, on whom Libya at that time relied for the bulk of its oil revenues (see Ch. 6, especially section 6.2).

18.   Petroleum Law, Article 2, as amended in 1963.

6 THE EVENTS LEADING TO THE 1965 PETROLEUM LAW AMENDMENT

6.1 The Discounting Practices of the Independents and the Majors

In September 1961, Esso Standard began regular exports of oil and so passed its effective date. The three Oasis partners — Marathon, Continental and Amerada — followed in July 1962 and Esso Sirte (50 per cent Esso, 25.5 per cent Liamco, 24.5 per cent Grace) in January 1963. Mobil, with its partner Gelsenberg (then having a 25 per cent interest), joined them as exporters late in 1963 and the two Amoseas partners — Texaco and Socal — in the second half of 1964.

The record of production from the beginning up to 1965 by individual operating companies was as shown in Table 6.1. Total annual production of crude oil and total exports in these years are given in Table 6.2.

Table 6.1: Crude Oil Production by Operating Companies, 1961-5 (thousands of barrels a day)

Company	1961	1962	1963	1964	1965
Esso Standard	18.2	126.2	250.0	408.9	471.7
Esso Sirte	—	—	43.6	73.1	95.4
Oasis	—	57.7	167.2	324.0	505.8
Mobil	—	—	2.8	45.6	100.7
Amoseas	—	—	—	13.1	43.7
Phillips	—	—	—	—	2.9

Source: Ministry of Petroleum Affairs.

Table 6.2: Total Annual Crude Oil Production and Exports, 1961-5 (millions of barrels)

	1961	1962	1963	1964	1965
Production	6.6	67.1	169.2	315.6	445.4
Exports	5.2	65.5	167.8	313.9	442.7

Source: Ministry of Petroleum Affairs.

Exports as a rule fall short of production because of operators' use

117

of crude in their own operations, and pipeline evaporation and other losses, as well as carry-overs of inventories.

Government revenues from oil received during each fiscal year (April-March) from the beginning until 31 March 1966, were as follows:

Table 6.3: Government Revenues from Oil, 1955/6-1965/6

Libyan Fiscal Year (April/March) £L'000			£L'000
1955/6	51	1960/1	115
1956/7	62	1961/2	2,000
1957/8	77	1962/3	7,200
1958/9	91	1963/4	23,800
1959/60	97	1964/5	56,000
		1965/6	116,000

Source: Ministry of Petroleum Affairs.

These revenues were a mixture of fees and rent on non-producing concessions, and of royalties and income and surtax on producing concessions − from 1961/2 onwards predominantly the latter two. It is not possible to correlate them exactly with production and export figures to obtain per barrel revenues because of the timing of the oil company payments. Royalties were paid every three months, 60 days in arrears, and surtax annually four months in arrears, so that the latter, in respect of operations in any one calendar year (say 1964), were not paid until the following fiscal year (1965/6).

The 1961 Amendment had been accepted, by the end of 1964, by all the concessionaires producing and exporting oil at that time. The price posted by Esso in 1961 had been US $2.21 a barrel for 39° API[1] gravity oil, with a drop of 2 cents a barrel for each degree of gravity less than 39° (but a ceiling price of $2.23 for 40° gravity and above). Of the other producing companies only Marathon had posted, at the same level as Esso. The others had followed Esso's postings in their financial statements to the Government (they were required to state a posted price in their fiscal accounts in the terms of the 1961 Amendment), but had not published a posting of their own.

The companies then proceeded in their accounts to deduct from the posted price, published or deemed, the 'marketing expenses as defined by Regulations', including 'rebates', in order to reach a figure for their income resulting from operations in Libya which, after deduction of allowed costs and expenses, was taxed at the rate of 50 per cent.

The following table gives the average per barrel prices, after deduction of marketing expenses, declared in their fiscal accounts by producing concessionaires for the years 1961-4:

Table 6.4: Fiscal Price per Barrel Declared by Libyan Oil Producers: 1961-4

	1961	1962	1963	1964
		US dollars per barrel		
Esso Standard	2.19	2.19	2.20	2.17
Marathon	—	1.64	1.62	1.59
Continental	—	1.71	1.50	1.64
Amerada	—	1.46	1.53	1.61
Esso Sirte[a]	—	—	2.17	1.96
Mobil and Gelsenberg	—	—	1.89	1.89

Note: a. Esso Sirte's junior partners — Liamco and Grace — sold their oil to Esso at this period. The accounting arrangements ensured that the tax reference price was the same as Esso Sirte's.
Source: Ministry of Petroleum Affairs.

The figures show that both the Esso companies (which were operationally, but not fiscally, one unit under a single management) observed the intent of the Law to relate their Libyan income to the posted price. The gravity of most Zelten oil exported was over 40°, of which the posted prices would be $2.23. The company deducted marketing expenses from posted prices of about 2 per cent, which was general practice in the Middle East and elsewhere at the beginning of the 1960s,[2] before arriving at their gross taxable revenue. The exception to this was in Esso Sirte's 1964 accounts, where the company appears in addition to have deducted the 8½ per cent discount agreed for 1964 in the OPEC formula (but not expensing royalties, as agreed in the same formula). Mobil and Gelsenberg appear to have followed a similar practice (but on a lower gravity and waxy high pour-point crude) and the Amoseas partners, who began production late in 1964, declared prices of the same order.

The Oasis companies, however, followed a very different course. The average declared prices of Marathon, Continental and Amerada for the three years 1962-4 were $1.58 on oil of which the posted price — in accordance with Esso's posting — would be $2.21, being on average about 39° gravity. Of the three companies, Amerada had no downstream operations and sold all its oil, first to Continental in 1962 and early 1963, and subsequently to Shell. Marathon and Continental disposed of their production in their own downstream operations, or in downstream operations in which they participated in varying degrees. They were thus selecting transfer prices more than 60 cents below posted price on average, to take into account the marketing expenses and rebates allowed by the Law and Regulation No. 6. The Petroleum Commission, and subsequently the Ministry of Petroleum Affairs, at no time received a demonstration to their satisfaction that the rebates were commercially reasonable, as required by the wording of the Regulation.

The low declared selling prices of the Oasis partners, together with high declared production costs, so reduced their taxable profits that even for 1964 — the third production year, by the end of which they had between them produced a cumulative aggregate of 200 million barrels — there was no income and surtax payable, with the exception of a small amount by Marathon, and in the case of the other two substantial losses and tax credits to carry forward to offset against 1965 tax liability. The combined accounts of the three companies for 1964 showed declared taxable profits of £L33.8m, giving a *prima facie* income and surtax liability of £L16.9m. But to offset against this liability were royalties for 1964 of £L12.3m and advance payments and losses brought forward from 1963 of £L8.6m. These completely wiped out the income and surtax liability and left £L4m to be carried forward and set against 1965 tax liabilities.

Thus the Libyan Government's revenue from these three companies for 1964 consisted — apart from minor amounts of surface rents and customs and stamp taxes — of royalty only. This amounted to 12½ per cent of the value at posted prices of production, i.e. about 28 US cents per barrel. In contrast to these companies, Esso Standard's income and surtax payments to the Libyan Government in respect of 1964 amounted to £L35 million, and Government revenue from Esso, including royalties, was approximately 92 US cents per barrel exported.[3]

It can readily be calculated that, had the Oasis companies been charged to tax on the basis of posted prices for these three years, the Libyan Government would have received an additional gross revenue from them of $60 million.[4] Such a sum was large in itself, and important in relation to Libya's total revenues, both fiscal and in foreign exchange. Even more important was the outlook for the future. Not only would these companies continue to make much smaller payments to Government than were envisaged in the revised Law, but it was certain that Esso and other producing majors would not for long tolerate their competitors obtaining oil from the same country as they at a much lower tax cost, and would undoubtedly follow suit if nothing were done to rectify the situation. Indeed they would be unable to take any other course as, during the period since the Oasis companies had been exporting, there had been a marked deterioration of product prices in many countries of Western Europe, at least partly caused by Continental's and Marathon's price-cutting to obtain a foothold in these markets. As has been mentioned above, these price cuts were passed back partially to be borne by the Libyan Government, and the majors would be unable to meet this competition for long if they did not adopt similar practices.

These facts and considerations were becoming widely known by the middle of 1965, after the producing oil companies had submitted their accounts and made their payments for 1964. They were the subject of analysis and discussion within the Libyan Government and the oil companies, and between these two interests. They were further mooted informally during the ninth OPEC Conference, which took place in Tripoli, Libya, in July 1965.

Libya had become a member of the Organization of the Petroleum Exporting Countries (OPEC) in 1962. In April of that same year OPEC passed a Resolution (No. IV.33) recommending 'that each Member Country should approach the company or companies concerned with a view to working out a formula whereunder royalty payments shall be fixed at a uniform rate . . . and shall not be treated as a credit against income tax liability'.[5] Following this, prolonged discussions on the subject took place with the companies concerned, who in effect comprised the eight majors with interests in Middle East concessions (in Venezuela a higher royalty was already expensed and not treated as a credit against income tax).

In 1964 the oil companies concerned offered to OPEC the acceptance of the expensing of royalties of 12½ per cent, to be offset by an allowance in fiscal accounts of 8½ per cent from posted prices in 1964, 7½ per cent in 1965, and 6½ per cent in 1966; thereafter the situation was to be reviewed in the light of market conditions.[6] Iran, and subsequently Qatar and Saudi Arabia, accepted the offer and negotiated with their concession-holders the amendment of the concessions accordingly. Kuwait followed suit after hesitation because of parliamentary opposition, but Iraq rejected it on the grounds that the offer was inadequate, and the non-financial conditions unacceptable.

The major oil companies who were parties to the offer were obligated to make the same offer to Libya, as a member of OPEC, and Esso and the Amoseas companies did so by letter to the Libyan

Government in the middle of November 1964. The terms of the offers, however, were not without strings attached. Amoseas expressly preserved the right to bring discounts or rebates into account; both companies required a quittance in respect of their past fiscal accounts, some of which had not yet even been received in the Ministry; and they both required access to all other producing companies' accounts to ensure that the latter did not receive more favourable fiscal treatment. If they did, then the treatment would also apply to themselves; in other words a 'most-favoured-company' clause. Such conditions were quite out of the question under the existing Law and Regulations. The terms of the offers, if they had been accepted, would have been nullified by the fact that the other producers did not conform to them. Indeed acceptance by the Government would have given formal consent to the offering companies to adopt the discounting procedures already practised by the Oasis companies.

In January 1965, the producing oil companies, at the request of the Ministry of Petroleum Affairs, provided estimates of exports of crude oil for the year 1965 and of payments to the Libyan Government in respect of these operations. It was made clear to the companies, who were naturally reluctant to do this sort of thing, that the estimates were given without any sort of commitment; the actual payments would be made in arrears in accordance with the Law and Regulations on the actual results of their operations. The payments themselves would consist of royalties on crude oil production and income and surtax (if any), plus minor amounts of rent and possibly fees. The oil company returns are shown in Table 6.5.

Table 6.5: Company Estimates of 1965 Oil Exports and Payments to Government, made in January 1965

	Crude Oil Exports (millions of barrels)	Payments to Libyan Govt. (£L millions)	US Cents per barrel
Esso Standard	171	51	83
Esso Sirte	17	5	82
Liamco/Grace	17	3	49
Amerada	58	10	48
Continental	58	5	24
Marathon	58	6	29
Mobil/Gelsenberg	27	3	31
Amoseas	16	2	35
	422mb.	£L85m	US¢56/b

Source: Ministry of Petroleum Affairs.

These estimates indicated that: (1) the Esso companies intended to introduce discounts into their 1965 accounts (probably the 7½ per cent allowed in the OPEC formula), thus reducing their per barrel payments (on larger production) from 92 cents/barrel for 1964 to 83 for 1965; (2) the junior partners in the Esso Sirte operation – Liamco and Grace – might apply much larger discounts; and (3) the other independent companies (with the exception of Amerada, whose estimate is questionable) would pay bare royalty only, or less, since there were unused credits carried forward from 1964 to set against 1965 royalty. The newcomers among the majors – Mobil and Amoseas – indicated payments somewhat in excess of royalty, but their income and surtax payments would be low because of their small initial production in relation to their operating expenses and overheads.

On the basis of the same level of crude oil exports as projected by the companies, the Ministry made estimates of payments to the Libyan Government if the OPEC formula were introduced and applied to all companies. They are shown in Table 6.6.

Table 6.6: Estimates of Oil Company Payments to Libyan Government for 1965 under OPEC Formula

	Crude Oil Exports (millions of barrels)	Payments to Libya				
		Gross	less b/f Losses and Tax Credits	Net	US $ per Barrel	
					Gross	Net
			£L millions			
Esso Standard	171	62	—	62	1.02	1.02
Esso Sirte	17	6	—	6	0.99	0.99
Liamco/Grace	17	6	(1)	5	0.99	0.82
Amerada	58	19	(2)	17	0.92	0.82
Continental	58	19	(2)	17	0.92	0.82
Marathon	58	19	—	19	0.92	0.92
Mobil	27	9	(3)	6	0.93	0.62
Amoseas	16	5	(2)	3	0.88	0.52
	422mb.	£L144	£L(10)	£L135	$0.95	$0.90

Source: Ministry of Petroleum Affairs.

The differing figures for Government revenue on a per barrel basis are because of the differing allowable costs and expenses of the producing companies (mostly overheads and including all drilling and exploration in Libya) in relation to the level of production and exports; and also to a minor extent to the differing posted prices and gravities of the oil produced. The estimate suggests that, even allowing for the deductions from payments because of brought forward losses and tax credits, under the OPEC formula the Libyan Government would receive £L50 million more oil revenue than the companies estimated they would pay under the existing Law, which in themselves were probably an over-statement.

Chart 6.1 gives a general picture of the per barrel revenue to be expected by the Libyan Government from oil (a) under the Law as it was at the beginning of 1965 and (b) with the application of the OPEC formula to all concessionaires; for comparison, average government per barrel take in the Middle East oil-producing countries that had accepted the formula at this time is also plotted. Since the discounts taken by the independent producers were expected to average at least 60 cents a barrel, even after 1965 — when it was hoped that the revenue would not be impaired to such an extent by brought forward losses and tax credits — under the existing Law Government revenue could be expected to be at least 40 cents a barrel less than under the OPEC formula.[7] On production and exports which were expected soon to rise to 500 million barrels a year and more, this would represent a loss to the Government of at least $200 million revenue a year.

6.2   The Entry of Libyan Independents into the Markets of Europe

Regulation No. 6 allowed the inclusion in marketing expenses allowable for tax purposes of 'rebates from the posted price which the concession-holder is obliged to grant for the purpose of meeting competition in order to sell Libyan crude petroleum to affiliated or non-affiliated customers', and went on to place the burden of a satisfactory demon-stration that the rebates were fair and reasonable on the company giving and claiming the rebates.

There was no objective criterion of 'obligation' to grant, nor of what the Petroleum Commission, and later the Ministry of Petroleum Affairs, might be satisfied was 'fair and reasonable'. As soon as the first accounts of the independent producers were received, revealing the the taking of discounts and rebates to the extent shown in Table 6.4, the Ministry expressed its strong dissatisfaction at this procedure even before it started to examine the accounts in detail — a lengthy process, and one which would give rise to even lengthier negotiations for adjustments.

It was to be expected that the independent Libyan producing

Chart 6.1: Comparison of Libyan Government Expected Oil Revenues in 1965 and after under 1961 Law and under OPEC Formula at various levels of Discount and Rebate[a]

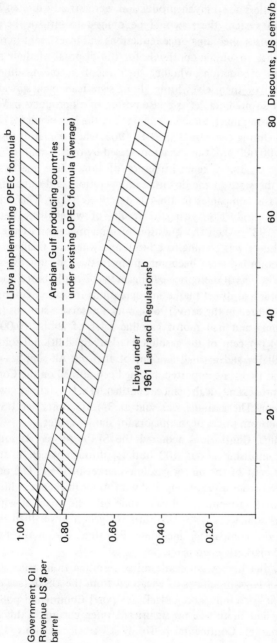

Notes: a. The diagram is indicative only; with constant oil company operating costs, Libyan Government revenue falls by 50 per cent of the discounts and rebates at all levels, plus 50 per cent of the non-expensed royalties less 50 per cent of the 7½ per cent discount allowed in 1965 under the OPEC formula.

b. The band in each case of Libyan Government revenue reflects differing allowable costs of production of different producing companies in relation to their levels of production, as well as different gravities of oil exported.

companies, who had not previously had oil business in Europe, and whose US outlets for Libyan production were strictly limited by the import quota system there, would be obliged to involve themselves in heavy expenses, including price reductions and investment in refining and marketing, to obtain footholds for the disposal of their rapidly rising Libyan production. Whether their supplies coming on to the market would of themselves bring about significant widespread price falls was not so predictable, as consumption of oil products in Western Europe was rising much more in volume than the independents' Libyan production. During the period 1961 to 1965, when the latter rose from nothing to 500,000 b/d, the former increased by over 2 million b/d.

In order to give a general picture of how these matters were developing, the state of the downstream operations and transactions of the three Oasis companies in 1964 is described below. This was their third Libyan production year, the results of which were becoming available in 1965, when the question of the application of the OPEC formula in Libya was coming to a head, and when the financial results of their discounting were becoming plain to the Libyan Government, as well as the effects of their price-cutting in the oil markets of Europe.[8]

Continental had direct marketing operations in several countries. In the UK it acquired in the early 1960s some 600 service stations (mostly Jet Petroleum) and had motor gasoline sales of about 10,000 b/d, comprising 4 per cent of the gasoline market. In addition it sold 3,400 b/d of distillates and a small amount of fuel oil. All supplies of products were at that time imported, having been refined on the Continent in various processing deals, since Continental's UK refinery was not yet on stream. The gasoline was sold at 3-4 US cents per US gallon below the uniform prices of the majors for similar grades.

In Belgium, Continental acquired the SECA service station chain in 1962, comprising about 100 outlets, through which it supplied some 6 per cent of the motor gasoline market in 1964. The products were acquired from a processing deal with Antar in France, which took 7,000 b/d of Continental's Libyan crude oil. The prices at which the gasoline was sold were 3-4½ US cents/US gallon lower than those of the major oil companies, including Petrofina, Belgium's principal refining and marketing company.

In Italy, due to low wholesale prices resulting from price controls, coupled with large purchases of cheap oil from the USSR (see note 12 — *c.* $1.25/b for crude f.o.b. Black Sea port) Continental policy was to go slow, and there was no significant price cutting in this already low-price market. Continental had only 18 service stations, all other products from a processing deal of 5,000 b/d with ENI at its Pavia refinery being disposed of wholesale.

In Federal Germany and Austria the SOPI chain of service stations was purchased in 1960, comprising some 400 outlets. The oil was processed in refineries at Karlsruhe and Heide and the gasoline sold with a wide range of discounts ranging from 3 to 11 cents per US gallon. Fuel oil was also sold at prices which 'gave away' the low-sulphur premium.

The above description is of Continental's direct marketing of oil products at the wholesale and retail level in 1964. Their main European business, however, at that time was the selling of crude oil to refineries in Germany and Italy. In Germany Continental had a 40 per cent share in the Karlsruhe refinery, the other shareholders being DEA and Scholven (Aral), both German companies. Continental had 100 per cent supply rights of crude oil to the refinery and, as described above, took from the refinery the products required for its own marketing. The capacity of the Karlsruhe refinery was 44,000 b/d; in addition there was a processing deal with DEA at the Heide refinery of 26,000 b/d. The prices Continental obtained for its crude oil delivered to these refineries, most probably calculated on a 'net-back' basis (the wholesale prices of products ex-refinery derived from a barrel of crude less refining costs, to give a price for crude at the refinery), showed substantial discounts on Libyan posted prices, of about 70 cents/b, after allowing for freight from Libya to destination.

At the Sincat refinery in Sicily Continental was supplying 50,000 b/d, the price being calculated as Continental's production costs plus tax costs, plus 15 US cents/b allowance for Continental's Libyan investment. It may be observed that such an arrangement could not justify the claiming of rebates in Continental's Libyan accounts since the build-up of the price of the crude included the tax paid in Libya, and moved up and down according to the amount of tax; since the tax should also depend on the price received for the sales it is not possible to derive the one from the other, and both depend on the sales prices declared in Continental's Libyan fiscal accounts.

Continental also had a US import quota of 14,000 b/d and traded in a further quota of 18,000 b/d.

Marathon's direct marketing of oil products was not large. In Italy the company purchased the ABC chain of service stations, comprising some 600 in late 1964. In Germany they operated about 100 service stations in the south-west, as well as bidding for the USAF supply contract at the Mannheim base. Their prices showed no significant price-cutting.

Marathon's principal outlets for Libyan crude were two. First, the La Coruña refinery in Spain in which they held 28 per cent equity, and in addition provided loans for foreign exchange requirements. They had long-term supply of crude rights (16 years) for 45,000 b/d 'at competitive prices'.

Second, Marathon had 100 per cent supply rights with the German refinery at Mannheim of 45,000 b/d. Marathon provided 40 per cent of the equity for this refinery and Wintershall (a German oil company) the remainder. The price arrangements were believed to be of the 'net-back' variety — from the prices of products sold by Wintershall and other marketers, marketing expenses were deducted (including a return on marketing investment) to give wholesale prices ex-refinery; from these were then deducted the refining cost and the freight cost of the crude from Libya, to give a Libyan export price.

Marathon also had processing deals in Italy amounting in all to 16,000 b/d, and in Switzerland of 10,000 b/d. In addition, they had a US import quota of 14,000 b/d and traded-in quotas of a further 12,000 b/d.

In the earliest days of production, Amerada, which previously in the USA had been a crude oil producer only with no downstream operations, sold all its production to Continental. Early in 1963 it switched to Shell, who thereafter took all Amerada's Libyan crude oil production until at the beginning of 1966 Shell acquired a 50 per cent equity interest in Amerada's Libyan operations. The price at which Shell bought Amerada's oil was believed to be similar to that already in operation in the much larger Shell/Gulf Kuwait Agreement, and provided for 50/50 profit-sharing; i.e. from the sales revenues of products derived from this crude oil were deducted all the applicable costs (including tax costs) of the total integrated operation, and the price paid by Shell to Amerada was calculated in such a way as to ensure a 50/50 division of the integrated profit. The prices declared by Amerada in its Libyan accounts would presumably reflect the price paid by Shell to Amerada for its Libyan oil calculated as described above. But, as with Continental's Sincat deal, since Amerada's Libyan tax was a cost element in the calculation, it must have been established by Amerada's fiscal accounts declaration as a start-point of the sales price to Shell calculation, and therefore would not *prima facie* meet the requirements of Regulation No. 6.

This description of the independent oil companies' sales of their Libyan oil production in one year, 1964, throws some light on the nature of oil markets at the time, as well as on the problems of the companies computing their total sales revenues for tax purposes in accordance with the Libyan Petroleum Law. The following observations are pertinent.

(1) There was no 'free market price for individual commercial sales of full cargoes' by reference to which a posted price could be established.[9] The integrated majors disposed of their production of crude in their own downstream operations at internally fixed transfer prices, whereas for the independents there were equally no individual commercial sales of full cargoes. The occasional sale of a 'distress' cargo, which, although not well documented, undoubtedly occurred, particularly with the advent of other small independents, could give no indication of a 'free market price'. The same could be said of all other crude oil at that time produced in the Eastern Hemisphere.

(2) The 'realisation' price for sales of crude oil, f.o.b. producing country, was not an easily identifiable figure derivable from a straightforward contract for the sale and purchase of crude oil. The idea that it was so is based on an erroneous impression that a widespread and homogeneous free market existed between parties making arm's-length commercial transactions in a straightforward manner through the interaction of supply and demand. The Rotterdam market developed some of these characteristics for product prices, for which data were regularly published from about 1960, but there was no analogous free market there for crude oil.

(3) Posted prices bore little relationship to realised prices, and after 1960 ceased even to reflect market conditions in the sale of oil products. The difference between posted and realised prices (it is assumed that 'realised' has some connotation of 'real' in its intended meaning) was seldom, if ever, a sum certain, but had to be calculated and deemed from complex and elaborate arrangements which, in the case of the independents, were made to dispose of their crude oil. These included take-overs of retail service station chains, investment in refineries and other considerations in money or kind to secure rights for the supply of crude over extended periods. Few of them were ever known to the public. The majority incorporated net-back provisions which derived a crude price from the sales proceeds of a deemed product yield from a barrel of crude, after deducting: (a) deemed allocated marketing costs of the purchasing entity, with or without allowances for return on marketing investment; (b) refining costs

presenting similar problems of allocation, capital consumption and return on capital employed; and (c) a freight for crude from origin to refinery (where it would be mixed with other crudes) which might vary from month to month according to the conditions of the freight market. Some deals (e.g. Continental/Sincat, Amerada/Shell) involved the sharing of all integrated costs (production including tax cost, transportation, refining and marketing) and the sales revenue, so as to share equally the integrated net profit.

With this background it is not surprising that the independents in Libya were both unwilling and unable 'to demonstrate to the reasonable satisfaction of the Ministry' that the rebates they took were 'commercially reasonable and fair'. The arrangements described were commercial secrets and access to the relevant contracts, although requested, was denied to the Ministry's Auditors during 1965.

6.3   The Impact of the Independents on Oil Prices

It has already been mentioned that the loss of revenue from discounting, and the threatened adoption of the practices by the majors, were by early 1965 matters of concern to the Libyan Government. Equally alarming were the effects of price-cutting on the markets for oil products in Europe. A representative picture of the trends in product prices and their meaning in terms of revenue to oil companies derived from a barrel of Libyan crude oil after transportation to market, refining and marketing is given in Table 6.7.

Table 6.7: Product Sales Income Derived from Libyan Crude Oil, 1961-5

Five key country average — UK, Italy, Germany, Sweden, Netherlands. Representative product income at refinery ($b)

	Premium Gasoline	Regular Gasoline	Diesel & Heating Oil	Heavy Fuel	Composite Product Revenue Derived from a Barrel of Libyan Crude Oil
1961	5.90	4.27	3.56	1.95	3.21
1962	5.95	4.27	3.52	1.99	3.20
1963	5.76	4.08	3.52	1.89	3.12
1964	5.73	3.97	3.02	1.64	2.82
1965 (1st half)	5.72	3.75	2.66	1.51	2.62

Source: Oil company documents based on price information from the markets. In the composite figure products are weighted in proportion to their average yield from a barrel of Libyan crude.

This shows that between 1961 and the first half of 1965 this revenue had fallen on average 18 per cent. If from the sales proceeds of products composing a barrel of crude a constant figure of per barrel costs for marketing, refining and transportation is deducted (say of $1 a barrel — which is somewhat high, but gives a start-point in 1961 of a crude net-back of $2.21/b, equal to the posted price of 39° gravity crude ex Mersa el Brega), the fall is 27 per cent. This, it may be noted, is somewhat less than the average discount of about 30 per cent taken in their tax accounts by the independents.

The majors, who were subject to the same competitive pressures on their prices, were not taking the discounts in their fiscal accounts. While the independents, in accordance with their interpretation of the Law and Regulations, passed on the bill for 50 per cent of their own estimate of the cut-price realisations to the Libyan Government in the form of tax relief, Esso, observing the intent of the Law, bore the burden themselves up to and including 1964. This situation was un-stable; hence the inauguration of discounting by Esso and the other majors beginning production at the time, and the alarm of the Libyan Government at the prospect of breaking the oil products markets of Europe at their own expense.

These facts are depicted in Chart 6.2, which shows an oil company calculation of the impact of lower product prices on the crude 'real-isation' in the years 1961 to 1965.

The falls in product prices in the markets were felt also in the sales of oil from the Middle East producing countries. A picture of the increasing discounts, derived from known sales of Arabian Gulf crude to European independent refiners (i.e. refiners not associated with the major oil companies) is given in Chart 6.3. These refer largely to sales of crude by the majors who not only had to meet the competition from the Libyan and Arabian Gulf independents but also, in some areas, particularly Italy, that of supplies from the USSR. Since the Middle East producing countries were all on a posted price basis with only small allowable discounts in their fiscal accounts, the discounting costs, that is the losses of sales income, were borne entirely by the oil companies without being offset by lower tax payments to producing country governments.

It could be argued, and was indeed put forward forcibly by the independents themselves, and some who supported them in Libya,[10] that the discounts and rebates were essential for them to gain a foot-hold in the markets of Europe to dispose of their rapidly rising Libyan oil production. Whether the validity of such an argument is accepted

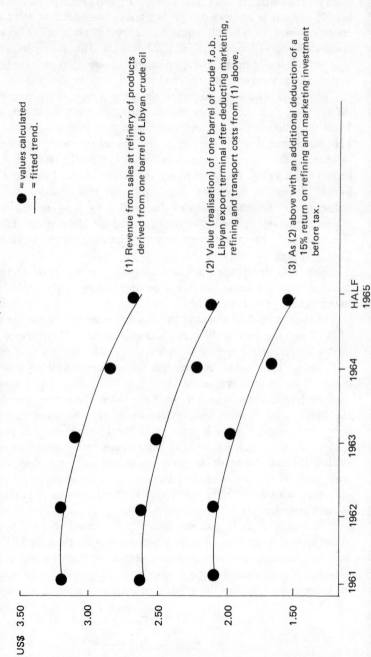

Chart 6.2: European Product Prices and Crude Netbacks to Libya, 1961-5

US$

● = values calculated
— = fitted trend.

(1) Revenue from sales at refinery of products derived from one barrel of Libyan crude oil

(2) Value (realisation) of one barrel of crude f.o.b. Libyan export terminal after deducting marketing, refining and transport costs from (1) above.

(3) As (2) above with an additional deduction of a 15% return on refining and marketing investment before tax.

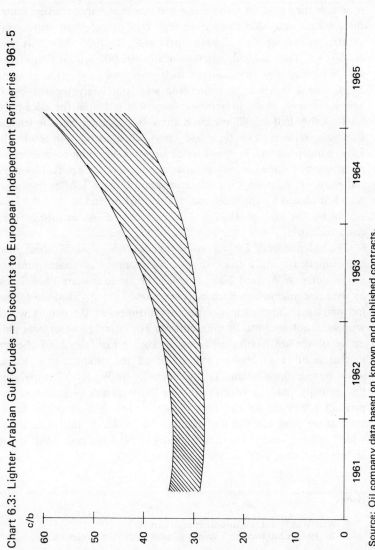

Chart 6.3: Lighter Arabian Gulf Crudes — Discounts to European Independent Refineries 1961-5

Source: Oil company data based on known and published contracts.

or not, the independents in aggregate made substantial advances in profit in the years 1962 to 1964. Although these profits include their US operations, there is a close correlation between their increase and the rise in their Libyan production.[11]

In summary, the independent Libyan producers established themselves in the markets of Western Europe during the years 1962 to 1964, and, while laying off part of the cost of this on the Libyan Government, to whom they paid no income and surtaxes, but only royalties, during these years, were able to improve their own consolidated profits very substantially from their Libyan operations. By 1965 they were well established. Then assured outlets of nearly 400,000 b/d for Continental and Marathon more than covered their combined production of about 340,000 b/d in 1965, and Amerada was completely secured by its agreement with Shell. In addition there was potential for sales of at least another half a million barrels a day to uncommitted independent European refiners. The time had come when encouragement to the Libyan independents, in the form of large tax allowable rebates, could no longer be justified on any grounds of commerce or equity, but could rather be regarded as discrimination against those Libyan producers who had abided by the intention of the 1961 amendment to the Law, which by the end of 1964 had been accepted by all oil-exporting concessionaires.

The independents' Libyan production of crude oil during these years only supplied a small proportion of the increases of consumption of oil products in Western Europe, which in the four years 1961-4 rose by over two million b/d. Such increases might have absorbed the Libyan independents' supplies in an 'orderly' manner, as the majors would wish, without recourse to price-cutting. The latter, however, was indicative of the difficulties of access to such a high threshold-of-entry market as oil. Furthermore, exports of oil and products from Russia were increasing substantially, particularly to Western Europe, and undoubtedly made a contribution to the weakness of crude oil and product prices during the early 1960s.[12] The falls in prices during these years took place in the context of a secular decline in oil prices which, it has already been noted, started in 1957 and continued – with an interruption in 1967 – throughout the 1960s.

Notes

1. American Petroleum Institute Specification.
2. By 1963 it had become ½ cent/b in most oil-producing countries.

3. The figures are from Ministry of Petroleum Affairs records.

4. $\dfrac{200 \text{ mb} \times 60 \text{ cents}}{2}$: this does not take account of losses brought forward to offset against surtax, which would have postponed the receipt of the additional revenue till later years.

5. M.S. Al Otaiba, *OPEC and the Petroleum Industry* (Croom Helm, London, 1975), p. 141 ff.

6. The seventh OPEC conference, held in Djakarta in November 1964, decided to leave it to member countries to accept or reject the offer, as each one thought fit.

7. The 40 cents/b shortfall is made up of loss of 50 per cent tax on profits lower by the amount of the discounts taken (50-60 cents/b) and of 50 per cent royalty (26-28 cents/b) resulting from treating it as a tax credit instead of expense of operations.

8. The information on this subject is from unpublished oil company records confirmed in part from contemporary journals and press comment.

9. Petroleum Law, Article 14.

10. The Minister of Petroleum Affairs in 1964 and 1965, Ess. Fuad al Kabbazi, accepted these arguments and was opposed to the revision of the Law intended to stop excessive discounting. The legislation of late 1965 was enacted during his tenure of office, but against his wishes.

11. The profits record and Libyan production of the three independents comprising the Oasis Group are shown in Table 6.8.

Table 6.8: Net Income and Libyan Production of Three Independents

	Net Income (US $ millions)	Libyan Production (millions of barrels)
5-year average 1957-61	132	0
1962	140	21
1963	178	61
1964	212	118

Sources: Companies' annual reports; Libyan Ministry of Petroleum Affairs published figures.

12. Soviet bloc exports of crude and products to Western Europe, compared with total Western European consumption, were as follows:

Table 6.9: Soviet Bloc Oil Exports to and Total Consumption of Oil in Western Europe, 1958-65

Million metric tons	1958	1959	1960	1961	1962	1963	1964	1965
Soviet bloc exports[a]	8	13	17	20	23	25	26	29
Total consumption – W. Europe[b]	153	173	205	228	264	303	345	389

Sources: a. *Petroleum Press Service*, Oct. 1963, Nov. 1966.

b. G. Jenkins, *Oil Economists' Handbook* (Applied Science Publishers, London, 1977)

The f.o.b. prices per barrel of crude oil shipped from the USSR to West Germany and Italy from 1960 to 1965 have been estimated as follows:

Table 6.10: Average Prices of Soviet Crude Oil, f.o.b. Export Point, to West
Germany and Italy

	1960	1961	1962	1963	1964	1965
To: West Germany	1.39	1.27	1.30	1.30	1.39	1.40
Italy	1.42	1.31	1.30	1.24	1.22	1.21

Source: M.A. Adelman, *The World Petroleum Market* (Johns Hopkins University
Press, Baltimore, 1972).

The gravities of the crude are not known. The prices are based on USSR official
trade figures and the greater part of the sales formed part of bilateral goods-for-
goods transactions.

7 THE 1965 PETROLEUM LAW AMENDMENT

7.1 The Summer of 1965 – New Concession Bids and the OPEC Meeting

In the early summer of 1965 two events were pending which for the time being diverted attention from the problems created by the unequal interpretation of the Petroleum Law. These were, first, the prospect of a new round of concessions being granted for areas surrendered by the early concessionaires, and second, the forthcoming ninth OPEC Conference at Ministerial level, which was to open at Tripoli on 7 July.

With the creation of a unitary State in 1963, a new capital had been designated at Beida, on the Jebel Akhdar, a few kilometres from the ruins of Cyrene. This was in the district in which King Idris had founded and led the Senussi Sect of devout Moslem revivalists. It was almost a 'green fields' site on which much construction was in progress. By 1965 it was the seat of Government and Parliament, the King himself residing at Tobruk, about 200 kilometres to the east.

Throughout the 1950s, Benghazi had been the principal centre of government activity, although most of the Ministries' offices were located at Tripoli. There had been some tension between Cyrenaican and Tripolitanian interests, and these were probably accentuated by the commercial discoveries of most oil being located in the Sirte basin in Cyrenaica. However, by 1965 the centre of administration had been firmly established at Tripoli, where the Ministry of Petroleum Affairs was located at this time, and to which the oil companies had moved, or were in process of moving, their head offices. Communications between the centres was not good – the telephone being unreliable over the 1,000 kilometres that separated Tripoli from Beida. The aeroplane was the best and quickest form of communication, and these were provided by oil companies.

The Minister of Petroleum Affairs, Ess. Fuad al Kabbazi, was normally resident at Beida, while the whole of the Ministry staff was at Tripoli. In the early summer the Minister appeared to devote himself entirely to making arrangements for the awarding of new concessions, for which bids were invited by published notice on 14 May 1965. This he did without the assistance or intervention of Ministry staff. At the beginning of June the Minister issued a statement containing 17 'elements of preference' to be taken into consideration in the granting of new concessions. These referred to the provision of the 1961 Amendment to the Law which stated that, in the awarding of concessions, the Commission (now Ministry) 'shall take into account such additional economic and financial benefits and advantages and other things which the applicant is willing and able to offer in addition to those stated' in the Law. They will be described in Chapter 8, where details of the subsequent concession awards are also given. Bids for new concessions were opened on 31 July 1965. But the award of concessions was overtaken by the storm brewing over the Petroleum Law and delayed until the early months of 1966, when the Amendment to the Law had been ratified, and all existing concession-holders had amended their own Concession Deeds, as well as bids for new concessions, to conform with it.

The OPEC Conference took place in July in an atmosphere of discomfort on the part of OPEC members at the falling of oil prices in world markets, and a will to try to stabilise them. In informal talks outside the meetings there was much criticism by OPEC members of the discounts known or believed to be taken by the Libyan independents, and the depressive effect of their actions on the general price levels of oil products (see Chapter 6). The attribution of lower oil prices to this cause was not shared by the Libyan Minister, who in his opening address made the following comments:

> Neither the petroleum exporting countries alone, nor in collaboration with the producing countries, can find a solution to this problem [sc. falling prices], because the old predominant system has collapsed by the entry of independents to the scene. There is no more an 'oliogopoly', or what I would call 'the Cartel' . . . The problem needs a tripartite co-operation between the producing country, the marketer and the consumer.

He went on to blame the low prices on consumer country governments taxing the oil products and thereby depressing prices so as to conserve their hard currency used to purchase crude; and to envisage a solution through consuming country governments becoming engaged in exploration and production, whereby they would 'care for stability in crude oil prices'; and for oil-exporting countries to acquire 'stocks and shares' in the downstream operations of the oil companies; this would mean 'integration downstream as far as we are concerned and integration upstream as far as they are concerned'.

The OPEC Ministers were not sufficiently in agreement with this analysis to endorse the Libyan Minister's proposals. The relevant resolution of the meeting was

> to adopt, as a transitory measure, a production plan calling for rational increases in production from the Opec area to meet estimated increases in world demand, and to submit a production programme to the Governments of member countries for approval.[1]

This resolution foreshadowed the course of events which culminated in the great changes in OPEC's power in the early 1970s. At that time the attempt to 'pro-rate' crude oil production among member countries was ineffective. As far as Libya was concerned the terms of the Petroleum Law would disallow restrictions on exports by concessionaires of their own oil.[2] Clause 1 of the Concession Deed gave them 'the right to take away petroleum whether by pipeline or otherwise from the concession area and to use, process, store, export and dispose of same'.

Even if Petroleum Regulation No. 3 had been invoked, which makes the concessionaire's right to export petroleum 'subject to such restrictions as the Government may impose . . . in cases of absolute necessity connected with the high interests of the State', the problems of allocation of such restrictions equitably between concessionaires, and of controlling them, would have been insoluble. The impositions themselves would have been of doubtful legal validity; if tested by arbitration, they would certainly have given rise to great embarrassment for the companies as well as the Government, which for reasons of national pride and prestige would have eschewed involvement in such a struggle.

The OPEC Ministers dispersed in the middle of July, having been conducted round the ancient Roman cities of Sabratha and Leptis Magna, without a firm plan to control and limit OPEC country production of crude oil, but having strengthened the foundations for the concerted measures to be taken in 1971 and the following years.

7.2 The Petroleum Prices Negotiating Committee and Preparations for the New Law

The Council of Ministers, meeting at Beida on 15 September 1965, under the chairmanship of the Prime Minister, Dr Hussein Mazegh, decided to set up a Committee to examine the problems created by the existing Petroleum Law and its interpretation by the independents resulting in a reduction of petroleum revenue below expectations and the intentions of the Law. The decision was conveyed to the members of the Committee and to the oil companies in letters from the Minister of Petroleum Affairs, Fuad al Kabbazi, who himself was not a member.

The members of the Committee were:

Khalifa Musa, Under-Secretary, Ministry of Finance, Chairman;
Muhammed Jeroushi, Director of Petroleum Affairs, Ministry of Petroleum Affairs;
C. Pitt-Hardacre, Economic Counsellor to the Prime Minister's Office;
Frank Waddams, Director of Companies' Accounts Dept., Ministry of Petroleum Affairs;
Professor Angelo Roca.

The Secretary to the Committee was Ibrahim Hangari, Secretary-General of the Supreme Petroleum Council.

Professor Roca, it appears, had been added to the membership of the Committee by Fuad al Kabbazi, but he was not in Libya, nor did he participate in any of the Committee's deliberations. He was described in the appointment letter as 'Counsellor for Marketing Affairs'.

The terms of reference of the Committee, according to the appointment letter, were:

1. To negotiate with petroleum exporting companies on posted prices for the purpose of reaching with these companies a principle for fixing that price in such a way as to realise the Government's interest in the light of economic circumstances prevailing in the petroleum market.

2. To negotiate on the extent of the equity of the discounts granted by some companies and the determination of the differences thereof that are due to the Government [*sic*].

The Committee was to submit the results of its 'operations' to the Council of Ministers.

These terms of reference made no mention of what was intended to be the main purpose of the Committee, namely to consider the adoption *in toto* of the OPEC formula in Libya, and make appropriate recommendations. In fact, for reasons which were never divulged, it appeared that the Minister for Petroleum Affairs was bent on steering events away from this course.[3] He followed up this letter with another, dated 21 September, to the producing oil companies, which informed them of the setting up of the Committee mentioned above, and called both members of the Committee and representatives of the oil companies to a preliminary meeting on 28 September.

The burden of the Minister's letter to the oil companies was that the posted prices of the companies were themselves unacceptable to the Government, which had protested against them to the companies to no avail; the discounts taken by some companies from these unacceptable posted prices had been excessive and the Ministry, under the terms of Petroleum Regulation No. 6, was entitled to receive proof to its satisfaction of their necessity and equity. The Committee had been charged by the Council of Ministers to 'consult with the companies concerned in this respect'.

This letter suggests that the Committee's function was merely to consult with the companies on the level of posted prices and on the level of discounts from posted prices, within the context of the existing 1961 Law and Regulations. The calling of a meeting of company representatives and of the Committee members to a meeting under the Minister's chairmanship provides further evidence of the latter's intention to steer decisions away from the OPEC formula. In the event, members of the Committee did not attend the meeting called by the Minister, which turned out to be uneventful and fruitless; instead it began deliberations under its Chairman, Khalifa Musa, at the Ministry of Finance and not at the Ministry of Petroleum Affairs.

The Chairman wrote to the companies early in October informing them of the true purpose of the Committee, which came to be called the 'Petroleum Prices Negotiating Committee'. The letter stated that

> it has been decided to negotiate now with *all* oil companies in Libya with a view to the introduction of the more equitable Opec formula . . . It is for that purpose that you have been called to negotiate with this Committee for the amendment of your concession in accordance with the Opec formula.

The first task which the Committee set itself was to establish the precise terms of the OPEC formula and the feasibility of its adoption in Libya. It became clear immediately that it could not be implemented without legislation, and under the terms of the existing concessions would have to be accepted voluntarily by all existing concession-holders to be effective.[4]

In its examination of the OPEC formula the Committee consulted with Esso, who was not only the principal producer of oil in Libya at the time, but also one of the companies, which comprised all the majors and CFP, to concede and implement the formula in other OPEC member countries. Esso made it clear early in the discussions that the offer was an 'all or nothing' package deal. There were two elements in it which appeared to be formidable blocks in the way of a smooth accomplishment by legislation of the intentions of the formula.

The first of these was a proposed change in arbitration from the 1961 provisions which stipulated that it should be governed by the laws of Libya and by the rules and principles of international law 'but only to the extent that such rules and principles are not inconsistent with and do not conflict with the laws of Libya'. The new proposal was that

the concession shall be governed by and interpreted in accordance with the principles of law of Libya common to the principles of international law and, in the absence of such common principles, then by and in accordance with the general principle of the law.

This change was hard for the Government to accept, but was insisted upon by the proposing companies as being that applicable in the formula implemented in other accepting countries.[5] It was ultimately accepted by the Libyan Government, and its acceptance was presented as a gesture by the Government of its intention to be fair and equitable in its dealings with the companies by putting arbitration outside its own jurisdiction and influence. In the event its effects were not tested until after the revolution, since both Government and companies were more than reluctant to invoke arbitration in the case of dispute.

The second block to smooth passage of the required Amendment was the entrenched right of the concession-holders to abide by the existing terms of their concession. It was out of the question that Esso and the other majors would accept the new arrangements while at the same time the independents did not. The former, in order to prevent this from happening, insisted on the inclusion in legislation of a 'most-favoured-company' clause. This was to provide that, in the event of any concession-holder being granted more favourable fiscal terms than those of the proposed amendment, such terms would apply also to the consenting concessionaires.

This dilemma made it abundantly clear that, for new legislation to be effective, it would have to be accepted by all existing and new concession-holders. Otherwise the result would be worse than the situation it was trying to mend. The dilemma underlines the difficulties of a host government dealing with a number of concessionaires on an equitable basis, with a commitment to honour with each one contractual terms which have become unequal in application and provide loopholes for evasion on a massive scale. There was no most-favoured-nation clause in the Libyan Law or contracts, as in Middle Eastern concessions.

It was believed by many, including some of the majors offering the formula, that the prospect of a quittance in respect of past years' accounts, which, so far as posted prices and discounts were concerned, was also included in the offer, would be sufficient to induce the reluctant independents to accept the new terms. The sum involved could have amounted to $60 million relief from claims for the Oasis companies.[6] This view was at no time shared by the present writer and, as will be described later, was disproved by events.

The Committee, having accomplished the drafting of the text of a proposed Amendment to implement the formula, distributed it to all companies, and proceeded to consult with each producing company on its acceptability. The producing majors, who by that time comprised Esso, Mobil, Amoseas and BP (shortly to begin production), signified their intention to accept. Gelsenberg, Mobil's minority partner, did the same. Among the other independents Amerada, who was associated with Shell,[7] first signified agreement then withdrew it, while Shell, who was not a producer, objected to the retro-activity of the proposal, which was intended to apply to 1965 operations and accounts.[8] The other independents rejected the proposals, requested discussions with the Prime Minister and prepared to submit counter-proposals. The non-assenting independents were seven in number, comprising Continental, Marathon, Sinclair (Liamco), Grace, Phillips, Pan-Amercian (Amoco) and N.B. Hunt. Continental and Marathon were substantial producers in the Oasis operation; Sinclair and Grace were minor partners in the small Esso Sirte-managed field; Phillips had just begun small production in late 1965 by joining their wells to existing pipeline systems; Pan-American was expected to start a comparable operation in 1966. N.B. Hunt was the 50 per cent partner with BP in Concession 65, production from which was to begin towards the end of 1966. Between them they accounted for 31 per cent of Libya's 1965 oil production, of which 27 per cent was supplied by Continental and Marathon, the remainder accounting for 4 per cent.

These seven independents sought and obtained an audience with the Prime Minister, Dr Hussein Mazegh, at which they submitted a memorandum explaining their opposition to the proposed measure. The memorandum was a brief summary of a long document drafted by Continental and contained the following assertions:

> The proposed Decree would retard Libya's economic growth by curtailing investment, impairing future crude oil production and reducing the total crude oil revenue. Reductions in exploration and development programmes would be felt in every sector of the Libyan economy because of fewer service contracts.
>
> The geographical and economic characteristics of the Libyan oil industry were such that it could not support the same system of taxes as Arabian Gulf oil.
>
> The Decree would cause Libya to lose its present strong market position, which was created to a considerable extent by the independent producers.
>
> The proposed Decree would involve increased taxes of unprecedented magnitude for the independent producers — many times greater than those involved in the Opec settlement in the Arabian Gulf.
>
> The independent producers were not responsible for the deterioration of market prices in Western Europe.

The memorandum ended by stating that 'because of its disastrous effects on Libya and the independent producers, our group seeks reconsideration of the proposed Decree and an opportunity to explain our opposition thereto'.

The meeting of the Prime Minister with the independents took place on 25 October. Dr Mazegh listened with sympathy and interest to the representations of the delegation, to the point of toleration without rebuke of a suggestion by one independent that Libya's geographical position between two stronger countries might become politically precarious if it aroused the opposition of American interests.[9] Subsequently the Prime Minister requested the Petroleum Prices Negotiating Committee to comment on the independents' representation to him in writing. The comments, which were submitted on the same day to the Prime Minister, contained a reasoned rebuttal of the independents' predictions and assertions — a rebuttal which was vindicated by subsequent events. The large increases in taxes for the independents under the new arrangements were cited in the Committee's comments as a measure of the extent to which they had been avoiding the payment of an appropriate level of taxes hitherto.

The draft Amendment, in the form acceptable to the consenting companies, was considered by the Council of Ministers on 27 and 28 October, and the problem came to centre on the point of acceptability of all the provisions by the Libyan Government. If the latter had altered the text in any significant manner, it would have become unacceptable to the consenting companies and therefore not applicable to them. There were several points in the draft to which objection was made in the Council, but none of them produced a conflict which was insoluble in terms of modified wording without change of basic meaning. However, the Council referred the consideration of the whole text to a Sub-committee of Ministers. This was chaired by Salem al Qadi, Minister of Finance, and included Fuad al Kabbazzi, Minister of Petroleum Affairs. The latter again diverted the issue from the formula to the consideration of discounts, and wished to call in the Petroleum Prices Negotiating Committee and the independents to pursue this line. The Chairman of the latter Committee declined to appear on this basis before the Ministerial Sub-committee, and for the time being it appeared that no further action on implementing the draft of the Amendment would be taken.

On 10 November the scene shifted to Beida, where the Council of Ministers once more assembled to consider the draft text submitted by the Petroleum Prices Negotiating Committee, as well as alterations and objections to it put forward by the Minister for Petroleum Affairs and the further representations and counter-proposals of the independents.

In the following days the dissenting independents submitted detailed counter-proposals to the Ministerial Sub-committee. Although independently submitted, they contained common features which, in brief, were as follows:

(1) an offer of acceleration of tax payments in the immediate future to help cover the deficit caused by the current shortfall of oil revenue compared with the budget estimate;
(2) a ceiling on discounts in the future varying slightly between companies but not substantially lower than those already taken in 1964 and previous years;
(3) a quittance on all accounts up to and including 1964.

These proposals offered no improvement on the existing situation; indeed, since they included a quittance for the past, they made matters worse. In the following days there developed a straight conflict in the Council of Ministers between the recommendations of the Petroleum Prices Negotiating Committee on the one hand and those of the Minister for Petroleum Affairs, assisted by some Iranian advisers, and representing the dissenting independents' views, on the other.

The Prime Minister and the Finance Minister were both convinced by 16 November that the best course was to introduce the OPEC formula measure without further change. On this and the following day the matter was referred to the King in Tobruk, who gave audience to the Prime Minister, the Chairman of the Petroleum Prices Negotiating Committee and the Minister for Petroleum Affairs. It is believed that the King, having heard the opposing viewpoints, expressed his view that legislation should be enacted in a form acceptable to the consenting companies, since this was necessary for its success. On subsequent days the draft Amendment was passed by the Council of Ministers and submitted to the King for signature on 20 November. It was broadcast by the radio the same day, published in Libyan newspapers on the following morning and in the *Official Gazette* on 22 November. It was issued as a Royal Decree on 20 November 1965, and was unanimously ratified by the Libyan Parliament meeting on 9 December.[10]

7.3   The Main Features of the New Law

The principal fiscal features of the new Law were, in brief:[11]

(1)   the expensing of royalties, hitherto treated as credits against future surtax payments;

(2)   discounts to be allowed on posted prices for tax purposes of 7½ per cent for 1965, 6½ per cent for 1966 (both adjusted for gravity[12]) and in subsequent years not more than 6½ per cent;

(3)   an allowance of ½ US cent a barrel marketing expense.

The expensing of royalties had the effect of increasing payments to Government by half the amount of the royalty, which was 12½ per cent of oil production valued at the applicable posted price.[13] This amounted to 13-14 cents a barrel extra payment to the Government, varying according to variations in posted price and gravity of the oil.

The discounts from posted prices for tax purposes were those agreed in the OPEC formula in 1964. After 1966 there was to be a further annual decision on the reduction of the discounts 'in the light of the competitive, economic and market situation', but in no case could the discount be increased.[14]

These new provisions, with the discount of 6½ per cent applicable to 1966 operations of the oil companies, would result in extra payments to Government for that year of approximately 5 US cents a barrel of crude oil exports, if the company concerned would otherwise have declared its sales at full posted prices and its tax-deductible costs and expenses had remained unchanged. In fact, the majors had already indicated that, in the absence of new legislation, even in 1965 accounts, they would have taken the discounts agreed in the OPEC formula, but would also have treated their royalties as an advance payment of surtax according to the terms of the existing law. They would thus pay an extra 14 cents a barrel over and above their payments as they would have been in the absence of the new legislation.

For the independents, whose fiscal sales price of posted price less marketing expenses including discounts and rebates would not have been more than $1.60 a barrel, the application of the new law to 1966 would mean extra payments of about 35 cents a barrel.[15]

The other features of the 1965 Amendment worthy of note were as follows:

(1) Article IX introduced provisions to try to close a loophole in the Law, as perceived by the companies, through which the Government might, as had happened elsewhere, impose extra taxes or levies on concessionaires over and above those stipulated in the Law, without actually violating the terms of the Law. Examples of such action, mentioned elsewhere, were the raising of Venezuelan income tax generally to high-profit companies in 1958, and the levying of extra port dues in Iraq in 1960. The Libyan Government was for a long time puzzled by the draft of the Law proposed by Esso containing these provisions; but as they had no thought at this or any other time of trying to find loopholes whereby the spirit of the Law might be violated to obtain uncovenanted advantages from the companies, they accepted this clause without demur.[16]

(2) The change in arbitration provisions and procedures has already been mentioned.

(3) Article XI of the Amendment stipulated that no new concessions would be granted to any concession-holder who did not amend all his existing concessions; the applications for new concessions opened on 31 July 1965 could remain in force under the terms of the new Law, with or without additions or deletions, if notice were given by the applicant in writing within 45 days of the publication of the new Law in the *Official Gazette*.

(4) The application of the most-favoured-company clause, detailed in Article XII, involved elaborate stipulations, and the right of companies, if they thought they were relevant, to have access to the records of other companies in order to monitor the position. In the event all companies amended, and these provisions were fortunately never called into use.

(5) Article XII contained provisions for a quittance in respect of periods before the new Law came into effect. The quittance depended on companies giving an undertaking in writing prior to 15 December 1965 to amend their concessions in accordance with the terms of the new Law not later than 26 January 1966. The provisions of the new Law would thus be effective as from 1 January 1965 and the quittance would refer to periods up to 31 December 1964. The quittance took the form of stating that the 'basis, including the levels of posted prices, rebates, discounts and allowances, used. . . is the proper basis for determining the Company's liabilities to the Government with respect to all the periods prior to the effective date of the agreement of amendment'. It did not include 'operating expenses and overheads as defined in Petroleum Regulation No. 6'. In effect, this wiped the slate clean not only in respect of discounts and rebates, which were the prime reason for the new law, but also posted prices for all companies, which the Government had hitherto contested.

7.4   Final Acceptance and Amendment of Concessions

In the Speech from the Throne opening Parliament on 7 December, the King referred to the Royal Decree Law of 20 November and commented in the following terms:

> It behoves my Government to announce that while it respects the companies' contractual rights, it can in no way tolerate any situation that might give rise to a reduction in the State's revenues from this important source, and it rejects any treatment that does not equate in this respect with other Opec member countries.

Nevertheless, by 15 December — the last day on which concessionaires were, according to the Law, to give their undertaking in writing to amend before 26 January 1966 in order to obtain the quittance — six of the producing independents, and among the majors Gulf, had not consented. The deadline was extended for two days, without further action on the part of these companies, who were Continental, Marathon, Grace, Phillips, Pan-American and N.B. Hunt.[17]

On 28 December, the Government announced that it had extended the deadline for written consent to 15 January 1966. This was reported in *The Times* of 29 December, which also reported that OPEC, meeting in Vienna, had passed a resolution recommending all OPEC members not to grant any new concession to Libyan non-assenters. OPEC also decided to approach non-OPEC members for support in implementing this course of action, and to contact the parent companies of the non-assenters to clarify its position in the matter.[18]

On 30 December, Continental submitted a further proposal to the Government. This proposal[19] 'accepted the principles of the Decree Law of 20th November, 1965' and agreed to amend in the following manner:

(1) a posting of $2.35/b for crude oil of 40° and above;
(2) full expensing of royalties for 1965 and after;
(3) the company's realisations to be based on sales to the ultimate consumer including marketing, refining and transportation profits attributable to Libyan crude oil; but not less than $1.70 for 1965 and $1.80 for 1966 or after;
(4) a quittance for 'marketing expenses' claimed for 1962-4.

The proposal drew attention to the opportunity afforded to Libya to share in the benefits of 'downstream participation' without investment, and expressed the view that other companies could not claim most-favoured-company treatment unless they were also willing to make a tax settlement on actual realisation including downstream profits.

This offer was not pursued by the Libyan Government. At the same time it became known[20] that a new Decree Law had been prepared which would place certain sanctions on non-assenters. The law was never published. With these pressures, the companies that had hitherto declined to amend to the provisions of the new Law now gave their undertakings to do so. The Agreements to amend the concessions were executed in the Ministry of Petroleum Affairs between the company representatives and the Acting Minister (the Minister being abroad at this time) on 20-22 January 1966. The new Law was thus to apply to all concession-holders as from 1 January 1965.

7.5   The Extension of the Quittance

The quittance given by the terms of the 1965 Amendment to those concession-holders who consented in writing before 15 December 1965 to amend their concessions to the new provisions before 26 January 1966 referred specifically to posted prices, rebates, discounts and allowances and royalty, but excluded operating expenses and overheads, for all accounting periods up to 31 December 1964. The deadline for assent was extended to 15 January 1966 by a measure announced on 28 December 1965, and approved by Parliament on 4 January 1966.

By this date all concession-holders had given their undertaking to amend, and so all became entitled to the quittance. After the concession deeds had been amended, the quittance was extended also to cover operating expenses and overheads. In a letter to each producing concession-holder in early March the Minister of Petroleum Affairs wrote:

> The Ministry of Petroleum Affairs, having examined the accounts submitted by your Company for the year or years up to and including 31st December, 1964, hereby informs you that . . . it accepts those accounts as final insofar as concerns deductions from income in respect of operating expenses and overheads.

This might appear to be an act of uncovenanted generosity. It was, however, within the administrative judgement of the Ministry whether or not to dispute and disallow operating expenses and overheads claimed by companies against taxable income, and the decision was taken that for these years it would not be expedient to do so. It was reasoned that more than 90 per cent of the sums hitherto in dispute were covered by the quittance in the new Law, and that the remaining comparatively small amounts which might be queried would not warrant the expense and effort involved in trying to collect them. Any Ministry disallowances would undoubtedly have been resisted by the companies, and in this case could not, in the last resort, be imposed short of successful arbitration. The processes of dispute and arbitration would take years to complete, and it was clear that the Government would not be prepared to embark on arbitration on small matters.

It was estimated in the Ministry that, with 100 per cent recovery of all potentially disputed items of operating expenses and overheads for the years up to 1964, a maximum of half a million Libyan pounds might be received. This compared with a potential of at least £L40 millions involved in the statutory quittance. But in fact it was probable that only a small percentage of disputed items would be recovered and these after long altercations and expensive arbitration. A further consideration was a six-year Statute of Limitation in tax matters, inherited from the Italian colonial era in the laws of the country. The likely benefits derived from goodwill generated between the Government and companies, though intangible, were also reviewed, and it was considered in the interests of all that the slate should be wiped completely clean for the past. A period of good relations between Government and companies followed, and this contributed to the prosperity of the Libyan oil industry and of the country during the next four years.

Notes

1. Resolution IX.61.
2. Other OPEC countries had different interests, which to some extent conflicted with each other. For instance, Venezuela, with high output and limited reserves, was for control; Iran, on the other hand, was pressing for an increase in its own share of Middle East production, and Iraq, where output had been comparatively low since 1960, also wished to regain its former position.
3. The Minister's attitude was influenced by the fact that the introduction of new oil legislation at this time clashed with the arrangements he was making for new concessions.
4. Clause 16 of the Concession in the 1955 Law stated that 'the contractual rights expressly created by this Concession shall not be altered except by mutual consent of the parties.' The Royal Decree of 9 November 1961 added to this that 'any amendment or repeal of these Regulations [sc. those introduced in 1961 allowing discounts and rebates] shall not affect the contractual rights of the Company without its consent.'
5. Iraq had not accepted the formula, its principal objection being that the arbitration provisions were inconsistent with the sovereignty of the Iraqi Government (see J.E. Hartshorn, *Oil Companies and Governments*, 2nd edn, (Faber and Faber, London, 1967), p. 342.
6. *Petroleum Intelligence Weekly*, 20 December 1965, p. 8, published this figure as coming from Libyan sources.
7. Shell purchased all Amerada's production and had been trying then for two years to obtain an assignment of 50 per cent of Amerada's interests, approval of which had hitherto been withheld by the Government. Both Amerada and Shell in fact tried to make acceptance contingent on the Government's agreement to the assignment. This was, of course, refused. Shell and Amerada both subsequently accepted and the assignment was approved by the Government, to operate as from 1 January 1966. Shell was also influenced in its attitude by the existence of a most-favoured-African-nation clause in its Nigerian concession contract. Nigeria was not a member of OPEC, and its concession terms at the time were more favourable to the companies than the OPEC formula.

8. In the OPEC formula agreement in other countries, it was a standard feature that the measure came into force on 1 January preceding the 12-month period ending 26 January in which the Agreement was made. This had been adopted in the Libyan draft version, as part of Esso's package offer. The Government aimed to have all producing concession-holders' assent before 26 January 1966, so that the new provisions would apply to the year 1965.

9. The writer was present at this interview.

10. *The Times*, 21 Dec. 1965.

11. This summary is quoted from an article by the writer in *The Times* of 21 December 1965. Although the objectives of the Law were simple, its actual text is long and complex. Reference is made in the main work only to points of broad significance for the Libyan oil industry in the context of the international oil industry situation. Some further comment is given below in these notes.

12. The adjustment for gravity, called the 'gravity differential allowance', was also part of the OPEC formula agreement. There was at that time a standard 2 US cents a barrel reduction in posted prices both in Libya and the Middle East for each degree of API gravity below 40° of the crude oil. The gravity differential allowance was, for 1966, of US $0.0026470 a barrel 'for each degree of API gravity by which the crude oil exceeds 27° API gravity'. This was introduced by the oil companies, and accepted by OPEC, to reflect the former's contention that the market for lighter crudes was not so firm as that for heavier crudes, and the 2 cents price differential per 1° should be reduced. Most of Libya's oil was light, and on a typical 39°API crude oil this stipulation meant an extra 3.2 cents a barrel discount. It was not so significant for other OPEC members, the gravity of whose oil was lower than Libya's. Libya, though accepting this as part of the OPEC package, was not in agreement with its rationale. As with the main discounts, after 1967 it became inapplicable to Libya (see note 14 below).

13. The amount that was to be expensed, usually referred to as royalties, was not strictly speaking so, but '12½ % of the value of crude oil exported . . . the value calculated on the basis of the applicable posted prices of crude oil exported'. In fact production was different from, and normally higher in volume than, crude oil exported, and included any amounts which were delivered in Libya for refining. There were also differences in gravity between production and exports. Any excess of royalty over 12½ per cent of the value of crude oil exported was still to be treated as a tax credit and not expensed.

14. This passage of the draft Law ran into stormy waters in the Council of Ministers because the company alone would make the 'determination' on any reduction in the discounts justified by market conditions. The final text of the Law, while defining as precisely as possible the criteria by which the company must be guided, retained the decision for the companies.

Discounts after 1966 were negotiated at OPEC level, and Libya would, under the proposed terms, be obligated – after discussion – to accept the oil companies' determination stemming from the OPEC level agreement. In the event the closing of the Suez Canal in 1967 changed the situation and resulted in the discounts being abolished in Libya, but not for Arabian Gulf oil.

15. The per barrel payments cannot be accurately stated across the board owing to differences in posted price and of gravity of different oils and even of the same oil between production (on which royalty is charged) and export (on which the sales price is based). The arithmetic in respect of a typical oil of 39°API would be as follows for 1966, when the discount was to be 6½ per cent:

		US dollars/barrel (to the nearest cent)	Comments
(1)	Posted price, 39°	2.21	
	Royalty	0.28	(12½% × $2.21)
	Extra tax payment by company due to expensing of royalty instead of treating it as advance tax payment	0.14	(50% of royalty)

(2) Tax reference price of crude oil per barrel under new law:

Posted price,			2.21	
Less: 6½% discount		0.144		
Gravity differential allowance		0.032		
Marketing expense		0.005	0.18	(½ US cent/barrel)
Tax reference price			2.03	

(3)	Saving in tax for company using OPEC discounts, compared with posted price	0.09	(50% × $0.18)
(4)	Extra tax for company from declaring at posted price less OPEC discounts, compared with declaring under old law 'marketing expenses including rebates'	0.21	($2.03 − 1.60) / 2

(5) Total extra payments

(a) By company declaring full posted price	0.05	(0.14 in (1) above less 0.09 in (3) above)
(b) By company declaring at $1.60	0.35	(0.14 in (1) above plus 0.21 in (4) above)

16. The text of Article IX contains the following passage:

The total income to the Ministry of Petroleum Affairs and other Libyan Government, Municipal and other authorities whether central or local in respect of the production, manufacture, dealings in oil or rights thereto, transport, sale, export, shipments and profits and distribution therefrom of crude oil produced in Libya by the Company and/or sold by the Company for export from Libya shall be equal in respect of any complete year to the amount which the Libyan Government would have been entitled to receive in respect of such year calculated in accordance with the Company's concession agreements as amended by this Decree, wherein this paragraph has been incorporated into the Concession Agreements. In the event any difference or dispute arises concerning this paragraph, such difference or dispute shall be referred to arbitration in accordance with Clause 28 below.

A similar safeguard had already been incorporated in Petroleum Regulation No. 6 on Esso's representations (see Ch. 5, note 15). The Regulation was presumably considered not sufficiently watertight, and this further passage — copied from the standard OPEC formula provisions elsewhere — was deemed to make it so.

17.   *Wall Street Journal*, 17 December 1965.

18.   M.S. Al Otaiba, *OPEC and the Petroleum Industry* (Croom Helm, London, 1975), p. 113.

19.   Letter from Continental to Ministry of Petroleum Affairs, dated 30 December 1965.

20.   *The Times*, 3 January 1966: but G.W. Stocking *Middle East Oil* (Vanderbilt University Press, Nashville, Tennessee, 1970), p. 379) states that the Decree was passed by Parliament unanimously on 26 December 1965, and included the imposition of a ban on exports and expropriation of physical assets for non-assenting companies.

Part IV

GOVERNMENT RELATIONS, OIL INDUSTRY
DEVELOPMENT AND THE LIBYAN ECONOMY 1961-1969

8 GOVERNMENT RELATIONS, INTERVENTION AND PARTICIPATION

8.1 The Posting of Prices — 1961

The first posting of a price for Libyan crude oil was made by Esso in August 1961, when the company was about to begin exports from Mersa Brega, its effective date being early in September. The price posted was $2.21 for 39° API gravity oil, with a 2-cents reduction for each degree of gravity of the oil under 39°, but a maximum of $2.23 for 40° and over.

The Chairman of the Petroleum Commission protested this posting even before it was published.[1] The 1961 Amendment to the Law which introduced the concept of posted prices and their definition into the Libyan legislation for the first time had only recently been enacted, and no concession-holder had yet signified acceptance of it. Regulation No. 6, defining posting procedures, was not to come into operation until the following December. The relevant legislation was the original 1955 Law, in which there was no mention of posted prices.

With the acceptance by Esso of the 1961 Amendments in early 1962, the company was under constraint to justify its posting in the terms of the amended Law and concession deeds and of Regulation No. 6. There were clearly no 'free market prices for individual commercial sales of full cargoes' of Libyan oil, and so the proper procedure to be used in posting was stipulated in the second part of the paragraph defining posted prices in the amended Law. This stated that

> posted prices shall mean a fair price fixed by Agreement between the Company and the Commission [later Ministry] or in default of agreement by arbitration having regard to the posted prices of crude oil of similar quality and gravity in other free markets with necessary adjustments for freight and insurance.

In Esso's posting there had been no agreement between the company and the Commission. That this state of affairs was a violation of the Law was disputed by Esso on the grounds that the Regulation gave the company the authority to 'establish and publish its posted price for Libyan crude oil', and that this was the Agreement referred to in the Law.

Esso thus concentrated on defending its position by maintaining that it had paid regard to the posted prices of crude oil of similar quality and gravity in other free markets with necessary adjustments for freight and insurance, and had come to its conclusions accordingly.

This it did in a memorandum dated 26 February 1962, to the Libyan Government's Petroleum Adviser (Dr Nadim Pachachi, who had played a leading role in preparing the 1961 Amendments and Regulation No. 6). The posted prices in other free markets to which Esso had paid regard were stated to be those of Saudi Arabian 34° crude at Ras Tanura and also at the Eastern Mediterranean pipeline terminal of Sidon, Iraqi 36° at the Eastern Mediterranean terminal of Banias, and Iranian 34° at Kharg Island.[2]

That the base postings chosen for the calculation were 'free market' prices was assumed on the grounds that they were prices at which oil was offered for sale to all buyers by the posting companies. It could well be argued that none of the Middle East or Eastern Mediterranean postings were free market prices, and there were no commercial sales of individual cargoes to third parties at these prices; and that the only posted prices of crude which approximately satisfied those conditions were in the USA.[3] If East Texan posted prices were used as basing points, a Libyan posting calculated according to the Law, with quality, gravity and freight adjustments, would be over $3.50/b. This was, however, an academic point, as neither of the parties to the dispute seriously suggested its application.

The calculations used by Esso to arrive at $2.21 show that the company gave no credit in the posting for the quality and gravity factors mentioned in the Law. One of the outstanding qualities of Libyan crude oil was its low sulphur content, which none of the oils used for the comparison shared. This was recognised by Esso in its memorandum; having mentioned that this quality 'may give fuel oil derived from Libyan crude an advantage of a few cents a barrel over regular grade fuel oil', and that such oil could be useful for blending with high sulphur oils, the company came to the conclusion that the value of low-sulphur crude 'in terms of a price penalty for high sulphur is not great'. The memorandum added that its advantage in this respect was offset by a high wax content, and that 'it may be necessary to further refine the product or to blend the Zelten distillate off with lower pour material'.

The premium commanded by low-sulphur oils was only then beginning to be recognised, and was to be further developed during the coming decade as consuming countries turned their attention to sulphur pollution, and in the USA and Japan legislation was introduced against burning high-sulphur fuels in industrial and domestic furnaces. When a sulphur premium was finally introduced into Libyan postings, in the Tripoli Agreement of March 1971, it was pitched initially at 10 cents to rise over the following three years to 25 cents a barrel.

The gravity of the oil was also mentioned by Esso in its memorandum, but not reflected in the posting. The gravity of the oils used by Esso in its calculation for comparison with Libyan 39° crude were 34°, and the fourth 36°. Esso asserted that market conditions did not favour the higher-gravity oils — the 'European market is one where gasoline already sells at distress prices and is a problem to refiners.' This assertion implicitly conflicted with Esso's own posting, which established a 2 cents difference in the posted price for each degree of gravity change up to 40° — a difference common to all Middle East postings.

The 'necessary adjustment for freight' was interpreted by Esso in a questionable manner. In applying this provision a net-back formula of the type outlined in Chapter 2, note 10, was used. This was done by Esso adding a freight from the basing points of the oils chosen for comparison to Rotterdam, and deducting from the resulting figure (which gave a price c.i.f. Rotterdam) a freight from Mersa Brega to Rotterdam, to arrive at an f.o.b. price Mersa Brega.

Esso applied Scale minus 50 per cent, claiming that it was 'a representative rate as evidenced by many charters made in the tanker market'. This must have referred to the spot market for single voyages, since at no time in the previous year had AFRA (used by Esso in its charges for crude oil to affiliates) fallen below Scale minus 16.6 per cent, and on average was above Scale minus 15 per cent. The adjustment for freight had a different impact on the posted price calculation depending on whether the basing point was the Arabian Gulf or the Eastern Mediterranean, as is shown by the calculations in notes 2 and 4.

Thus Esso in its posting, as well as giving Libyan crude oil no credit for its high quality and gravity, included only an exiguous one for its freight advantage to European markets. The Libyan Government protested the posting, and repeated its protests many times during the coming decade. The quantitative expression of the quality, gravity and freight factors to be applied in the terms of the Law were open to wide differences of opinion, and the variables that could be used large in number. Esso had combined the variables in its evaluation to give a very low posting, and had defended them by reference to its commercial and technical experience, which it would be difficult for the inexperienced Libyan officials to gainsay. In the opinion of many a posting higher by about 30 cents a barrel would have interpreted the legal provisions adequately.[4]

The story of this posting illustrates two points of significance. One, that the oil company interest was no longer in pitching posted prices high, as it had been in the early years after the war, but to keep them as low as possible in order to reduce royalty and tax payments to governments. The other, that in spite of what the Law stated about host government agreement, the company unilaterally fixed the posted price. After 1960, the formation of OPEC prevented further falls, but Libya, at that time not a member of OPEC, was starting from scratch. Within the terms of the concession contracts there were no means short of arbitration of changing the company's decision.

It may well be asked why, if the case was so strong, the Libyan Government did not have recourse to arbitration. This was provided for in the Law, and indeed was urged on the Libyan Government many times by the present writer in later years, as being the most reasonable and civilised way of settling a dispute. There was, however, an unmovable reluctance on the part of the Government to do so. This may have been caused by a number of factors, of which the relationship between a sovereign power and a multinational company of the private sector was one, and a lack of confidence in the outcome if an inexperienced developing country contended in a court with the sophistication of a long-established international giant another.

8.2   After the Initial Posting

Only one other producing company posted a price for crude oil between 1961 and 1965. It was Marathon, one of the partners in the Oasis operation, who published a price in 1963 at the same level as Esso. Continental did not follow suit, and in answer to criticisms asserted that the Law did not require it to do so.[5] It used prices similar to Esso's postings in its fiscal accounts submitted to the Ministry. The third Oasis partner, Amerada, also did not post. It was selling all its oil first to Continental and after 1963 to Shell; as all its crude oil was committed in this way it would have been a fiction to post a price as though it were available to buyers generally (as it was required to be by Regulation No. 6).[6] Liamco and Grace, the junior partners in the Esso Sirte operations, sold all their production to Esso, and also did not post. Mobil and Gelsenberg, who began production in

1963, Amoseas in 1964 and Phillips in 1965 all for the time being followed Esso's posting without publishing a price of their own.

The enactment of the 1965 amendment and its acceptance by all concession-holders gave a quittance for all posted price disputes as far as the end of 1964. The amended Law stated that, if a concession-holder undertook in writing to amend his concession to accord with the new Law before 15 December 1965 (later extended for a month), then

> the basis including the levels of posted prices ... used by the Company in determining the amount of payments, including royalty, made to the Government by the Company is the proper basis for determining the Company's liabilities to the Government with respect to all the periods prior to the effective date of the Agreement.

The effective date of the Agreement was 1 January 1965.

The wording of the quitttance gave no indication that the Government accepted the posted prices as proper after the beginning of 1965. However, the matter was quiescent for a few months until Mobil started producing from its Amal field towards the middle of 1966, when it posted a price of $2.10/b for 36° oil — 5 cents below the Esso postings — on the grounds of its waxy content, which gave it high pour-point characteristics. These characteristics would, it was stated, make it less marketable because special heating equipment would have to be installed in refineries and pipelines in Northern Europe to ensure fluidity much of the year. Mobil was followed by Texaco and Socal (the parent companies of Amoseas) with a similar posting for its Nafoora crude, and for similar reasons. And at the end of the year BP posted its Sarir oil at a price 2 cents lower than the Mobil/Amoseas postings on similar grounds plus a higher freight.

The Ministry formally protested all these postings as soon as they were made, but no further action was taken either by the companies or the Government. The Arab-Israeli war in the first days of June 1967 and the closing of the Suez Canal gave rise to a quite new situation in petroleum markets. An Arab embargo on oil shipments to the Western Powers sent oil prices sky-high, and when shipments were resumed from Libya in July, the closing of the Suez Canal and soaring freights gave its oil an immense freight advantage over Middle East oil, particularly as the Mediterranean terminals from Iraq and Saudi Arabia remained closed for some time.

On 1 August 1967, the Minister of Petroleum Affairs, Khalifa Musa (who had succeeded Fuad al Kabbazi earlier in the year), sent a letter to all companies producing oil in Libya requesting them to submit proposals for increases in posted prices during the week beginning 14 August. The letter quotes the definition of posted prices embodied in the Law, and continues:

> There are three factors in the present situation which call for a review and adjustment of posted prices in accordance with the above provisions of the Law and your Concession:
> 1. The world-wide increase in prices of petroleum and petroleum products, particularly in European markets.
> 2. The more favourable geographical position of Libya for the supply of these markets in comparison with the Arabian Gulf owing to the closure of the Suez Canal.
> 3. The rise in freight rates which increases the favourable situation and demand for Libyan oil compared with oil from the Arabian Gulf.

This letter adds that, if and when circumstances again change, a further review and adjustment to posted prices may be necessary; and that new prices should be operative 'for the purpose of your Libyan Financial declaration as from the date of resumption of export of crude oil from Libya at the beginning of July, 1967'.

The high freight rates, together with the longer journey of Arabian Gulf oil round the Cape of Good Hope instead of through the Suez Canal, had increased the freight advantage of Libyan oil over Arabian Gulf oil to North-West Europe from about 40 cents a barrel to at least $1.10/b. This suggests that this cause alone would justify a price rise, as long as the conditions lasted, of about 70 cents/b. On representative figures given to the press to illustrate this point, it was reported that this was Libya's claim, but this was denied by the Libyan Government, which had not quantified a claim, but asked for oil company proposals. The old quality and gravity points were not even mentioned.

The Minister's letter envisaged that conditions would change again, and that posted prices would change with them. The oil companies pleaded that as the present situation was temporary it did not call for immediate action. But the terms of the Law did not make any provision for temporary situations, nor was there any knowledge of how long temporary conditions would last. The legal requirement for posted prices to be adjusted for freight, rates of which were always subject to fluctuations, surely implied that Libyan posted prices should be changed from time to time to take into account freight rate changes, even if other posted prices remained static. This situation was envisaged in Regulation No. 6, which required concession-holders to establish and publish their posted prices 'from time to time'.

At about the same time the Ministry made a proposal to the companies for a procedure which incorporated the current AFRA rate in the posted price formula, so that the posted price would fluctuate with AFRA (as did the oil companies' charges for crude oil to their affiliates in consuming countries). Such a procedure, after the details of basing points and other variables had been settled, would take the posted price out of dispute between companies and Government, make it a matter of routine accounting, but at the same time would meticulously implement both the wording and intention of the Law. No response was received from the companies to this proposal.[7]

The war and the closing of the Suez Canal had a major effect on oil prices in Europe. These are illustrated in Chart 8.1 which shows that, in the Rotterdam products market, when oil became available again in July, the immediate rise in price of a composite barrel of products was of the order of 100 per cent. Prices in this market, however, soon fell back, and by 1969 had reached their pre-Suez levels again. Average composite prices, as calculated by Adelman (p. 190) for this period at Rotterdam were:

1967 (Jan. − May) $2.05/b; 1967 (July − Dec.) $3.24/b; 1968, $2.53/b; 1969, $2.04/b.

The downward trend was not prolonged into 1970, when the comparable prices are given by the same sources as $2.24 for the first half and $3.19 for the second.

If these prices are taken as a reflection of market realisations of integrated companies, as is argued by Adelman, it may be inferred that those companies with Libyan oil, particularly those with shipping requirements covered by their own vessels or long-term charters, were able to reap large rewards in 1967 without any appreciable increases in costs. The Libyan Petroleum Law's intent was that the Libyan posted price should be set at a level which resulted in comparability of prices of Libyan oil with those of oil from other sources − particularly from the Arabian Gulf, the major source − at a point of delivery. The claim for an increase in posted prices on these grounds, while high price and high freight conditions lasted, was difficult to contest.

The oil companies, however, did not respond, and the talks with the

Ministry on posted prices were fruitless. Instead of adjusting the posted prices, the companies, under Esso's leadership, offered the temporary elimination of the OPEC formula discount and of the gravity differential allowance[8] while the Suez Canal remained closed. This in effect increased the tax reference price of Libyan crude oil by about 15 cents a barrel, and consequently the Government take by about 7.5 cents/b, without altering posted prices themselves. This proposal was implemented to apply from the resumption of shipments in July, 1967. The oil companies did not move on posted prices. In January, 1968, Occidental, coming into production from its new Idris and Augila fields, posted at the same level as Esso, and this posting too was formally protested by the Ministry. In addition to the long-standing grounds for protest, there was an additional one in that Occidental's oil was likely to be about $42°$ gravity, and the posting did not allow for any 2-cents increase per degree of gravity over $40°$.

Chart 8.1: Rotterdam Oil Prices, 1960-71

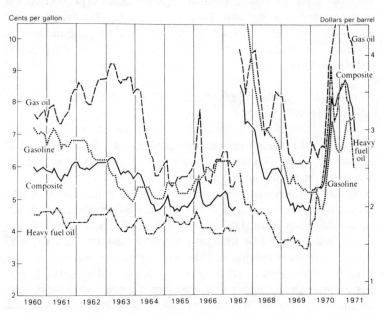

Figure VI-1.   Rotterdam product prices and realization per barrel of crude charge, by months, 1960–1971. (Source: Appendix Table VI–B–1.)

Source: M.A. Adelman, *The World Petroleum Market* (Johns Hopkins University Press, Baltimore, 1972, published for Resources for the Future, Inc.)

8.3 New Concessions — 1966

Applications for new concessions in areas surrendered by the original concessionaires had been invited by notice published on 4 May 1965, and opened on 29 July 1965. The awards had been delayed because of the intervention of preparations for the new Law, which would clearly affect the terms of grant of the concessions and require their revision to conform with its provisions. In the draft of the Law, and in the Law itself, applicants were given the option of withdrawing their bids, or of notifying the Ministry of the revision of their bids to conform with the new Law. They also might be changed in respect of other benefits offered over and above the conditions required in the new Law.

The offer of extra benefits in concession bids had been legalised in the 1961 Amendment,[9] and on 2 June 1965 the Minister distributed a Ministry notice enumerating 'Elements of Preference between Applicants for Obtaining Concession Contracts'. These elements number 17, consisting of a remarkable *mélange* of miscellaneous points, the evaluation and weighting of which according to their comparative economic merits might be considered an insoluble task. As published, they were as follows:

1. That posted prices be taken as a basis for fixing the amount of royalty and income for the concessionaire, and that these prices may not be modified except by approval of the Council of Ministers.

2. That posted prices shall be fixed once semi-annually by agreement between the Ministry of Petroleum Affairs and the concessionaire, provided that they be not less than prices posted in the Middle East for crude oil of a similar type and specific gravity after making necessary adjustments, when deemed necessary, for freight rates, insurance premiums, A.P.I. gravity and type of crude oil.

3. That each concession contract be considered an integral unit completely independent of other contracts accorded to the concessionaire for the purpose of calculating the income derived by the concessionaire and his expenditures, as well as the prescription of working obligations provided for in Article 11 of the Petroleum Law.

4. That the concessionaire pay in full and in advance the rent provided for in the Petroleum Law, and that he does not reduce royalty due for payment during any year for the concession

area by amounts equivalent to the sums paid by him as rents
during that year.

5. That royalty be calculated on the basis of all quantities of petroleum extracted from the field without regard to quantities used
   by the company for its own operations.

6. That the concessionaire does not deduct from the profits realized
   any expenses incurred prior to the date of granting him the concession, reconnaissance expenditures included.

7. That the concessionaire notify the Ministry of every tender
   exceeding the value of £L200,000 before its announcement and
   that he call a Ministry representative to attend the opening of
   tenders; and that the tender conditions provide that the contract
   shall not become effective except after the approval of the
   Minister if the contract amount exceeds £L200,000 and after the
   approval of the Council of Ministers if the contract value exceeds
   £L1 million.

8. That the concesionaire deposit all amounts necessary for local
   expenditure with one of the banks operating in Libya.

9. That the concessionaire undertake to give priority to the utilisation of oil tankers owned by the Libyan Government or
   Libyan nationals when freight charges and conditions are the
   same.

10. That the concessionaire undertake to supply the Ministry with
    all statements, information and technical conclusions related
    to the concession and that he fill all forms decided by the
    Ministry for this purpose from time to time.

11. That the concessionaire undertake to follow most modern
    technical methods and to adopt all safety measures for the
    preservation of natural gas in compliance with laws and regu-
    lations or as directed by the Ministry for this purpose from
    time to time. And that he undertake to obtain prior approval
    from the Ministry in respect of means of production, completion
    of wells, and their abandonment, rates of extraction and limit-
    ation of distance between wells and the limits of concession
    areas.

12. That the concessionaire undertake to surrender the whole
    concession area after fifteen years from the date of granting
    the concession if no oil or natural gas in commercial quantities
    has been found.

13. That the concessionaire offer a percentage of profit exceeding
    50% and that he expense the greater part of royalty.

14. That the concessionaire accord the Government the right to obtain crude oil within a limit not exceeding 50% of its share of profits.
15. That the concessionaire owns markets for disposal of petroleum.
16. The capability of the applicant and his readiness to erect petroleum refineries and to construct petrochemical industries in the country.
17. Any other conditions more favourable to the Government.

The awards of the new concessions were announced by the Minister of Petroleum Affairs by Ministry notice issued on 20 February 1966. He had been absent from Libya from the time of the promulgation of the new Law in November until after the completion by the companies of the Amendments to their concessions late in January 1966. The Amendments had been executed on the Government side by the Acting Minister.

Forty-one new concessions were allotted, and subsequently, when the deeds were executed over the following months, numbered from 96 (the last concession, No. 95, having been awarded in 1961) to 136. They are listed in Appendix 8.1. The final conventional concession – No. 137 – was awarded to the French Aquitaine/Erap in 1968, at the time of the signing of the first joint-venture deal between the Libyan National Oil Company and this French State enterprise. After this, no further concessions under the terms of the Petroleum Law were awarded.

Notable for their absence from the list of awards were Esso and the Oasis partners. Esso were bitterly disappointed at this, particularly in view of their co-operation with the Government in the formulation of the new Law, and of their patent and proven capability to fulfil their obligations and undertake benefits additional to those required by the law itself.

Among the other majors, Gulf and BP did not apply, nor did CFP; Mobil, Shell, Texaco and Socal (the latter two jointly) each succeeded in some of their applications. Among the successful independents, European State enterprises and other European companies were more prominent than hitherto. Aquitaine (a mixed French State enterprise with shareholders in the private sector), together with the French Auxerap (a subsidiary of Erap, 100 per cent State-owned) and Hispanoil (a Spanish State oil company), combined, with a new US independent, Murphy Oil Corporation, holding a 16 per cent interest, to form a single operating unit under Aquitaine's leadership. This joint enterprise successfully discovered oil and began production in Concessions 104 and 105 in 1969. The Italian State Agip also obtained two concessions, one of which was to prove productive.

West German companies were notably successful in their applications. In addition to Gelsenberg, the 35 per cent partner of Mobil, Elwerath and Wintershall, acting together, added three to their already existing areas; Union Rheinische, a newcomer, obtained four new concessions, and Scholven Chemie three.

Few of the US independents already in Libya were successful. Phillips Petroleum on its own obtained two areas, and jointly with Atlantic – with whom it was already in partnership in Concessions 86-89 – one further area.

The rest of the successful bidders were American-based newcomers. Of these the most notable was Occidental, whose quick success in discovering and developing oil production on a large scale in Concessions 102 and 103, as well as extra benefits offered to the Government – in particular the development of the Kufra oasis – were to become legends.

Libyan Clark, sponsored by a small US refiner, obtained two areas, and subsequently assigned a 75 per cent interest to Texaco/Socal. Libyan Desert Oil company, which was traced back to Tex Feldman, an American oilman, through a company set up in Switzerland, obtained a concession, but performed no work on it, and it was revoked in 1968. Circle, Lion and Mercury were all companies set up in Switzerland by a Mr Jett for the purpose of acquiring concessions in Libya. Circle obtained three concessions and the other two companies one each. The last two were revoked in 1968 for not fulfilling working obligations. Circle was purchased by Ashland Oil and Refining and Whitestone Petroleum in 1967 on a 50/50 basis, changed in 1969 to a 75/25 basis. Ashland was successful in obtaining a joint-venture deal with Lipetco in 1969.

Libya Texas Oil and Refining, which obtained two concessions, was jointly set up by the Anderson-Pritchard Refining Company of Texas, Bell Refineries, J.P. Driscoll and Merritt D. Orr (both Dallas independents). These concessions were also revoked in 1968 on similar grounds. The other two successful applicants were American Mining and Exploration Co., owned by Continental Grain Company of Chicago (which obtained one area), and Bosco Middle East Oil Corporation (two areas), an American enterprise based in Texas primarily concerned with geographical and geophysical exploration and surveying.

It is doubtful whether any of the seven last named concessionaires could fulfil the requirements of eligibility as stated in Article 5 of the Petroleum Law, which required the Ministry, in considering applications, to have regard to the applicant's previous activities in the petroleum industry, his previous experience in the conduct of similar operations, and his financial and technical capacity to conduct the contemplated operations. The awards to these companies caused considerable comment and some dismay.

According to Article 2 of the Law the High Council of Petroleum Affairs should be concerned with the granting of concessions, and their recommendation should be passed to the Council of Ministers for approval, before any final decisions were taken. It is not known to what extent this procedure was complied with, but it was widely believed at the time that the Royal Court had substantial influence in the awards. It soon became evident that the majority of these seven concessionaires had embarked on their applications, not with the intention of developing them, but in the hope of acquiring valuable assets at small cost to dispose of for values substantially greater than the outlay incurred in acquiring them.

8.4 Negotiations and Agreement on Accelerated Tax and Royalty Payments – 1968

On 8 July 1968, the Minister of Petroleum Affairs sent a letter to all concession-holders requesting them to make their tax and royalty payments earlier than hitherto. The Law required royalty to be paid quarterly within 60 days of the end of each quarter, and the income and surtax payments to be made annually within four months of the end of the year.

The Minister pointed out in his letter that this arrangement was 'very unfavourable to the Government in comparison with any other major oil producing and exporting country'. He went on to propose that royalties should be paid monthly within 15 days of the end of the month and tax payments quarterly within 30 days of the end of each quarter. This, he wrote, 'will result in Libya being on a parity basis only with the least favourable practice in other oil producing countries'. The Government, he added, 'is desirous of concluding an amicable agreement with concession-holders along these lines ... without the necessity of enacting legislation or other statutory measures'. He invited concession-holders' views before proceeding to detailed arrangements.

For the Government it was essential that the concession-holders should act uniformly in this matter, if only to avoid complications arising from the 'most-favoured-company' provisions introduced in the 1965 amendment to the Law. Having addressed the letter to all concession-holders, it expected them to give an answer agreed among themselves. Such a method naturally required consultation and collaboration among concession-holders, and these were carried out informally in Libya and, more particularly, in New York, where the parent company representatives could most conveniently assemble. Their views were expressed to the Government by Esso, who was the largest single producing concession-holder and by implicit consent their leader.

The negotiations not unexpectedly involved counter-proposals and bargaining. The oil companies took the opportunity to obtain Government concessions on various points at issue described below in return for their agreement on accelerated tax and royalty payments. The outcome of the negotiations was that the concession-holders consented to pay tax and royalties quarterly, within 30 days of the end of each quarter. This change in payments was to be phased in over 3 years, beginning in 1969. Agreement was reached by the beginning of October 1968. The Government announced this to the press on 19 October, stating that the agreement

> has the effect of advancing tax payments one year on a permanent basis and the Government will accordingly receive an extra year's taxes during the period of the phase-in. On present estimates of production and oil revenue the extra amounts to be received by the Libyan Government over the next five years amount to $1,064 million as a result of these earlier payments alone.

The Agreement was in the form of a letter from the Minister to each concession-holder which the latter signed and returned together with two supplementary letters from the Minister to concession-holders on other matters settled at the same time.

In the main letter the Government conceded three points to the companies.

(1)   The companies would be allowed to use, for 1969 and future years, commercial exchange rates in converting the dollar values in their fiscal accounts into Libyan pounds, instead of IMF par rates, as some of them had been doing. In 1965 companies had been given an option to select

either method, but once having made their election, they had to apply it consistently.[10] At the time this option was taken, the IMF rate appeared more favourable to some companies in the resultant tax liability, but by 1968 the opposite was the case. In deciding to allow these companies to switch again, the Government considered that the amounts involved were negligible in relation to the benefits of the main agreement. Continental was the principal company involved in this concession.

(2)   Direct taxes within the meaning of the Law were to include customs duties, stamp taxes and road licences on company-owned vehicles; but not social insurance contributions 'to the extent that they do not exceed the present rates'. Under the terms of the amended Law, direct taxes were still to be treated as credits against surtax and not as operational expenses, and a definition of direct taxes had been unsatisfactorily attempted in the Regulations. The Government, in conceding this point to the companies, adjudged again that the amounts of money involved were nugatory in relation to the benefits of the Agreement; but in the full knowledge that such a classification was not in accordance with the generally accepted meaning of 'direct taxes'. Esso was the principal contender for this concession, for reasons given in Chapter 5, section 5.1.

(3)   The Ministry waived its claim against some companies for improper treatment of inventory when switching from the old Law to the amended Law at the beginning of 1965. This was a complicated accounting point connected with the calculation of '12½% of the value of crude oil exported', which under the new Law was to be expensed. By not including inventory carried over into 1965 in this calculation (since it was not produced but nevertheless exported in 1965) some companies diminished the amount to be expensed and so increased residual gross royalty and rents payments (from which the 12½ per cent of exports was deducted) still to be treated as tax credits. This was a once-only concession, again small in relation to the main issue. The independent producers were the companies principally involved.

Thus in the outcome, all the producing companies were able to bid for and obtain satisfaction on some points at issue. There were two additional points of general interest in which the Government was able to meet the producing companies' wishes. One was to satisfy a complaint by the companies that, at the time they made remittances to Libya for the large surtax and royalty payments, the exchange rate, which was *de facto* set by the Bank of Libya alone, moved against them. The Minister, in a separate letter to the Companies, stated that 'the bank of Libya had agreed to provide the oil companies . . . the most favourable rate of exchange available and in any event a rate which does not exceed the arithmetic average of the daily rate of exchange during the previous three months'. He refrained from pointing out that it was always open to the companies to buy Libyan currency in advance, instead of leaving it till the last minute before payments were due; and that the new accelerated tax agreement would spread company payments more evenly throughout the year.

The other point was a clearance on 1965 accounts so far as the deduction of operating expenses and overheads was concerned. This was also given in a separate letter which stated that 'the Ministry is prepared to treat the year 1965 as closed . . . on the basis of the calculations as originally submitted by your Company and as subsequently adjusted up to and including today's date'. The letter was withheld in the case of some companies until outstanding points had been settled satisfactorily. The principal company involved was Continental, with a substantial disputed Home Office charge, which was settled within a month.

The accelerated tax agreement was notable as an example of co-operation between Government and companies. The contrast between the rancour of the chronic posted price dispute and the ease with which this settlement was achieved is worthy of remark. The whole negotiations were concluded within three months between the time when the subject was broached to the companies by the Government and that of final agreement. It may be observed in partial explanation that the acceleration of tax payments did not affect the oil companies' profits, only their cash flow. Indeed, in the small concessions given to the companies in the agreement there was some slight improvement of profits to the parent company involved. It may be inferred that at the time cash did not have such significance in the eyes of the parent companies as profits.

8.5   Employment in the Libyan Petroleum Industry

Numbers employed in the Libyan petroleum industry in the first six years of activity are given in Table 4.1. They show a continuously strong rising trend — from 1,150 Libyans and 350 expatriates in 1956 to 7,950 Libyans and 2,700 expatriates in 1961. The record in the following decade is shown in Table 8.1.

Table 8.1: Employees in the Libyan Petroleum Industry — 1961-9

	Libyan	Foreign		Libyan	Foreign
1961	7,950	2,700	1966	3,772	1,897
1962	8,150	2,850	1967	3,536	1,842
1963	9,000	3,000	1968	3,327	2,070
1964	9,500	3,100	1969	3,465	2,135
1965	3,902	1,970			

Source: Ministry of Petroleum Affairs/Ministry of Petroleum publications — *Libyan Oil* .

For the years 1961-4 the figures are for persons employed in the petroleum industry in Libya. For 1965 and after the figures are for persons employed by the concession-holders and exclude contractors' employees.

So far as can be judged from this discontinuous series of figures, a high point both of Libyan and overseas employees was reached in 1964 or 1965. Thereafter both categories fell back slightly, except for rises — more in expatriates than Libyans — in 1968/9; these rises were attributable to the development of the 1966 concessions, in particular Occidental's. After the revolution of September 1969, there was a big increase in Libyan employees.

The original concession contract contained in Schedule II of the 1955 Petroleum Law stipulated in Clause 18 that concession-holders should, after 10 years of operations, employ Libyans to the extent of at least 75 per cent of the total number employed by the company in Libya 'provided that the requisite number having adequate skills and ability is available'. There was no mention of the obligation of a company's contractors in this respect.

So far as training was concerned, the concession contract stipulated that from the date of commencement of regular exports from Libya of petroleum in commercial quantities the company should spend annually between £L2,500 and £L5,000 on technical training of Libyans.

In its booklet, *Libyan Oil*, published in 1973, the Ministry of Petroleum comments (p. 137) that these amounts were 'not sufficient to finance a short training course for one trainee only'. These conditions 'provided the companies with enough instrument and justification to disregard the development of national elements working in the oil sector . . . the training of Libyans and their development have been left to the conscience of the companies who showed no concern whatever'.

In the colonial era before the second world war, the Italians had neglected the education of Libyans. During the war period no progress had been made in this field, and little during the military occupation that followed. The booklet quoted above recognised that 'the domestic manpower market lacked national technical elements required by the oil industry due to poor educational circumstances in general and to neglect of vocational training in particular'.

The wish of the Libyan Government — before the revolution as well as after — that Libyan nationals should participate in the Libyan oil industry as much as possible was a manifestation of a trend visible in all developing oil-producing countries, in most of which the pressure on the companies during the 1960s to replace expatriates with nationals was much stronger than in Libya. In the list of extra benefits enumerated in 1965 by the then Minister of Petroleum Affairs as 'elements of preference' in the award of new concessions (see p. 165) there was no mention of employment or training of Libyans as one of these. Only later was more attention given to these matters. In the first joint-venture agreement with the French companies of April 1968, the companies undertook to provide substantial sums for the training of Libyans at home and abroad and to assist in this training and in the establishment of a Libyan Petroleum Institute. In 1969 the Minister of Petroleum Affairs, commenting on the various joint-venture deals which had been entered into in 1968 and 1969, mentioned that they contained provisions for training of Libyans at home and abroad, preference for the appointment of Libyans especially to senior positions, and also for the employment of Libyan contractors.

Throughout the 1960s there were effectively few Libyans employed in management positions in oil companies, although the more responsible concession-holders carried out extensive training programmes for Libyans both in Libya and abroad. The joint-venture deals and the establishment of Lipetco provided the first indications of positive formal moves towards the Libyanisation of senior posts and more intensive training of Libyans. The movement was to be strongly accelerated soon after the revolution.

8.6   The Libyan General Petroleum Corporation — 1968

The Libyan General Petroleum Corporation was established as the

National Oil Company by Law No. 13 of 1968, issued as a Royal Decree on 14 April. In creating a State-owned oil company Libya was following the example of other major oil-producing countries in the Eastern Hemisphere. The immediate occasion for setting it up was that it should be the Government Agency for carrying out its participation in a joint-venture agreement being negotiated at that time — the first such agreement embarked on in Libya. This deal was with the French State-owned Erap/Aquitaine group, for which Heads of Agreement had been signed at the beginning of April during a State visit of the Prime Minister, Abdel Hamid Bakush, and the Minister of Petroleum Affairs to Paris.

The Corporation, according to the terms of the Law, should

> endeavour to promote the Libyan economy by undertaking the development, management and exploitation of oil resources in the various phases concerned, the establishment of national petroleum industries, and the distribution of locally manufactured and imported petroleum products, as well as by participating with the authorities concerned in planning and executing the general oil policy of the state, determining the prices of crude oil and products, and safeguarding price levels.

To carry out these objectives the Corporation was to

> operate within the Kingdom of Libya or outside it, in the petroleum industry or any of its various phases including prospecting, exploration and drilling for oil, natural gas and other hydrocarbons, production, refining, transportation and storage of these substances or any of their derivatives including chemicals extracted from crude oil.

It could act either directly or in participation with other operating companies in exploration and production, and could establish and operate refineries and petrochemical industries, construct pipelines and oil ports, acquire and charter Libyan flag tankers, undertake the marketing of crude oil, and the distribution, selling and exporting of oil products. Not the least important of the Corporation's duties was the 'training of Libyan nationals to occupy technical and administrative posts in the petroleum industry' and to supervise 'the implementation of the concession holders' obligations' to do the same.

The first Chairman and Director-General of Lipetco, as the national company came to be called, was Ess. Mohamed Jeroushi, who had hitherto been first Director-General and subsequently Under-Secretary at the Ministry of Petroleum Affairs. The Head Office of the Corporation was located in Tripoli, separate from the Ministry of Petroleum Affairs. In an introduction to the published text of the Law Jeroushi wrote that, in establishing Lipetco, the Government was creating a practical instrument for 'efficiently and positively utilizing the Libyan experience in exploiting our petroleum wealth', which hitherto had been done exclusively by the oil companies within the legal framework under government supervision and control.

During the first eighteen months of Lipetco's life its major activity was concerned with joint ventures. The first of these has been mentioned, and will be described in greater detail below. Four others were embarked upon in the summer of 1969 — with Shell, Agip, Ashland Oil and Refining Co. and Chappaqua Oil Corporation. All these agreements were negotiated in the Ministry, under the supervision of the Minister, and handed over to Lipetco only at signature. During this time there was in fact little 'participation with the authorities concerned in planning and executing' policy, supervision and control of the industry, which continued to be carried out almost entirely in the Ministry.

8.7   Joint-Venture Agreements

The first joint-venture agreement was made in the spring of 1968 with the French State companies mentioned above — Erap (later called Elf) and SNPA (Aquitaine), who at the same time were awarded the last conventional concession — No. 137. The Agreement stipulated that the French partners (with Aquitaine as operating company) would undertake exploration with very substantial minimum working obligations ($22.5 million expenditure in 10 years) — Lipetco's share of which would not be reimbursable, but the whole would be amortisable for tax purposes when profits were earned.[11] A decision to develop an oilfield after commercial discovery was to be the point at which Lipetco would take up its share. This share was to be 25 per cent of production up to 200,000 b/d, increasing by steps until it reached 50 per cent at a production level of 550,000 b/d. Lipetco was to finance the development costs of its share, but the French companies would procure finance for Lipetco at favourable interest rates.[12]

If oil was produced the French partners undertook to market

Lipetco's share, at the latter's option, at the best price available, for a commission fee of 2 per cent of realised price below a total production of 550,000 b/d, and ½ cent a barrel over 550,000 b/d.

Lipetco's Law stipulated that 'a pre-requisite for any participation contract shall be that the rights, benefits and privileges accruing therefrom to the Corporation shall exceed whatever is due to the Government under the Petroleum Law'. At the time of the signing of the Agreement with Erap it was claimed on the Libyan side that the terms of the joint venture would give Libya more than 80 per cent of the profits from any oil discovered. The figures put out for this and many other joint-venture deals in other oil-producing countries at the time, which attributed to the Government a share in the profits from joint-venture operations usually of over 80 per cent, were largely conjecture, based on optimistic estimates of the national company's realisations from sales of its oil, and usually ignoring the cost of the large capital required to be invested by the national company in the development of the joint operation. In this case, the estimates were sufficiently accepted for no one to query whether the legal requirements were being violated.[13]

As long as Lipetco's share of the joint venture was less than 50 per cent, the management of operations and investment decisions was in the hands of the oil company partners. Thus Lipetco was committing itself to shoulder large liabilities for investment undertaken on the decision of others. It was also in the position of a minority shareholder — of a junior, if not a sleeping, partner. For Libya, nevertheless, the venture was the first step along the way of taking a share in the operations and management of the country's petroleum industry, which it was the object of the Law, as well as the ambition of most Libyans, to achieve.[14]

After the French joint-venture deal, the Libyan Government gave every indication that in future it would favour more of them, rather than award new conventional concessions. Speaking at the opening of the new Zueitina terminal by the King on 21 April 1968, the Prime Minister, Abdel Hamid Bakush, said that there were plans for the conclusion of joint-venture deals in the future, which were intended to provide Libya with a greater income from oil.

As a result of this encouragement, in the summer of 1968 proposals were made by a number of oil companies for joint ventures with Lipetco. After months of negotiation, in May and June 1969 four agreements were announced — with Shell, ENI (Agip), Ashland Oil and Refining and an unknown company named 'Chappaqua'.

The Council of Ministers had approved certain general conditions to be applicable to all joint ventures, which were communicated to applicants in letters from the Minister of Petroleum Affairs, as follows:

1. No exploration expenditure shall be re-imbursable by Lipetco in any circumstances.
2. The maximum amortization allowed for cash bonuses will be:
   (i) signature bonus not amortizable
   (ii) subsequent production bonuses may be amortized up to a maximum of 50% and at a maximum rate of 10% per annum. If production reaches 550,000 b/d, no further amortization of cash bonuses will be allowed.

   Any application already made containing more favourable terms than the above for Libya will not be subject to alteration.
3. Expenditure by joint-venturers on extra benefits offered (e.g. industrial plants, pipelines, etc.) shall in no case be a current deductible from taxable income under the Petroleum Law. Amortization allowed, if any, in petroleum accounts will be clearly defined in the individual joint-venture agreement.
4. Expenditure on a joint venture may not be consolidated with existing production operations but must be treated separately for accounting purposes.
5. Rents may not be deducted from royalties on reaching production, but will continue to be paid in addition to royalties. Such rents may not be treated as tax credits, but as deductible expenses under the Petroleum Law.
6. Royalty shall be fully expensed and no part of it treated as a tax credit.
7. The joint-venturer shall finance Lipetco's share of appraisal and development expenditure and recover Lipetco's share of expenditure from proceeds of Lipetco's oil at an agreed rate (say 10¢ a barrel) with an appropriate interest charge.
8. The joint-venturer shall, if Lipetco so wishes, purchase Lipetco's share of oil, or undertake to market it at a price guaranteed to equal current Libyan realization prices in general.

These provisions were common to all the deals. The 'extra benefits' offered by the successful companies varied greatly from each other. To all appearances Shell's agreement was the most favourable to Lipetco. Shell undertook to spend £L11 million ($30.8 million) on exploration within nine years, to provide cash bonuses of £L2 million on reaching 100,000 b/d production and £L3½ million at 500,000 b/d production. The company agreed to finance Lipetco's development costs at 6½ per cent interest, repayable by Lipetco from 50 per cent of the proceeds of sales to Shell of its own oil. Lipetco's participation was to be 25 per cent up to 500,000 b/d production and 50 per cent above that figure. Shell undertook to buy Lipetco's oil, when it had a 25 per cent share, at an agreed market price which would be derived from the going 'realisation' price of oil.

In addition Shell undertook to build a refinery of 25,000 b/d initial capacity, rising to 40,000 b/d, and a luboil plant of 600 b/d capacity. The company would be reimbursed for the costs of these over a period of 10 years and would manage the plant for a similar period. In marketing Shell was to hand over to Lipetco 15 of its existing service stations at an agreed price and build 10 more for Lipetco in Libya.

The commitment to launch Lipetco into refining and marketing was attractive. But perhaps the most significant undertaking on Shell's part was to buy Lipetco's oil at the going price. Shell had always been short of owned crude in its world-wide operations, at the same time being the leading marketer in the Eastern Hemisphere. The guarantee of a market at the going price for Lipetco's oil was a potential asset of great importance.

Agip's agreement was similar in many respects, the additional benefit in it being the construction of a gas line from the Sirte basin to Benghazi and, as with Shell, the handing over of service stations to Lipetco in Libya. Agip also undertook to buy Lipetco's crude at an average going rate for third party sales.

Ashland undertook as an additional benefit to erect a carbon black plant in Libya, but the terms of finance and repayment of cost both of this and of Lipetco's share of development were unsatisfactory. They need not detain us here, as the joint venture did not last long after the revolution.

Chappaqua offered to Lipetco more limited participation than the others in production, but a 57½ per cent share in profits in lieu of participation. It also offered Lipetco participation in downstream operations (of which it had none); and royalty increasing to 19 per cent at 500,000 b/d production. As Chappaqua had produced no evidence of previous activities or experience in the petroleum industry, nor of the financial and technical capacity to conduct operations, as required by Article 5 of the Petroleum Law, it is astonishing that the joint-venture agreement was made. It subsequently transpired in July that a contract existed between Shaheen Natural Resources Inc. for the latter to acquire 20 per cent of Chappaqua's stock and to be operator in the joint venture. As this arrangement was contrary to the assurance given by Chappaqua in the Agreement that, among other things, the company was 'not subject to a contract limiting its right and power to execute the Agreement', steps were taken to cancel the deal almost before the ink was dry. It was in fact annulled in the following November, and this marked the first direct intervention in the oil industry by the new Revolutionary Command Council.

8.8   Conservation and Other Regulations

The XVIIIth Conference of OPEC, meeting at Baghdad in November 1968, approved a 'pro-forma' Conservation Regulation for the use of member states. It comprised no less than 47 Articles, laying down in impressive detail the role of governments of oil-producing countries in supervising concessionary companies' operating practices in exploration, drilling, production and handling of oil.

On 8 December of the same year, the Under-Secretary of the Libyan Ministry of Petroleum Affairs, Ess. Ibrahim Hangari, who was also Libya's representative at OPEC, issued to concession-holders, as Petroleum Regulation No. 8, this conservation regulation. At the same time he informed the press of the regulation, pointing out that Libya was the first country to adopt it.

In issuing the document as though it were a valid Regulation which would be applicable to all concession-holders, two considerations were ignored. The first was that, to be valid, it must be published in the *Official Gazette* under the signature of the Minister. The second was that, according to the terms of the amended concession deeds, no amendment to the petroleum regulations would affect the contractual rights of the companies without the latter's consent. Even if it were to be published in the *Official Gazette*, therefore, it would not apply to existing concession-holders without their consent, though it would apply to new concessions subsequently granted.

The passages in the existing concession deeds referring to conservation and governmental supervision of operations were few. Clause 5 stipulated that

the Company shall carry on all its operations under this Concession in accordance with good oil field practices and so that when petroleum is found it shall be produced in reasonably substantial quantities having regard to the world demand for petroleum and economic exploitation of the petroleum resources of the concession.

Clause 20 enumerated the reports to be furnished by the company to the Ministry, and these were made flexible in the Ministry's favour by the addition, to 7 individual subjects, of 'such further information relating to its operations in the concession area as the Director shall reasonably require'.

The proposed Regulation, in its detailing of good oilfield practices, might be considered faultless and, apart from the irritation and frustrations of submitting large numbers of documents to a slow-moving and not very experienced bureaucracy, such as a concessionary company could not reasonably oppose. But the stumbling-block in the way of acceptance was that the text gave the Ministry *de facto* management control of all aspects of the concessionaire's operations, particularly drilling, since it required prior permission of the Ministry in writing for the drilling of any well.[15] This was unacceptable to existing concessionaires, whose freedom to manage their own operations, and to extract and dispose of their oil, was assured under their concession deeds, subject only to the obligation to follow good oilfield practices and to make the reports which the Ministry might reasonably require.

The companies immediately protested to the Ministry, pointing out that the Regulation would not apply to them without their consent. Some, including Esso and Mobil, submitted counter-proposals. The Minister let it be known quietly that the text issued was only a draft, subject to discussion and change. It was not published in the *Offical Gazette*.

This incident would not have been of sufficient significance to describe had it not been indicative of underlying problems of government-oil company relations which have been manifested, with growing force, in many oil-producing countries, not least in the North Sea in recent years. It is also worth mentioning because after the revolution the Government used this legally invalid regulation to provide a validation for their actions in cutting back production of various companies from time to time. They had no need to, since reference to 'good oil field practices' would have provided as adequate a pretext for their actions, and one based on the Law. In the 1970s all vestiges of company independence in the control of their own operations had vanished, but in 1968 that condition was neither foreseen nor tolerable to concessionaires. In the Tripoli Agreement of March 1971 compliance with this regulation was mentioned, and it thus became *de facto* accepted by the companies.

In the first half of 1969 much work was done in the Ministry on revising the whole of the Petroleum Regulations. Proposals were made to consolidate Regulations 1-7[16] into a new one — Regulation No. 9. Drafts were prepared and submitted to the concession-holders for comment and discussion. But it was clear by the middle of the year that it would be impossible to obtain the consent of all 40 separate concession-holders to all the proposed amendments, however sensible they were, in the interests of rationalisation. The work was overtaken by events since, after a lull during the summer months, its resumption was prevented by the revolution which occurred on 1 September.

Notes

1. S.M. Ghanem, *The Pricing of Libyan Crude Oil* (Adams Publishing House, Malta, 1975), p. 67, where it is stated that the protest was announced on 12 July 1961. See also *The Economist*, 28 Oct. 1961, p. 369.

2. The Esso memorandum was not available to the writer, and the extracts below and in the text are taken from the account of it in Ghanem, *Pricing of Libyan Crude Oil*. The calculations by which Esso arrived at its posting were, according to the memorandum, as follows:

$/b	Saudi Arabia Ras Tanura 34°	Sidon 34°	Iran Kharg Island 34°	Iraq Banias 36°
Posted price f.o.b. export terminal	1.80	2.17	1.73[a]	2.21
Freight to Rotterdam	0.58	0.26	0.69[a]	0.26
c.i.f. Rotterdam	2.38	2.43	2.42	2.47
less:				
Freight Mersa Brega/ Rotterdam	0.22	0.22	0.22	0.22
Value of oil at M. Brega	2.16	2.21	2.20	2.25
Average of previous line figures	2.16	2.21	2.20	2.25

$$\frac{}{4}$$

$$= \$2.205$$

The company rounded up $2.205 to $2.21 and chose 39° as the gravity of Libyan oil commercially equivalent to the four oils used in the calculation.

Note: a. There appear to be errors in the statement of figures here: Iranian 34° oil ex Kharg Island was posted at $1.79, but after this date. The freight to Rotterdam at Scale minus 50 per cent was $0.59, not $0.69/b.

3. For a description of the nature of US crude postings see M.G. de Chazeau and A.E. Kahn, *Integration and Competition in the Petroleum Industry* (Yale University Press, New Haven, 1959), Ch. 8.

4. Ghanem, *Pricing of Libyan Crude Oil*, estimates the appropriate posting to have been around 40¢/b higher than the actual, after bringing in calculations involving a number of other basing points (Algeria, Qatar and Kuwait). In his calculations a sulphur premium is attributed to Libyan oil calculated in detail from the characteristics of each oil used for comparison. Figures for this are taken from a study completed in 1968 by Dr M.M. Al Hashimi, then Director of the Ministry of Petroleum Affairs Technical Department. The sulphur premium for Libyan oil arrived at by Ghanem, though different for each comparison, is on average 25¢/b, and more than explains the conclusion that a posting higher than actual by 40¢/b was justified.

The support for a 30¢/b higher posting can be derived by using Esso's chosen basing points, applying the normal 2¢ per degree gravity differential, a 12 cents premium for low sulphur and AFRA at Scale minus 15%.

| | Saudi Arabia | | Iran | Iraq |
| | Ras Tanura | Sidon | Kharg Island | Banias |
$/b	34°	34°	34°	36°
Posted price f.o.b. export terminal	1.80	2.17	1.79	2.21
Freight to Rotterdam	0.91[a]	0.44	0.92[a]	0.44
c.i.f. Rotterdam	2.71	2.61	2.71	2.65
Freight Mersa Brega/ Rotterdam	0.37	0.37	0.37	0.37
	2.34	2.24	2.34	2.28
Gravity differential	0.10	0.10	0.10	0.06
Quality premium	0.12	0.12	0.12	0.12
Value of 39° oil at M. Brega	2.56	2.46	2.56	2.46

Average of previous line
figures = $2.51

Note: a. Including 12¢/b Suez Canal dues.

The c.i.f. delivery point chosen of Rotterdam was never questioned as being appropriate. If a delivery point in the Mediterranean had been chosen, the Arabian Gulf oils would have shown larger differences.

5. Regulation No. 6, Article 14, however, requires a concession-holder to 'from time to time establish and publish its posted prices . . .' The words 'from time to time' were sufficiently imprecise for Continental to excuse their delays in posting.

6. Article 14, para 1, states 'its posted price . . . shall be the price at which crude petroleum . . . is offered for sale by the concession holder or its affiliates to buyers generally in cargo lots f.o.b. Seaboard Terminal'; and in para. 3; 'The Ministry shall be entitled to call upon a concession-holder to establish . . . that the applicable posted prices apply to Libyan crude available to buyers generally.'

7. This proposal was outlined in an Article in *The Times* of 26 September 1967, by the writer. After the June war a new AFRA rate was set monthly, to reflect rapid changes in the market. The principle of fluctuating short-haul freight premiums in posted prices was adopted in the 1971 Tehran and Tripoli Agreements.

8. The discount agreed in OPEC was to be 5½ per cent for 1967 and the

gravity differential allowance 0.2647 cents/b for each degree of gravity in excess of 27° API. The calculation of an extra 7½ cents/b government take from their elimination is, on a 39° crude oil,

$$\frac{\$(2.21 \times 5\tfrac{1}{2}\%) + 12° \times 0.002647}{2} = \$0.07627$$

For later years the agreement between OPEC and the oil companies made in the Autumn of 1968 was to phase out the discount and at the same time to raise the gravity differential allowance to a maximum of 0.56 cents per degree of gravity over 27°. This would have been unacceptable to the Libyan Government, who maintained that the gravity differential allowance had no commercial justification. A Ministry paper dated 25 November 1967 concluded that a price differential of 3.97 cents per degree of gravity was justified, calculating the value of gravity from current Rotterdam product prices and product yield patterns of Libyan crude oils.

As the Suez Canal remained closed for several years, the discount and allowances negotiated for the Arabian Gulf oils did not apply to Libya.

9.   Article 1 of this Amendment had changed Article 7 of the original Law (see p. 102) to read: 'The applicant may include in his application particulars of any economic and financial benefits and advantages and other things which he is willing and able to offer in addition to those stated in this Law and the Second Schedule hereto'.

10.   See Article 14 (8) − 'In computing profits . . . sound and consistent practices . . . shall be employed.'

11.   See *Middle East Economic Survey*, 19 Apr. 1968. Since, according to the Petroleum Law, the accounts of all of a concession-holder's operations in Libya were allowed to be consolidated for tax purposes, and since for a producing concession-holder exploration expenses in all his concessions were 100 per cent tax deductible in the year in which they were incurred, the French companies were able − as soon as they began earning profits in their conventional concessions (104 and 105 began production in 1969) − to charge the exploration expenses of the joint venture against the taxable profits of their conventional concessions, and thus recover 50 per cent of the costs in the form of lower tax payments currently. This privilege was not given in subsequent joint ventures, in which the company partner was not permitted to consolidate his expenditures with existing conventional concessions.

12.   There was also to be a progressive royalty payment beginning at 12½ per cent and rising to 15 per cent when production reached 500,000 b/d. Bonus payable was $1 million on signature, $3 million on commercial discovery and $9 million when production reached 300,000 b/d.

The Heads of Agreement were signed in Paris on 4 April 1968. These were followed by signature in Tripoli of the Contract of Agreement at the beginning of May (*Middle East Economic Survey*, 10 May 1968) and Financial and Operating Agreements on 28 July (*Middle East Economic Survey*, 16 Aug. 1968).

13.   See *Middle East Economic Survey*, 19 Apr. 1968. The figure of over 80 per cent for Libya's share of profits was given by the Minister of Petroleum Affairs in the press announcement of the signing of Heads of Agreement in Paris. In August Lipetco published a study (*Middle East Economic Survey*, 9 Aug. 1968) which calculated that the State's share in net income per barrel would be over 85 per cent at a production level of 550,000 b/d, compared with 67 per cent in a conventional concession.

The figure-work to support this was as follows:

Lipetco (50 per cent of output)		French Group (50 per cent of output)	
	$/b		$/b
Realised price	1.700	Posted price	2.210
Marketing allowance	0.005	Cost of production	0.400
Cost of production	0.400	Royalty (15 per cent)	0.330
		Net taxable income:	1.480
Lipetco's net income	1.295	Tax (50 per cent)	0.740
		French group's net income after tax	0.740
		Government take (royalty + tax)	1.070

(a) Weighted net income per barrel

$$\frac{1.295 + 1.480}{2} = 1.3875$$

(b) Weighted Government take per barrel

$$\frac{1.295 + 1.070}{2} = 1.1825$$

$$\frac{(b)}{(a)} = 85.225 \text{ per cent}$$

The calculation of Government take for a conventional concession in the Lipetco study was as follows:

		$/b
	Posted price, 39°	2.210
	Cost of production	0.300
	Royalty (12½ per cent)	0.276
(a)	Net taxable income	1.634
	Tax (50 per cent)	0.817
	Company profit	0.817
(b)	Government take	0.276 + 0.817 = 1.093

$$\frac{(b)}{(a)} = 66.89 \text{ per cent}$$

Such simplistic calculations as these, which are widely used in the oil industry, are a convenient and practical, but somewhat subjective, way of making this type of analysis. In this particular study, the method by which the Government's percentage share in profits is reached both in the conventional concession calculation and in that for the operating surplus to the company (sales realisations less operating costs and expenses, before payments to Government including royalty) represents the profit to be divided with the Government.

The operating surplus on this basis is the sales revenue less operating costs. In the conventional concession calculation above, using posted price as sales revenue and 30 cents/b as operating cost, the operating surplus to the company before payments to Government is $1.91/b. Government take as a proportion of this is approximately 57 per cent.

However, since Lipetco's oil is assumed to be sold at $1.70/b, it is to be expected that with the conventional concession, and in the French Group's share of the joint venture, 'realisations' (i.e. proceeds of actual third party sales or net-back-to-crude in an integrated operation) are of the same order in competitive petroleum markets. (This price was not out of line with quotations at Rotterdam and net-back-to-crude calculations for Libyan 36° high pour-point crude during the summer of 1968). Using this figure, instead of posted price, for sales revenue in the conventional concession, Government take ($1.0936) expressed as a percentage of operating profit ($1.70 minus $0.30 operating cost = $1.40) is 78 per cent. For the French Group with operating costs assumed in the Lipetco calculations of 40 cents/b, and higher royalty, Government take would be 82 per cent of profit.

It would be sufficient to leave the calculation at this point, if all that were needed were to support the requirement of Lipetco's Law that the rights, benefits and privileges of the participation contract should exceed whatever was due to the Government under the Petroleum Law. The excess of Lipetco's income from its own share in the joint venture over the Government take from the French Group's share might with reason be regarded as Lipetco's cost of capital or the return on its capital invested. The Government makes no investment in the conventional concession, nor in the French Group's share of the joint venture.

In addition to the extra benefit from the joint venture shown above, derived from higher royalty, there were also additional benefits accruing from Lipetco's exemption from pre-discovery exploration expenditure, and from bonuses, neither of which are allowed for in the calculations.

A further point – the cost of production of 30 cents/b in the conventional concession and 40 cents/b in the joint venture is pure surmise. It is true that at that time the cost per barrel in the largest producing concessions of Esso and Oasis in Libya was of the order of 30 cents, as reported in fiscal accounts drawn up in accordance with the provisions of the Law and concession agreements on an annual basis. A fiscal accounting cost is the correct one to use in these calculations since the figure of taxable profit, on which actual tax is levied, is derived from it. But as explained in Chapter 2, the fiscal accounting cost per barrel gives little indication of economic cost. As a point of interest, and for comparison, a figure for the 'long-run supply price' of Libyan oil in the years 1966-8 is calculated by Prof. Adelman to be 54 cents/b (*World Petroleum Market*, p. 76). In the Lipetco calculation 40 cents/b used for the joint venture assumes a higher cost in the new enterprise than in the established conventional concession.

In addition to the comparison described above, the Lipetco study also evaluated Government share of net income per barrel during the earlier stages of the venture before production reached 550,000 b/d. The calculations need not detain us – the final figure was 75 per cent. The figure for this period in respect of the French Group in isolation, calculated using a sales revenue of $1.70/b, royalty 12½ per cent and costs of production 40 cents/b, is approximately 80 per cent. The difference between this and that of 78 per cent for the conventional concession is entirely explained by the higher costs of production assumed in the joint venture.

An issue of potentially great importance, which was never satisfactorily settled, was the control of management of the joint-venture agreements. In the exploration stage, and while Lipetco was a minority partner, management was controlled by the company partner. In the case of the French deal, the management committee, from the beginning until the 50/50 partnership was reached, consisted of two Lipetco and four French representatives. The decisions on development and production were thus in the last resort in the hands of the French (although there were arrangements in the Agreement for each partner to opt out if it chose to do so, and for the other to take up the relinquished share and commitments).

14. With numerous joint-venture agreements entered into by 1969, Lipetco was undertaking contingent liabilities of great size for investment decisions made by others. The cumulative effect of these commitments on Lipetco's financial status was never put to the test, as some of them were cancelled and those that survived did not develop into major operations.

The problem of management control if 50/50 partnership were reached disappeared when the venture was changed to an 85:15 production-sharing agreement in 1976.

15. Article 10 of the Regulation states: 'Before undertaking any operations relative to the drilling of a well, the operator shall obtain from the Ministry permission in writing, and to this end shall submit a report in triplicate to the Ministry.'

As an example, taken almost at random, of the degree of control proposed, Article 6 stipulates:

> Prior to the construction and installation of facilities for drilling, gathering, separation, storage, transportation, loading, supplementary recovery and any other facilities referred to in this regulation, the operator shall submit to the Ministry, *for its decision within a reasonable period of time*, a description of the project which shall include . . . etc. etc. Upon completion of any stage of the work . . . the operator shall inform the Ministry in writing in order that the latter may verify . . . etc. etc.

On oil production the Regulation states:

> no well shall be allowed to produce above its most efficient rate and to this effect the gas-oil ratio and water-oil ratio for each individual well shall be strictly controlled. The Ministry shall notify . . . etc. etc., if no improvement the Ministry may order the well shut in.

The sentiment of this last passage is unexceptionable; but the oil companies would find it difficult to accept that the Ministry was a better judge of a well's most efficient rate of production than they themselves, since it was in their interests to produce their fields as efficiently as possible. Occidental, whose increase in production, unprecedented in its rapidity, to over 600,000 b/d within a year of beginning, caused misgivings in the Ministry, and not disinterested criticism of other producing companies about good oilfield practices in the Idris field. Too rapid withdrawals can cause 'coning' of a field, resulting in the overlying gas being drawn down to the place of extraction of the oil and thus impairing recovery of the oil from the whole field.

16. Regulation 7, which has not previously been mentioned, was issued in April 1962, and refers only to procedures in applying for concessions under the amendment to the Law in this respect in 1961.

Appendix 8.1: Concessions 96 - 137

Number of Concession	Date of Execution	Name of Parent Organisation of Concession-Holder	Shareholding	Operating Company in Libya	Abbreviated Name	Area Zone	Area Granted sq.km.	Comments
96.	29.3.66	Wintershall AG	50%	Wintershall AG Libyen	Wintershall WIAG	II	1,033	
97.	29.3.66	Elwerath AG	50%			II	2,487	Oil discovered, 28.7.70
98.	29.3.66	"				IV	4,065	
99.	29.3.66	"				IV	25,277	
100.	29.3.66	Agenzia Generale Italiana Petroliche, S.p.A.	100%	AGIP S.p.A.	Agip	II	3,014	Oil discovered, 5.12.68. Producing/50 per cent participation, 1972
101.	29.3.66	"	100%	"	"	IV	5,243	Surrendered, 21.9.70
102.	29.3.66	Occidental Petroleum Corp.	100%	Occidental of Libya Inc.	Occidental or Oxy.	II	1,567	Oil discovered, 12.11.66. Producing 1968. 51% nationalisation, 1973
103.	29.3.66	"	100%	"	"	II	1,880	Oil discovered, 30.5.67 Producing, 1968. 51% nationalisation, 1973
104.	5.4.66	Société Nationale des Pétroles d'Aquitaine	28%	Aquitaine Libye	Aquitaine	II	2,500	Oil discovered, 13.12.68 Producing, 1969
		Société Auxilaire de l'Entreprise de Recherches et d'Activités Pétrolières	14%		Auxerap			

Appendix 8.1 *(continued)*

	Date	Company	%	Operating company	Marketing	Group	Area	Notes
104 (cont.)		Hispanica de Petróleos, SA / Murphy Oil Corp.	42% 16%	Aquitaine Libye	Hispanol Murco			
105.	5.4.66				"	II	1,507	Oil discovered, 13.1.68 Producing 1969
106.	5.4.66	Union Rheinische AG	100%	Union Rheinische Libyen	Union	I	2,732	
107.	5.4.66	"	100%	"	"	II	2,577	
108.	5.4.66	"	100%	"	"	II	1,730	
109.	5.4.66	"	100%	"	"	IV	3,861	
110.	18.4.66	Phillips Petroleum Co.	100%	Phillips Petroleum Libyan Branch	Phillips	IV	4,589	Surrendered, 5.10.70
111.	18.4.66	"	100%	"	"	IV	4,849	Surrendered, 5.10.70
112.	19.4.66	Mercury Petroleum Co. SA	100%	None	—	I	2,646	Revoked, 1968
113.	16.4.66	Lion Petroleum Co. SA	100%	None	—	I	2,661	Revoked, 1968
114.	18.4.66	Royal Dutch/Shell Group	100%	Sirtica Shell	Shell	II	4,583	
115.	18.4.66	Scholven Chemie AG	100%	Scholven Chemie Libyen	Scholven	II	5,305	
116.	18.4.66	"	100%	"	"	II	4,952	
117.	18.4.66	"	100%	"	"	II	11,780	
118.	16.4.66	American Mining & Exploration Co.	100%	Amexco	Amexco	I	2,594	
119.	19.4.66	Clark Refining Co.	100%	Libyan Clark	Clark	II	2,979	75% assigned in May 1968 to Texaco/Calasiatic in equal shares
120.	19.4.66	"	100%	"	"	II	9,975	
121	19.4.66	Circle Oil Co.	100%	None	—	II	4,875	Acquired by Ashland Oil & Refining and Whitestone Petroleum
122	19.4.66	"	100%	"	—	II	4,918	

Appendix 8.1 *(continued)*

Number of Concession	Date of Execution	Name of Parent Organisation of Concession-Holder	Shareholding	Operating Company in Libya	Abbreviated Name	Area Granted Zone	sq.km.	Comments
123.	19.4.66	Circle Oil Co.	100%	None	–	II	2,185)	eventually 75/25. Surrendered, 1971
124.	16.5.66	Mobil Oil Co.	65%	Mobiloil Libya	Mobil	I	4,445	
125.	16.5.66	Mobil/Gelsenberg	35%	"	Gelsenberg	I	5,267	
126.	16.5.66	" "		"		II	1,959	Oil discovered, 25.4.68
127.	16.5.66	Libyan Desert Oil Co.	100%	None	–	I	5,117	Revoked, 1968
128.	21.5.66	Libyan Texas Petroleum Refining Co.	100%	None	–	I	3,153	Revoked, 1968
129.	21.5.66	"	100%	"		I	3,573	Revoked, 1968
130.	21.5.66	"	100%	"		II	2,302	Revoked, 1968
131.	18.7.66	Texaco Inc. Standard Oil Company of California	50% 50%	American Overseas Petroleum Ltd.	Amoseas	I	4,050	Surrendered, 1974
132.	18.7.66	"	"	"	"	I	4,933	"
133.	18.7.66	"	"	"	"	I	3,570	"
134.	18.7.66	Bosco Middle East Oil Corp.	100%	Bosco Middle East	Bosco	III	2,661	
135.	18.7.66	" "	100%	"	"	III	2,813	
136.	29.12.66	Atlantic Richfield Co. Phillips Petroleum	50% 50%	Libya Atlantic	Arco Phillips	I	2,986	
137.	30.4.68	Société Nationale des Pétroles d'Aquitaine Entreprise de Recherches et d'Activités Pétrolières. (Later combined to form Société Nationale Elf-Aquitaine)		Aquitaine Libye	Aquitaine Elf/Erap	I	6,846	Off-shore – conversion to 81/19 production-sharing, 1974. Oil discovered, 1976

9 OIL INDUSTRY DEVELOPMENT IN LIBYA DURING THE 1960s

9.1 Exploration and Drilling

The course of development of oil operations in terms of exploration work and drilling activity is indicated in Table 9.1, which continues the series of Table 4.1, p. 75.

The geological and seismic survey work was at its most intense in 1960 and 1961, and this reflects high activity in the early concessions before the first surrender of 25 per cent of acreage five years after the original grant. Subsequently survey activity was on a falling trend, with the exception of 1966/7 for geological and 1967/9 for seismic; increase in activity then being associated with the 41 new concessions of 1966 allocated from surrendered acreage. New concession-holders frequently negotiated with those who had surrendered the area for survey information, thus avoiding duplication of work. After these times both geological and seismic survey work diminished, as more of the total area became covered by geological survey, and more of the favourable structures revealed by this were subjected to seismic survey. In 1964 a geological map of Libya was published by the US Geographical Survey, as mentioned in Chapter 1, to which the oil companies contributed.

Drilling activity rose to its highest levels in 1963/4 in exploration and 1964/5 in development. These levels reflect the culmination first of wild-cat drilling, followed by development of discovered fields, in the early concessions awarded between 1956 and 1961. The subsequent falling off of well completions was to be expected, as the more promising prospects were tested and the more favourable finds developed. There is no evidence to associate the lower levels of drilling activity with the 1965 Amendment to the Law which introduced the OPEC formula. Decisions on drilling programmes were taken many months before the completions of wells reported, and those on lower levels of drilling activity in this case before early 1966, when it was clear that the new legislation would be effective. There were smaller increases of exploration drilling in 1968/9 and of development drilling in 1969/70 attributable to the rise in activities from the 1966 concessions. The causes of the major fall in drilling in 1970 and 1971 will be described in Part V.

Table 9.1: Pre-Drilling and Drilling Activities 1961-71

	1961	1962	1963	1964	1965	1966	1967	1968	1969	1970	1971
Surveys — Party/months											
Topographical	76	41	44	45	29	27	9	7	9	10	3
Geological	356	334	312	284	94	221	289	127	172	99	73
Magnetometric	8	13	1	1	–	–	–	3	–	–	1
Gravimetric	27	20	12	–	–	1	14	18	12	8	1
Seismic	439	359	333	246	216	144	186	149	244	126	45
Drilling Activity											
Exploration wells completed	97	109	146	135	117	57	42	105	92	46	25
Development wells completed	130	122	211	273	243	188	149	105	235	198	26
Footage drilled — thousands of feet	1,332	1,581	2,425	2,553	2,400	1,789	1,533	1,637	2,553	2,355	485
Percentage of exploration wells in which oil/gas found	19	21	9	13	8	11	18	25	18	9	15

Sources: Ministry of Petroleum Affairs, Kingdom of Libya, *Libyan Oil, 1954-1967*; Ministry of Petroleum, Libyan Arab Republic, *Libyan Oil, 1954-1971*.

9.2   Pipelines and Terminals

From the large numbers of oil and gas discoveries, a record of which is given in Appendix 4.2 of Chapter 4, five separate trunk pipeline systems to sea terminals emerged, as appraisals matured into decisions on feasibility of commercial development. The network of pipelines leading to export terminals is shown in Map 9.1. The principal pipelines and terminals, with data on their capacity and operations, are described in Table 9.2.

The total pipeline delivery capacity to terminals was, with the completion of the Occidental line to Zueitina, in excess of 4 million barrels a day. Actual exports by terminals are given in Chart 9.1. At the terminals themselves, none of which, except Harega, provided the protection of an enclosed harbour, loading was done with the tankers moored at deep-water buoys, around which the tanker was able to revolve to adapt its position to weather and current conditions.

The decisions to embark on a pipeline and terminal project, or to join a new field into an existing pipeline, were the principal objective evidence of the 'finding of oil in commercial quantities' which, in the terms of Article 13 of the Law, called for greatly enhanced rents on the whole of the relevant concession. As mentioned in Chapter 3, section 3.4, this provision may have had an effect opposite to that intended by the Law — concession-holders may have delayed the decisions to embark on pipelines and terminals in order to avoid paying a greatly increased rent, which for the periods before production would be unrecoverable as an offset against surtax, and subsequently amortisable at only 5 per cent p.a. In the case of Gulf, who in Concession 66 had discovered substantial oil (see Chapter 4, Appendix 4.2), it was a factor, perhaps decisive, in inhibiting a pipeline from being built, as is described below.

The 1955 Law, in Article 12, stipulated that any concession-holder having surplus pipeline capacity should make it available to others on agreed terms, which were to conform with those normally prevailing in the petroleum industry. The July 1961 Amendment enlarged this provision, by requiring the Commission's (later Ministry's) approval to an inter-company agreement on such matters, and its proposal of terms in case of failure to agree.[1] If there were an impasse, the matter would be referred to a Committee of three, comprising representatives of: (1) the concession-holder having surplus capacity; (2) the Ministry; and (3) the President of the Supreme Court of Libya. The decision of this Committee, on a majority vote, would be binding.

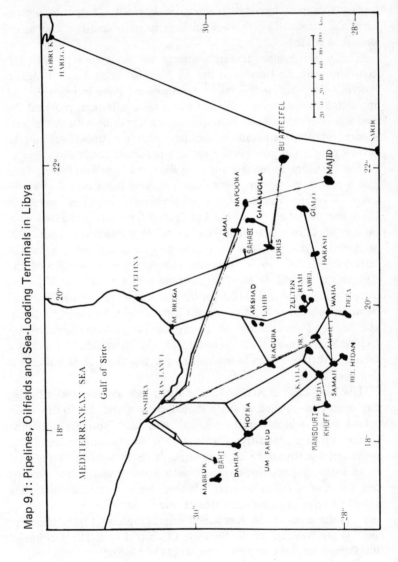

Map 9.1: Pipelines, Oilfields and Sea-Loading Terminals in Libya

Table 9.2: Principal Pipelines in Libya

Year of inauguration	Operating Company	Sea Terminal	Principal Oil Fields	Concession	Approx. Trunk Length km	Diameter inches	Approx. Maximum Capacity b/d	Comments
1961	Esso	Mersa Brega	Zelten and minor fields	6	172	36	805,000	A second 30″ pipeline was constructed to carry sea water from sea to field for injection to maintain pressure, but was never used for this purpose. It was converted into a gas line to supply the gas liquefaction plant at Mersa Brega which was inaugurated in 1971.
			Raguba	20	88	20	150,000	
1962	Oasis	Es Sidr	Dahra	32	210	30	823,000	This network linked all the Oasis fields. The final stretch of 58km from Bahi Junction was looped.
1963			Samah	59	139	32		
1963			Waha	59	160	30		
1964			Gialo	59	152	30		
1969			Defa	59	33	30		
1969			Bahi	32	46	20		
1969		Es Sidr	Zaggut	59	270	24	220,000	Direct additional line to Es Sidr from concession 59 fields.
1963	Mobil	Ras Lanuf	Hofra	11	145	30	200,000	The Hofra line (initially 24″) and Ora line, which also carried Amoseas' Beda/Katla oil, converged at Saida Junction, 88km from Ras Lanuf.
1965			Ora	13	136	24		
1966			Amal	12	273	30	664,000	Line duplicated to accommodate Amoseas' oil from Nafoora.
						36		
1966	BP	Harega (Tobruk)	Sarir	65	514	34	505,000	
1968	Occidental	Zueitina	Idris	103	212	40	1,000,000	
1968			Gialo Augila	102	66	24	150,000	
1970			Intisar (Idris)	103	216	20	68,000	For natural gasoline, naphtha etc.

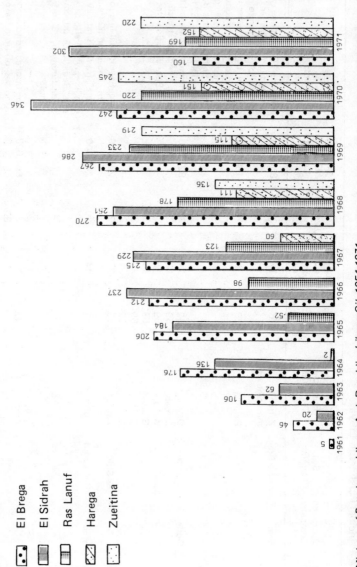

Chart 9.1: Crude Oil Exports by Terminals, 1961-71 (million bbls)

El Brega

El Sidrah

Ras Lanuf

Harega

Zueitina

Source: Ministry of Petroleum. Libyan Arab Republic. *Libyan Oil, 1954-1971*.

These provisions were never used — an indication that the oil companies themselves were reluctant to air differences or refer them to a body outside their control for settlement. Moreover the increased commercial rent provision of the Law mentioned above would inhibit a concession-holder contemplating development of a field by linking it to an existing pipeline from referring the problem to the Ministry, since he would *ipso facto* imply that the field was commercial and the concession liable to enhanced rents.

It is unlikely that a company intending to develop a field would embark on construction of a pipeline with capacity surplus to their own foreseen peak needs, in spite of pipelines exhibiting archetypal characteristics of economies of scale. A pipeline, if not entirely dependent on gravity for its flow, must be full in order to operate, but its rate of throughput can be increased greatly by extra pumping facilities. All trunk pipelines in Libya required pumps, since they had to rise before their descent to the sea.

Although no claims for usage of spare capacity were referred for arbitration to the Committee, several producers did link in to the trunk pipelines constructed, owned and operated by other concessionaires. The most important was Amoseas, all of whose fields, beginning in 1964, were linked to the Mobil system with terminal at Ras Lanuf. Esso Sirte and partners linked the Raguba field in Concession 20 to Esso's main pipeline in 1963. Others were Amoco which in 1966 linked Khuff, Concession 93, to Amoseas at Beda, and in 1970 Sahabi, Concession 95, to Occidental's line to Zueitina. Phillips in 1965 linked Umm Farud in Concession 92 to Mobil's pipeline; Aquitaine linked Mansour in Concession 104 to Amoseas (Beda), and Majid in Concession 105 to Amoseas (Nafoora), both in 1969; Agip which discovered oil in Concession 100 at Bu Atteifel, linked to Occidental in Concession 103 in 1971.

The construction of pipelines in the case of Libya comprised, with associated pumping and terminal facilities, a substantial element in the total cost of production of the oil (as much as 30 per cent), as well as being one of the heaviest single front-end investment costs involved in field development. The pipeline decision was critical in oilfield development. It is fitting to end this brief review with a reference to the pipeline which was never built, since it sheds some light on the problem of marginal fields.

There were many discoveries of oil in Western Libya, which in the earliest days had been considered the most promising area because of commercial oil having been located at Edjele, just over the border in

Algeria. Indeed, the first discovery in Libya had been Esso's in Concession No. 1 in the far south-west. There were other discoveries in the west, the most substantial being by Gulf in Concession 66 — no less than 13 separate discoveries resulting in 27 potential producing wells with a rated potential of some 30,000 b/d. In addition there were several discoveries by CPTL in Concession 23 with a potential of 20,000-40,000 b/d, and smaller discoveries by Shell in Concession 52, Oasis in 26, and Phillips in 90 (from a surrendered part of 26).

In 1964 the Ministry had contended that Concession 66 was commercial and that Gulf should therefore pay enhanced rents on it. This Gulf had successfully resisted, demonstrating to its own, if not the Ministry's, satisfaction that development was not profitable — distance from the sea being about 425 km, and the oilfields being small, fragmented and faulted in a complex manner.

In February 1966, after the amendment of concessions to the new Law, Gulf proposed to the Ministry that the Government should finance a pipeline to be constructed and operated by Gulf, the charging of tariffs to be based on operating costs only, without capital cost or recovery element. This would enable the profitable development of fields in Concession 66 to take place. Such a pipeline might also take in other concessions in which discoveries had been made, and would undoubtedly stimulate further exploration effort in its vicinity. The Government would be rewarded by revenues from oil which otherwise would not be developed, and this would more than offset the subsidy on the pipeline, whose tariffs would not cover full cost. It might be added that the enhanced rents on Concession 66 alone, which would immediately be declared commercial, would have gone some way to offset the cost to the Government of the subsidy covering the servicing costs and amortisation of capital.

The Government regrettably did not pursue the proposal, although on reasonable premises of costs and production it may have proved financially rewarding. A further attempt to develop the western concessions was made by Esso in 1967. At that time they entered into an agreement with Gulf for Concession 66 and CPTL for Concession 23 to take a 50 per cent interest in these concessions in return for conducting further exploration work there, and laying a pipeline to the coast if sufficient recoverable oil were identified to make the project commercial. The great advantage to Esso from this deal was that, having failed to obtain new concessions in 1966, and with dwindling hopes of expansion on their existing ones, they obtained entry into promising areas, and all exploration costs incurred by them could be expensed against their income from their producing concessions, according to the Petroleum Law. Thus in effect, by reduction in tax receipts the Libyan Government would finance half of this exploration expenditure.

Government agreement to this temporary assignment was required, in terms of the Law, and given. Esso, having embarked on this project — it seemed to some observers in a half-hearted manner — abandoned it in 1969 and turned back the areas to their original owners, as they were entitled to do under the agreement, which has been described as a 'farm-out'.[2]

The feasibility of a Western pipeline was still being examined in the 1970s by the National Oil Company,[3] after the revolution and after Gulf had surrendered all its Libyan concessions and left the country. In 1976 tenders were invited for its construction, which was begun in 1977 for completion in 1980.

9.3   Utilisation of Gas

The problems of utilisation of gas produced in association with crude oil were common to Libya and other oil-producing countries where the fields were far from inhabited centres which might provide markets. In addition to associated gas there were several gas fields discovered. Of these the most notable were in Concessions Nos. 6 and 20 of Esso, which were eventually made use of in the great gas liquefaction plant constructed at Mersa Brega and completed towards the end of the decade. Others with substantial potential gas production were discovered by Libyan Atlantic off-shore in Concession No. 88; Gulf in 66, Oasis in 26 and CPTL in 23 — all in Western Libya; Mobil in 72 in Zone III in the far south; and Pan-American (Amoco) in 95. None of these fields were developed.

Gas associated with oil production was flared, except for that part used by the companies in their own operations. The wells in the gas fields were plugged and the fields abandoned.

Esso's project for gas liquefaction at Mersa Brega and for export of LNG (liquefied natural gas) was described as the largest single investment that the parent company had ever made, and at the start of construction the largest such plant in the world. It was begun in 1965 for completion in 1968, when its initial capacity would be 345 million cubic feet of gas a day. The cost of the project was estimated at inception to be $200 million.

In the early stages of construction Esso made two contracts for sales of gas: one of 235mcf/day to Snam,[4] a subsidiary of ENI (Ente Nazionali Idrocarburi — the Italian State energy enterprise) for delivery at Genoa; the other of 110mcf/day to Catalaña de Gas for delivery at Barcelona.

The supply of gas from the fields in Concession No. 6 was through a 30-inch pipeline originally laid to take water from the sea back to the fields for re-injection. This became available when the water re-injection project was abandoned. A further line to bring gas from Raguba in Concession 20 was joined to the main line at km110 from Zelten. Operation, originally planned for 1968, was delayed until 1970 by technical and logistic problems, and then further until 1971 by Government intervention on fiscal matters.

9.4   Refining and Marketing of Oil Products in Libya

One of the first ambitions of the government of a country which becomes a significant oil producer is that oil products for consumption within the country should become available at low prices. A widely held view is that, as the marginal costs of producing extra oil over and above a big oil-exporting operation are low, such oil should be made available for internal consumption, which is small in relation to oil exported; consequently, there was no reason why oil products in the country should not be sold at very low prices to cover the bare production, refining and distribution costs of that oil.

This was the case in the major producing countries of the Middle East in the 1960s, and the example of the Iranian Consortium may be mentioned to illustrate it. The Consortium Agreement stipulated[5] that the oil company members would supply the National Iranian Oil Company with its requirements at cost (which meant at an accounting cost of production and refining the oil products supplied). In the costs there was no royalty or profits tax included. NIOC was the sole marketer of oil products in Iran and the prices at which NIOC sold the products in Iran were low.

In Libya the Petroleum Law of 1955 had made provision for refinery development in Article 21, by giving any concession-holder who discovered petroleum the right to construct and operate a refinery in Libya; and further stipulating that if refineries were established the producing concession-holders might be required to contribute *pro rata* the crude oil required by the refinery to meet domestic consumption.

This crude would be made available at 'field storage', and a concession-holder would not be required to furnish or build additional handling or transportation facilities for this purpose.

The Law also required the crude to be made available at 'field storage price'. Royalty would be paid on this oil, but even after the 1965 Amendment would be recovered as an offset against surtax due, since this Amendment stipulated that the amount of royalty to be expensed was 12½ per cent of the value of crude oil exported and not of crude oil produced (and not exported).

These provisions might have laid the foundations for the supply of oil for internal consumption in Libya at bare cost of production and refining. But in the event no satisfactory implementation of these measures was achieved. Esso constructed a refinery in the conditions and terms described below, and other producing concession-holders were not required, either physically or in the form of exchange trans-actions, to deliver their shares of refinery input at 'field storage price'.

Marketing of oil products in Libya during the 1950s and 1960s was in the hands of three companies – Shell, Esso and Asseil (an affiliate of the Italian Agip) – with approximately equal shares of the market. All products were imported up to 1966, when the Esso refinery came on stream, and were subject to import duties which, together with the companies' own charges, made prices to the public comparable with retail price levels of oil products in Western European countries. There was no price competition between the marketers, and Libya provided a market which, though small, ensured a comfortable profit to the marketers and avoided the losses on the downstream operations of refining and marketing which were typical of Western European countries at this time.

In 1958 the Petroleum Commission's approval was sought for the assignment of a 50 per cent interest in Concessions 16, 17 and 20[6] to Esso. The Government stipulated as a condition of the assignment that, in the event of discovery and development of commercial oil, Esso should construct a refinery in Libya to supply the market requirements of the country. Esso undertook to do this, but only on conditions which, in its turn, the Government accepted. Two of these were that the refinery should be established on a purely commercial basis; and that its products should be sold at free competitive prices which would permit the realisation of a reasonable margin of profit.[7]

Commercial oil from Concession 20 was produced and exported through Esso's Mersa Brega terminal in 1963. Construction of a refinery was subsequently embarked upon in Holland, and the completed plant was floated out to Mersa Brega, its Libyan location, by raft, to begin operations in 1966.

Esso, though carrying out its undertakings, did not exceed them. The refinery investment was the minimum which, at the time, would provide a refinery of the size to meet Libya's consumption. Its rated capacity was 8,000 b/d of crude oil input, which could be increased to not more than 10,000 b/d. Consumption of oil products in Libya, which in 1962 had been around 5,500 b/d, had already risen by 1965 to 8,300 b/d and by 1967 to over 11,000 b/d. The product pattern of the refinery inevitably did not coincide with the consumption pattern in Libya. There was no constraint on the other two marketers to buy their supplies from the refinery, and they were unlikely to do so, since it was more profitable to them to provide outlets for their own parent organisations' crude than to buy in supplies from Esso at full cost (posted price of crude less allowable discounts, plus refining costs including a refining profit). This was a very different situation from that in Iran, where NIOC was able to buy its product requirements at production cost (without profit or tax) from the output of the great refinery at Abadan, the rest of which was exported by the participant companies.

The refinery was from the outset a high-cost operation, since there were many diseconomies of small scale,[8] and of the limitations on types of crude supplied (which were to be solely Libyan crude according to the agreement) in relation to product requirements. In addition, the freight from Mersa Brega to Tripoli and Benghazi was exceptionally high, as the harbours in these two places, to which the refinery output was shipped for internal distribution, could take only 16,000-ton tankers. One tanker was allocated by Esso to ply permanently on these runs and, as with the refinery operation itself, was costed in the price build-up of products to show a 'reasonable profit'.

Esso's interpretation of their conditions that the refinery should be established on a commercial basis and that the output should be sold at prices which would permit the realisation of a reasonable profit margin was different from the expectation of the Government in accepting this condition to approve the concessions assignment. The company charged the refinery, for its crude input, the same prices as it was declaring for its exports of crude after the 1965 Amendment to the Law (posted prices less allowed discounts). It then built up its product prices by adding refinery costs plus return on refinery investment, and shipping costs, including cost of capital. This was in accordance with normal practice in all consuming countries in the international oil industry (see Chapter 2, section 2.4), but whereas since the early 1950s oil companies had seldom been able to obtain full recovery in the markets of prices calculated in this way, they were able to do so in Libya, as were the other Libyan marketers.

So far as taxation was concerned, the Petroleum Law as amended in 1965 stated that the taxable income from petroleum operations of the concession-holder other than from the export of crude oil was 'to be ascertained in a manner to be agreed between the concession-holder and the Ministry'. This agreement was implicit in Esso's conditions for establishing the refinery, which had been accepted by the Government, with the added bonus for Esso that royalty on the crude oil refined remained, even after 1965, as a credit against surtax payable on the company's total operations in Libya, and was not expensed, as was the case with royalty on crude oil exported.

Thus little reduction of oil product prices could be expected from the establishment of a refinery in Libya under these conditions. Shell and Asseil continued to import their own products for marketing as before. Esso supplied its marketing requirements from the Brega refinery, exporting any surpluses and doubtless entering into exchange deals with the other two marketers, which were not publicised and did not affect prices of products charged in the market.

In 1967 the Government called in consultants (Economist Intelligence Unit) for advice on pricing of oil products in Libya. Their recommendations, which took into account Esso's conditions for refinery operations, resulted in a lowering of retail prices of gasoline, kerosene and gas oil prices by about 6 milliemes a litre, and equalisation of prices between Tripoli and Benghazi.[9] These lower prices were introduced on 1 May 1967. The prices of heavy fuel oil, mostly sold under contract to large industrial users (e.g. power stations), for ships' bunkers and for export, were not controlled. The irony of these reductions in price was that two-thirds of the savings to consumers, in the cost of petroleum products, of about £L2 million a year on current consumption, came from lower duties. Import duties on petroleum products were lowered, and excise duties on refinery products were pitched at 2 mils/lt lower than the import duty. Only one-third of the savings from the lower prices were attributable to cheaper oil products from the companies.

As part of a joint-venture deal with Shell in 1969, a refinery of initial capacity of 25,000 b/d was to be constructed by Shell at a suitable site west of Tripoli. Even after the revolution of September 1969 Shell proceeded with design and ordering of plant and materials.

Thereafter, however, the whole project was taken over by the re-vamped National Oil Company, which in May 1971 commissioned the Italian firm of Snam Progetti to construct a 60,000 b/d refinery, with a unit for the manufacture of lubricating oils, at Zawia, west of Tripoli, to be completed by the end of 1973 at a cost of 25 million Libyan Dinars (the new currency introduced to replace the Libyan pound at par).[10] The crude for the refinery was to be shipped from the export terminals of Mersa Brega and Es Sidr.

9.5   The Kufra Agricultural Project

One of the extra benefits undertaken by Occidental in its tender for concessions awarded in 1966 was to 'earmark 5 per cent of its net profits from the sale of crude oil produced from its concessions for agricultural development in the Oasis of Kufra or in any other area'.[11]

Kufra was chosen for this attention by Occidental for two reasons. First, the existence of groundwater there, in spite of virtually no rain-fall, suggested the presence of a large aquifer capable of supporting extensive agricultural activities. Second, Kufra, before its occupation by the Italians in 1931, was the last Senussi stronghold in Libya, and as such was a place of symbolic importance to King Idris, whose father was buried there. A proposal to develop it was likely to be regarded with favour.

Kufra is the name of an area in the far south-east of Libya (see Map 1.1, p. 22) which contains a number of separate oases inhabited by some 6,000 settlers. Occidental would not have taken further action on its undertaking if it had not discovered commercial oil. But it did do so, and this with a speed and in quantities which had seldom been seen in the history of the oil industry. Its first major discovery was in December 1966 – the Augila field on Concession 102 – and this was followed by even more prolific wells on Concession 103, which heralded the Idris field. In 1968, Occidental exported 136 million barrels of crude oil through its pipeline to Zueitina terminal, both the pipeline and terminal having been constructed in a notably short time. By 1969 Occidental was contending with Esso for the leading place as a producer among the concession-holders, exporting over 600,000 b/d of crude oil.

Thus the 5 per cent of its net profits committed to the agricultural development of Kufra quickly amounted to many millions of dollars. The company thereupon undertook the development of Kufra with a vigour and speed comparable to that displayed in its oil operations. With large amounts of money earmarked, the great difficulties and costs of supplying heavy equipment and maintaining operations were of small importance. By 1968 major underground sweet water resources had been discovered, estimated to be sufficient to irrigate some thousands of hectares for many decades without serious fall in the level of water table.

Having made what progress was possible by irrigation and crop improvement in the oases themselves, the company set up an experimental desert farm some 10 kilometres from the oasis base. By the end of the decade much progress had been made in formulating suitable farming methods, crops and livestock. In 1970 the company handed the management of the project to the Government, which proceeded with further development as mentioned in Chapter 15, section 15.8.

Notes

1. Petroleum Regulation No. 6, Article 3, enlarges on the Law and gives the principles on which tariff charges to a user of spare pipeline capacity should be based.

2. *Petroleum Intelligence Weekly*, 21 July 1969.

3. Ministry of Petroleum, Libyan Arab Republic, *Libyan Oil, 1954-1971*, p. 107.

4. Snam Progetti, an affiliate, was the main contractor constructing the plant.

5. Consortium Agreement, Article 14.

6. These concessions were originally granted to Liamco, which had already assigned a 49 per cent interest to Grace. These two companies now invited Esso to take a 50 per cent undivided interest overall and become operator. Oil was discovered in Concession 17 (Mabruk field, which was not developed) in 1959 and in Concession 20 in 1961 (Raguba field, which was to produce at a peak rate of about 130,000 b/d).

7. Ministry of Petroleum Affairs, Kingdom of Libya, *Libyan Oil, 1954-1967*, p. 71.

8. Optimum refinery size at the time was considered to be at least 100,000 b/d crude input.

9. 6 milliemes/lt was equivalent to about 1.7 US cents and just under 1½ old pence. Maximum prices before and after the implementation of this proposal were:

| | | Gasoline | | Kerosene | Gas oil |
		Premium	Regular		
Milliemes/lt					
Before 1 May 1967	Tripoli	40	37	20	27
	Benghazi	42	39	22	29
After 1 May 1967		34	31	15	23
The new prices were equivalent to:					
shillings & pence/imperial gallon		3/1d	2/10d	1/4½d	2/1d
US¢/US gallon		36	33	16	24½

Sources: Ministry of Economy and Trade and Bank of Libya, *Annual Report 1967/8*

10. Source as in note 3.

11. Annex 2 to Occidental's Concession Agreement.

10 LIBYAN OIL PRODUCTION, EXPORTS AND MARKETS

10.1 Production and Exports of Crude Oil

The record of Libyan oil production from its beginning in 1961 until 1971 is given in Table 10.1, which also shows each operating company's contribution to the total. By the middle of 1969 Libya was exporting, on a monthly basis, 3.1 million barrels a day — a level comparable with the other leading oil exporters of the time — Iran, Saudi Arabia and Venezuela. Libyan leadership in this field was very temporary, but as Government take per barrel in Libya was higher than in Iran and Saudi Arabia, total oil revenues at the time were about the same level as those of the two Middle Eastern producers, though still behind Venezuela.

On an annual basis 1970 production was the highest. An immediate increase in production and exports after the revolution of 1 September 1969 was not surprising. Oil exports were not stopped at the time of the revolution. In the light of assurance given by the Revolutionary Command Council, most concession-holders were bent on exporting all the oil they could while the going was good. Moreover Oasis was in the course of opening up two new fields at Defa (Concession 59 — 1969) and Bahi (Concession 32 — 1970), having recently completed the required pipeline capacity, and in early 1970 was producing above one million b/d; Occidental was due to bring into production its 'C' structure on Concession 103 in early 1970, and Aquitaine's two fields of Majid (Concession 105) and Mansour (Concession 104) started production towards the end of 1969.[1]

The subsequent course of oil production and exports is described in the final section of this work. In terms of its share of OPEC and world crude oil production for the years 1961-70, Libya's record is given in Table 10.2.

10.2 Distribution of Exports

Exports to individual countries during this period are recorded in Table 10.3. Throughout these years the bulk of Libyan production — 93 per

10.1: Libyan Crude Oil Production by Operating Companies 1961-71 ('000 b/d)

Company	1961	1962	1963	1964	1965	1966	1967	1968	1969	1970	1971
Esso Standard	18.2	126.2	250.0	408.9	471.7	488.1	495.9	615.4	618.3	570.6	349.1
Esso Sirte	—	—	43.6	73.1	95.4	95.8	107.2	128.0	127.9	121.4	98.2
Oasis	—	57.7	167.2	324.0	505.8	650.5	630.0	687.9	789.0	946.1	824.4
Mobil	—	—	2.8	45.6	100.7	170.5	204.2	237.7	264.2	252.9	186.5
Amoseas	—	—	—	13.1	43.7	81.9	128.9	244.5	369.1	322.9	261.5
BP/N.B. Hunt	—	—	—	—	—	4.0	168.5	304.9	321.3	412.9	419.6
Phillips[a]	—	—	—	—	2.9	8.2	4.8	7.5	6.0	4.2	3.7
Amoco	—	—	—	—	—	8.3	4.4	1.1	0.4	7.7	14.6
Occidental	—	—	—	—	—	—	—	382.1	607.8	659.4	586.4
Aquitaine	—	—	—	—	—	—	—	—	5.1	19.9	16.8
Total	18.2	183.9	463.6	864.7	1,220.2	1,507.3	1,743.9	2,609.1	3,109.1	3,318.0	2,760.8

Note: a. Phillips' concession was turned over to NOC in November 1970.
Sources: Ministry of Petroleum Affairs, Kingdom of Libya, *Libyan Oil, 1954-1967*; Ministry of Petroleum, Libyan Arab Republic, *Libyan Oil, 1954-1971*.

Table 10.2: Libyan Crude Oil Production and Exports, 1961-70, and its Share of OPEC and World Production

| | Crude Oil | | Crude Oil Production | |
	Production mb	Exports mb	Share of OPEC per cent	Share of World per cent
1961	7	5		
1962	67	65	1.8	0.8
1963	169	168	4.2	1.8
1964	316	314	7.0	3.1
1965	445	443	9.1	4.0
1966	550	547	10.3	4.6
1967	637	627	11.2	4.9
1968	952	945	14.1	6.8
1969	1,135	1,120	15.5	7.5
1970	1,211	1,209	15.0	7.3

Sources: as for Table 10.1.

cent over the decade — was exported to Western European countries, of which West Germany received the largest single share, followed by Italy and the United Kingdom. In 1968 and 1969 Libya was supplying over a quarter of Western Europe's total oil requirements. A smaller proportion of total exports went to Western Europe in 1971, and this was offset by more going to the USA, Canada (5mb), the Bahamas (36mb), Trinidad (26mb), Egypt (4mb) and Bulgaria (3mb). This shift reflected the early stages of the greater import requirements of the USA. The oil going to the Bahamas and Trinidad was for processing in 'off-shore' refineries, probably for destination in the USA.

10.3 The European Markets for Libyan Oil

Libyan oil in the markets of Europe during the years 1961-5 has been described in some detail in Chapter 6, sections 6.2 and 6.3. This description portrays a marked erosion of product prices between 1961 and the early part of 1965, which reacted to give falling crude real-isations for Libyan oil, if shipping and refining costs are deemed to be stable.

From 1965 to June 1967, at which point the Arab-Israeli war upset the economics and logistics of oil supply, prices and realisations in Europe were reasonably firm as a whole. The trend is depicted in Chart 8.1, p. 164; in addition to this information, annual figures are given in a study by Gelsenberg[2] relating to Libyan crude only, from

Table 10.3: Countries to which Libyan Crude Oil Exports were Delivered, 1961-71 (millions of barrels)

	1961	1962	1963	1964	1965	1966	1967	1968	1969	1970	1971	1966-71 Total
West Germany	0.01	10	53	105	169	188	149	260	274	285	212	1,705
Italy	0.8	11	22	38	44	65	129	183	242	275	219	1,230
United Kingdom	3	21	47	72	88	76	76	172	153	179	163	1,049
France	0.2	2	13	18	42	64	81	75	122	120	112	648
Netherlands	0.5	7	13	26	34	53	58	68	113	123	57	552
Spain	–	–	2	15	16	21	28	57	59	59	46	302
USA	–	7	8	14	15	27	18	53	57	34	56	290
Belgium	0.7	7	6	10	12	21	33	30	45	47	26	236

Smaller amounts in total to:

	mb
Switzerland	76
Trinidad	68
Denmark	56
Bahamas	48
Norway	47
Turkey	20
Canada	20
Egypt	17
Brazil	13

Amounts less than 10mb in total to Austria, Bulgaria, Canaries, Curaçao, Finland, Ghana, Greece, Ireland, Japan, Morocco, Panama, Romania, Sweden, Tunisia, Uruguay, Yugoslavia.

Total exports of crude oil 1961-71: 6,447 million barrels.
Percentage of total delivered to Western European countries – 93.

Sources: As for Table 10.1.

which figures in Table 10.4 have been extracted.

Table 10.4: Sales Value per Barrel of Products Refined from Libyan
Crude 1964-7

	1964	1965	1966	1967 (Jan.-April)
Dollars				
France	3.10	2.96	2.90	2.77
United Kingdom	3.03	2.73	2.66	2.50
Italy	2.24	2.17	2.50	2.47
W. Germany	2.74	2.60	2.50	2.09
Average	2.79	2.44	2.65	2.45

The average values may be taken as a continuation of those given in
Chart 6.2, p. 132, though the two studies are quite independent of
each other. In France, the United Kingdom and West Germany, prices
continued to fall, but the firmness of the average sales value of products derived from a barrel of Libyan crude between 1965 and 1967
may be attributed to a marked hardening of prices in Italy, which
hitherto had been a depressed market. Italy was the nearest large
market to Libya, and prices there may have been affected by the
amendment to the Libyan concessions in early 1966. This, by raising
the variable costs of the Libyan independents, was a disincentive to
supplying oil to the Sicilian and Sardinian refineries at distress prices.

At the time of the June 1967 war the Libyan Government placed an
embargo on exports of oil. After a short time the general embargo
was lifted, but maintained, for a period of some three months, on
exports to West Germany, the United Kingdom and the USA only.

These events caused an immediate doubling of product prices in
Europe. This great rise was ephemeral, but prices on average remained
much higher in 1968 than before the war, although on a falling trend.
By 1969 they had dropped once more to 1965 levels or below.

With the Suez Canal closed, the pipelines to the Eastern Mediterranean
temporarily out of action, and soaring freights, Libya's favourable
position to supply Europe with oil was greatly enhanced. Even with
the fiscal discounts from posted prices cancelled, the tax-paid cost
of Libyan oil delivered in North-West Europe or the Mediterranean
in 1968 was much lower, and the quality higher, than any oil from the
Arabian Gulf. The oil companies fortunate enough to have this oil
at their disposal reaped a rich harvest. Libyan crude oil production
as a whole rose in 1968 by 50 per cent over 1967 average levels.

The majors — Esso, Mobil, Texaco, Socal and BP — increased their

Libyan output in 1968 over 1967 by 36 per cent on an annual basis, which masks the considerable rise that occurred in the last part of 1967. The higher prices obtainable induced Liamco and Grace to sell their entitlement from Raguba field in Concession 20 on the market, instead of to Esso at a 'half-way' price; and N.B. Hunt, whose 50 per cent entitlement to BP production in Concession 65 was growing rapidly, followed suit.[3]

The Oasis companies' production in 1968 rose 9 per cent over 1967 but only 6 per cent over 1966 because at that time their field production and pipeline capacity were fully exploited, and the new fields and pipelines, which enabled their output to rise greatly in 1969 and 1970, not yet ready. Among the independents the most notable contribution to increased Libyan production in 1968 came from Occidental, which made its first shipment on 28 February, and grew at such a pace that its exports averaged nearly 400,000 b/d for the year as a whole.

Occidental launched into downstream operations by acquiring the European refining and marketing facilities of Signal Oil and Gas. These comprised an 84 per cent interest in Raffinerie Belge de Pétroles, of 40,000 b/d capacity, a 75 per cent interest in asphalt plants at Ostermoor and Essen, and a chain of about 1,000 VIP service station in the UK, West Germany and Belgium. In addition, Occidental reportedly contracted sales of crude to independent refiners in Spain, West Germany and Italy of 250,000 b/d at $1.80 − $1.85/b f.o.b. These and the outlets acquired through Signal brought its placements of crude oil to 400,000 b/d by mid-1968.[4]

Occidental, and to a less extent Bunker Hunt, were remarkably fortunate in the timing of their Libyan production. They were enabled to break into the European market without incurring the costs and encountering the difficulties which had been experienced by Continental and Marathon (described in Chapter 6, sections 6.2 and 6.3).

By the middle of 1969 prices and realisations had again fallen to their 1966 levels. The reversal of this downward trend, which took place in 1970, and the part played by Libya in bringing it about, will be examined in the final section of this book.

Notes

1. *Petroleum Intelligence Weekly*, 8 Sept. 1969 and 15 Sept. 1969.
2. W. Cipa, 'Realizations Obtained by German Refineries and Consumer Prices for Petroleum Products in Germany Compared with the Situations in Other Member Countries of the European Common Market and in Great Britain'

(Gelsenberg AG, Essen, 1967). The average is weighted by volume of exports to each of the four countries.

    3. The 'half-way price' was derived from a formula on a per barrel basis of: posted price + cost of production divided by two. Thus if posted price of Raguba 40° crude was $2.23 and cost of production 33 cents/b, the half-way price would be $ \frac{2.23 + 0.33}{2} = $1.28. From this realisation Liamco would pay royalty (12½ per cent of $2.23 = 28 cents) and cost of production (33 cents), leaving a taxable income of 67 cents, on which tax would be 33.5 cents, leaving a net income per barrel of 33.5 cents. Esso would pay, as tax, 50 per cent of the difference between posted prices (less allowable discounts — after mid-1967 of only ½ cent/b) and the acquisition cost of the oil from Liamco or Grace.

    Thus the Ministry of Petroleum Affairs would receive the full government take per barrel and Liamco and Grace would make a profit of 33.5 cents/b. To obtain a per barrel after tax profit to match this on direct sales to the market they would have to realise a price of around $1.75/b. Their per barrel accounts (to the nearest cent) would be as follows:

		$/b
Sales price		1.76
Less cost of production, 0.33		
	Royalty, 0.28	0.61
Tax		0.81*
Net profit to company		0.34

*Half of (posted price less costs of production and royalty)

Liamco and Grace sold their oil to Esso on this basis at their own option, and chose this option up to June 1967. After this time they could obtain prices above $1.76/b on the market, and did so until in February 1970 prices obtained were falling below the opportunity cost of not selling to Esso. At this time they reverted to selling their crude to Esso.

    A similar arrangement held between BP and N.B. Hunt on Sarir oil from Concession 65, but with a limitation of 50,000 b/d which BP would take at a half-way price. Above these amounts, the price paid by BP to Hunt would be lower. The posted price of Sarir oil was lower than Raguba oil and costs of production higher. There was thus a lower break-even point for Hunt of between $1.65 and $1.70/b, at which it would pay him to market his own oil (see *Petroleum Intelligence Weekly*, 23 Feb. 1970).

    4. *Middle East Economic Survey*, 8 Mar. 1968.

11 THE IMPACT OF OIL ON LIBYA'S ECONOMY

11.1 Foreign Exchange Practices of the Oil Companies

The Petroleum Law and the Concession Deeds allowed a concession-holder to 'retain abroad all funds acquired by it abroad including the proceeds of sales in so far as such funds may exceed the Company's requirements for the purposes of its operations in Libya'. This clause also stipulated that concessionaires should 'be subject to the normal exchange control applicable in Libya', but the proviso allowing them to retain funds abroad exempted them *de facto* from this control. They were free to use their earnings overseas for whatever purpose they thought fit, including payments abroad for services provided in Libya by overseas contractors, emoluments to their expatriate staff in Libya, their own home office expenses attributed to Libya and dividend payments to parents.

This practice was in accordance with normal procedure in Middle East concessions, and was of paramount importance to oil companies operating in countries other than their homeland. A confidence that, in an essentially international business, they could freely dispose of their earnings from sales of oil in many countries, without interference from the government of the oil-producing country, was a prerequisite for them to invest in oil production operations in the first place. The parent company required all surplus funds to deploy on other operations world-wide, and to provide activities which were not directly profit-making, such as research and head offices, and dividends to shareholders.

Oil company practices in this respect, however, appeared in a different light to many in the oil-producing countries. The Government of Libya, it is true, recognised the importance of allowing the companies a free hand in this matter, but others saw only the disappearance overseas of a great deal of the wealth of the country derived from the exploitation of its wasting and irreplaceable national asset; and in so far as earnings from Libyan oil were being used for exploration and development of oil in other countries, Libya appeared to be providing funds for rivals who might well damage and eventually replace its own industry.

Oil concessionaires were not permitted to borrow money from banks in Libya to cover their local expenses, and followed the practice of remitting to Libya in advance the amounts of money needed for these, and for royalty and tax payments to Government. These latter were paid to the Ministry of Petroleum Affairs in Libyan currency — this being also the currency in which fiscal accounts were compiled. The normal practice of the companies was to retain funds surplus to their Libyan requirements in a current account with their parent companies, through which (or through a separate loan account) they also received funds to finance their operations in Libya; from these accounts also they made payments for equipment, materials and services purchased outside Libya, and that part of their contractors' expenses and ex-patriate staff emoluments which were paid abroad. Surplus funds in these accounts were paid to the parent companies as dividends. The parent companies were thus chief bankers to their Libyan subsidiaries, as well as being their shareholders. Parent company officers were invariably directors of the Libyan subsidiary.

The policy of the oil companies was to hold in Libya only sufficient funds to cover their near requirements. They were not allowed to earn interest on their bank deposits in Libya, and since there was no short-term money market, they kept their Libyan balances to a minimum. Indeed the problems of last-minute remittances to make the periodical big tax and royalty payments, and the unfavourable exchange rates available at these times, caused company complaints, on which they received official reassurances from the Government at the time of the accelerated tax and royalty payments Agreement in 1968 (see Chapter 8, section 8.4).

The oil companies themselves were not above pursuing tactics to their own advantage in exchange transactions. It was a common, if not universal, practice to present cheques to the Ministry in payments for taxes after the banks had closed at 2p.m. and on Thursdays (the banks being closed on Fridays), so that their presentation and clearance would be delayed; on sums of many millions of pounds the interest earnings involved could be significant.[1]

On one occasion an attempt was made by the Bank of Libya, influenced by an active Deputy Governor, Ess. Ali Mouzughi, to inter-vene in oil company foreign exchange practices permitted by the Pet-roleum Law. In 1968 an instruction was sent to concession-holders to remit in advance to Libya the funds budgeted for a complete year of operations. This aroused oil company resentment and resistance, and was quickly scotched by the Ministry of Petroleum Affairs. The Ministry realised that the quickest way to damage an oil industry, as evidenced in the past in other countries, was to try to exercise control over oil companies' disposal of their funds, and more particularly to force oil concessionaires to submit to a common feature of exchange control regulations throughout the world — of repatriating proceeds of exports.[2]

11.2 Libya's Balance of Payments

Taking into account that the oil companies retained abroad revenues derived from their sales of Libyan oil, an attempt has been made in Table 11.1 to gauge the impact of the companies on the Libyan economy so far as their investments in and earnings from oil operations are concerned, without for the moment considering the secondary effects of their expenditure, activities and payments to Government on the Libyan economy. The table has been compiled in a manner different from the conventional balance of payments statement and is intended to give a simplified picture of the oil company revenues derived from Libyan oil and how they were disposed of — in capital and operating expenses both inside and outside Libya, in royalty and tax payments and finally, as the industry developed, in recovering their investment and in profits.

The first line gives revenues derived from crude oil exports. As these are expressed at tax reference prices (i.e. posted prices less allowed discounts) they may be considered, for the years 1965 onwards, an over-statement, to the extent of about 15 per cent on average, of the value of the export oil at 'realised' prices (i.e. net back to crude after deducting downstream costs and expenses from the sales revenues of final products). Lines (2) (a) and (b) give the oil companies' actual expenditures in, and therefore remittances of funds to, Libya. In the early years all these expenditures were for operations. The companies had no royalties or profits taxes to pay (but only some customs duties, stamp and road taxes, which are included in their expenses, and concession fees and rents as recorded in Table 4.3). In 1964 royalty and tax payments exceeded operational expenses for the first time, and thereafter became predominant in oil company payments in Libya.

Lines (3) (c) - (e) indicate oil company expenditures for their Libyan operations outside Libya. Their imports of equipment and supplies, payments for contractors (including drilling contractors, pipeline and terminal constructors) and for services from their home offices and third parties, and even expatriate emoluments paid in their home countries, are all deemed to be contributions to the Libyan oil industry,

Table 11.1: Oil Companies' Investment in Libya, Earnings therefrom and their Disposal, 1958-70

£L million	1958	1959	1960	1961	1962	1963	1964	1965	1966	1967	1968	1969	1970
(1) Exports of crude oil and other Libyan earnings	–	–	–	4	48	117	216	281	355	417	665	772	850
(2) Payments in Libya for:													
(a) royalties and taxes	–	–	–	2	7	24	56	82	142	191	286	363	469
(b) capital and operating expenses in Libya	10	13	21	25	28	38	38	47	46	40	56	97	100
(3) Total payments in Libya:	10	13	21	27	35	62	94	129	188	231	342	460	569
Payments outside Libya for:													
(c) imports	8	13	21	13	25	24	22	22	14	32	56	54	32
(d) contractors' and other services	5	8	17	29	33	29	41	47	50	50	56	93	77
(e) expatriate emoluments	1	1	2	2	4	5	6	6	8	9	10	12	14
(4) = (2) + (3) Capital and operating expenditure and payments to Govt.	24	35	61	71	97	120	163	204	260	322	464	619	692
(5) = (4) – (1): Net investment of oil companies in Libya (+), or net recovery of their investment in, plus profits from, Libya, (–)	+24	+35	+61	+67	+49	+3	–58	–77	–95	–95	–201	–153	–158

Sources: IMF, *Balance of Payments Yearbooks*; Libyan Ministry of Petroleum, *Libyan Oil, 1954-1971.* The values of exports of crude oil in line (1) are probably over-stated by the difference between declared tax reference values and 'realised' prices, which may be as much as 15 per cent. Thus oil company recovery of investment and profits will be over-stated by similar amounts. For further comments see note 3.

the last three being conventionally classified, in balance of payments statements, as invisible imports. These were made without payment of foreign exchange by Libya, and may be regarded as investment in Libya by the oil companies, whether the expenses were of a capital or current nature.

By deducting all capital and operating expenses and payments to Government from export revenues, a figure of net oil company investment in Libya year by year is obtained. The investment, of course, started long before the revenues. The first year in which oil company revenues in aggregate exceeded their expenditures for Libyan operations was 1964, and this was attributable largely to Esso and Oasis production, which in 1964 comprised 85 per cent of the total. The break-even point for the industry as a whole, after adding in 1956/7 figures of expenditures from Chapter 1, note 8, occurred in 1967.

After extracting oil industry transactions, the remainder of Libya's balance of payments is given in summary form in the conventional manner in Table 11.2. This shows that the non-oil balance of payments deficits on current account − and from 1967 onwards on capital account also − were amply covered by oil company remittances of foreign exchange to Libya. As a result the Bank of Libya's reserves of foreign exchange increased each year from 1958 to 1970, rising from £L19m in 1958 to £L568m at the end of 1970. Further comments on items in the tables are given in notes 3 and 4.

11.3 Inflation and Employment

The balance of payments constraint on Libya's economic growth was thus first mitigated and then removed by the advent of oil revenues and oil company expenditures in Libya. The swelling volume of this money inflow from overseas did not have a major inflationary effect on the economy.[5] A price index for consumer goods and services is available from 1964 and is recorded in Table 11.4. This record shows an average annual price rise between 1964 and 1970 of about 5 per cent. The earlier food price index for Tripoli shows an average annual increase between 1955 and 1964 of about 4 per cent.

Inflation was mitigated by much increased spending, in both the public and private sectors, on imports of goods (including food) and services (including overseas engineering and construction contractors), all of which were acquired at internationally competitive prices. In sectors which relied on home stock, materials and labour, there were larger

Table 11.2: Libya's Non-Oil Balance of Payments, 1958-70 (£ Libyan millions)

	1958	1959	1960	1961	1962	1963	1964	1965	1966	1967	1968	1969	1970
Current Account													
(1) Exports f.o.b.	+ 5	+ 4	+ 4	+ 4	+ 3	+ 2	+ 3	+ 3	+ 2	+ 2	+ 2	+ 2	+ 3
(2) Imports c.i.f.	−16	−31	−42	−42	−49	−61	−77	−93	−132	−140	−176	−221	−205
(3) Trade balance	−11	−27	−38	−38	−46	−59	−74	−90	−130	−138	−174	−219	−202
(4) Travel	− 2	− 2	− 1	− 2	− 3	− 3	− 3	− 4	− 5	− 8	− 12	− 21	− 21
(5) Military receipts	+ 7	+ 7	+ 7	+ 7	+ 9	+ 7	+ 7	+ 8	+ 5	+ 1	+ 3	+ 4	+ 1
(6) Other services and transfers	− 5	—	+ 2	− 4	− 5	− 14	− 15	− 18	− 31	− 46	− 78	− 36	− 67
(7) Current Account Balance	−11	−22	−30	−37	−45	−69	−85	−104	−161	−191	−261	−272	−289
Capital Account													
(8) Official grants & loans received	+ 9	+15	+13	+13	+13	+11	+ 8	+ 3	+ 1	− 27	− 29	− 42	− 37
(9) Other (net)	− 3	—	—	− 1	—	+ 6	—	− 1	+ 5	+ 3	+ 3	− 10	− 3
	+ 6	+15	+13	+12	+13	+17	+ 8	+ 2	+ 6	− 24	− 26	− 52	− 40
(10) Total balance of payments—current and capital accounts	5	− 7	−17	−25	−32	−52	−77	−102	−155	−215	−287	−324	−329
(11) F/E remittances to Libya by oil cos.	+10	+13	+21	+27	+35	+62	+94	+129	+188	+231	+342	+460	+569
(12) Increase in Libya's F/E reserves	+ 5	+ 6	+ 4	+ 2	+ 3	+10	+17	+ 27	+ 33	+ 16	+ 55	+136	+240
(13) Total of Libya's F/E reserves at year end	19	25	29	31	34	44	61	88	121	137	192	328	568

Source: IMF, *Balance of Payments Yearbooks.*
For further comments, see note 4.
The + and − signs in items (1) - (11) show foreign exchange earnings and outgoings respectively, and not increases and decreases.

price increases, more especially in land, rents, building, construction, domestic services and other labour-intensive activities. There are no official figures on these, nor on wages, and few on employment. The records of the Ministry of Labour and Social Affairs show that there was virtually no unemployment — all able-bodied males offering themselves for employment obtained it, and there was a significant influx of workers from neighbouring countries to supplement domestic labour resources.

11.4 National Income

Growth of the Libyan economy after 1965 is recorded in Table 11.5. In five years, including the oil sector, money GDP at factor cost increased 2½ times. When deflated by the consumer price index — defective for this purpose, but the only one available to give an approximation of 'real' terms — it nearly doubled (15 per cent p.a.). Excluding the oil sector, in money terms it doubled and in real terms it rose 54 per cent (9 per cent p.a.). There is a series of figures given by UN statistics of GDP from 1958 to 1964, which show an average annual increase for these years of 12 per cent in money terms. They are not on a comparable basis with the later figures and, for the sake of consistency of presentation, have been omitted.

To estimate GNP at factor cost, net factor income paid abroad — much of it oil industry employee and profits payments — is deducted from GDP in Table 11.5. The GNP figure derived from this gives an estimate of Libya's own share in the growth of its economy. It shows at constant prices a rise of 93 per cent over the five years — an annual average rate of 14 per cent. On a *per capita* basis, using the *'de jure'* population figures in Table 11.4, individual income rose in money terms from £L261 in 1965 to £L548 in 1970. In real terms this was 61 per cent, on average 10 per cent p.a.

When one looks at the real growth in individual sectors, the following picture emerges.

Table 11.3: Growth of the Libyan Economy by Sectors, 1965-70

| | Percentage Increase | | | Percentage Increase | |
	5-year	Annual Average		5-year	Annual Average
Agriculture	6	1	Public administration		
Manufacturing	37	6	and defence	112	16
Construction	78	12	Education	133	18
Transport and			Health	170	22
communications	58	10	Ownership of		
Wholesale and retail			dwellings	53[6]	9
trade	1	—	Petroleum	198[7]	24

Table 11.4: Population, Prices, GNP and Per Capita Income 1958-70

	1958	1959	1960	1961	1962	1963	1964	1965	1966	1967	1969	1970	1971
(1) Population (*de jure*[a]) mid-year, millions	1.26	1.30	1.35	1.40	1.45	1.50	1.56	1.62	1.65	1.76	1.84	1.91	1.99
(2) (a) Food prices, Tripoli (Jan. 1955 = 100)	111	114	128	136	133	149	146						
(b) Consumer price index All items (Jan. 1964 1964 = 100)							100	105.8	114.3	118.4	123.6	134.2	137.3
(3) GNP, £L million								423	525	633	843	1,002	1,063
(4) *Per capita* income £L								261	313	364	468	536	548

Note: a. Sc. of Libyan nationality.
Sources: (1) *UN Monthly Bulletin of Statistics,* derived from Ministry of Planning and Development
(2) Bank of Libya Economic Research Department, *Economic Bulletin.*
(3) National Accounts Dept., Ministry of Planning and Development.

For items (2) and (3) there are some conflicting figures, none of which alter the trends or magnitudes significantly. In such cases the apparently more reliable figure has been chosen for these and other tables. A few alterations from sources have been made when, in the opinion of the writer, from personal knowledge or conflict of sources, an error of copying or calculation has been made at source.

Table 11.5: Gross Domestic and National Product at Current Prices, 1965-70 (£L millions)

Sectors	1965	1966	1967	1968	1969	1970
(1) Agriculture, forestry and fishing	25.0	27.1	30.3	33.4	37.4	34.6
(2) Petroleum extraction	272.3	342.9	406.6	648.6	754.7	812.6
(3) Other mining and quarrying	1.0	1.1	1.3	1.5	1.4	2.0
(4) Manufacturing	12.6	14.4	16.4	20.0	20.8	22.5
(5) Construction	35.4	46.5	66.4	89.2	86.6	81.8
(6) Electricity and gas	1.5	1.7	1.9	3.0	4.0	6.0
(7) Transportation and communications	18.5	24.7	31.2	39.3	40.2	38.0
(8) Wholesale and retail trade	33.3	42.2	49.0	45.5	48.5	43.9
(9) Banking and insurance	7.0	8.7	10.5	6.3	7.9	12.0
(10) Public administration and defence	35.5	44.8	54.3	77.1	86.7	98.0
(11) Educational services	13.1	16.8	20.4	25.6	32.4	39.7
(12) Health services	4.5	6.4	7.7	10.9	19.2	15.8
(13) Ownership of dwellings	36.6	45.2	55.4	59.7	64.2	59.5
(14) Other services	8.5	9.9	10.6	11.6	11.8	12.7
(15) Gross Domestic Product (at factor cost)	504.8	632.4	761.4	1,071.7	1,215.8	1,279.1
(16) Less net factor income paid abroad	81.6	106.9	128.3	228.3	214.0	216.0
(17) Gross National Product (at factor cost)	423.2	525.5	633.1	843.4	1,001.8	1,063.1
(18) Add indirect taxes	28.1	34.0	35.6	46.3	50.0	49.7
(19) Less subsidies	1.1	2.1	2.8	8.3	8.4	11.0
(20) Gross National Product (at market prices)	450.2	557.4	665.9	881.4	1,043.4	1,101.8

Source: National Accounts Department – Ministry of Planning and Development.

These figures suggest that, contrary to widespread belief,[8] agricultural production did not decline, but remained fairly steady. Private-sector manufacturing also rose by a modest amount, and this may be attributed in part to oil company requirements met by local manufacture, and to workshops providing for the great increase in consumer durables such as cars and electronic goods. The high level of construction activity occurred principally in the neighbourhoods of Tripoli, Beida, the oil terminals and other oil installations, and was mixed private and public sector — the latter being particularly evident in the building of many mosques.

The greatest increases, apart from petroleum, were in the public sector. Transport and communications — mostly roads — public administration and defence, education and health all expanded fast. More details of this expenditure are given in the government development expenditures in Table 11.6. Ownership of dwellings also rose at 9 per cent p.a., and this reflects a mixture of villa and apartment construction, much of it around Tripoli, but also at oil company installations, engendered by the oil and related industry requirements; and of government-sponsored building at Beida and elsewhere for officials and public servants, and several low-cost housing schemes for the greatly increasing urban population.

11.5 Public Finance and Development

Table 11.6 gives the record of federal government revenues from 1959/60 to 1970/71, and expenditures from 1963/4. This latter year was the first in which the three provinces were merged into a unitary Government, which established a Ministry of Planning and Development and embarked upon a five-year plan for development.

Over the years from then to the end of the decade the budgets were by and large in balance. There was in fact almost an exact balance cumulatively over the seven years to 1969/70, which relieved the country from deficit financing and removed a potential source of inflation.

In accordance with a law made in 1963, 70 per cent of petroleum revenues were to be appropriated for economic and social development. Although the figures suggest that this intention was not fully translated into accomplishment, even by relating oil revenues of one year with development expenditures of the following, there were nevertheless large sums available for development expenditure and much was

Table 11.6: Government Revenue and Expenditure, 1959/60 – 1970/1 (£L millions)

	Fiscal Years, April-March											
	1959/60	1960/1	1961/2	1962/3	1963/4	1964/5	1965/6	1966/7	1967/8	1968/9	1969/70	1970/71
(1) Revenue[a]												
(a) Oil	0.1	0.1	2	7	24	55	116	139	191	279	363	469
(b) Other	13	12	17	17	30	35	42	53	59	79	84	83
(2) Expenditure												
(a) Ordinary					50	64	83	113	166	239	292	288
(b) Development					13	23	52	82	120	140	113	146

of which:

	Actual Expenditure 1963/4 – 1966/7	Appropriations				
		1966/7	1967/8	1968/9	1969/70	1970/71
Agriculture	20	8	8	11	16	50
Industry	7	5	5	8	8	20
Transport and communications	33	20	20	24	23	27
Public works	48	24	24	29	25	18
Education	16	10	10	14	15	11
Health	3	3	3	4	7	6
Labour and social affairs	9	6	5	2	2	1
Planning and development	7	5	5	4	2	1
Interior	12	5	5	1	1	1
Housing	12	19	2	12	22	33

Note: a. Federal revenues only before 1963/4, when the unitary system of government was adopted.

Sources: (1) (a) Ministry of Petroleum Affairs) 1959/60 — 1966/7, as reported in Min. Pet. Affairs, *Libyan Oil, 1954-1967.*
　　　　　　 (b) Ministry of Finance 　　　　　　)

　　　　　(2) (a) Ministry of Finance 　　　　　　　　　　) 1967/8 – 1970/1, Diwan of Audit as reported in Central Bank, *Economic*
　　　　　　 (b) Ministry of Planning and Development) *Bulletin* (Mar./Apr. 1977).

accomplished. Major recipients of this expenditure were public works, transport and communications and housing, but it was widely distributed throughout public-sector economic and social activities.

Notes

1. The writer was on more than one occasion – as then Director of Companies' Accounts Dept. at the Ministry – saddled with such cheques of up to £L50 million to carry around in his pocket over the weekend, there being no suitable safe available in the Ministry.

2. In both Indonesia and Algeria there had been measures taken at various times to force oil companies operating there to repatriate the proceeds of their sales of oil. This had been an element in destroying the confidence of concessionaires in these countries, causing further investment in oil development to wither.

A new Law on foreign investment in Libya other than in petroleum was promulgated on 31 July 1968. It guaranteed remittance of profits and repatriation of capital to investors from abroad, as well as transfer abroad of the Libyan earnings of their overseas employees.

3. Notes on Table 11.1. The figures for this table have been adapted from a number of sources as indicated below. As different sources use different bases, there are minor discrepancies between the sources according to whether the figures are:

(1) in respect of oil operations in a calendar year on an income and expenditure basis;
(2) receipts and payments in any calendar year on a cash basis;
(3) Government receipts on a fiscal year basis (April-March).

Notes on and sources of individual aggregates:

Line (1) IMF Balance of Payments Yearbooks derived from records of Ministries of Finance, Economy and Trade, Industry and Central Bank of Libya. They include oil company revenues from operations in Libya other than crude oil exports – more especially Esso's refinery and the Esso, Shell and Asseil (Agip) marketing in Libya of petroleum products. These are insignificant in relation to total figures. There is a close correspondence of these figures with those of oil exports valued at prices declared for tax purposes in companies' fiscal accounts.

Line (2) (a) Ministry of Petroleum Affairs.

Line (2) (b) IMF Balance of Payments Yearbooks as above.

Line (2) Totals. There is a close correspondence between these figures and Central Bank of Libya records of oil company sales of foreign exchange for Libyan pounds to meet their expenses in Libya, royalty and tax payments. The years in which these sales were made differ slightly from those in which the payments are recorded.

Line (3) IMF Balance of Payments Yearbooks as above. The totals (2) + (3) are confirmed by Ministry of Petroleum Affairs figures of annual expenditure of oil companies given in Chapter 1, note 8, after deducting tax payments (not royalty), which are not included in the latter figures.

4. Notes on Table 11.2. This table gives Libya's balance of payments without oil industry transactions. Against the net balances on capital and current account are offset the oil company remittances of funds to Libya, to arrive at

the change in Libya's foreign exchange reserves each year.

The table is compiled in the conventional manner, adapted from IMF Balance of Payments Yearbook figures. For 1958 it ties in with the net figures for 1958 given in Table 1.3. Comments on individual items are given below:

(1) Exports, mostly of agricultural produce, diminished somewhat, but did not by any means cease with the arrival of the oil era, even allowing for inflation.

(2) The great rise in imports over the years suggests that increased demand resulting from higher earnings and the presence of a large and affluent expatriate population was met largely from imports; this is confirmed by figures of agricultural and manufacturing production in Table 11.5, which did not rise to anything like the same extent.

(5) Military receipts were, until 1970, the costs incurred and payments made for the presence of US and British forces — the former at Wheelus Airbase near Tripoli, the latter in Tripoli, Benghazi, Tobruk and elsewhere.

(6) Other services and transfers contain numerous types of payments, mostly outward, and increasing sharply with the increase of oil revenues. This is in fact a balancing item and undoubtedly many transactions of a capital as well as a current nature are included.

(8) Official grants comprised aid, mostly from the UK and the USA. The negative figures in 1967 and after are explained by Libyan assistance to other Arab countries after the 1967 war.

(11) The figures of foreign exchange remittances to Libya by oil companies are taken from Table 11.1.

(12) The increases in Libya's foreign exchange reserves are mostly those of the Bank of Libya, including changes in position in the IMF. They also include changes in position of banking institutions operating in Libya.

5. Important determinants of changes in the money supply, which may also shed some light on inflationary tendencies, are indicated in the banking figures for these years, as follows:

Table 11.7: Libya — Money Supply Determinants, 1965-70

End of Year	1965	1966	1967	1968	1969	1970	Increases (1969) minus (1965)	(1970) minus (1965)
£L millions								
Assets of Banking System								
Foreign assets	87	120	134	188	324	572	+237	+485
Advances to private sector	35	47	54	73	93	96	+ 59	+ 61
	122	167	188	261	417	668	+296	+546
Liabilities of Banking System								
Money Supply[a]	67	91	117	150	202	241	+135	+174
Quasi-money [b]	29	37	42	47	74	80	+ 45	+ 51
Government deposits	16	24	15	41	97	280	+ 81	+264
Other (net)	10	15	14	23	44	67	+ 34	+ 57
	122	167	188	261	417	668	+295	+546
Velocity of money[c]	1.8	2.0	1.5	1.4	0.9	0.8		

Notes: a. Currency in ciruclation plus demand deposits.
   b. Time and savings deposits including margins on letters of credit and guarantees.
   c. Total debits to demand deposits divided by average total demand deposits.
Source: Central Bank of LAR, *Economic Bulletin* (Mar./Apr. 1977).

The above table shows that, up to 1969, little more than half of the rise in foreign exchange reserves during this five-year period engendered increases in the stock of money. A quarter was reflected in increased government deposits, representing the unspent balances of oil revenues, not part of the money supply as conventionally defined. A large but unstated portion of the quasi-money comprised deposits on opening letters of credit and was, as such, pre-payment for imports, also money taken out of circulation prior to purchase of goods overseas.

There was no net bank lending to Government and no public-sector net borrowing requirement during the period. The increases in government deposits had a deflationary affect.

In addition to this there was a marked fall in the velocity of circulation of money as measured by the turnover of current accounts, and this is confirmed by relating stock of money figures to GNP at constant prices over the period. These factors give sufficient evidence to explain the smallness of price rises by reference either to the crude quantity theory of money or to Keynesian liquidity preference.

Determinants of the money supply are examined for six Middle East countries by Edith Penrose in 'Money, Prices, and Economic Expansion in the Middle East, 1952-1960', published in *Rivista Internazionale di Scienze Economiche e Commerciali*, Anno XI (1962, no. 5); reprinted as Chapter XVI in *The Growth of Firms, Middle East Oil and Other Essays* by the same author (Frank Cass, London, 1971).

6. As conditions were radically altered after the revolution by enforced rent reductions, four-year figures from 1965 to 1969 are taken here. The five-year figures reduce those given to 25 per cent and 5 per cent respectively.

7. As petroleum prices did not follow the price index trend, being geared to posted prices for exports, these increases are calculated at current prices.

8. E.g. Ministry of Petroleum Affairs, Kingdom of Libya, *Libyan Oil, 1954-1967*, p. 50: 'The inevitable result of migration of population from rural areas to employment in the towns and the [oil] companies was a fall in agricultural production.'

Ministry of Petroleum, Libyan Arab Republic, *Libyan Oil, 1954-1971*, p. 122: 'agriculture started to decline as a result of expansion in the building industry.'

Part V:

AFTER THE REVOLUTION, 1970-1976

12 THE REVOLUTIONARY GOVERNMENT AND THE OIL COMPANIES

12.1 The First Year

The almost bloodless revolution which took place on 1 September 1969 scarcely affected oil operations. Production and exports of oil continued normally, apart from a two-week interruption of air and postal communications. Early comments by those in authority were reassuring. The new Prime Minister, Dr Mahmud al Maghribi, who had been a lawyer with Esso previously, stated to a French news agency on 17 September,

> there will be no spectacular changes in our oil policy, and I can confirm that we shall endeavour to cooperate with the oil companies, provided that the interests of the Libyan people — which were completely neglected by the former regime — are taken into account. It is possible to safeguard these interests by means of a more effective control over oil operations.[1]

In another press interview with the Tripoli daily, *al Thaurah*, reported on 29 October, Ess. Isa al Ghiblawi, the newly appointed under-secretary of the Ministry of Petroleum (which the Ministry of Petroleum Affairs was now called) stated:

> We shall continue to respect our agreements with the companies so long as they continue to operate within the limits of the law. We have no intention of nationalising oil. We consider ourselves bound by the agreements concluded with all the oil companies in Libya.

These remarks were made apropos of the cancelling of the recently concluded joint-venture agreement between Lipetco and Chappaqua — action which, as described in Chapter 8, section 8.7, was initiated by the previous regime. The decision was made by the Council of Ministers on 27 October on account of 'substantial breaches' of the terms of the contract on the part of Chappaqua.[2] There is little doubt that there were irregularities on the Government side in awarding the joint venture and on the company's side in its representations and undertakings, which have already been described. The under-secretary added, in his comments on this affair, that 'the joint-venture . . . was the result of pressure from one of the most notorious personalities of the time' and went on to name a Colonel al Shalhi, who had been a member of King Idris' entourage. This is one of the few recorded instances of a public specific accusation of corruption, rumours of which had been rife and fully exploited in general terms by the new regime and its supporters.

On posted prices Ess. Ghiblawi said that their revision would be agreed upon through negotiations with all the oil companies operating in Libya and would no doubt be satisfactory to both parties. On joint ventures, he said that 'the Ministry of Petroleum plans to continue the policy until such time as a change-over to the service contract state becomes possible.'

Apart from these references to posted prices, no further action was taken until towards the end of the year. On 22 December a committee was established, with membership drawn from officials of the Ministry of Petroleum, to negotiate with oil companies to adjust the posted price of Libyan crude oil.[3] It was another month before negotiations started in earnest. They were initiated by an address on 20 January 1970 to oil company representatives by the new Minister of Petroleum and Minerals, Ess. Izzedin al Mabruk, who had succeeded the first post-revolution Minister, Ess. Anis Shtaiwi. This was followed by a further meeting of heads of oil companies on 29 January, which was addressed by Colonel Mu'ammar al Qadhafi, who had emerged as Leader of the Revolutionary Command Council. In his address to the companies he made the remark which was to become famous, that 'the Libyan people, who have lived for five thousand years without petroleum, are able to live again without it.'

The Pricing Committee proceeded to negotiate with the companies, but without positive result. Two rounds of meetings took place with individual companies before the Government decided to strengthen its approach. On 4 April Dr Maghribi, who had ceased to be Prime Minister, was appointed Chairman of the Committee. Behind the Committee, the decisions were to be guided by Major Abdu Salem Jalloud,[4] who had emerged as second-in-command to Colonel Qadhafi, and had presided over the negotiations with the United States and United Kingdom Governments which resulted in the accelerated evacuation of the American and British air and military bases and presence in Libya. This development signified that the Revolutionary Command Council was itself to handle the matter as one of high priority.

In spite of the pressure on the companies, Amoco (Pan-American), who had brought into production the small Sahabi field in Concession 95 and begun exporting via Occidental's pipeline, posted a price for this crude, in the middle of April, identical with Occidental's existing postings. This was done although, a few days earlier, both Occidental and Esso had agreed in principle on a price adjustment, and had made some proposals for small increases to be phased in over a period of years. These had been dismissed by the Pricing Committee as 'trivial'.

Early in May, the policy of cutting back oil companies' production began. Such actions were, in normal circumstances, contrary to the Petroleum Law, which gave concession-holders the right to take away, export and dispose of petroleum in their concessions, restricted only 'in cases of absolute necessity connected with the high interests of the State'.[5] The Revolutionary Government, which had repeatedly affirmed its adherence to the existing oil laws and the concession contracts concluded in accordance with them, did not support their actions by reference to this proviso. Instead, they had recourse to the conservation regulation, circulated but never validated in 1968 (see Chapter 8, section 8.8) as Regulation No. 8. The cuts were imposed by the Technical Department of the Oil Ministry on the grounds that the companies concerned were producing wells at above their most efficient rate, for which, according to the regulation, the Ministry might order them to be shut in. Subsequently, on 26 April 1971 Law No. 32 was promulgated which imposed fines by decision of the Minister of Petroleum on any person violating the provisions of the Petroleum Law and Regulations, including indemnification for losses of hydrocarbons and damage to deposits arising therefrom.

Occidental was the first company to receive orders to cut back its production. This company's rapid increases in production, and the misgivings to which they gave rise in the Ministry as early as 1968, have already been mentioned. They provided some rationale for the cut-backs in the eyes of the Ministry, but not in those of Occidental itself, who stated that they would cause a permanent loss of 55 million barrels of recoverable oil in the fields affected.[6] It was widely expected that the Government would first turn its attention to Occidental, since this company had no oil resources other than its Libyan fields and was thus most susceptible to pressure.

In May Occidental's production was cut in successive stages by nearly 400,000 b/d. In June Amoseas was ordered to cut back production by 120,000 b/d. In July Oasis was subjected to similar treatment, having its production allowable reduced by 125,000 b/d (after having reached over 1 million b/d production earlier in the year), and in August Mobil's output was reduced by 55,000 b/d. Further cutbacks were imposed on Occidental (bringing the total to 425,000 b/d) and on Esso (110,000 b/d) at the beginning of September.

Furthermore, during this period Esso was prevented from beginning exports of LNG from Mersa Brega, pending an adjustment of prices, and also from drilling twelve fill-in wells on the Zelten field. New port dues of 1 cent/b were imposed on tankers shipping oil — a levy which was considered illegal by the companies in terms of Article IX of the amended Petroleum Law and Article 6 of Regulation 6. In addition, a decree of 4 July nationalised the marketing of oil products in Libya and took over all distribution installations and service stations. This affected the three companies Esso, Shell and Asseil (ENI), who distributed and marketed oil products in Libya. The memorandum accompanying the decree mentioned that it was 'the inception of a series of similar revolutionary measures in numerous economic fields'. Finally, in a decree issued at the end of August, overseas payments by oil companies to employees and contractors were banned.

The effect of these events on petroleum markets will be described in Chapter 13. In brief, they gave rise to scarcities and to fears for future supplies which stimulated stockpiling in consumer countries. The consequent rise in prices of both oil and freights created conditions in which a demand for increases in Libyan posted prices in terms of the existing law could not be resisted with any degree of plausibility by the oil companies.

The other major result of the events was a drastic fall of exploration and development investment by the oil companies. By May 1970 the number of rigs in the country had fallen by half from the summer of 1969 — from 52 to 26, and by August to 18. In May the Ministry of Petroleum sent an 'urgent request' to concession-holders to start drilling in inactive areas within a month 'to make business for idle contractors'.[7] This apparently had little effect since the working obligations of the Law had apparently been fulfilled. Nor was exploration and drilling activity encouraged by the possibility of a mooted 51 per cent Government acquisition of contractors, including Schlumberger, Dowell-Schlumberger and Geophysical Services International.[8]

After prolonged discussions and further rejected offers, and in conditions which were later described by Occidental as 'under duress',[9] Occidental made an offer, early in September, which was accepted by the Libyan Government. It was later named the 1 September Agreement — to coincide with the first anniversary of the revolution. The details of it, and the following of its pattern by the other oil-producing companies, will be described in Section 12.2 of this chapter.

The decision by Occidental to concede higher posted prices marks, in a sense, the end of an era in the international oil industry, and the beginning of a new one. The creation of OPEC in 1960 had blocked any downward movement in posted prices throughout the world after that date. The oil companies themselves had blocked any upward move. Posted prices were a world-wide issue. The Libyan subsidiaries of the major oil companies had no discretion in the matter, whatever local considerations required or equity demanded. The decisions, if any — and for ten years there was only one decision, to do nothing — were made in the Head Offices of these groups in London, New York, Houston or San Francisco. None of these Head Offices was prepared to take the initiative in breaking the line, although, as events proved, they would follow a leader. The natural inertia built into this system ensured that, so long as the concession agreements in the oil-producing countries were strictly honoured by host governments, there would be no change, whatever the commercial or legal justification for it.

The independents in Libya were quite content to follow the majors' lead in this matter. But Occidental was exceptional in that not only were its Libyan operations the major part of its business, but the head of the company, in whose hands the power of decision lay, intervened personally many times in its dealings with the Libyan Government. This the Libyan leaders. were shrewd and forceful enough to make use of and to exploit. The market prices of oil had been driven up to such an extent by the autumn of 1970 — largely by Libyan actions — that the raising of posted prices absorbed only a small amount of the extra revenue derived by the companies from this movement. The international oil companies made good profits in 1970,[10] and it became clear after the event that they had been holding the line on posted prices for ten years, not for themselves, but for consumers of oil.

The Government's actions were the more effective in that they were untrammelled by any delay of legislative procedures. A proposal reviewed by the Revolutionary Command Council one evening could become law before dawn on the following day. The insecurities and fears engendered by this situation undoubtedly affected the oil companies' courses of action and, more importantly, the reactions to Libyan events and expectations in the petroleum markets of the world.

12.2 The 1970 Price and Tax Settlements

The basic Agreement with Occidental was for an increase in posted prices of 30 cents/b, to be raised by a further 2 cents/b on 1 January of each of the following five years.[11] The other measures included in it, which might have the superficial appearance of little more than a tying up of loose ends on outstanding matters, were in fact of equal importance and had just as far-reaching consequences as the rise in posted price.

The most important of these was a rise in the rate of tax, from 50 per cent to 58 per cent in the case of Occidental. This was rationalised as the consolidation of 5 per cent of pre-tax profits which Occidental was contributing towards the development of Kufra (Chapter 9, section 9.5) in accordance with the extra benefits offered to Libya in its original concession; and 3 per cent in lieu of back payments of tax on the higher posted price, which was to apply retroactively to the beginning of Occidental's production in 1968 (and to 1965 in the subsequent agreements with other companies).

The 5 per cent increase in tax in lieu of the Kufra expenditure doubled these payments, as Occidental had been treating them as a tax deductible and recovering half as a tax credit. As for the other 3 per cent, an option was given of making the retroactive tax payments in cash, or increasing permanently the rate of tax. The rate applicable in the subsequent agreements with other companies varied according to the different amounts involved for each company.

This tax increase, and those of the agreements that followed with other companies, was seen by the world, and particularly by other members of OPEC, to have destroyed the 50/50 profit-sharing principle which had been predominant for 20 years. The pretext for it was the willingness of the Libyan Government to allow large retroactive tax payments to be eased by spreading them over the years. The companies themselves had to make a difficult choice. Most of them, who had been producing in large quantities in 1965 and before, would be faced with very large payments if they chose to settle the arrears in cash.[12] If they opted for the higher tax rate instead, they hoped they would be able to recover the extra payments through escalation clauses in their sales to third parties, and in integrated operations through their price build-ups, which in most countries had to be justified to price control authorities. This hope was not altogether realised, since subsequently the Libyan Government refused to remove from the Agreements the reference to retroactivity, and thus made it difficult for the companies to include them in their price escalations, in which there were no provisions for retroactivity adjustments.

Another element in the Agreement which had big consequences was a change in the base gravity and in price differentials for different gravities. Hitherto the base gravity, which Esso had used for posting at \$2.21/b, was 39°, with a 2 cents fall in price for each degree below this, and a 2 cents increase for 40° oil only (and no increase above 40°). The new Agreement made 40° the base gravity for price, extended the 2 cents differential to each degree of gravity above 40°, and reduced the differential to 1½ cents for each degree of gravity below 40°.

This altered the whole gravity differential structure with a vengeance. It will be recalled that, in the OPEC settlement applicable in the Arabian Gulf countries, and to Libya before the closing of the Suez Canal in 1967, discounts from posted prices included a gravity differential allowance, which had the effect of narrowing the price differential per degree of gravity from 2 cents to, at this time, about 1½ cents. But the base used was 27° oil, so that the higher the gravity of the oil above 27°, the greater the gravity differential allowance. Now the differential was to be applied to a base oil of 40°, so that the lower the gravity of the oil below 40° the greater would be the increase in its posted price.

After the Occidental Agreement, the other producing companies followed within 6 weeks. First the Oasis companies — Continental, Marathon, Amerada-Hess and Shell[13] — were invited to make an offer similar to Occidental's in the third week of September. Continental, Marathon and Amerada-Hess, for each of whom their Libyan production was more than 50 per cent of their total world-wide, consented after a week. Shell demurred and immediately received an embargo on its exports — an embargo which had no pretence of support from conservation considerations, since it was an undivided part of Oasis' total production. For Shell its Libyan production was only 3 per cent of its total, and its reluctance was fortified by consideration of a most-favoured-African-nation clause in its Nigerian concessions. However, it subsequently agreed to make the offer in the middle of October, and had its production restored, but still subject to the cut-backs applicable to all Oasis production.

The Government then called on Gelsenberg, Hunt, Liamco and Grace — all independents — to 'capitulate'. The four companies did so at the beginning of October, together with the first of the majors — the two Amoseas companies, Socal and Texaco. This latter event broke the resistance of the majors, and after a further week Esso, Mobil, BP and Aquitaine accepted. Phillips was the only producing company that did not do so, choosing to surrender its small field which, it reported, was not 'breaking even'.

The lower postings for high pour-point waxy crude of Mobil and

Gelsenberg, Amoseas, BP and Hunt were eliminated at the same time, so that, in addition to the general increases, these companies raised their posted prices by a further 5 cents/b in the case of Mobil, Gelsenberg, Socal and Texaco, and 7 cents/b for BP and Hunt, who in addition made good a 2 cents freight differential (their oil being shipped at Tobruk, some hundreds of miles east of the other terminals).

Since the retroactive payments for the higher posted price differed between the companies, the agreements incorporated different tax rates. Mobil and Gelsenberg, on account of the retroactive extra 5 cents/b for waxy crude, were obliged to adopt a new tax rate of 55½ per cent. Esso, BP, Hunt, Liamco, Texaco and Socal, 55 per cent; the Oasis Group and Grace, 54 per cent. Aquitaine, whose group included Erap, Murco and Hispanol, opted for cash payment, since they had only recently started producing and their retroactive payments were not large; Amoco (Pan-American) — which was not in a profit situation on its small production of 15,000b/d — did the same, and thus retained the 50 per cent tax rate.

When Occidental had made the Agreement, most of its cut-backs in production were restored — perhaps to encourage the others. However, this favour was not granted to the others when the time came, and they were left protesting and dismayed.

The new base posted price for all Libyan oil thus became $2.53/b for 40° API from 1 September 1970, applied retroactively to 1 January 1965. This was to rise by a further 2 cents/b on 1 January each year for the next five years. The new gravity differentials of 2 cents per degree above 40° and of 1½ cents per degree below 40° raised the price of all oils other than 40° by more than the basic 30 cents/b. The tax rate of profits was raised from 50 per cent to an average of over 54 per cent.

12.3   OPEC and the Tehran Agreement of 14 February 1971

Most other OPEC countries stood aloof while the Libyan negotiations were in progress. OPEC had supported the implementation of the conservation regulation,[14] and no doubt viewed with satisfaction the cut-backs in Libya, which stimulated sharp increases in petroleum prices. Iraq and Algeria alone issued statements supporting the Libyan actions. But when the Libyan settlement was achieved, the breached line of oil company defence became vulnerable everywhere and OPEC countries, both individually and collectively, were not slow to attack.

In November Iran was conceded an increase in profits taxes from 50 per cent to 55 per cent, a rise of 9 cents/b in the posted prices of heavy crudes and an additional annual payment of $125 million. In the same month the oil companies themselves increased posted prices of what had come to be termed the 'short-haul' crudes. The prices of Iraqi and Saudi crudes piped to the Eastern Mediterranean terminals were raised 20 cents/b and of Nigerian 25 cents/b. This move was aimed at re-forming a tenable line by creating a semblance of comparability (in conditions of very high freights) between the prices of short-haul and long-haul crudes delivered in Europe and the USA, as well as between the different short-haul crudes themselves. The 5 per cent increase in tax rates and the price increase of heavier crudes, implemented in Iran, were subsequently offered to the other Gulf States and Nigeria.

Meeting at Caracas on 9-12 December 1970, OPEC passed a resolution aimed at consolidating all these gains. The Resolution, No. XXI. 120, referred in its preamble to the principle 'that the reference price for the purpose of determining the tax liability of the concessionaire companies should be determined by the Governments of member countries'.

It then enumerated under five headings the objectives that all member countries should adopt:

1. To establish 55% as the minimum rate of taxation on the net income of the oil companies . . .
2. To eliminate existing disparities in posted or tax reference prices of the crude oil in member countries on the basis of the highest posted price applicable in the member countries, taking into consideration differences in gravity and geographic location and any appropriation escalation in future years.
3. To establish a uniform general increase in the posted or tax reference prices in all member countries to reflect the general improvement in the conditions of the international petroleum market.
4. To adopt a new system for the adjustment of gravity differential of posted or tax reference prices on the basis of 0.15 cents/b for each 0.1° of gravity for crude oil of 40° and below, and 0.2 cents/b for crude oil of 40.1° and above.
5. To eliminate completely the allowance granted to oil companies as from 1st January, 1971.[15]

The objectives were to be pursued on a regional basis, the Arabian Gulf States comprising one region and being represented in negotiations by

Iran, Iraq and Saudi Arabia. A tight timetable was set for the negotiations, with the threat of unilateral enforcing action if the objectives
were not met.

The OPEC Resolution was also reflected in action by individual
countries. Even before its publication on 28 December, Venezuela
passed laws raising the tax rate from 52 to 60 per cent and giving
the Government the right to raise unilaterally its tax reference
prices.[16] The Franco-Algerian talks bogged down in Algerian demands
for control and massive price increases. Libya itself began again to
attack in early January with a statement that its previous agreement
had been solely a settlement of outstanding matters and did not reflect
recent changes in market conditions. The Government therefore
presented a 'non-negotiable' demand for a further 5 per cent rise in tax
rates and another big price rise.

The oil companies, under the leadership of the majors, and with the
support of their home governments, responded promptly to these
events. The quickness of their reactions was in notable contrast to the
inertia, which, as has already been mentioned, governed their conduct
in considering the representations on posted prices made to them by
the Libyan Government before the revolution. On 16 January 1971,
they delivered to the Governments of the ten OPEC member countries
a message proposing an 'all-embracing negotiation' between themselves
and OPEC countries for the achievement of an 'overall and durable
settlement'. At the same time they made an agreement between themselves, known as the Libyan Producers' Agreement, of 15 January
1971, the gist of which was a commitment to act in concert *vis-à-vis*
the Libyan Government by mutual assistance, to prevent the latter
from forcing further concessions from individual companies by exerting
pressure on them at their weakest point. This agreement, although its
existence became known to the Libyan Government,[17] was kept secret
at the time, and the text was made public only in 1974 when Hunt filed
a claim for damages against Mobil for breaking it.

Both the letter to OPEC countries and the Libyan Producers' Agreement required and obtained clearance from the US Government in the
form of an assurance that it would not take action against the US
signatories for violation of the anti-trust laws.[18] Both documents
were signed eventually by all the companies producing oil in Libya
(including Gelsenberg and Hispanol after the event) except the two
State concerns, Erap and Eni. The message to OPEC was endorsed by
some companies without Libyan interests, making 24 signatories in all;
the Libyan Producers' Agreement was signed by 17 companies.

The message to OPEC countries stated that the companies 'could not negotiate further the development of claims by member countries of Opec on any other basis than one which reaches a settlement simultaneously with all producing governments concerned'. It then proposed the 'broad lines of a settlement', as follows:

A. A revision to the posted prices of all crudes in all member countries of Opec and with provision that the new levels should be subject to a moderate annual adjustment against the yardstick of 'worldwide inflation' or similar criterion.

B. A further temporary transportation adjustment for Libyan crudes, with appropriate adjustments for other 'short-haul' crudes, such adjustments to vary both up and down by reference to a freight escalator.

C. No further increase in the tax rate percentage beyond current rates [sc. 55 per cent], no retroactive payments and no obligatory re-investment.

D. The foregoing all to be firm for a period of five years from the date of settlement, after which the terms would be subject to review.

The aim of the companies to reach a settlement with all the governments concerned simultaneously was a non-starter, since the OPEC Caracas Resolution had already designated concerted negotiations only for the Gulf States, and for other members to act individually. Libya, in fact, declined to accept the letter, or to negotiate with the companies collectively.

Negotiations between the companies and the Gulf States began on 19 January, but, after much haggling, broke down on 2 February. A full OPEC meeting was called on the following day and passed Resolution XXII. 131, which set 15 February as the deadline for agreement with the companies, failing which OPEC members 'shall take appropriate measures including a total embargo on the shipments of crude oil and petroleum products'.

Discusssions were therafter resumed and agreement was reached on 15 February, which became known as the Tehran Agreement. It incorporated the substance of OPEC demands, as listed in Caracas the previous December, as well as most of the safeguards for stability requested by the oil companies in their message of 16 January. The tax rate was stabilised at 55 per cent, and posted prices were raised by 35 cents/b. These posted prices were to be increased by 2½ per cent plus 5 cents/b on the following 1 June, and a further 2½ per cent plus 5 cents/b on 1 January in each of the years 1973-5. The price differentials for different gravities were to be those proposed in the OPEC Caracas Resolution, and there were to be further tidying-up adjustments for claims from individual States in respect of existing posted price disparities. The allowances dating from the OPEC formula of 1964 were to be eliminated immediately.

The companies obtained assurance of stability for the next five years and an undertaking on the part of the Gulf States not to seek further increases in government take during the term of the Agreement if there were to be different terms in other countries (a practice described as 'leap-frogging'); nor to support by action any other state demanding better terms — a measure clearly aimed at Libya. The companies also obtained their objectives of no retroactivity and no obligatory re-investment, since no reference to these was made in the Agreement.

12.4 The Libyan Producers' Agreement and the Tripoli Settlement of 20 March 1971

In the Libyan Producers' Agreement of 15 January 1971, each party to it 'declared its intention not to make any agreement or offer of agreement with the Libyan Government with respect to "government take" as applied to crude oil without the assent of the other parties thereto'. If the Libyan production of any of the parties was further cut back as a result of Libyan Government action, then the other companies which were parties to the Agreement would make good the loss of oil *pro rata* from their Libyan production, or other production if Libyan oil was not available, at cost. The amount of crude oil so supplied would be 100 per cent of the cut-backs in 1971, 80 per cent in 1972 and 60 per cent in 1973.

This Agreement, which was later extended to 1974 and to cover matters other than government take, as will be described below, undoubtedly affected the course of the negotiations in Tripoli which took place during and after the Tehran Agreement. These had begun early in the new year with 'non-negotiable' demands and a refusal to deal with the companies collectively. By late March the discussions in Tripoli were reported to be 'real negotiations, not just re-statements of non-negotiable demands'.[19] The Libyans were dissatisfied with Tehran, both on the grounds of inadequate price increases and because of the value of the short-haul freight premium for Libya quantified and agreed there. On the first count it was pointed out that Libya was taking from the companies royalty oil in kind and selling it at substantially more than posted prices,[20] thus demonstrating that posted prices were too low. On the second, it was widely opined that agreement in Tehran on a Libyan short-haul premium was unwarrantable intervention in Libyan affairs, to achieve an all-embracing solution which the companies wanted but Libya had rejected. Moreover, OPEC support of Libya was limited to the objectives embodied in the Caracas Resolution plus an additional reasonably justified short-haul premium.

The other oil-producing countries with Mediterranean outlets — Iraq, Saudi Arabia and Algeria — agreed to give full support to Libya to negotiate separately with the oil companies operating in Libya.[21] In these negotiations it was reported that

> Libya used to the full her previous tactics of seeking confrontation, attempting to divide the companies from each other and constantly taking negotiations to the brink in order to gain the utmost compromise from the companies. By 2nd April, after several deadlines had passed and talks had climaxed in a last-minute refusal by the Revolutionary Command Council to ratify the agreements negotiated, a settlement was reached.[22]

The settlement was called the Tripoli Agreement of 20 March 1971, and took the form of each company submitting an offer of amendment to its Deeds of Concession which, in the words of the offer, comprised 'one integrated proposal'. The companies would not consent to deviation from the offer in any respect, and thus achieved a united front, even though it was a long way back from their original positions.

The principal headings of the settlement were as follows:[23]

(1) The posted price for 40° crude oil was raised to $3.32/b.
(2) The companies' Concession Deeds, as amended by the proposal, were to continue to be valid.
(3) Profits taxes were to be stabilised at 55 per cent.
(4) The additional surtax rates prescribed in the previous Agreement in lieu of retroactive payments were to be commuted into supplementary per barrel payments equal to what the extra surtax would have been under the previous agreement.
(5) Royalties and taxes were to be paid monthly instead of quarterly, as stipulated in the 1968 Agreement.

Since this arrangement did no more than spread the previous quarterly payment into three equal instalments — one a month in advance, the second at the same time as before and the third a month in arrears, it was purely cosmetic and made no practical difference to these payments.

(6) The allowance embodied in the 1965 Amendment, i.e. the discounts of the OPEC formula, the gravity differential allowance and the marketing expenses allowance of ½cent/b, were to be permanently eliminated. As the first two had been suspended since the Suez Canal was closed in 1967, the marketing expenses allowance of ½cent/b was the only item involved in this.

(7) The companies agreed to provide at cost plus a fee their *pro rata* shares of crude for refining and consumption in Libya. This undertaking was a re-statement of an already existing obligation of concession-holders to provide oil for this purpose 'at field storage price', contained in Article 21 of the original 1955 Petroleum Law, but was hereby deemed by the Government to be extended to include oil refined overseas for Libyan consumption.

(8) During the period from the Operative Date of the proposal to 31 December 1975, the provisions of the companies' concession deeds as amended by the present proposals were to be 'the provisions applicable for determining the total financial obligations in respect of the companies' crude oil'. Accordingly they constituted a final settlement of all subject matters of recent discussion between the Government and the companies and those referred to in past OPEC resolutions. In addition, they constituted, for the period before the Operative Date, a final settlement of all matters concerning posted prices, taxes, claims for retroactivity, methods of payment of royalty and taxes, claims for re-investment undertaking and supply to Government of oil.

The above is a summary of the main proposal. An Annex gave further details of elements in the new posting and future escalations. In this Annex the posting of $3.32 for 40.0° gravity oil was broken down into a Base Posting[24] of $3.07, a Suez Canal allowance of 12 cents and a temporary Freight Premium of 13 cents. The Base Posting was to be increased by 0.2 cents for each full 0.1° of gravity above 40.0°, and decreased by 0.15 cents for each full 0.1° gravity below 40.0°. Libya thus adopted the gravity differential prices embodied in the

OPEC Caracas Resolution and the Tehran Agreement, changing for each one-tenth of a degree, instead of for each one full degree as fixed in the September 1970 Agreement.

The Base Posting itself included, for the first time, a low-sulphur premium of 10 cents/b, applicable as long as sulphur was less than 0.5 per cent by weight of Libyan crude. This sulphur premium was to be increased by 2 cents on 1 January of each of the years 1972-5.

The Base Posting was to be increased by 5 cents/b plus 2½ per cent as from the Operative Date; and was to be further increased by the same amounts on 1 January of each of the years 1973-5. The only difference between this and the Tehran Agreement was the advancing of the first increases from 1 June to 20 March 1971, the Operative Date.

The Suez Canal Allowance would be reduced to 4 cents/b on the first day the Canal was re-opened to ships of 37 feet draft, and eliminated entirely if and when it was open to commercial ships of 38 feet draft, or if the Canal Authority formally announced that the Canal was not to be deepened to a draft of 38 feet.

The Temporary Freight Premium would be varied quarterly by 0.058 cents/b for each 0.1 per cent by which the AFRA LR2 exceeded Worldscale 72 in the previous quarter.[25] A permanent short-haul freight premium was incorporated in the Base Posting. This temporary premium was intended to reflect the excess of current high freight rates over the norm (which was deemed to be WS 72), and would fall when AFRA LR2 fell, as it soon did. Thus a proposal made by the Ministry of Petroleum Affairs in 1967 for the proper implementation of the Petroleum Law provisions that posted prices should include 'necessary adjustments for freight', which had been ignored by the companies at the time, was now introduced.

A final element of the Agreement, which went beyond the Tehran Agreement and was counter to the companies' conditions for a settlement as emunerated in the 16 January letter to OPEC countries, was a commitment to undertake certain minimum exploration activities. This took the form of a 'Note on Expenditure for Exploration' and, unlike the main Agreement, which was in the form of a proposal from each individual company, was a collective undertaking on the part of all the producing companies.

The commitment was that the companies would 'together average [each year of the Agreement] at least one exploration rig in operation on concessions held by them jointly or individually'. If at any time there were no untested proven prospects then an equivalent financial obligation would be undertaken in secondary recovery or gas utilisation.

The total obligation so involved was eight rigs — one each from Esso, Occidental, Mobil/Gelsenberg, BP/Hunt, Oasis and Amoseas in the first place, joined by the Aquitaine Group and Amoco subsequently. The expenditure commitment, although not mentioned in the Note, was reported to be $3.5 million a year for each rig.[26] The Note also refers to carrying out these operations in compliance with the Petroleum Law and Regulation No. 8, thus for the first time explicitly accepting the validity of this Regulation.

It is clear that the companies gave way reluctantly on this principle, although the financial commitment was small in relation to the moneys involved in the main settlement. It may be inferred, from the fact that the commitment was in the form of a Note, and even a Supplement to the Note (about alternative expenditure as above), that it was the subject of last-minute disagreement, and that the companies stead-fastly refused to make any formal money commitment to re-investment. The matter is indicative of the Libyan Government's alarm at the rapid fall in exploration and development, as well as the companies' reluc-tance to commit their free funds to a country which, whatever its oil prospects, did not give them confidence in the future security of their investments.

The posted price of $3.32/b for 40° crude oil determined by the Agreement was at the same time raised to $3.447/b by the imme-diately effective 2½ per cent plus 5 cents/b increase. This compared with the posted price of the Arabian Gulf 'marker' crude — Arabian Light, Ras Tanura, 34° — after the 2½ per cent plus 5 cents/b increase due on 1 June 1977 — of $2.285/b. These prices gave a differential in favour of Libya of $1.162/b, compared with $0.73 after the Sep-tember 1970 Agreement, and $0.43 in the years before this.

Similar Agreements were concluded with Iraq and Saudi Arabia for their Mediterranean oil, and with Nigeria, by the companies concerned; and from the same date Algeria set her tax reference price at $3.35/b, with temporary short-haul and Suez premiums raising this to $3.60/b.

Thereafter the differences between Libyan and Arabian Gulf prices varied as the temporary freight premium changed and the low-sulphur premium for Libyan oil rose by 2 cents a year. The contrast between the price differentials after the Tripoli Agreement and those prevailing before the revolution suggests that Libya's advantages over Arabian Gulf oils in gravity, quality and geographical position had by then been more than adequately recognised in prices. Libya had by now lost the cost advantage which previously she had had in the markets of Europe and North America. By May 1971 it was reported that Middle Eastern oil was 'gaining the edge over Libya in Europe', and that Libyan sales of royalty oil had been 'put out of court',[27] since the Government was selling the oil at prices well below the new posted prices, which is what they would receive from the companies by taking the royalty in cash instead of in kind.

12.5 Currency and Exchange Problems

On 15 August 1971, President Nixon suspended convertibility of the US dollar into gold, and thereafter the value of the dollar depreciated in terms of most of the major currencies of the countries in which Libyan oil was sold. The depreciation became a *de jure* devaluation by the Smithsonian Agreement of 18 December 1971, at which the dollar was devalued by 8.57 per cent in terms of gold, and some other currencies, notably the Yen, Deutschmark, Swiss and Belgian Francs and the Dutch Guilder, were revalued or floated upwards.

Since posted and tax reference prices of oil from all OPEC countries were expressed in terms of US dollars, the members were concerned to protect their oil revenue against losses from the falling value of the dollar. This concern was expressed in Resolution XXV. 140 of 22 September 1971. The steps taken thereafter culminated in the First Geneva Agreement of 20 January 1972, which raised posted prices in the countries which were parties to it by 8.49 per cent. The Agreement was between the Arabian Gulf States and the oil companies who were parties to the previous Tehran Agreement, and was supplemental to and incorporated in it. In addition to the raising of posted prices by a fixed percentage, it provided for further quarterly adjustments, up or down, in line with future variations of the value of the dollar in terms of the other nine currencies of the countries which comprised the 'Group of Ten', who were parties to the Smithsonian Agreement.

In September 1971, the Libyan currency was changed from the pound to the Dinar at par, and at the same time the Libyan Dinar was revalued in terms of the US dollar from the middle rate of $2.80 = LD1 to $2.90. This was done just before the oil companies were due to make large payments to the Libyan Government, and caused confusion about how much payment was due.

Unlike the Middle Eastern concessions, in which payments to government by oil companies were made in dollars or pounds sterling, in Libya all such payments were made in Libyan currency. This had given rise to its own currency conversion problems from the outset.

In 1965 concessionaires had been given a once-for-all choice of applying the IMF par rate for the US dollar ($2.80 = £L1) in converting their accounts into Libyan pounds, or of using a current commercial rate. Later, as part of the 1968 Accelerated Tax Agreement, those who had chosen the former were permitted to switch to the latter method, which was more favourable to them in the event of a depreciating dollar, as well as being more equitable, since the rates used in the accounts would approximate those at which the companies had to buy Libyan pounds for expenses in Libya and payments to government.

By revaluing the new Dinar to $2.90 the Government ensured that the companies should buy at this rate to pay their Dinar dues which had already been calculated in accounts at the $2.80 rate, thus costing them 3½ per cent more in dollars, which would accrue to the Bank of Libya — the sole seller of Libyan currency. On 26 September the Minister of Petroleum ruled that the companies should continue to use the $2.80 rate in their accounts, while at the same time they had to buy Libyan currency at $2.90 or more. This they declined, pointing out that to do so would be contrary to the 1968 Agreement, and they continued to use the (higher) commercial rate in the compilation of their accounts. Towards the end of November the Government attached Esso's bank accounts in Libya and transferred to the Ministry the amounts which were in dispute under this heading (about $900,000). The companies, however, continued to contest the Ministry's ruling.

Libya had remained aloof from the OPEC negotiations, attempting once more to achieve a better result on its own. OPEC's activities, together with the Libyan demand of 26 September, had caused the companies to come together again to extend the Libyan Producers' Agreement of January 1971. By Memorandum of Intent and Confirmation of 18 October 1971, the 'safety net', which had previously been applicable only to cut-backs imposed by the Libyan Government to call the companies to heel on posted prices, was extended to cover similar action to enforce adjustments for currency. The same memoranda applied the measures also to analogous situations with respect to demands for participation, as will be described below.[28]

At the beginning of February 1972, the Libyan Government fixed a new dollar rate of LD1 = $3.04. They thus retained the old parity of the Libyan pound with gold, and revalued it in dollar terms by 8.57 per cent, which was identical with the dollar's devaluation in terms of gold. Whether the companies thereafter accepted this as Libya's action to match the OPEC agreement, and prepared their Libyan accounts at the $2.80 rate is not clear. In any event, a final agreement, again in the form of a proposal for settlement by each company, was reached at the beginning of May containing the same features and effective from the same date as the Geneva Agreement of 20 January. The Libyan Agreement provided for adjustments of accounts and payments already made in respect of 1972 to conform with its terms, which included a guarantee that the companies would be permitted to compile their Libyan accounts at the applicable commercial rate of exchange.[29]

The revaluation of the Libyan Dinar in terms of dollars, taken by itself, had a mixed effect on Libya's dollar earnings and the Government's Dinar revenue from oil. Since oil company revenues were earned and expressed in dollars, the conversion of these revenues into Libyan Dinars at the new rate, both in the books and in transactions, gave a lower value of these revenues in Dinars. The same applies to royalty and tax payments derived from these dollar prices and earnings from oil. The oil companies' Dinar costs and expenses of production, however, if they do not change, require higher dollar remittances to finance them. On the other hand, the overseas part of their production expenses is, like their revenues, translated into Dinars at the new rate in their accounts and, if they do not change, give smaller Dinar amounts than before charged to expenses in the accounts.

Thus the foreign exchange earnings, which accrued to the Bank of Libya, increased — with dollar devaluation but with no change in posted prices — only to the extent that the companies needed to sell more dollars to meet their Libyan costs of production. The Dinar payments to Government fell by the amount of the devaluation of the dollar.[30] In this respect an analogy may be made with a country whose exports are priced in overseas currencies; if the country revalues its currency and the export prices do not change, the country receives the same amount of overseas exchange as before, but the individual exporters receive lower values in their own currency for their exports.

The increase in posted prices compensated for this. It increased Libya's foreign exchange earnings by the extra revenue derived from the higher prices and at the same time restored the Dinar expressions of these earnings to their pre-revaluation level. The only slight discrepancy was that the increase in posted prices was of 8.49 per cent, while the Dinar/dollar revaluation was 8.57 per cent.

A further revaluation of the dollar in terms of gold, amounting to 11.1 per cent, occurred in February 1973, in addition to which other currencies concerned (with the principal exceptions of the UK and Italy) had been revalued or floated upwards, to make an average appreciation of all of them against the US dollar of 22.5 per cent by May

1973 compared with April 1971.[31] OPEC was dissatisfied with the adjustments of the First Geneva Agreement of 20 January 1972, since the formula agreed there did not apply to posted prices the full percentage increases matching the average depreciation of the dollar in terms of other currencies. This was rectified in the Second Geneva Agreement between the same parties as the first, dated 1 June 1973. It specified new posted prices higher than before by approximately 12 per cent, applicable to second quarter 1973 operations, and made provisions for future changes to meet the requirements of OPEC members to obtain full compensation in posted prices for future changes in the value of the dollar.

The Second Geneva Agreement was, like the first, tied into the Tehran Agreement as an amending supplement to it. Libya signed a separate Agreement with its oil companies — as was necessary, since it had to be supplementary to the Tripoli Settlement and the First Libyan Currency Settlement. On this occasion, however, it was identical with the Geneva Agreement, *mutatis mutandis*, and signed by the Minister of Petroleum in Geneva on the same day as the other, but with a clause that an Arabic text would also be signed by Libya and the company.

Thus OPEC countries, including Libya, had both inflation and dollar depreciation escalation factors built into their posted prices until the end of 1975. These were soon to be superseded by new and more radical alterations in the structure of the industry.

12.6 The End of Price Negotiations — Autumn 1973

The events of the international oil industry between June and December 1973 have been recorded elsewhere, and will be briefly summarised below. Libya did not set the pace in this period, which was marked by the end of negotiations on prices with the oil companies, and the assumption by OPEC and its members of complete control over the setting of prices for their oil exports. In the years 1970 to 1972 Libya had shown other members of OPEC what could be obtained from the companies in negotiation when adequate pressures were brought to bear, and OPEC had learned its lessons. Now, when OPEC took the power of price-setting altogether from the oil companies and into its own hands, Libya's policies, after a period of trial and error, became directed towards keeping its oil prices competitive with those of other oil-exporting countries in the markets of the world. It was able to express its views in OPEC's deliberations, which resulted in price decisions and co-ordination between OPEC members, and then to pursue its own pricing policies to achieve its desired levels of oil sales in this context. This period was also marked by moves towards participation and nationalisation, which will be described in the next section of this chapter.

During the first nine months of 1973, the oil importing countries saw themselves in the midst of crisis, as both they and the exporting countries struggled to adjust to the new situation created by the price and participation agreements, by rapidly changing market conditions, as each of the oil companies attempted to secure its own supplies, and by continued monetary instability and inflation.[32]

In spite of the rises in the cost of oil to the oil companies, they were seen to be increasing their margins to an unprecedented extent, particularly the majors, with the result that OPEC countries perceived themselves as obtaining a much reduced share of oil profits than that envisaged in the Tehran, Tripoli and Geneva Agreements.

Negotiations between the OPEC Gulf States and the oil companies to revise the Tehran Agreement began on 8 October — two days after the outbreak of hostilities between Israel and Egypt. On 12 October the oil companies asked for an adjournment for inevitable consultation, co-ordination and clearance, and on 16 October the OPEC Gulf States issued the communiqué which marked the end of price negotiations with oil companies.

The communiqué stated that these six Gulf members 'decided to . . . establish and announce the posted prices of crude in the Gulf', which were to be 'based on actual market prices'. The actual market prices would 'from that day on determine corresponding posted prices, keeping the same relationship between prices as existed in 1971 before the Tehran Agreement [sc. 1.4:1] . . . The corresponding market price for Arabian Light crude is hereby established and announced at $3.65', which 'represents only a 17% increase over the actual sale of the same crude recently'. The sulphur premium was to be determined individually by member states, the Geneva Agreement was to continue in force, and in the case of oil company refusal to take crude on the new basis, the producing countries would make it available to any buyer at prices computed on the basis of the 'marker' crude.

The new posted prices were 70 per cent above the old. But this proved to be only the prelude to a larger increase. As a result of the cut-backs on production and embargoes on oil shipments to the USA and the Netherlands imposed by the Arab States on 27 October, oil was sold at auctions by the Iranians at $17/b, and by Nigeria and Libya at over $20/b — mostly to American independents. On 23 December the OPEC Gulf States announced their decision to increase posted prices in such a way as to yield a government take of $7/b. This resulted in a posting for the Arabian Light 34°, which was the marker crude, of $11.651/b, as from 1 January 1974.

It also resulted in the fiction of profit-sharing, which had been adopted in the early 1950s, being abandoned. It was a return in concept to the old royalty agreement — of a fixed take per barrel for the government of the host country. The difference now was that, instead of being negotiated (some might say imposed) by the oil companies, it was decided upon by the oil-producing country governments. And instead of being 4 shillings (gold) per ton as in the original Iraqi Concession of 1925, it was $7 a barrel. This was approximately a fivefold increase in terms of gold and fiftyfold in terms of dollars.

Libyan posted prices were changed to accord with the change in the marker crude price, with adjustments for freight and low-sulphur premium. Libyan crude of 40° rose from $4.604/b at the beginning of October 1973 to $8.925 on 19 October and to $15.768 on 1 January 1974. The relationship with the marker crude prices of the last two postings were as follows:

	19 Oct. 1973 $	1 Jan. 1974 $
Posted price, Arabian light 34°, Ras Tanura	5.119	11.651
Gravity differential	0.120 (2¢/1°)	0.360 (6¢/1°)
Permanent freight differential	1.740	1.811
Low-sulphur premium	1.336	1.336
Suez Canal premium	0.152	0.152
Temporary freight premium	0.458	0.458
Posted price, Libyan 40°	$8.925	$15.768

The low-sulphur premium was determined by the Libyan Government, as proposed in the Gulf States' communiqué of 16 October, and was increased by $1.196 from the previous level of 14 cents/b. The gravity differential applied for 1974 was 6 cents per degree below as well as above 40°, although the Gulf States decided only to double existing gravity differentials from 1½ to 3 cents per degree below 40°, and from 3 to 6 cents per degree above 40°.[33] In other respects the rationale of the elements in the new postings was based on the principles of the Tehran, Tripoli and Geneva Agreements.

12.7 The Nationalisation of BP and N.B. Hunt

Quite soon after the revolution in Libya, rumours of impending nationalisation were widespread, and they grew after the nationalisation of distribution and marketing of oil products in Libya on 4 July 1970. But nothing further occurred until, quite suddenly, BP was nationalized on 7 December 1971, by decision of the RCC. This was done in retaliation for Britain's failure to act to prevent Iran's seizure of the Tumb islands in the Arabian Gulf.[34]

The nationalisation decision included provisions for compensation to be fixed by a 3-man committee set up under the chairmanship of a Counsellor of the Libyan Courts of Appeal whose decision would be final. BP was prevented from loading oil at Harega terminal, but N.B. Hunt, its 50 per cent partner (but not operator) in the Sarir field of Concession 65 — total production of which at the time was about 430,000 b/d of high-pour crude — was unaffected. Other oil companies' production was frozen at existing levels so as not to supply BP. The latter's personnel were ordered to stay in their posts, and Libyans were drafted in from other companies, which were to continue to pay them. The decision established the 'Arab Gulf Exploration Company (INJAZ)', a subsidiary of the NOC, to take over the assets and business of BP.

BP 'reserved its rights' and formally invoked arbitration under the provisions of the Petroleum Law. This was not responded to by the Libyan Government, although the Law required it. The UK Government approached governments of other OECD countries with requests not to abet Libya in moving BP's oil. Thereafter BP initiated a number of proceedings in various courts for attachment of cargoes of crude oil from the Sarir field shipped by Injaz. The first of these was in January 1972, at Syracuse, for oil which had been shipped by the National Oil Company to Sincat as part of a processing deal, the products being returned to Libya for marketing. It was not successful, but the fact that title to such oil was disputed deterred buyers and depressed prices which Libya could obtain for it in the markets.

The Libyan Producers' Agreement (see section 12.4) had been extended, in October 1971, to ensure collective action by the parties to it in matters concerning participation demands, as well as those connected with claims of OPEC members to offset depreciation of the dollar. On 16 December 1971 the companies concerned signed a 'Further Memorandum of Confirmation' to the effect that there came 'within the purview' of the original Agreement the

> total or partial nationalization of the properties of any party hereto by the Libyan Government in contravention or breach of the applicable provisions of the Petroleum Law or the terms of any of the concession agreements of such party (including the action by the Libyan Government by decree dated 7th December, 1971, with respect to the properties of BP Exploration Company (Libya) Limited in Concession 65).

N.B. Hunt was a party to this Agreement, and since it sold much of its oil to BP it found itself in an invidious position, particularly in respect of the Libyan ban on companies increasing production to make good BP's loss. A few days after the seizure Hunt's allowable was fixed at 228,000 b/d (compared with its own exports averaging 160,000 b/d in the first half of 1971, the remainder having been sold to BP). In May 1972 this was cut to 150,000 b/d, and in June further still, so that Hunt was unable to fulfil all his sales contracts.[35] In October 1972 Hunt received a demand from the Government for a half-share of all oil sold by him since the nationalisation of BP, and a 50 per cent State participation thereafter (this was at the time of pressure on other companies for 50 per cent State participation). This demand was accompanied by a ban on Hunt's exports which lasted until January 1973, when liftings were resumed.

In June 1973, following Hunt's refusal to accept participation terms and to market BP's (now Injaz's) share of Sarir crude, his interest was nationalised. This action was described by Col. Qadhafi as a 'slap in the face' for the USA for its support of Israel. The subsequent suit filed by Hunt in April 1974, in the US District Court of Alexandria, Va., against Mobil and other oil companies for breach of contract of the Libyan Producers' Agreements brought these Agreements to publication.

BP, as well as pursuing claims for its oil through the courts whenever it could (much of the oil went to Eastern Europe,[36] where it was safe from pursuit, even if it returned to Western Europe from there, as some of it did) also initiated arbitration proceedings against the takeover in the International Court of Justice. This the company was entitled to do under Clause 28 of its Concession Agreement, since the

Libyan Government had not responded to its request for arbitration. In October 1973, the sole arbitrator appointed by the President of the International Court in accordance with the provisions of the Concession Deed — Gunnar Lagergren, a Swedish judge — delivered judgement. It was to the effect that the nationalisation of BP's interests in Concession 65 had been a clear violation of international law, made 'for purely extraneous political reasons, and was arbitrary and discriminatory in character'. The fact that, after two years, no compensation had been offered 'indicates that the taking was confiscatory'.

In November 1974, the Libyan Government reached a full and final settlement with BP, whereby the latter received a net payment of £17.4 millions. This represented £62.4 millions compensation for the value of the assets seized, less £45 millions retroactive payments assessed as due from BP according to the terms of the posted price agreement of October 1970.[37]

N.B. Hunt, two months before its nationalisation, had initiated arbitration on the points at issue, and the Libyan Government — for the first time — accepted to arbitrate. After the nationalisation, and the International Court's sole arbitrator's judgement in the BP case, the Government cancelled the arbitration. Hunt pursued claims to his oil in various courts, and claims against the Libyan producers for breach of contract, as mentioned above.[38] In September 1975 Hunt came to an agreement with the Libyan Government by which he received an undisclosed sum of money. He announced that after that date he had no further rights in his concession or the oil from it, but that cases initiated prior to the settlement would continue.[39]

12.8 General Participation/Nationalisation

There is no clear dividing line between nationalisation and participation, nor between their connotations as defined in this work. Here nationalisation will be taken to mean compulsory acquisition of part or all of an oil company's business by the Government, and participation will refer to negotiated joint ventures, production-sharing, service contracts and other forms of co-operation between Government and company. The distinction is blurred when Government participation is forced on a company under pressure, and the company acquiesces either at the time or subsequently. These cases will be classified here as nationalisation.

The quest for and negotiations on government participation in existing concessions by OPEC countries generally began in earnest in

1968, when Sheikh Zaki Yamani of Saudi Arabia referred the matter to OPEC, after some years of representations to the oil companies had proved fruitless. In Resolution No. XVI.90 of 25 June 1968, OPEC declared that in existing conventional concessions, if they do not provide for Government participation, 'the government may acquire a reasonable participation, on the grounds of the principle of changing circumstances.'

In June 1971 OPEC set up a Ministerial committee,[40] consisting of the Oil Ministers of Iran, Kuwait, Saudi Arabia and Libya 'to draw up the basis for the implementation of effective participation by member countries'. The Committee recommended that participation should be implemented, without committing itself to a precise percentage figure, that compensation should be at net book value, and the companies should be obliged to buy back participation oil to the extent required by governments.

The principal negotiations for participation were conducted between Saudi Arabia, represented by Sheikh Yamani, and Aramco, in which Exxon, Texaco, Socal and Mobil were partners. Agreement was reached at the end of 1972, and provided for 25 per cent government participation at the beginning of 1973 to rise in steps to 51 per cent by January 1982.[41] Compensation was to be assessed at updated book value, which envisaged an element of revaluation of assets for inflation. The companies agreed to buy back government crude in 3 categories — (1) bridging crude, to enable the companies to fulfil their existing commitments; (2) phase-in crude, which the companies were obligated to purchase from the Government; and (3) crude at government disposition, which was to rise from 10 per cent of total in 1973 to 30 per cent in 1976.

The Agreement was offered by the companies to Abu Dhabi, Kuwait and Qatar, but only Abu Dhabi accepted. It was not long before its terms — negotiated with the companies, and in retrospect moderate — were overtaken by events in other countries, not least in Libya; participation soon became subject to the 'leap-frogging' already manifested in prices and, being negotiated under duress, became indistinguishable from compulsory nationalisation.

After the establishment by OPEC of the Ministerial committee on participation, Libya, together with Nigeria, announced that they intended 'to pursue negotiations for participation with their concessionaires on an individual basis'.[42] Apart from the BP nationalisation — which is in a different category — the first agreement on participation in an existing concession was with the Italian Eni and its subsidiary, Agip. Agip had developed the Bu Ateiffel field in Concession No. 100, with an ultimate potential of some 300,000 b/d, but it was shut in by Ministry order, which insisted on satisfactory utilisation of associated gas. In September 1972, after two years of desultory negotiations, Eni proposed 50 per cent State participation to combine with its already existing joint venture, where there had been 43 wells drilled resulting in 8 non-commercial discoveries, and also with Concession 82, on exploration in which another Eni subsidiary — Cori — had spent some $40 millions without success.

This was accepted by the Libyan Government, who thereby acquired a 50 per cent interest in Concessions 100 and 82. The terms were[43] that the Government would pay in cash 50 per cent of approved expenditure already incurred in Concession 100. This was agreed at $62.4m to be paid over 5 years. The output target for the Bu Ateiffel field for 1973 was put at 200,000 b/d. There was to be a management committee of 3 Italians and 3 Libyans, the Chairman being Libyan and the Managing Director Italian. An advantage to Agip of getting Bu Ateiffel into operation was that it would be enabled under the Petroleum Law to amortise its unproductive exploration expenditure in Concession 82 amounting to $40 millions against the earnings from oil from Bu Ateiffel at the rate of 5 per cent p.a. There had been an arrangement for some time with Occidental for Agip to pipe its gas in a separate line from Concession 100 to Occidental's Concession 103A, where it would be processed at the gas plant and the liquids go forward by the latter's pipeline to the coast. The putting into operation of this project had been prevented for some time by cutbacks on Occidental's production from 103A. Cori's Concession No. 82, dating from 1959, was unique in that it incorporated an offer by the concessionaire of a 30 per cent State 'carried' interest in the event of development and production.

Immediately after the Agip participation agreement, N.B. Hunt received a similar demand — for 50 per cent government participation plus 50 per cent of all income from oil sold by Hunt since the BP nationalisation 10 months earlier. Hunt did not respond and his exports of oil were embargoed. At the same time it was made clear by the Government that general 50 per cent State participation was 'not negotiable', and was a preliminary step to a greater portion being acquired by the State later; and that such participation would apply only to profitable concessions.

In December 1972, Occidental's allowables were once more cut — to 360,000 b/d. During the early months of 1973 negotiations with companies took place in which the Libyans proposed 50 per cent take-overs at net book value, and buy-back of Government oil so acquired at a price half-way between posted price and tax-paid cost to the companies. In May it was reported that 100 per cent national-isation was being demanded, but Colonel Qadhafi expressed himself against it in an interview with a Beirut newspaper.[44] In the same month the Government requested the companies to make their own proposals along the lines of the service contracts/production-sharing arrangements similar to the new arrangements in Iran and elsewhere. This was followed by a one-day stoppage of loadings as a protest at the situation in the Middle East.

Early in June 1973, Hunt's production, which had re-started in January, was stopped once more, and two shipments already loaded pre-vented from leaving. The pretext for this action was Hunt's refusal (a) to accept participation terms, and (b) to market BP's Sarir crude. This action was followed by the nationalisation of Hunt's assets and business.

In August Major Jalloud intervened as leader of the Libyan side in the participation negotiations and immediately made it clear that 51 per cent was demanded by the Government at net book value. On 11 August the Government decreed a partial nationalisation of Occidental, and the company formally signified its acquiescence. Immediately afterwards, Oasis was subjected to similar treatment — 51 per cent nationalisation and compensation at net book value. Continental, Marathon and Amerada, the concession-holders who between them owned $83\frac{1}{3}$ of Oasis, acquiesced, but Shell, who owned the remaining $16\frac{2}{3}$ per cent, did not. Shell's decision not to do so was undoubtedly influenced not only by its involvement in the much milder Middle East participation settlements, but also by its position in Nigeria, where it was bound to a most-favoured-African-nation clause in its concession. Shell's liftings of oil were embargoed from 12 August. The Oasis settlement also included a company undertaking to maintain three rigs in operation in Libya.

Having achieved 51 per cent participation in the operations of the leading independents, the Government turned to the majors. Amoseas — the operating company of Texaco and Socal — almost immediately had its allowable production cut by 50 per cent to 100,000 b/d, and at the same time strong pressures were put on all the majors to acquiesce in nationalisation on similar terms. They were placed in a dilemma similar to that of Shell — acquiescence would prejudice their Middle East settlements, refusal would be likely to result in total shut-down of their Libyan operations.

The general nationalisation decree of 51 per cent of the assets and business of the producing majors came, as expected, on the fourth anniversary of the revolution — 1 September 1973. It comprised all the producing majors — Esso, Mobil, Texaco and Socal — and their partners — Liamco (Arco), Grace and Gelsenberg. By the same decree Shell was 'considered' to be a party to the Agreement with the other Oasis companies.

All the nationalisation decrees (or Laws as they were officially termed) comprised similar provisions.[45] They took 51 per cent of the assets and business of the companies concerned for the Government, with the exception of Esso's gas liquefaction plant. Compensation was to be decided by a committee of three, headed by a Justice of the Courts of Appeal and including NOC and Treasury representatives; the companies were to continue to operate in the concessions under a management committee of three appointed by the Minister of Petroleum, two of whom, including the chairman, were to be Libyans, the third the resident manager of the operating company; all employees of the companies, regardless of nationality, were to continue at their posts; the parties were to make arrangements within a month for the lifting of the NOC's share, including the quantities and prices involved. Fines and/or imprisonment were stipulated for offences in contravention of the terms of the decree.

On the promulgation of the nationalisation decree the majors immediately protested and gave formal notice of arbitration under the terms of the Petroleum Law. No arrangements were made about the shipping of the NOC's share of oil as specified in the decree, but the companies were not restrained from lifting and continued to do so without interference. It was intimated to them in the middle of September that if they did not pursue lawsuits they would be permitted to continue. This would not, of course, affect the ultimate prices and ownership of the oil lifted in accordance with the nationalisation decree, which would be determined retroactively when final settlement was reached.

In the middle of September Occidental was allowed to increase its production to 475,000 b/d. With a stipulated buy-back price of $4.90/b for its nationalised oil — which seemed high at the time — and with market prices soaring once more as a result of events in Libya, Occidental claimed that it was making as much money with a 49 per cent share as it had previously done with 100 per cent of its concessions.[46] By the end of September it was reported that Libyan crude was being sold for $5.50/b and there were rumours that Occidental's high-gravity oil was fetching $5.85-$5.90/b. The economics of participation were already looking more tolerable to the majors. As well as this, their dilemma was resolving itself to the extent that Abu Dhabi, which had accepted the Saudi settlements, at this time announced that it would seek a 51 per cent interest in its concessions before 1982, and Kuwait, which had not, was already demanding the same proportion.

Before 1 October, which was stipulated as the date by which agreements on prices and production of the nationalised oil were to be reached, Gelsenberg and Grace acquiesced in the nationalisation decree. The majors did not, and were compelled to load participation oil at their terminals. They proceeded to place advertisements in newspapers asserting their ownership of oil so shipped and their intention to lay claim to it.

The events which followed occurred in the context of the Egyptian-Israeli October war, the embargoes on oil imposed by the Arab States and the great price rises of the last quarter of 1973. Libya decreed a 5 per cent reduction in production and banned shipments to the USA before the end of October. Iraq, which had already nationalised the Iraq Petroleum Company in June 1972, proceeded to do the same to the US and Dutch (60 per cent of Shell) interests in the Basrah Petroleum Company. In November Sheikh Yamani joined the demand for higher percentage participation, saying that 51 per cent was not adequate. In February 1974 Kuwait reached an agreement with its concessionaires — BP and Gulf — to take over a 60 per cent interest in the concessions, and later in the month Qatar followed suit. In July Saudi Arabia made a similar interim arrangement, to operate from the beginning of the year.

Until February 1974 the majors had been continuing to lift their Libyan oil as fast as they could, and to pay Government dues on the old concession basis. In the middle of February the Libyan Government seized the Amoseas operation (Texaco and Socal) and the Liamco (Arco) share of Esso Sirte (25.5 per cent) as a reply to President Nixon's call for the Washington Energy Conference. In the middle of March Mobil acquiesced in its 51 per cent nationalisation and Esso signified its willingness to do the same if the gas liquefaction plant were included (which would involve large compensation, the great expense of construction being of recent date). At the beginning of April the Government seized the Shell 16.7 per cent interest in Oasis, bringing its total interest in this partnership operation to 59.16 per cent. In the middle of the month Esso acquiesced in 51 per cent nationalisation (which excluded the gas plant). At the same time both Esso and Mobil entered into production-sharing arrangements with new acreage, which will be described in the next section.

The 51 per cent nationalisation of Esso marked the end of the period of State acquisition of interests in producing concessions, with the exception of the Elf-Aquitaine joint venture, which began production in February 1975 and continued at a level of some 10,000 b/d. This was converted from the original joint-venture terms of 1968 to an 85-15 production-sharing deal along the lines then devised in April 1974, together with off-shore Concession No. 137 on an 81-19 per cent sharing basis.

By 1975 the State had acquired 100 per cent of BP-N.B. Hunt's Sarir field in Concession 65, and of Amoseas' (Texaco-Socal's) production from all its fields, also 59.16 per cent of all Oasis operations and 51 per cent of Esso Standard, Occidental and Mobil/Gelsenberg. Esso Sirte's operations were acquired up to 63.5 per cent by virtue of 100 per cent nationalisation of Liamco's 25.5 per cent interest and 51 per cent of the remainder belonging to Esso (50 per cent) and Grace (24.5 per cent). Agip handed over to the State 50 per cent of its operations in Concession 100 by agreement and in 1974 Elf/Aquitaine converted their joint venture so as to give the State an 85 per cent share of production. Of the producing concessions only the Aquitaine-operated fields in Concessions 104 and 105 (which included Erap, Hispanol and Murco as partners) and Amoco's small production in Concession 95 remained untouched[47] (see Table 13.1, p. 274).

The State's share of total Libyan production in 1975 of 1.5 mb/d and in 1976 of 1.9 mb/d amounted to 64 per cent, excluding royalty oil. The Libyan Oil Minister, Izzedin al Mabruk, who had held this position since the beginning of 1970, is reported to have expressed the view, in May 1975, that circumstances were not right in the world oil picture to continue nationalisation

> beyond the 51 per cent acquired in 1973. With 51 per cent we have effective control of production and prices — what more do we need? We can operate the fields, but we need the companies for marketing in a situation of sagging demand, and for new investment and expertise in wildcat exploration.[48]

Shell reached an accord with the Government on compensation for nationalisation in June 1974. The agreement provided for payment in oil at a rate of 40,000 b/d and for liftings by Shell of the NOC's oil at a discounted price. Thereupon Shell dropped all legal complaints against the Government.[49]

The full amount of the compensation was no doubt the book value of Shell's share of Oasis' net assets, as was that to Continental, Marathon and Amerada, there being variation between the concession-holders according to the companies' amortisation and depreciation practices in the early days. Amerada had received $19.4 million compensation, Conoco and Marathon $42.5 million each.[50] Towards the end of 1977 Texaco and Socal reached a settlement on their nationalisation, which amounted to $76 million payable in oil over 15 months.[51]

12.9   Production-Sharing Joint Ventures

Within six months of its 51 per cent nationalisation, Occidental signed a production-sharing agreement with the Libyan NOC covering 21 widely spread areas of new land. It was described as a 'pace-maker' for several other similar ventures that followed. The principal provisions of the agreement of February 1974 — when the nationalisation battle with the majors was still raging — were that Occidental undertook to spend $90 millions on exploration in the new areas and would be entitled to 19 per cent of the oil produced from them, free of Libyan taxes and royalties. The NOC (Linoco) would pay to Occidental its own 81 per cent share of development costs, but would be reimbursed for this at a rate of 5 per cent p.a. interest-free after oil exports from the areas allocated reached 100 million barrels.

This and the agreements that followed demonstrated the Libyan Government's method of tackling the problem of dwindling exploration and development — a problem which had been growing ever since the early days of the revolution, when the companies' confidence in the security of their investments and operations in Libya started to be impaired.

This production-sharing agreement was quickly followed by others, which were agreed in principle in April 1974, and signed in the following October. The Agreements so concluded were with Exxon, Mobil (later joined by Gelsenberg), CFP, Elf-Aquitaine and Agip. In essence they were similar to each other and to the Occidental venture. They all provided for production-sharing between the NOC and the company in the ratio of 85:15 on-shore and 81:19 off-shore. The company expenditure commitment on exploration was $90 millions over six years for Esso, $70 millions over five years for CFP, $45 millions over four years for Elf/Aquitaine and $82 millions over five years for Agip. The NOC was to provide its share proportion of development costs on-shore and 50 per cent of them for off-shore development. These would be reimbursable to the NOC by the company at a rate of 5 per cent a year beginning after three years of exports or 80 million barrels. Most of the outstanding amounts on this account were to carry interest at 1 per cent under a commercial rate, but some, like Occidental's, were interest-free.

It is not easy to quantify the expected profitability to the companies of these agreements, made at a time of great disturbance in the oil companies' command over their oil resources, of volatility in price levels and uncertainty about their future course, together with escalating exploration and development costs, royalty and tax rates. It is, however, clear that to establish title to even 15 per cent of oil reserves established through their exploration commitment, at cost and free of taxes and royalties, would be of substantial benefit. Their outlay on drilling and other development expenses — which normally comprise far the greatest part of costs of production — was limited in the early stages to their own share entitlement. The obtaining of this entitlement free of tax and royalty would go a long way towards paying back the whole of their costs of exploration, development and operations before a total production of 80 million barrels was reached.

After this the cash payment to the NOC of the latter's share of development costs at 5 per cent p.a. would be nearly treble their depreciation charges at 10 per cent p.a. for their own development costs. Even in the 1960s under the 1965 Petroleum Law Government take per barrel on the most profitable concessions had been more than three times operational costs per barrel, while at the time of the signing of these ventures it was between 10 and 20 times the per barrel cost of production of those parts of the old concessions left to the concessionaires. Thus even after the initial period the economics of the operation were highly attractive to the companies, provided that the large outlays on exploration were successful in establishing good oilfields. It is not surprising that Occidental requested the Libyan Government in May 1975 to take over 100 per cent of its remaining conventional concessions and allow the company to operate them on a per barrel fee basis. The request was not granted. This 'service contract' type of arrangement has certain affinities to the production-sharing ventures, the difference being that in the former the company is reimbursed in money and in the latter with oil. In fact this might be termed royalty in cash or kind, the roles of the company and the Government having been reversed from the traditional concession — both in the matter of payment of royalties and in management control of the operation.

The companies, in venturing on these new-style deals, had the political risks to consider, particularly since they were made at a time when, within the past year, the Government had seized control of pricing, royalty and tax rates and majority interests, including management control, of existing concessions. In brief, it had demonstrated again and again that the original concession contract was worthless. What then were the chances of survival of any new contract beyond the time when it would suit the Government to abrogate or force changes in its terms?

Such a question is not possible to answer. The oil companies concerned in these ventures protected themselves from exposure to excessive losses by limiting their development expenditure to 15 per cent of the total for any field. The exploration commitment was at risk in any case, but was the easier to incorporate in their world-wide exploration budgets since these were relieved of much of their previous burdens because of the nationalisations which had already taken place and were continuing to do so. The drive of the companies to secure long-range supplies of oil was undiminished, and over-rode the fears of further harassment if the ventures were commercially successful.

Only majors and State oil enterprises entered into these ventures (CFP may be classified under both these headings and Gelsenberg had always been associated with Mobil in Libya), by virtue of the fact that they had the financial strength, or access to financial resources, to accept the large exploration risks and expenditures involved. Towards the end of 1976 BP also intimated that it would consider entering into a service contract arrangement with the Libyan Government, its dispute over the 1971 nationalisation having been settled in 1974. Early in 1976 Elf/Aquitaine took in as partners two other companies with State backing in their own countries — Austria's OMV (15 per cent) and West Germany's Wintershall (10 per cent) — and thereby spread their exploration commitment of $45 million in four years over a wider base.[52]

On the Libyan side, the agreements provided a satisfactory answer to the problem of stimulating exploration by using the large funds, the high technical skills and expertise in execution which the oil companies possessed, and by giving them strong incentives to achieve success. The large investments required by the NOC in case of development were by no means beyond the financial capacity of the State. In addition to the pay-back of these investments from the NOC's share of production, they would be recouped from the oil company partners over 20 years in case of establishment of sizeable fields. By 1976 Occidental had made two discoveries in the areas covered by its production-sharing agreement, at depths of less than 4,000 feet and within five kilometres of existing pipelines. These were expected to come into production before the end of the year.[53]

Notes

1. *Middle East Economic Survey*, 19 Sept. 1969.

2. The new Oil Minister, Ess. Anis Shtaiwi, who had previously worked as a petroleum engineer with Oasis, made these comments. He was also Minister of Labour and Social Affairs. In this latter capacity he was responsible for implementing an early decision of the Council of Ministers to double all wages of workers and to abolish 'trafficking in the supply of labour'. This latter referred to the system by which contractors provided labour to the oil companies and their contractors for projects, such as the pipelines, gas liquefaction plant and terminal facilities at Brega (*Middle East Economic Survey*, 31 Oct. 1969).

The sequence of events delineated in the following pages was fully reported in the contemporary issues of journals dealing with the international petroleum industry, particularly *Petroleum Intelligence Weekly* and *Middle East Economic Survey*. Separate note references for each single event are not always necessary, and will be given in this section only when identification of source is of significance.

3. *Al Thaurah*, 23 Dec. 1969, quoted in S.M. Ghanem, *The Pricing of Libyan Crude Oil* (Adams Publishing House, Malta, 1975), p. 148.

4. Ghanem, *Pricing of Libyan Crude Oil*, p. 150.

5. Concession Deed, Clause 1, and Petroleum Regulation No. 3, Article 1.

6. *Petroleum Intelligence Weekly*, 25 May 1970; Occidental published this from a report prepared for them by the oilfield consultants De Golyer & McNaughton.

7. *Petroleum Intelligence Weekly*, 18 May 1970.

8. *Petroleum Intelligence Weekly*, 10 Aug. 1971.

9. In September 1975, when further demands were made on Occidental, supported by a complete stoppage of production, the company published its reply to the Libyan Government which stated that the production restrictions 'followed a continued pattern of arbitrary action by the Government to restrict drastically Occidental's production and then restore it once the demands have been met under duress'. It cited the 1970 events as an example, adding that in each case of production restriction 'there was no technical basis for the cut-backs', and that the Government 'by its own action in restoring production when it had secured the acquiescence it desired proved that it had been arbitrary in imposing the cut-backs'.

However, Armand Hammer, Head of Occidental, in the BBC television programme 'Tonight', transmitted on 1 December 1978, referred to his dealings with Major Jalloud in 1970, and to saying to him during the negotiations that it was not reasonable for the company to pay the Libyan Government an extra 20 cents/b tax in view of the high prices which oil commanded in markets around the world.

10. A review of operations of the seven major international oil companies published by the First National City Bank in March 1971 showed that their net earnings in the Eastern Hemisphere rose 7 per cent in 1970 over those for 1969, in spite of the fact that payments to host governments in 1970 rose to 72 per cent

of net earnings compared with 70 per cent and were 19 per cent higher than in the previous year.

In the same year – 1970 – mainly US domestic oil company profits fell by over 8 per cent (*Petroleum Intelligence Weekly*, 8 Feb. 1971). Continental's net income rose nearly 10 per cent and it had 'substantially' increased earnings in the Eastern Hemisphere (mostly from Libyan oil). Marathon, however, suffered a fall in profits of 5 per cent from its combined US and Eastern Hemisphere operations. It is probable that for all companies with Libyan interests the net earnings were struck after provisions for the greater part of the large retroactive payments involved in the Agreements with the Libyan Government.

11.   The generalised Agreement, later accepted by the other producing oil companies, and couched in terms of an 'offer' by the companies, was published by the Arabian Gulf Exploration Company in *Petroleum Agreements* (Benghazi, January 1973). This company – whose acronym was Injaz – was formed by the Libyan Government to take over the business of BP, nationalised on 7 December 1971. The Agreement is reproduced in Ghanem, *Pricing of Libyan Crude Oil*, p. 302.

12.   The years before 1965 were exempted because of the quittance on posted prices contained in the 1965 Law and amended concession Deeds, which in 1970 was honoured by the Government.

13.   Amerada had merged with Hess – a major distributor and refiner on the US Eastern Seaboard – in 1969. Shell had acquired one-half of Amerada's one-third interest in Oasis in 1966.

14.   Resolution XIX. 110, 16 December 1969.

15.   This referred to the discounts, gravity differential allowances and marketing expenses (0.5 cents/b) written into the 'OPEC formula' Agreement of 1964.

16. C. Tugendhat and A. Hamilton, *Oil – the Biggest Business*, rev. edn (Eyre Methuen, London, 1975), p. 186.

17.   See *Petroleum Intelligence Weekly* special supplement on this subject (6 May 1974).

18.   Testimony of James Akins, Director of Office of Fuels and Energy, US Department of State, before the US Senate Foreign Relations Sub-Committee on Multinational Companies, 1974.

19.   *Petroleum Intelligence Weekly*, 15 Mar. 1971. It was also reported in the same issue that the companies were preparing for a Libyan shut-down, if necessary.

·20.   *Petroleum Intelligence Weekly*, 18 Jan. 1971, reported that a Swiss brokerage firm, 'Perola, S.A.', had bought 5 million tons of Libyan royalty oil, some at $2.90/b (cf posted price $2.55), and that Libya had now placed 213,000 b/d of royalty oil – about 57 per cent of its royalty entitlement.

21.   Joint communiqué issued after a meeting of the oil Ministers of these countries at Tripoli, on 23 February 1971. The next day Algeria nationalised 51 per cent of its oil companies and all pipelines – see Ghanem, *Pricing of Libyan Crude Oil*, p. 175.

22.   Tugendhat and Hamilton, *Oil*, p. 193.

23.   The full text of the Agreement was published in 1973 by the Arabian Gulf Exploration Company – see note 11 of this chapter.

24.   A façade of making the same basic posted price increase as in the Tehran Agreement was maintained by expressing the new Libyan posted price as consisting of:

Posted price as in September 1970, 40°:	$2.55 ($2.53 + 2¢ on 1.1.71)
Low sulphur-premium:	$0.10
Increase in permanent short-haul freight premium:	$0.07
Increase in posted price at Tehran:	$0.35
	$3.07

25. See Chapter 2, notes 16 and 17. By this time there were four AFRAs —
for General Purpose, Medium, Large Range (LR)1 and Large Range (LR)2 (vessels
of 80,000-159,999 DWT). In 1969 Intascale had been replaced by Worldscale and the
percentages above or below the 'Flat' rate were expressed as a figure, instead
of as a plus or minus per cent. Here WS72 = freights 72 per cent of the Worldscale flat level.

It appears that the Temporary Freight Premium of 13 cents/b was agreed after
bargaining. Having determined WS72 as the freight at or below which a temporary
premium would not be justified (as the short-haul freight advantage below that
point was built into the Base Posting differential between Libya and Gulf
postings), by increasing the TFP 0.058 cents for each 0.1 increase in Worldscale
above 72, it appears that the 13 cents TFP would apply to an AFRA of WS94.4;
this corresponds to the LR2 AFRA for December 1970 and January 1971. By
March 1971 this AFRA had fallen to WS91.2.

26. *Petroleum Intelligence Weekly*, 5 Apr. 1971.

27. *Petroleum Intelligence Weekly*, 19 Apr. 1971 and 10 May 1971.

28. *Petroleum Intelligence Weekly*, Special Supplement, 6 May 1974.

29. *Petroleum Agreements*: Arabian Gulf Exploration Company; see note 11.

30. Local production costs did not fall in terms of Dinars, as did the revenues;
thus an additional diminution of oil company profits expressed in Dinars occurred,
leading to a further fall in Dinar values of surtax on these profits.

31. The figure is quoted in Annex B to the Second Geneva Agreement
referring to an 11-currency average (the Australian and Canadian dollars having
been added to the original 9), compared with 9.85 per cent for these same currencies on 20 January 1972.

32. Edith Penrose, 'The Development of Crisis', *Journal of American
Academy of Arts and Sciences* (Harvard), vol. 104, no. 4 (Fall 1975), p. 46.

33. Ghanem, *Pricing of Libyan Crude Oil*, p. 222.

34. This happened at the time when the UK's treaties of protection of the
Trucial Sheikhdoms terminated. The Libyan action presupposed that BP represented the UK Government, which held approximately half of its ordinary shares
but in fact never exercised its potential controlling interest to intervene in BP's
commercial operations.

35. *Petroleum Intelligence Weekly*, 19 Jun. 1972.

36. *Petroleum Intelligence Weekly*, 22 May, 12 June, 31 July 1972, where it
is reported that Soviet liftings of Sarir crude rose to more than 100,000 b/d.

37. In the Agreement of October 1970, BP raised its tax rate from 50 to 55
per cent in lieu of payments for the retroactive increases in posted prices. In the
Tripoli Agreement of March 1971, the 5 per cent extra tax rate was commuted
to equivalent extra per barrel payments on exports. BP was particularly hard hit
by these arrangements as, although its exports of oil had begun only in 1967,
its posted prices were 7 cents/b lower than the equivalent gravity main postings
because of high-pour and freight differential; this 7 cents differential was abolished
retroactively in the 1970 Agreement, which also raised the Base Posting by 30
cents/b.

Just before the nationalisation — in October 1971 — BP had made a promising
discovery in the Sarir area — the discovery well flowed at 10,000 b/d, which

upgraded the reserve estimate of the field to 15 billion barrels, of which 14 per cent was said to be recoverable.

BP surrendered most of its remaining concessions – Nos. 34, 36, 37 and 64 – in March 1972, but retained Concessions 80 and 81. In Concession 80 a substantial discovery had been made in 1967 but not developed, and in 81 Wintershall had acquired a 25 per cent interest.

In October 1976, BP stated that its dispute with the Libyan Government was ended, and that it would consider 'service contracts' with the Libyan Government – of the type which had then been entered into by many of the oil companies operating in Libya: *Petroleum Intelligence Weekly*, 11 Oct. 1976.

38.   This suit was dismissed by the court, and this was confirmed by the Supreme Court, on the grounds that a trial would require investigation of policies and conduct of the Government of Libya (*New York Times*, 6 Dec. 1977).

39.   In 1978 BP obtained an award of £17 million in the High Court in London for costs of oil lifted by Hunt from the Sarir field after BP's nationalisation. The development costs of the field had been borne by BP and were reimbursable in respect of his share by Hunt. At the time of writing Hunt is to appeal and to claim $2 billion from BP in a Dallas court on various counts (*Financial Times*, 10 Apr. 1979).

40.   Resolution XXIV. 135 (13 July 1971).

41.   The full text of the Agreement was published as a Supplement to *Middle East Economic Survey*, 22 Dec. 1972.

42.   *Middle East Economic Survey*, 10 Mar. 1972.

43.   *Petroleum Intelligence Weekly*, 9 Oct. 1972 and 5 Mar. 1973.

44.   *Petroleum Intelligence Weekly*, 14 May 1973.

45.   The text of the general Law was published as a Supplement to *Middle East Economic Survey*, 14 Sept. 1973.

46.   *Petroleum Intelligence Weekly*, 17 Sept. 1973.

47.   Amoco pulled out of Libya and sold its assets and business to the Government in March 1976.

48.   Statements made to *Petroleum Intelligence Weekly* representative and reported in the issue of 12 May 1975.

In contrast to the proportion of oil production now *owned* by Libya, 'some 85% of Libya's oil production *operations* are conducted by American firms with the rest being conducted by NOC together with French, Italian and Spanish companies'. (*Arab Oil and Gas*, 16 Jun. 1979).

49.   *Petroleum Intelligence Weekly*, 17 June 1974).

50.   Central Bank of Libya, *Annual Report 1973/4*.

51.   *Petroleum Economist* (Nov. 1977).

52.   *Petroleum Intelligence Weekly*, 26 Jan. 1976.

53.   *Petroleum Intelligence Weekly*, 12 Jan. 1976.

13 PRICES, MARKETS AND OPERATIONS

13.1 Libyan Influence and Competitiveness in the Markets

In the early 1960s the advent of Libyan oil had been a contributory factor in weakening prices in the markets of Europe (see Chapter 6, section 6.3). By the end of the decade Libya was supplying more than a quarter of Western Europe's requirements of oil and a significant and increasing proportion of North American imports, either directly or indirectly through 'off-shore' refineries. In this latter use it was becoming especially attractive not only for its cheapness but also because of its low-sulphur fuel oil derivative, which met the new anti-pollution measures at that time coming into force in the USA.

Conversely, the withdrawal of Libyan oil from the markets in the 1970s had the opposite effects. The restrictions on production imposed on the Libyan oil companies in the summer of 1970 gave rise to increases in market prices and freights, which made the 30 cents/b rise in posted prices conceded by the companies from September 1970 patently justifiable in terms of the Petroleum Law. These restrictions reduced Libyan exports from a high level of 3.7 million b/d in April, 1970, to about 3 million b/d in August and September. The cut-backs imposed on the companies concerned amounted to nearly 900,000 b/d, but were partially offset by other increased production.

To this reduction of 'short-haul' supplies,[1] as they came to be called, was added another, resulting from damage to Tapline in Syria on 3 May 1970. The closure of this line reduced Eastern Mediterranean supplies by 475,000 b/d. By August there was in total a contrived reduction in Mediterranean supplies of over one million b/d. The likely effects of this were pointed out by William Laird, Director of the US Oil and Gas Division of the Department of the Interior, in a warning to the US Senate in that month. He expressed the view that, with soaring freights, the tankers were not available to make good this deficiency with long-haul oil, nor for further requirements for the coming winter heating season.

The effect on oil prices in consuming countries was first felt in freight rates. Their movement is shown in Chart 13.1. The May cut-backs of Occidental's production, plus the Tapline closure, were enough to stimulate a sharp rise in spot freights, as oil companies strove to

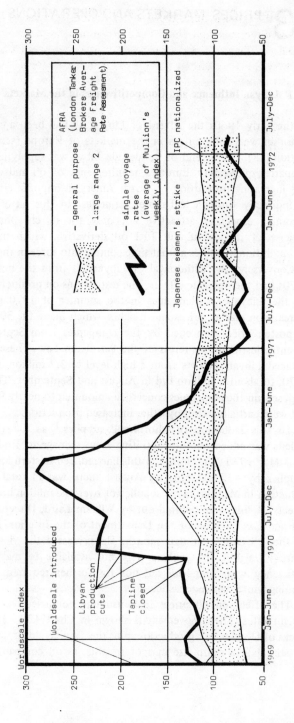

Chart 13.1: Tanker Freight Rates, 1970-2

Source: *Petroleum Press Service* (September 1972), p. 334.

secure the tonnage necessary to carry the oil to replace that lost from the Mediterranean on the far longer journey from the Arabian Gulf round the Cape of Good Hope. AFRA followed, so that by the end of 1970 even for the largest size of vessels it was Worldscale 100 and for smaller tankers much higher.[2]

By June there was a shortage of Libyan oil in Europe, yet because of the contractual arrangements for its sale, and with higher freights, its price was some 55 cents/b lower than Arabian Gulf oil delivered to Rotterdam. The crude oil sales contracts of Occidental and others normally included protection for the seller against cost rises from posted price and tax increases, but these had not yet taken place. Company resistance to them in Libya, therefore, was as much for protection of their customers as themselves, so far as contracts of sales of crude to third parties by independents with escalation cover was concerned.

The Libyan Government, in concentrating their pressure on the independents, particularly Occidental, showed more astuteness than they are usually credited with, and probably more than they themselves realised. It is widely believed that the whole reason for this concentration was the vulnerability of the independents and their fear of losing their Libyan supplies which comprised all or a large part of their resources of crude oil outside North America. But in addition, being protected in their contracts by escalation clauses, they had least to fear from consenting to posted price and tax increases in a rising market and with restrictions on supplies. When the summer cutbacks had engineered price rises in the markets, above all in freights, which more than absorbed the Libyan posted price demands, there was no defence against accepting the demands (though there could be against retro-activity). The majors, anchored to their built-in inertia on posted prices, might well have continued to resist pressure, as they did in 1967, on the grounds that the high prices in the markets were temporary. They too would have been protecting their customers more than themselves, and in the outcome their profits benefited substantially from the rises in market prices even after they had acceded to higher posted prices.[3]

Between mid-July and mid-August prices of products derived from Libyan oil rose in Rotterdam by 23 per cent on a composite barrel basis − from $2.60 to $3.20/b.[4] Allowing 50 cents/b for refining costs and losses and 40 cents for freight, the latter would give a net-back price for crude oil in Libya of $2.30/b. At the end of August the National Oil Company (abbreviated now to Linoco) took royalty oil in kind for the first time and sold it − to Austria's OMV − at $2.17/b for 37° gravity − 2 cents above the posted price. It was not delivered until some time after the posted price had risen to $2.485/b.

The increase in posted prices in September appeared at first to arouse buyer resistance. Occidental was seen to be producing little more than half of its restored allowables and its storage tanks were reported to be full to the brim. But this appearance was short-lived. In October Linoco agreed to sell[5] Occidental's royalty oil to Egypt at $2.55/b, which was the posted price to come into effect in the following January.

At the same time the lack of supplies in Europe forced buyers to accept the higher Libyan prices, and by December European prices were soaring at the refinery level. In that month a Swiss brokerage firm contracted to buy over 2 million tons of Brega 40° royalty crude at $2.90/b, compared with the new posted price of $2.55/b. By this time OPEC had adopted the Caracas resolution and the expectation of further price rises dominated market sentiment.

With the conclusion of the Tehran and Tripoli Agreements, the relationship between Libyan and Arabian Gulf crude oil prices was changed. Until September 1970 the posted price of Libyan 40° Brega crude had been $2.23/b − 24 per cent higher than Arabian Light 34° ex Ras Tanura, the posted price of which was $1.80/b. This difference, in terms of the Libyan Petroleum Law, was intended to be a measure of the freight, gravity and quality advantages of Libyan oil in its principal markets of Europe. That it did so adequately was argued by Esso in defending its 1961 posting, but at all times strenuously opposed by the Libyan Government.

The excess of the Libyan over the Arabian Gulf posting was widened to 40 per cent by the September 1970 rises in Libyan prices. The Libyan Government always maintained that these increases were corrections of the previous levels to accord with the requirements of the Law, which hitherto had not been observed, and the retroactivity clauses of the Agreement were taken as an admission of this by the companies. There was little opportunity to test the impact of these new posted prices on the market, since their application was accompanied by constraints imposed on the free flow of short-haul oil, high freight rates, and the expectation of higher prices both in the Gulf and Libya, which became a certainty after the OPEC Caracas resolution of 20 December 1970.

After the Tehran and Tripoli Agreements the Libyan posting for Brega 40° was $3.447/b and the Arabian marker crude − including the June 1971 upward adjustment of 2½ per cent plus 5 cents/b − $2.285/b. The differential had thus risen to 50 per cent. In money terms, before September 1970, Libyan 40° crude at export terminal was posted 43 cents/b higher than Arabian 34°; in June 1971 this difference had risen to $1.16/b.

The Government take per barrel at the two periods and for the two oils was approximately as follows:

	Libyan Brega 40° $/b	Arabian Light 34° $/b	Difference $/b
Before September 1970	1.10	0.96	0.14
June 1971	1.925	1.330	0.595

If a constant cost in both periods of 10 cents/b for Arabian and 30 cent/b for Libyan is assumed, then the tax-paid cost of the two oils to the companies was:

	Libyan 40°	Arabian 34°	Difference
Before September 1970	$1.40	$1.06	$0.34
June 1971	$2.225	$1.430	$0.795

The payments to Government were variable costs to the companies, payable in cash within a comparatively short time of production and export of the oil. The greater part of costs of production were normally 'sunk' costs and programmed costs of exploration, drilling and development. Although this average cost concept was widely used by oil companies in the pricing of contracts for sale of oil, there were times when incremental costing, cash-flow analysis and cash recovery of investment were equally relevant in their decision-making. For short-run incremental sales there was no significant increase in costs of production. Such incremental production and sales had the effect of reducing the average per barrel cost of production, but increasing the government per barrel take, as the income or surtax was levied on higher revenue (the incremental exports valued at posted prices) without any appreciable offset from higher incremental costs of production.

The royalty and tax payments on an incremental barrel of crude were thus as follows:

	Libyan 40°	Arabian 34°	Difference
Before September 1970	$1.255	$1.013	$0.242
June 1971	$2.090	$1.385	$0.705

Assuming no change in short-run costs of production, these figures indicate that Libyan crude in 1971 would have to make up in lower cost of transport and higher value of products at least 79 cents/b before it could be competitive with Arabian Gulf oil in the market on a full cost basis, and 70 cents/b on an incremental cost basis. But in addition to this, the retroactivity elements of the Libyan 1970 settlements, quantified then as an extra profits tax varying between the companies from 4 to 5½ per cent, had been converted by the Tripoli 1971 Agreement into an extra per barrel payment equal in total to the amount derived from the extra profits tax hitherto applicable. This added between 11 and 15 cents/b to the average costs of most Libyan producers and between 12 and 16½ cents/b to their incremental costs. They also undertook to spend $3.5 million a year per operation on exploration, and this added a small sum of between one and two cents a barrel, depending on size of production, to their fixed programmed costs.

From March 1971 for more than two years the differential between Libyan and Arabian Gulf costs and prices was maintained, subject only to the adjustments for the temporary freight premium in Libya as freights fell. Because the annual increases built into the Tehran and Tripoli Agreements were partly percentages, as were those of the Geneva currency settlements, the absolute differentials in posted prices rose – from $1.16/b in June 1971 to $1.59/b on 1 October 1973.

On 1 January 1974, by which date the whole pricing structure was managed by governments, the Saudi Arabian Government posted the marker crude at $11.651/b and the Libyan Government posted Brega 40° at $15.768/b. This gives a difference in posted price between the two of $4.12/b. By that time a simple measure of the differences between the posted prices of Libyan and Arabian crudes no longer gave a valid measure of cost difference, since the participations and nationalisations which were taking place in the two countries, and the arrangements made by governments about the prices of government-owned crude sold to the companies and to the world at large, had become an important factor in the cost of crude oil.

The higher Libyan prices and costs after March 1971 brought about a marked substitution of Arabian Gulf oil for Libyan oil in the markets of Europe.[6] The majors were able to carry this out in their supply planning.[7] The partially integrated independents – Continental and Marathon – were for the most part tied to their Libyan supplies of crude, and therefore had to make the best of it in their downstream operations. Amerada was tied to Shell. N.B. Hunt, after the nationalisation of its partner BP, to whom it had been selling 50,000 b/d, was on its own, but soon beset with troubles culminating in its nationalisation in the middle of 1973. Occidental, the largest independent, sold much of its crude under contracts which contained price and tax escalation clauses, but gave the buyer the option to seek his supplies elsewhere in the event of cost rises.

From the spring of 1971 to the end of 1974 — with the exception of the confused period from summer 1973 to the spring of 1974 — reports confirm that Libyan oil had lost its cost advantage over Gulf oil, and that there was a continuing shift away from Libya to the Arabian Gulf.[8] The declining trend in Libyan production and sales up to the end of 1974 is illustrated in the company production figures of Table 13.1. Most of the cut-backs in allowables occurred in the summer of 1970. With the exception of further cut-backs on Occidental in 1973 and 1975 and the temporary harassment of Hunt (1972-3) and Esso (1974), much of the falls in production in the non-crisis years may be attributed to the growing cost disadvantage of Libyan oil compared with others, as the petroleum markets became adjusted to the new supply conditions and freights fell. The falls in new investment in exploration and development after the revolution, for new oil to replace the older fields becoming exhausted, also played a part.

Following the action of OPEC in October 1973, of wresting from the oil companies their control over the posting of prices, the pricing of crude oil became a matter of 'fine tuning' by OPEC member governments to maintain their sales of oil at the levels they wished, within the context of OPEC agreement on the general level of prices. Having obtained at auction $20/b at the outset for royalty oil and $16/b for oil of disputed title (the majors had not yet accepted 51 per cent nationalisation) the Libyan Government aimed its sights high. The posted price for Brega 40° was set at $15.768, and the price for oil bought back by the companies from the nationalised portion of their concessions was to be $16/b. This made the 'acquisition cost' to the companies — a new term to describe the average cost to them of their own concession oil (tax paid) and the oil bought back from the nationalised portion of their concession — about $13/b.

At the start of 1974 companies selling Libyan crude were reported to be obtaining between $14 and $15/b. But as conditions became more stable, embargoes lifted and freights fell, the Libyan price was soon seen to be too high. It compared with $8-$9½/b acquisition cost[9] of the Arabian marker crude, where buy-back prices to the companies for the participation oil had been pitched at 93 per cent of the posted price of $11.651/b. Beginning in April 1974, the buy-back price for

Table 13.1: Average Daily Production of Libyan Oil Companies, 1970-6

'000 b/d	1970	1971	1972	1973	1974	1975	1976	Percentage Nationalised as at end of 1976
Esso Standard)	692	447	364	312	216	200	246	51 (Esso Standard)
Esso Sirte Group)								63.5 (Esso Sirte Group)
Oasis Group	946	824	797	723	551	550	682	59.2
Occidental	659	586	425	353	320	273	320	51
BP/Hunt	413	420	214	236	137	167	304	100
Mobil Group	253	186	164	144	104	88	92	51
Amoseas Group	323	261	233	192	74	90	106	100
Agip	–	–	24	110	107	146	156	50
Aquitaine Group	20	17	16	12	9	9	8	0
Elf-Aquitaine joint venture	–	–	–	–	–	11	10	85
Amoco	8	15	9	6	6	7	n/a	100
Phillips	4	4	3	2	–	–	–	100
Total mb/d	3.3	2.8	2.2	2.2	1.5	1.5	1.9	64
Percentage world production	7.23	5.60	4.15	3.79	2.76	2.83	3.33	

Sources: 1970-1 Ministry of Petroleum; 1972-6 Central Bank of Libya, *Economic Bulletin* (March/April), 1977. Production is shown as for the operating company of the original concessionaires irrespective of nationalisation or State participation and its timing. The percentage nationalised excludes royalty oil.

40° oil was lowered in Libya by stages to reach $11.86/b at the beginning of 1975.

Meanwhile many changes had been made elsewhere in percentage government participation. Kuwait and Qatar had agreed with the companies concerned on a 60 per cent nationalisation in early 1974, followed by Saudi Arabia and Abu Dhabi. The OPEC Gulf States, meeting in September, had agreed on a weighted average government take for the marker crude, on the basis of 60 per cent nationalisation, of $9.74/b, increased from $9.41/b previously. To achieve this, royalty was raised   to 16.67 per cent in the Gulf States and profits taxes to an average of 65.7 per cent, posted prices remaining unchanged. Libya followed the increase in royalty but raised its tax rate to only 60 per cent. At the same time the buy-back price for companies was reduced to $12.50/b, making an average acquisition cost to them of $11.66/b and average government take $11.16/b.

On 1 January 1975, the Gulf States raised the government take on the marker crude to $10.12/b. Libya kept its share at $11.16, but altered the components by reducing direct sale and buy-back oil from $12.50/b to $11.86/b, and increasing company tax to 65 per cent. This left average acquisition cost to the companies unchanged at $11.66/b, compared with that for the marker crude of $10.24/b.

The manipulation of prices by raising royalties and tax rates resulted from the judgement of OPEC countries – particularly of Sheikh Yamani – that in spite of the hammering the oil companies had received and were receiving, they were seen to be making enormous profits. This was because the higher the posted price, the higher the oil company profit on that part of their concessions left to them, to the extent that their realisations in the market were maintained reasonably close to government sales prices. The raising of royalty and tax rates diminished the profit margins of the companies on their owned oil. Sheikh Yamani is said to have remarked that if consuming countries did not curb the companies' excess profits, the producing countries would do so.[10] Saudi Arabia followed up the September action in November by raising royalty to 20 per cent and the tax rate to 85 per cent; at the same time reducing the posted price by 40 cents/b, and hence the buy-back price, which was 93 per cent of posted price.

Libyan exports of oil in December 1974 had fallen to 800,000 b/d. The declining trend was attributed to its relatively high price, diminishing demand for oil and the continuing embargo on shipments to the USA. This had been cancelled by other Arab producers early in the year, and was unostentatiously lifted by Libya in December. In

February 1975 Libya abandoned the 'one price' system by introducing variations of price for the different crudes over and above those agreed for gravity. At the same time Linoco cut most of its sales prices — which were the same as the buy-back prices to the companies — by between 15 and 29 cents/b, to reduce the average acquisition cost to the companies by 10 cents to $11.56/b. This was further reduced in stages to $10.90-$11.00/b in June. At this time Brega 40°, at $10.97/b acquisition cost, was only 73 cents/b more costly to the companies than the Arabian marker crude at $10.24/b.

At about this time Continental expressed the view that Libyan oil was still uncompetitive in the open market.[11] The company stated that Libyan oil retained a quality premium of 50 cents/b on the Rotterdam spot products market, and at spot rates then prevailing also enjoyed a 15 cents/b freight advantage. Using an acquisition cost for Libyan oil of $11.16/b and for Arabian Light of $10.24/b, the company pointed out that, after allowing for its advantages, Libyan oil still had a net cost disadvantage of 27 cents/b. The company added that, even so, it was able to earn a moderate profit in its integrated operations because of the high value of the light products derived from Libyan oil, its petroleum coke and its low content of residual fuel oil (prices of which had fallen 50 per cent in the past year). In addition to its other advantages 90 days credit was given on buy-back sales of Libyan oil, compared with 60 days for most other supplies. With money costing around 10 per cent p.a. this concession could be valued at 25 cents/b.

Also at this time — spring 1975 — Occidental revealed in an SEC declaration that the prices of sales in its contracts, which contained escalation clauses, had been higher in recent months than market prices, and that its customers were consequently refusing to take delivery. The company was therefore obliged to sell spot in order to comply with the Government's insistence on its increasing production. In April Occidental was reported to be selling crude at 55 cents/b below its acquisition cost, thereby providing evidence of the amount by which Libyan prices exceeded the going market prices.[12] In May the company was selling at $11.00/b — again under cost, and was warned not to do so by the Ministry of Petroleum. It was at this time that Occidental unsuccessfully requested 100 per cent nationalisation of its concessions and to continue as operator on a per barrel fee basis.

Occidental's dilemma — of being obliged to increase production and at the same time to maintain prices dictated not by the market but by the Government — resolved itself in a dramatic way. In August new major cut-backs were imposed on the company, amounting to over 300,000 b/d, and a month later its production and exports were stopped. The company responded by suspending payments due to Libya of $440 million and stated that it would seek damages of over one billion dollars for continuous breaches of contract. The dispute was settled in December in Occidental's favour by the company being guaranteed minimum allowances for a ten-year period.[13]

The incident may have convinced the Libyan Government that, if Libyan production was to be increased, prices must be pitched at a level competitive with other oils, particularly those from the Arabian Gulf. The necessity for competitiveness was clear in the case of a largely non-integrated producer, which had to dispose of its crude in arm's-length transactions with third parties. It was somewhat masked in the case of the integrated majors, who nevertheless had the ability to substitute one crude for another to the extent that the spread of their producing interests and buy-back operations allowed it.

The Libyan price cuts of the first half of 1975 proved effective in stimulating oil production and exports, which had by now become the principal objective of Libyan oil policy. In June output had recovered from its low of 800,000 b/d to 1.5 million b/d, and for the third quarter exports averaged 1.9 million b/d.

In October 1975 Libya raised its sales prices, posted prices and hence company acquisition costs by 10 per cent, in line with the OPEC decision. In July 1976 OPEC attempted to adopt a new system, on the lines used by Algeria, of replacing the fixed gravity differentials and sulphur premium with prices derived from net-back calculations of the value of different oils in the markets, and Libya followed suit. As a result the price band of the various oils was widened from 22 cents to 57 cents. The waxy crudes were lowered by 5 cents/b, thus re-introducing the lower prices for high-pour waxy crudes which had been abolished in the 1970 Agreement and for which the companies concerned had had to make, and were still making, retroactive compensation. The prices of lighter crudes were raised between 15 and 30 cents/b, but they were still considered cheap and this was stated by a Libyan spokesman to be 'consistent with Libya's stated objective of maximizing production and sales'.[14] A rise in posted prices of 29 cents to $16.35/b added 20 cents/b to the cost of the companies' equity crude.

For 1976 as a whole exports of crude oil averaged 1.9 million b/d. At the end of the year they were running at 2 million b/d, and this recovery continued into 1977.

On 1 January 1977, Libya followed the majority of OPEC members in raising all prices by 10 per cent, as opposed to Saudi Arabia and Abu Dhabi, which limited themselves to a 5 per cent increase.

The principal destinations of Libyan exports are shown in Table 13.2. Throughout the period the major part was delivered to Western European countries, though this was on a declining trend, falling from 93 per cent in 1970 to 61 per cent in 1976. Reasons for this may be found in: (1) the emergence of North Sea oil which, being by and large of a quality and gravity comparable with Libyan, replaced Libyan oil in 1975 and 1976 in Northern Europe, particularly in the UK; and (2) the great increase in Libyan exports to the USA which, after 1975 when the embargo was lifted, became Libya's principal customer.

13.2 The National Oil Corporation

Law No. 24 of 5 March 1970 replaced Lipetco with a new National Oil Corporation, which has subsequently been called, in English, either the NOC or — to distinguish it from the national companies in other oil countries — Linoco. Apart from the change in name, its prerogatives, fields of activity and duties were similar to those of Lipetco. It continued to be an 'independent body operating under the supervision and control of the Minister [of Petroleum] in order to achieve the development plan objectives in the oil sector'.[15] The Corporation's first Chairman and Director-General was Salem Mohammed Amesh; his deputy was Omar Muntasir who subsequently replaced him and has remained Chairman until the present time. The new Law limited any new joint ventures to those in which the foreign partner took the whole of the risks in the pre-commercial exploration period — which meant that exploration costs would not subsequently be amortisable; and insisted on Linoco's share being fixed at a given percentage from the start of operations, and not on a sliding scale as in previous joint ventures. It also authorised Linoco to enter into 'contract-type' agreements, which bore fruit in the production-sharing ventures embarked upon from 1974 onwards.[16]

Law No. 69 of 4 July 1970 transferred all marketing of oil products in Libya to Linoco. It gave the Corporation the sole right to import and sell oil products, and nationalised all the oil companies' marketing properties, installations and assets against compensation. In 1971 the 'Brega Petroleum Marketing Company' was set up as a subsidiary of Linoco to carry out these activities.

Table 13.2: Country Destinations of Libya's Crude Oil Exports,
1972-6 ('000 b/d)

Destination	1972	1973	1974	1975	1976
North America	208.9	239.7	9.6	330.9	508.6
of which:					
Canada	35.3	34.5	8.3	11.5	12.5
USA	173.6	205.2	1.3	319.4	496.1
Latin America	194.1	122.4	146.1	169.7	103.1
of which:					
Bahamas	113.2	87.1	37.9	71.9	31.6
Brazil	10.3	25.5	67.6	43.7	32.6
Trinidad & Tobago	70.6	9.8	–	13.2	–
Western Europe	1,738.7	1,701.9	1,247.0	841.2	1,136.0
of which:					
Austria	12.7	12.4	11.1	2.8	13.1
Belgium and Luxembourg	25.8	54.5	29.7	5.6	5.2
Denmark	1.9	3.5	4.5	2.3	0.4
France	196.1	121.2	88.8	53.7	97.5
Germany (FR)	553.4	497.1	329.9	284.8	371.6
Italy	441.9	566.0	502.8	294.1	344.6
Netherlands	103.6	86.1	13.4	28.9	44.8
Spain	56.3	32.9	54.8	64.5	95.0
Switzerland	36.8	32.5	20.9	6.5	7.5
United Kingdom	300.2	249.1	182.9	50.4	41.8
Eastern Europe	65.9	77.8	9.3	24.5	54.2
of which:					
Bulgaria	11.6	16.5	5.3	2.3	4.4
Romania	16.4	26.0	4.0	17.3	34.1
USSR	38.3	35.3	–	–	–
Middle East	–	–	–	–	2.1
Africa	–	15.0	13.7	15.6	1.7
of which:					
Egypt	–	14.5	3.1	–	–
Asia and Far East	6.6	17.7	64.6	49.2	40.9
of which:					
Japan	6.6	17.7	64.6	47.5	36.8
Total	2,214.2	2,174.5	1,490.3	1,431.2	1,846.6

Source: OPEC, *Annual Statistical Bulletin*; figures provided directly by Libyan
Government.

The principal activities of Linoco that have been reported during the
post-revolutionary period are as listed below.

13.2.1 Exploration and Production. Apart from the joint-venture and
production-sharing deals which are described elsewhere, Linoco

acquired most of the relinquished areas and surrendered concessions. The land under direct exploration by Linoco was recorded as 234,000 square kilometres at the end of 1971.[17] Little news of subsequent activities in these areas was reported until 1974. By an agreement with Saipem, Eni's subsidiary, in early 1972 a joint drilling company was formed. Saipem was to provide Linoco with 18 drilling rigs, 12 of which were for exploration. The oil strikes and development of new production reported in Linoco-controlled areas are described in section 13.3, below.

Linoco's production operations included the Sarir field after the nationalisation of BP (1971) and Hunt (1973); the former Amoseas fields after their nationalisation in 1974, to be operated by Linoco's subsidiary, Umm al Jawabi;Phillips' Umm Farrud field relinquished in 1970, and Amoco's Sahabi field sold in 1976. Linoco's total production and exports from 1973, as reported, are shown in Table 13.3.

Table 13.3: Libyan National Oil Corporation — Production and Exports of Crude Oil, 1973-6

	Production[a] '000 b/d	Exports[b] '000 b/d
1973	441	640
1974	214	815
1975	281	908
1976	408	1,201

Notes: a. Includes only fields 100 per cent owned and directly managed by Linoco. Source: *Petroleum Intelligence Weekly* reports from Libya.
b. Includes State oil from all operations and oil bought back by companies. Source: Central Bank of Libyan Arab Republic, *Economic Bulletin* (March/April, 1977).

13.2.2 Shipping. In the 1966 concessions most applicants had offered, as an extra benefit, priority to Libyan tankers, provided their terms of charter were on a par with others available. Libya thus had a ready-made potential for tanker usage and from 1971 onwards Linoco began ordering vessels. Orders for two vessels of 47,000 tons each from Spain (for the Zawia refinery) as part of a barter deal for oil, and two of 86,000 tons from Japan, at a cost of *c*.$14 million each, were reported in 1972, and two further tankers of over 100,000 tons were ordered in 1973. In March 1975 it was reported that three of the orders had been delivered, and towards the end of 1976 plans were announced to increase the fleet by 50 per cent to 12 vessels of a total tonnage of 686,500 tons.[18]

13.2.3 Refining and Marketing in Libya. The refinery at Zawia, of 60,000 b/d (see Chapter 9, section 9.4), was completed and commissioned in 1974. Thereafter a doubling of its capacity was undertaken, for completion in 1977. Plans announced in 1976 for three new export refineries at Tobruk, Zueitina and Misurata, adding over 600,000 b/d to capacity, appear to have been shelved for the time being.

Concessionaires were obliged by the Petroleum Law to supply crude oil at 'field storage price' for a refinery in Libya producing for Libyan consumption (see Chapter 9, section 9.4). In 1971 Linoco arranged a processing deal with Sincat in Italy for refining oil products for Libyan consumption. The companies were called upon to supply the crude at 'field storage price' (which presumably was interpreted as bare operating cost) for this purpose. Not unnaturally they demurred, since such arrangements were not stipulated in the Petroleum Law. This was at the time of the Tripoli settlement, which reiterated the concessionaires' supply obligations contained in the Law (see Chapter 12, section 12.4); by July a compromise was reached whereby the companies supplied 70 per cent at cost and 30 per cent from royalty oil.[19]

Thus the Government achieved what the previous regime had failed to do − a cheap supply of oil for internal Libyan consumption. This was made even less costly when Linoco acquired its own crude oil supplies and when the Zawia refinery came on stream in 1974, to which concession-holders would be obliged by the Law to supply feedstock at cost. Consumption of oil products in Libya, which had remained fairly stable at around 20,000 b/d in the years 1968-71 rose to 25,000 b/d in 1972, 30,000 b/d in 1973, 34,000 b/d in 1974 and to over 50,000 b/d in 1975 and 1976.[20] The average value of a composite barrel of products sold in Libya fell in 1972 by 12 per cent − from LD3.73 in 1971 to LD3.29 in 1972[21] in a period when crude oil posted prices rose some 40 per cent.

13.2.4 Petrochemicals. From the early days of oil production in Libya, the construction of chemical plants using petroleum and natural gas as feedstocks was contemplated. In its 1966 concessions Occidental had offered, in addition to the development of Kufra, to construct and pay 50 per cent of an ammonia plant, to provide fertilisers for Libyan agriculture and for export. It was to have an initial production capacity of 600 tons a day, capable of expansion to 1,200 t/d, and to use gas supplied by the Libyan Government.

Occidental had made its offer contingent on the plant being economically viable, and in 1969 commissioned a feasibility study which reported unfavourably, in the light of probable impending world surplus of ammonia production. The company thereupon requested to switch to a methanol plant on similar terms, and this was agreed by the Government after the revolution.

Subsequent developments in petrochemicals were controlled by Linoco. A complex was first planned near Benghazi, to which Agip had offered to construct a gas ·line as part of its joint-venture deal. The site was subsequently changed to Mersa Brega where royalty gas would be readily available, and British firms — which included Power Gas Company and ICI — were retained by Linoco as consultants.[22]

In 1972 the National Methanol Company was created to implement the agreement with Occidental. The plant was to have a capacity of 1,000 tons a day of methanol, but it was not until 1974 that a contract for construction was entered into — the cost involved being $88 million. Occidental, as part of its production-sharing agreement of 1974, was relieved of further financial obligations at a time when costs had amounted to $20 million.[23]

In June 1975 a plan to construct an ethylene plant to produce 300,000 tons a year at a cost of LD60 million was announced. The original ammonia plant offered by Occidental and taken over by Linoco when Occidental switched to methanol was begun late in 1976.

13.2.5 Sales of Crude Oil. Linoco made several contracts for the sale of royalty oil abroad between September 1970 and March 1971. The quantities involved amounted to 9 million tons, of which 1.5 million tons had been delivered by the end of 1971.[24] These sales were made in times of great uncertainty about the future course of prices, and the prices stated were at or above the posted prices of the oil at the times the sales were agreed in principle. In each case where the price is known, the posted price of the oil — and hence the cost of the royalty oil to Linoco, which was posted price — caught up and overtook within a short period the prices of the sales originally agreed. Whether the contracts had clauses in them providing for part or full recovery by the seller of such increased costs was not revealed, nor whether the buyer in such a case was able to decline delivery. The small proportions of the contracted amounts delivered to three of the buyers by the end of 1971 suggest that this may have happened.

The rise in posted prices caused by the Tripoli Agreement of 20 March 1971 put further sales of royalty oil out of court as a viable commercial operation for Linoco. After BP's nationalisation in December 1971, Linoco had available Sarir oil, but its purchase in

Western Europe was inhibited by the legal actions inaugurated and threatened by BP to claim ownership. One such action – for oil shipped by Linoco to Sincat in Sicily to process for the Libyan market – was eventually decided against BP. But the threat of being involved in such proceedings successfully deterred most buyers, even at discounted prices.

After a visit of Brezhnev and Kosygin to Libya, and of Jalloud to Moscow in March 1972, Linoco made large sales of Sarir crude to the USSR and Eastern Europe, which provided ready buyers in spite of UK Government protests to them that BP claimed title to this oil. Much of such oil is believed to have found its way back to Western Europe, but the pursuit of claim to it in the courts would have been a difficult, if not hopeless, undertaking.

It was not until the middle of 1973 that the gathering storm over prices and nationalisations brought other ready buyers of 'hot' Libyan oil at rising prices.[25] Then again began a period when Linoco made many sales of royalty oil at higher than posted price. Sales were made at above posted price in August (but below Occidental's recently agreed buy-back price of $4.90/b) to Sohio: at the beginning of October, Linoco's crude was fetching $5.50/b and at the end $9.00/b.[26] In each case the going price of oil soon overtook that at which these sales were made.

The problem of disputed title dwindled and eventually disappeared, apart from back claims, with the nationalisations of 1973, after the companies concerned had acquiesced – all except Amoseas and Liamco by mid-1974.[27] From that time Linoco had far more oil of undisputed title than it could sell, at least after the frenzied bidding for supplies at the turn of the year 1973/4 had died down.

In April 1974 Linoco was selling direct to customers 70 per cent of its settlement. There were some barter deals reported .– one with France (3/74) of 7 million tons a year, another with Argentina (11/74) of 50,000 b/d in exchange for food. Subsequently, with the falls in oil prices and consumption experienced during the course of 1974, and with Libya maintaining its own prices at uncompetitive levels, it appears that most of Linoco's shares of production in the companies that had acquiesced in partial nationalisation were sold back to them.

Nevertheless for 1974 as a whole, Linoco's direct sales averaged 393,000 b/d. This amounted to some 25 per cent of a shrunken total of Libyan production, and the Corporation was the largest single exporter of crude in that year. The remainder of its entitlements, amounting to 425,000 b/d, was sold back to the companies.

In 1975 a pact was made between Linoco and Eni whereby the latter would buy 240,000 b/d at a market price. The oil was to come from increased production at Bu Ateiffel (160,000 b/d) and from Linoco's entitlements from other companies (80,000 b/d); as part of the pact Linoco was to enter downstream operations in Italy.

13.3 Exploration, Drilling and Production

Production figures for the years 1970-6 are given in Table 13.1. The turning-point in the secular decline from the peak in April 1970 of 3.7 million b/d occurred in the first half of 1975. At the beginning of 1975 production was at a rate of 800,000 b/d, and by the start of 1977 it had climbed back to over 2 million b/d.

In terms of drilling activities, exploration and development work is measured in Table 13.4. From a peak in 1969 (which was even so below the high level of 1964, when over 400 wells were completed) the number of wells drilled fell rapidly to a fraction of their former levels, but recovered somewhat from 1973 onwards.

Table 13.4: Drilling Activities in Libya, 1969-76

	1969	1970	1971	1972	1973	1974	1975	1976
Number of rigs, year-end	55	13	18	9	8	14	9	18
Number of wells completed	327	244	51	55	72	72	84	88

Sources: 1969-71 Ministry of Petroleum;
1972-76 Central Bank of Libya, *Economic Bulletin* (March/April 1977).

As early as May 1970 — when the first restrictions on Occidental's production were imposed — the Libyan authorities had expressed concern about the decline of drilling. In that month the Ministry sent an 'urgent' request to companies to start drilling on inactive concessions within a month.[28] This apparently met with little response; indeed it probably accelerated surrenders of concessions — particularly the early ones, where greatly enhanced rents (of £L3,500 per 100 km^2) would become payable after 15 years, and this limit would be reached within a few months.

The new demands for higher prices put forward in January 1971 included a 'supervisory edict' by the Ministry of Petroleum instructing concessionaires to re-invest in Libya a specified proportion of company profits derived from oil operations. This was strongly resisted by the oil companies who, in their Message to OPEC countries of 16 January 1971, offering terms for an 'all-embracing' settlement of outstanding matters, specifically required 'obligatory re-investment' to be excluded from any agreement, and this was so done in the Tehran settlement.

Nevertheless, in the Tripoli Agreement of March 1971 each operating group undertook to keep one rig in operation in Libya during the years 1971-5, or to spend an equivalent amount ($c.$\$3.5 million p.a.) on other things in lieu. The battle to avoid compulsory re-investment was thus lost by the companies in Libya, as were so many others. But the price was small, amounting to not more than 1 or 2 cents/b addition to production costs, which were also tax deductibles. In the Oasis nationalisation settlement of August 1973 the three accepting companies concerned undertook to maintain 3 rigs operating on exploration in Libya for the following 3 years.

Early in 1972 a joint drilling venture was established between Linoco and Eni by which the latter's subsidiary, Saipem, was to operate 18 drilling rigs in Libya for Linoco — 12 of them on exploration.[29] Two of these were already in the country, and therefore sixteen more would have been added to the already existing total. Bearing in mind that there were other rigs in Libya (6 alone derived from the Tripoli Agreement), the figures suggest that the full number was slow to come, and had not been reached by 1976. At the end of 1973, it was reported that only one rig was operating on exploration.[30] In 1974 the number was increased by the extra rigs of the Oasis companies and from then onwards more rigs were added as a result of the new production-sharing deals. There was thus some recovery in exploration, as well as production drilling in and after 1974, but by 1976 these operations were still far below their pre-revolutionary level.

Between 1970 and 1976 there were two new fields developed. The first — Agip's Bu Ateiffel field in Concession 100 — was announced in early 1969. It promised to be a major operation of 300,000 b/d production, over 40° gravity, low sulphur, very high wax and also gas content. It was far from the seaboard ($c.$ 350 km) and the decision was made to pipe it to Occidental's line to Zueitina in Concesssion 103A. To meet the Government's requirements on gas utilisation a gas line was also constructed. On Concession 103 the liquids were to be separated to join Occidental's in the products pipeline to Zueitina, where they were treated and marketed at home and overseas as naphtha, butane and propane. The gas was injected into Occidental's field. Production was held up for a long time because of the Libyan insistence on proper gas utilisation. Early in 1972 some shipments were made, but they were stopped until the 50/50 participation pact was made in October 1972 — after two years of dickering. Production in quantity began thereafter and reached 110,000 b/d in 1973, rising to 156,000 b/d in 1976.

The other development was in the Elf/Aquitaine joint venture. Early in 1971 the existence of a small field was established in this operation. It was developed to start production in 1975, when it averaged 11,000 b/d: by this time it was an 85/15 production-sharing deal.

There were several discoveries reported from time to time, but few in the years 1972-4. The most significant was one of 10,000 b/d by BP 18 miles north of the Sarir field, as a result of which the reserves were re-assessed at 15 billion barrels, 14 per cent of which was deemed recoverable.[31] Soon after the discovery the Sarir field was nationalised; the new field, now called Mussalla, is being developed by Linoco's subsidiary, Arabian Gulf Exploration Co.

Mobil was reported in June 1971 to have made a major discovery (6,000 b/d) 10 km north of its original declining field of Hofra in Concession 11, and brought it into production the following October. Although no new significant discoveries or development were reported during the next three years, half of the 200 wells completed during that time were reported as producers. In 1974 Linoco announced new oil strikes (amounting to one billion barrels potential) in the Ghadames basin and several 'relatively huge fields' in the Ras as Hilal area.[32]

In 1975 and 1976 the discovery rate started to rise. In 1975 Oasis achieved 7 successful exploration wells in the Gialo and Dahra areas of Concession 59,[33] doubtless as a result of employing the three rigs agreed upon in 1973. In late 1975 Linoco too was reported to have made a 4,000 b/d strike in the west on the Hammada al Hamra plateau — Gulf's former Concession 66. Early in 1976 Linoco announced the discovery of potentially the largest oilfield in Libya in off-shore Concession 137 — the last conventional concession awarded in 1968 to Elf-Aquitaine, since 1974 worked on an 81/19 production-sharing basis.[34] This claim has not yet been confirmed by any development, which may have been inhibited by a boundary dispute with Tunisia (see Chapter 14, section 14.5). In addition two new discoveries were reported in the former Amoseas Concession in May 1976, one near Beda of 100 million barrels recoverable oil, and the other near Nafoora of 50 million.

Finally the Occidental production-sharing venture appears to have repeated the success — if in a less sensational manner — of its first concessions. After unusually intensive activity, in which three seismic parties and three drilling rigs were used, two new discoveries 5 km from Oasis' Es Sidr pipeline were announced early in 1976. The oil was of 52.8° gravity. The field — named Almas — was developed and, by leading into the already existing pipeline, was expected to be in production by the end of the year. The speed with which this field has been developed is an indication of the incentive effect of the production-sharing type of agreement.

Production from two small fields terminated during the period. Phillips in 1970 sold its Umm Farud field in Concession 92, then producing at about 4,000 b/d, to Linoco, rather than accept the 1970 increases in posted prices which, it asserted, made production uneconomical. Production was carried on for a long time by Linoco. In 1976 Amoco, who had not undergone any nationalisation because of its small operation, and had already shut down its Khuff field in Concession 93, sold its Sahabi field in Concession 95 to the State. The company stated that, with only 6,000 b/d production, it was no longer profitable.

Many concessions were surrendered between 1970 and 1972, partly because of the imminence of the high 15-year rents, as already mentioned, and partly because of Government pressure during this period to 'drill up or give up' — at a time when further investment in the country for the oil companies was of doubtful wisdom.

In August 1970 Gulf surrendered all its concessions, including the Hammada field on Concession 66 in Western Libya, which had a potential of 30,000 b/d if linked to the sea. Gulf was followed at the end of the year by CFP, who in spite of several discoveries in Concession 23 which could be linked to a Western pipeline, surrendered all its Libyan interests. In 1976 the Libyan Government, which had from time to time emphasised the importance it attached to such a pipeline, was taking action to embark upon it.

Other non-producing concessions were surrendered by many companies. These were selective, even by companies that had had their production 100 per cent nationalised. BP, for instance, surrendered Concessions 34, 36, 37 and 64, but retained 80 and 81, where oil had been discovered some years previously. Shell relinquished its concessions in Western Libya, but retained No. 114 and continued with its modified joint venture — without success. Phillips relinquished five concessions, one of which contained the Umm Farud field, mentioned above, but not its off-shore interests, where gas had been discovered but not developed. Oasis relinquished Concessions 26 and 30 in Western Libya and 76 in Zone IV in the far south.

Proven reserves of oil, which were assessed at 36 billion barrels in 1969,[35] were reported to be 24.5 billion barrels in 1977.[36] This latter figure comprised at the time 4.45 per cent of OPEC countries' recoverable reserves,[37] and about 33 years' supply at the current levels of Libyan production of about two million barrels a day. Too much significance should not be attached to such aggregates and calculations; all the quantities involved are variable – the proportion of oil-in-place recoverable, the future levels of production, future exploration, its success rate and the development to be achieved. The variables are functions of technical, political and economic factors yet to be determined.

It is clear, however, that, judged by traditional standards, Libya has adequate reserves in relation to existing production levels.[38] It is equally evident from a survey of events related in this last section, that for much of the 1970s maximum finding rates and development have neither been aimed at nor achieved. In fact the fall in the estimated reserves between 1969 and 1977 is some 66 per cent more than the total amount of oil withdrawn from the fields during this period. Since 1976 Government policy has been to aim at the highest possible rates of finding, development and production of oil. The results of pursuing these aims are being unfolded on a continuing basis, the trend of which so far appears to be positive.

13.4 Gas Utilisation

In Chapter 9, section 9.3, the construction of Esso's natural gas liquefaction plant at Brega was described. It was ready to start up, after many delays and increased costs, in the middle of 1970. But its commissioning was then held up by the Government on the question of prices.

The Petroleum Law stated that the income of a concessionaire from operations in Libya other than crude oil exported was to be 'ascertained in a manner to be agreed between the concession-holder and the Ministry'.[39] Esso had contracted prices for its sales of gas to Italy and Spain in 1969 – the original target year for operations – of 38.5 cents per million British thermal units for Eni and 42 cents to Cataláña de Gaz delivered.[40] The securing of firm long-term contracts

(20 years for Eni and 15 years for Cataleña de Gaz) was a necessary condition for Esso to undertake the great investment involved, in order to give some assurance of adequate profitability.

The company would pay royalty on the gas and this was defined in the Law as

12½% of the value of all natural gas derived from the concession area and exported by the concession-holder, the value of the natural gas for this purpose being the sales price after deducting any handling charges, duties and imposts and the cost of transport from the well-head paid by the concession-holder and not received from the purchaser.[41]

This latter provision thus gave a lead for agreement between the Ministry and the concession-holder on the level of net income which would be taxable at the rate of 50 per cent, although it made no attempt to define the production cost of the gas. This is a tricky problem since gas could be deemed to be a by-product of the production of oil, or of drilling for oil, and its costing could vary between nil and full allocated oil production costs on a deemed equivalence of so much gas equal to one barrel of oil.[42]

In 1969 additional plant to produce LPG (Liquid Petroleum Gases – butane and propane, of lower calorific value in liquid form, but on a volume basis richer, than LNG) and NGL (Natural Gas Liquids – naphtha) was installed, for both domestic market and export, at an extra cost of $14 million. This plant began operating in 1970, during which six shipments were made altogether to the Lebanon, Cyprus and Spain, amounting to some 23,000 metric tons.[43] In 1971 there were no exports, but only local shipments to Benghazi and Tripoli, since this operation too was caught up in the prices dispute.

By the time the LNG operation was ready to start, the necessary LNG carriers delivered and the customers waiting, the 1970 posted price dispute was coming to a head, and restrictions on oil production had already been imposed. It was therefore to be expected that there would be no easy agreement on the fiscal price of gas. The Government refused to allow shipments until the price was settled, and thereby was able to inflict damage on the project's profitability, which was already impaired by the operational delays and escalation of costs previously encountered. A government committee was established to examine and report on the price of gas. It recommended that exports of gas continue to be banned and that the price issue be referred to the crude oil pricing committee, thereby 'hoping to pressure the Company'.[44]

After the 1970 oil price settlement, the Government demand for higher gas prices to both customers was dropped, but it insisted on the prices to the Italian and Spanish customers being the same, thereby claiming to dictate prices, not only to Esso, but also to the purchasers of the gas from Esso.

At the time of the 1971 oil price negotiations culminating in the Tripoli Agreement, a price of 43 cents/mbtu[45] was accepted by the Spanish customer. The royalty and tax reference price in Libya was agreed at 34 cents/mbtu, raised from the original proposal by Esso of 20.6 cents/mbtu. In accepting this, Esso reduced its freight deduction from 11¢ to 9¢ per thousand cubic feet and abandoned its attempt to obtain an investment allowance.

The delivered price compared with one of Algerian gas to Eni of 42.5 cents/mbtu, which had been adopted after years of negotiation, but the Algerian gas was said to be better adapted to Eni's needs than the Libyan. An Eni spokesman, at the time of the price settlement with Spain, is reported to have stated that they 'could do without Libyan gas at that price'. Nevertheless seventeen shipments of LNG to Spain and four to Italy were reported in the second half of 1971.[46]

From the middle of 1971 the gas liquefaction plant was in use and exports of LNG rose. By the spring of 1973 the plant was working at 80-90 per cent capacity,[47] and was expected to continue at this rate for the rest of the year. Esso, whose oil production was at a lower level than was needed to supply the liquefaction plant with its full complement of gas, contracted at this time to buy 120 mcfd of gas from Occidental and 100 mcfd from Amoseas. After the great rises in oil prices in the closing months of 1973, the Libyan Government made demands for increases in gas prices. Such rises would bring the price of gas some way towards that of oil, calculated on equivalent thermal properties of the two. A new f.o.b. price of $1.62/mbtu was decreed in October 1974, but Eni refused to lift it at that price level.[48] Thereupon Esso's operations were shut down to enforce the price rise — including the associated oil production operations since, if they had continued, Esso would have had to flare the gas and incur penalties for doing so under Regulation 8. Within a month enough production was again allowed to supply the Spanish customer, who perforce submitted to the price increase.

Early in 1975 agreement was reached with Eni for a price of $1.14/mbtu to be phased in over three years, the first-year price being

$1.04/mbtu. The Spanish customer thereupon demanded similar treatment. Whether he obtained it or not was not reported. After a fall in production of LNG in 1974 of 15 per cent because of the price dispute, record exports were achieved in 1975 and again in 1976.[49]

Towards the end of 1976 Esso announced *force majeure* on its operations at Mersa Brega, since its work-force there was reduced by 25 per cent because of conscription, but no major problems appear to have developed as a result.

The gas liquefaction plant was not subjected to 51 per cent nationalisation, as were Esso's oil operations, in spite of an attempt by Esso to have this so. If it had been, Esso's compensation at net book value would have been much higher than it was, since the plant had been very costly — about $300 million of expenditure on the plant and equipment in Libya — and at the time of the nationalisations would have been little depreciated in the books of the company.

Plants for the extraction of natural gas liquids from the gas separated from crude oil at the fields were embarked upon by BP and Occidental before the revolution, and both came on stream in 1970. At Sarir the liquids so extracted were injected into the crude oil stream, thus 'spiking' it, and the gas re-injected into the fields. The spiking of crude oil normally raised its gravity, thereby increasing its value, but also raising its posted price for taxation purposes. The BP operations at Sarir added 12,000-15,000 b/d of liquids to the crude stream of about 400,000 b/d at this time.

Occidental's plant on Concession 103 had a capacity of 68,000 b/d liquid extraction, but full capacity working was seldom, if ever, reached. After 1972 the liquids were piped separately to Zueitina where they were treated and sold commercially both for domestic consumption and for export. Agip was able to use these facilities after Concession 100 started producing in late 1972. Both Agip's and Occidental's gas were re-injected.

Exports of LPG began in 1970, when 23,000 tonnes were shipped. They rose to 115,000 in 1972 and between 140,000 and 150,000 tonnes in each of the years 1973-5.[50]

As already mentioned, the problem of gas utilisation persisted, and gave rise to a number of warnings from the Ministry requiring oil producers to use it, give it to the State under Regulation 8 or suffer penalties for waste. In August 1971 when one such edict was issued, it was reported that current gas production was 1.7 billion cubic feet a day.[51] Besides the NGL operations already mentioned, which at that time produced 45,000 b/d of liquids, both Oasis and Mobil had installed gas injection wells in some of their fields. Production from Eni's new field was delayed pending satisfactory use of its gas, which was assured towards the end of 1972. For the year 1972, 55 per cent of associated gas in Libya was used or re-injected and the rest flared. By 1973 the proportion used had risen to 66 per cent.[52]

13.5 Employment, Education and Training in the Oil Industry

The movement towards replacing expatriates with Libyans in the oil industry was strongly accelerated after the revolution. Within three months a new department was established in the Ministry of Petroleum for dealing with employment and training, which also decided on applications for the admission of new expatriates and the extension of old contracts. In doing this they considered first the availability of Libyans to perform the work for which the permits were asked.

By the end of 1971 the aim of placing Libyans in 'all administrative positions such as services, personnel, accounts, materials, procurements and training' had been accomplished.[53] There was also a number of Libyans on the Boards of Directors of the oil companies. The longer-term objective of 'Libyanising' all positions of a technical nature was being pursued.

Numbers employed by the oil companies did not greatly change from 1970 to 1974,[54] but within the total there was a fall of 30 per cent in the number of expatriates. Oil company employees numbered 6,720 at the end of 1974. This figure does not include Linoco, whose management and employees were entirely Libyan, nor oil company contractors, who at the end of 1974 employed 3,626 of whom 2,476 were Libyan.[55]

In the matter of training, considerable pressure was brought on the companies to intensify their own training schemes. The evidence available suggests that the companies responded to the government requirements in on-the-job training, company courses and sponsoring employee training abroad.[56] Linoco has pursued its own training objectives through the facilities offered in joint ventures, through joining the 'Oil Companies' Training and Languages Centre' and in sending employees and scholarship-holders abroad on training courses, seminars and for higher studies at university level.

The Government established the Institute of Petroleum Affairs by Council of Ministers' decision of 26 August 1970, to give 'practical and theoretical education in petroleum affairs' at the high school level. Subsequently, in 1971, the Higher Petroleum Institute was established by Law No. 105 of 2 December, at Tobruk. The objective was to provide similar education at pre-university level. It was located at Tobruk to be near the oil installations and terminal of the pipeline from the Sarir field. It opened its doors to 200 students initially on 1 January 1973.[57]

These institutions were developed in close co-operation with the French, who had undertaken substantial practical and financial aid in the original Erap/Aquitaine joint venture of 1968. In addition a Faculty of Oil and Minerals was established at the Libyan University in 1972.

Notes

1. 'Short-haul' referred to the shorter sea voyage from Mediterranean terminals (and Nigeria to a less extent) to South Europe, North Europe and North America, compared with the longer voyage to these destinations of oil loaded in the Arabian Gulf, particularly when the Suez Canal was closed.

2. For description of AFRA see Chapter 2, section 2.4, and of Scale see Chapter 2, note 16. In 1962 'Scale' was changed to 'Intascale' and in 1969 to Worldscale (WS). After the latter change, variations from the flat rate (WS100) were expressed, without plus or minus sign, as an indexed percentage of the flat rate: e.g. WS 120 describes a freight 20 per cent higher than WS100, and WS 80 gives a rate of 20 per cent lower. By this time also there were four different quarterly AFRA awards — for general purpose tankers, medium, large range 1 and large range 2.

Worldscale 100 gave a freight advantage to Libyan oil over Arabian Gulf oil delivered in North-West Europe of approximately 85 cents/b which, according to the Petroleum Law, should be reflected in Libyan postings.

M.A. Adelman, *The World Petroleum Market* (Johns Hopkins University Press, Baltimore, 1972), p. 123, stated 'Worldscale 40 was still expected as the long-term rate as late as the end of July 1970'.

3. See Chapter 12, note 10.

4. *Petroleum Intelligence Weekly*, 24 Aug. 1970. The price information in this chapter in most cases follows that in *PIW* reports.

5. Ministry of Petroleum, Libyan Arab Republic, *Libyan Oil, 1954-1971*, p. 116. Occidental's temporary glut was probably caused by technical and logistical problems, e.g. lack of available tankers, at this period of disrupted operations.

6. The following figures of crude oil imports into the principal countries of Western Europe (W. Germany, France, Italy, UK, Netherlands, Belgium, Denmark, Spain and Sweden) illustrate the substitution of Middle Eastern for African oil in these markets:

Table 13.5: Crude Oil Imports to Principal West European Countries, 1971-6

		1971	1972	1973	1974	1975	1976
Total crude oil imports in tonnes		568	621	545	512	521	572
Proportion from North Africa	%	25.1	19.9	19.4	15.6	12.3	12.9
Proportion from Middle East	%	59.3	64.2	66.9	70.4	72.6	72.3

Source: *Petroleum Economist/Petroleum Press Service* (June 1973), p. 217; (June 1975), p. 226; (June 1977), p. 215.

7. The Libyan crude oil supplies, produced and acquired, of the five majors with Libyan interests after 1971 (Exxon, Shell, Mobil, Texaco and Socal), expressed as a proportion of their total Middle Eastern plus Libyan crude oil supplies, were as follows:

Table 13.6: Libyan Five Major Oil Companies — Crude Oil Supplies. Libyan as a Percentage of Total Middle Eastern plus Libyan, 1968-76

	Average 1968-70 %	1971 %	1972 %	1973 %	1974 %	1975 %	1976 %
Exxon	32	17	12	11	8	10	10
Shell	15	13	11	8	4	2	5
Mobil	14	8	7	4	4	4	4
Texaco	12	7	5	4	0.1	–	–
Socal	12	7	5	3	0.1	–	–

Source: *Financial and Operational Statistics*, Supplements to Annual Reports of the Companies.

8. Such reports were made in *Petroleum Intelligence Weekly* on 10 May 1971, 25 Oct. 1971, 15 Jan. 1972, 21 Feb. 1972, 19 Jun. 1972, 26 Jun. 1972, 25 Dec. 1972, 25 Feb. 1974, 20 May 1974, 19 Aug. 1974, 26 Aug. 1974, 6 Jan. 1975.

9. An acquisition cost of $8/b would be on the basis of 25 per cent participation. The higher figures would apply to 60 per cent participation which was being introduced in early 1974 and applied retroactively to 1 January 1974.

10. The pertinence of this remark, which was reported verbally to the writer, was borne out by the profit figures for 1974 of the oil companies subsequently published. These in aggregate were, over the relevant period, as shown in Table 13.7.

Table 13.7 : Profitability of Oil Companies in Operations outside the USA, 1970-6

	1970	1971	1972	1973	1974	1975	1976
Aggregate net income, $'000 millions	3.0	3.8	3.2	7.5	10.0	5.5	5.6
Return on average invested capital	11%	12%	10%	21%	24%	13%	12%

Source: Chase Manhattan Bank, *Financial Analysis of a Group of Petroleum Companies* (1977). The companies included in the analysis comprise all the majors and the US independents with substantial international operations, except Occidental and Hunt.

Occidental's profit record in international operations was as shown in Table 13.8.

Table 13.8: Net Income of International Operations, Occidental Petroleum Corporation, 1970-6

	1970	1971	1972	1973	1974	1975	1976
Net Income in $ millions:							
Production of oil and gas	79	46	42	43	101	59	80
Marketing, refining & shipping	49	35	(6)	67	(3)	(20)	(26)

Source: Company *Annual Reports*. Figures in brackets denote losses. In and before 1974 the production profits refer solely to Libyan operations.

11. *Petroleum Intelligence Weekly*, 19 May 1975.

12. *Petroleum Intelligence Weekly*, 7 Apr. 1975. Linoco itself was reported to be selling at discounts from the official price and giving 90-120 days credit in addition.

13. See Chapter 12, note 9.

14. *Petroleum Intelligence Weekly*, 5 July 1976.

15. Ministry of Petroleum, *Libyan Oil 1954-1971*, p. 16.

16. Ibid., p. 13.

17. Ibid., p. 104.

18. The information about tankers is taken from *Petroleum Intelligence Weekly*, *Petroleum Economist* and Central Bank reports of various dates.

19. *Petroleum Intelligence Weekly*, 5 July 1971.

20. Central Bank of Libya, *Economic Bulletin* (March/April 1977). The 1975/6 figures are those given by OPEC, *Statistical Bulletin*, and are higher than those of the Central Bank.

21. Central Bank, *Economic Bulletin*. Values are not given after 1972.

22. Ministry of Petroleum, *Libyan Oil, 1954-1971*, p. 113.

23. Occidental disclosed this in its *Annual Report* for 1975.

24. Ministry of Petroleum, *Libyan Oil, 1954-1971*, p. 116. The buyers, quantities contracted and delivered, and dates were as follows:

Date of Contract	Buyer	Quantity Contracted '000 tons	Delivered up to 31 Dec. 1971 '000 tons
Sept. 1970	OMV (Austrian)	300	304
Oct. 1970	Witco (Austrian)	4,700	118
Oct. 1970	Egyptian Pet. Authority	750	467
Dec. 1970	Perola S.A. (Swiss)	2,250	100
Mar. 1971	Naphthachem (Bulgarian)	1,000	493

25. *Petroleum Intelligence Weekly*, 25 June 1973.

26. These and subsequent sales and the price information were reported in the contemporary issues of *Petroleum Intelligence Weekly*.

27. Amoseas' parents − Texaco and Socal − claimed arbitration in accordance with the terms of the Petroleum Law (1965). As a result, the International Court appointed a sole arbitrator who ruled in March 1977 that the nationalisation was illegal and that the Libyan Government should implement the award before 30 June 1977. Subsequently, the Government reached agreement with the companies on compensation. *Petroleum Economist* (November 1977).

28. *Petroleum Intelligence Weekly*, 18 May 1970.

29. Ibid., 17 Jan. 1972.

30. Central Bank of L.A. Republic, *Annual Report 1973/4*, p. 145.

31. *Petroleum Intelligence Weekly*, 11 Oct. 1971.

32. Central Bank reference as in note 30 above. Ras al Hilal is on the Cyrenaican coast near Cyrene. It was not stated whether the strikes were on or off-shore. There has been no information about further development.

33. Conoco, *Annual Report*, 1975.

34. *Petroleum Economist* (November 1976), p. 425.

35. *Oil and Gas Journal*, 28 Dec. 1969.

36. De Golyer and McNaughton, *Twentieth Century Petroleum Statistics*, 1977.

37. OPEC, *Annual Statistical Bulletin*, 1977. This source also states that in 1976 Libyan crude oil production was 3.33 per cent of world production.

38. Adelman, *World Petroleum Market*, p. 217, after examining the

available evidence, suggests that the 'Persian Gulf-North African optimum lies somewhere between 10 and 15 (reserves times production), but it is safer to make it 15 to 20'.

39. Article 14, 5(b) of the Petroleum Law as amended (1965).

40. *Petroleum Intelligence Weekly*, 10 Nov. 1969. There are significant differences in the calorific values of different natural gases; as a rule of thumb one cubic foot of natural gas is often taken as producing 1,000 btu: thus, one million British thermal units (1mbtu) is taken to be roughly equivalent to one thousand cubic feet of gas. In this case the thermal value of the gas was higher than this.

41. Article 13, 1(e).

42. A widely used conversion basis is that one barrel of crude oil provides between 5.5 and 6 million btus and therefore is equivalent to between 5,500 and 6,000 cubic feet of gas. On the other hand, it might be argued that, in the case of associated gas production, the only alternative to using it was to flare it – as was done widely in the Middle East and Libya. In this case its opportunity cost at field gas separator is zero, and the total costs consist solely of those incurred in conveying it in an acceptable and usable form to the customer. If, on the other hand, the gas by re-injection could improve recovery of oil from a field, its opportunity cost would be its value for this purpose.

43. Ministry of Petroleum, *Libyan Oil, 1954-1971*, p. 100.

44. S.M. Ghanem, *The Pricing of Libyan Crude Oil* (Adams Publishing House, Malta, 1975), p. 151. Shukri Ghanem was the Chairman of this gas pricing committee.

45. *Petroleum Intelligence Weekly*, 15 Mar. 1971. The price of LNG, at 43¢ mbtu on a thermal equivalent basis, was equal to about $2.50/b of crude oil. In March 1971 Libyan 40° crude under the Tripoli Agreement was posted at $3.447/b. This was f.o.b., while the gas price was delivered. Also the gas when delivered was ready to use after re-gasification in a reticulation system, but the crude oil needed refining and distribution of products.

46. Ministry of Petroleum, *Libyan Oil, 1954-1971*, p. 100.

47. *Petroleum Intelligence Weekly*, 23 Apr. 1973.

48. *Petroleum Intelligence Weekly*, 14 Oct. 1974. On a thermal basis this price would equate a barrel of crude oil at $9-$10/b.

49. OPEC, *Annual Statistical Bulletin*, gives a figure of 3.8 billion cubic metres commercial production for 1975 and 4.0 bcm for 1976: these are equivalent to 368 and 387 m cu ft/day respectively. Libyan reserves of natural gas given by the same source amounted to 28 trillion cubic feet in 1976; this is c.200 years' supply at existing production levels.

50. Figures for 1971 exports are given in Ministry of Petroleum, *Libyan Oil 1954-1971*, p. 100, and for 1972-5 in *Petroleum Economist* (July 1977), p. 258.

51. *Petroleum Intelligence Weekly*, 16 Aug. 1971. The Central Bank of Libya in its *Annual Report* for 1972/3 states that only a small proportion of this (2 per cent) was marketed: the remainder of that reported as used was presumably either consumed in their field operations by the companies or re-injected into the fields.

52. *Petroleum Intelligence Weekly*, 11 Mar. 1974.

53. Ministry of Petroleum, *Libyan Oil, 1954-1971*, p. 139.

54. The following figures given by the Central Bank are shown in Table 13.9.

Table 13.9: Numbers of Employees of Oil Companies Holding Concession Areas, 1970-4

Classification of Employees – at Year End	1970	1971	1972	1973	1974[a] Number	Percentage of Total
(1) Libyan Employees	4,308	4,750	4,854	5,032	5,140	76.5
(a) Supervisors	1,096	1,248	1,197	1,644	1,674	24.9
(b) Skilled labourers	1,940	1,896	2,096	2,357	2,416	36.0
(c) Trainees	311	565	605	149	150	2.2
(d) Unskilled labourers	961	1,041	956	882	900	13.4
(2) Foreign Employees	2,170	2,013	2,018	1,611	1,580	23.5
(a) Expatriate (contracts)	2,010	1,849	1,863	1,449	1,415	21.0
(b) Local	160	164	155	162	165	2.5
Total:		6,478	6,763	6,872	6,643	6,720	100.0

Note: a. Totals of Libyans and foreigners are actual: details about types of jobs are estimates based on figures of the preceding year.
Source: Central Bank of Libya, *Annual Report*, 1974/5.

The above figures continue the series in Table 8.1 provided by the Ministry of Petroleum; they show the same trends, but where they overlap, these figures are consistently higher than the Ministry's. It may be assumed that they have a wider coverage – perhaps including concession-holders not in production who may be omitted from the Ministry's figures: and a different basis of computation – average annual *v.* year-end figures.

55. Ibid.
56. An account of these company activities to the end of 1971 is given in Ministry of Petroleum, *Libyan Oil 1954-1971*, pp. 139-45, with the following figures:

	1968	1969	1970	1971
(a) Libyans benefiting from training programme in Libya	1,003	971	1,011	1,156
(b) Libyans going on courses abroad (5 companies):				
(i) Training	54	85	121	308
(ii) Academic	33	25	59	51
(c) Expenditure on training Libyans (one company) – LD	196,000	162,000	287,000	275,000

57. *Petroleum Intelligence Weekly*, 1 Jan. 1973.

14 OVERSEAS RELATIONS IN PETROLEUM AFFAIRS

14.1 Organization of Petroleum Exporting Countries (OPEC)

Libya joined OPEC in 1962. Membership of this body has been highly conducive to Libya's oil interests. The OPEC background played a decisive part in Libya's adopting the 1965 amendment to the Petroleum Law, which was based on the OPEC formula. On the other side, OPEC was able to take advantage of Libyan posted price and tax rate increases of 1970 — the price rises in the oil markets engendered in this struggle and the oil shortages resulting from it greatly facilitated the 1971 Tehran settlement. This in its turn enabled Libya to make the Tripoli Agreement.

These last two events altered the price relationship of Libyan to Arabian Gulf oil, in that the former lost its competitive advantage over the latter, which it had enjoyed throughout the 1960s. Libya was thereafter content to play its part in bringing about, and to adopt, the OPEC Geneva currency settlements. But again in the second half of 1973 the great rises in market prices stemming partially from Libyan nationalisation contributed to the ending of OPEC negotiations with the oil companies, and the inauguration of the period, which has lasted to the present day, of OPEC countries forming an unchallenged cartel manipulating oil prices world-wide. Libya is a member of this organisation and benefits accordingly.

14.2 Organization of Arab Petroleum Exporting Countries (OAPEC)

Libya was a founder member of the Organization of Arab Petroleum Exporting Countries. OAPEC was established in January 1968 by three conservative Arab oil-producing countries — Saudi Arabia, Kuwait and Libya. Its aims were co-operation and close ties between members, and the safeguarding of their legitimate interests in petroleum affairs; unification of efforts to ensure the flow of petroleum to markets on equitable and reasonable terms; and the creation of a suitable climate for the capital and expertise invested in the petroleum industry in the member countries.[1]

The original membership of OAPEC was confined to Arab countries for whom oil constituted 'the major and basic source of national income'. After the revolution in Libya, the new Government applied to OAPEC for an amendment to this qualification, and this was accepted, to embrace any Arab country for whom oil constituted an important source of national income. Subsequent to this broadening of membership, Algeria, Abu Dhabi, Bahrein, Qatar and Dubai joined the original three in 1970, and Egypt, Iraq and Syria in 1972. Article 3 of the OAPEC Agreement ensures that members are bound by the ratified resolutions of OPEC, even if they are not members of OPEC.[2]

Besides attending to the specialised interests of Arab countries in oil matters, OAPEC agreed on the establishment of four companies by its members. These are:[3]

(1) The Arab Maritime Petroleum Transport Co., set up in 1972 to own and operate a tanker fleet; its authorised capital was $500 million, of which $411 million had been paid up by 1977.

(2) The Arab Shipbuilding and Repair Yard Co., 1974, with an authorised capital of $340 million, of which $270.5 million had been paid up by 1977. The company has constructed and will operate a dry dock at Bahrein for completion in 1977.

(3) The Arab Petroleum Investments Corp., 1975; authorised capital $340 million, paid up $170 million.

(4) Arab Petroleum Services Co., 1977; authorised capital $50.6 million, paid up $25.3 million.

All these companies conduct their business independently of the OAPEC Secretariat, their Boards of Directors reporting direct to shareholders. In the Transport Co. Libya's shareholding, at 13.5 per cent, was equal to that of the other OPEC members. In the Investment Co. it holds 15 per cent and in the Services Co., whose headquarters are in Tripoli, the largest single interest of 17 per cent. In the dry dock company it has only a small 1.1 per cent interest.

More recently OAPEC has launched a series of training seminars, which have taken place in Baghdad, Cairo and elsewhere. In 1979 Egypt was expelled from membership.

14.3 Arab League Petroleum Congresses

Libya had played a part in the Arab Petroleum Congresses since their inception in 1958. Their proceedings and resolutions have been generally marked by radical proposals and hostility to the major oil companies. OAPEC, with its original membership of three conservative-minded Arab countries, provided a counterbalance to the more extreme pronouncements of the Congresses. Its enlarged membership made it almost identical in representation with the Congress, and it has subsequently tended to supplant the latter in influence. The eighth Arab Petroleum Congress held in Algiers in June 1972 was notable in recommending that Arab oil-producing states take direct control of their oil industries and that they establish, through their national oil companies, direct links with countries importing Arab oil.

14.4 Co-operation with Algeria

Relations with neighbouring Algeria in so far as petroleum affairs were concerned had been friendly during the 1960s. In this period Algeria developed an aggressive and regulatory attitude to the oil companies. It joined OPEC only in 1969 and had not adopted OPEC formula arrangements. In April 1969 Algeria served notice on the companies that both posted and tax reference prices were to be increased, and in this way anticipated by several years the practices to be adopted by other OPEC countries at the end of 1973.

After the Libyan revolution, the two countries conferred on oil matters more frequently. In December 1969 a co-operation agreement was concluded 'to co-ordinate their positions and unify their efforts to create a powerful front capable of preserving the interests of the two peoples against the monopolies that exploit their riches'.[4] Since Libya was at that time beginning its efforts to obtain rises in posted prices, Algeria's influence was exerted on Libya to follow the example it had set and impose new prices on the companies. The prices decreed in Algeria earlier in the year made its oil — typically of a similar quality and gravity to Libya's — more expensive and less competitive than the latter.

In March 1970 the two countries were reported to be co-ordinating price demands, and in April they formed a joint exploration company, possibly with the hope of developments in Western Libya to join the Trapsa pipeline from the Algerian fields across the border to the coast.

The Libyan and Algerian oil Ministers were joined by their Iraqi colleague in a meeting in May 1970, called to concert the action of the three countries on oil problems. The communiqué promised 'legislative or regulatory measures' instead of the 'interminable and sterile negotiations with producing companies'.[5] Shortly thereafter the Algerian Government nationalised all the operations of Shell and Phillips in the country[6] — amounting to production of 100,000 b/d — thus leading the way among OPEC countries in this sort of action, as well as in government control of posted prices. In July of the same year Algeria ordered a 'definite and irrevocable' rise in tax reference prices (referring to the 1969 fiat which had not been implemented by the companies) and it was expected that Libya would emulate this action, albeit having a far greater assortment of companies to deal with than Algeria. The timing and tactics of the Libyan Government in their actions which followed are described in Chapter 12.

When the OPEC negotiations culminating in the 1971 Tehran Agreement began, Algeria agreed with Libya to co-ordinate their own demands separately from the main OPEC discussions. Libya in fact led with the oil companies in negotiating the Tripoli Agreement and Algeria followed by setting its prices on a par with the Libyan and following the latter in subsequent variations resulting from freight changes.

After the 1971 Tripoli Agreement the two countries were concerned with keeping oil (and gas) prices reasonably in step. This preoccupation was common to the other countries with Mediterranean-delivered oil — the short-haul crudes. These included Iraqi oil at Tripoli and Banias and Saudi Arabian at Sidon.

Algeria nationalised 51 per cent of the French companies in March 1971, with the result that, by 1972, the Algerian oil industry was 77 per cent nationalised. Thus it not only preceded Libya in nationalisation but also acquired for the State a larger percentage of oil operations than did Libya.

14.5 Other Overseas Relations

Libya's oil markets have always been, and still remain, predominantly in Western Europe, joined latterly by the USA as its oil import requirements have grown. Table 13.2, p. 279, shows the principal destinations of Libyan crude. The relationships at government and national oil company level have been strongest with France and Italy, the two largest markets across the Mediterranean. The joint-venture, production-sharing and marketing accords at this level have been mentioned in Chapter 12. The purchase of a 9.6 per cent equity interest in Fiat by Libya at the end of 1976 for $207 million plus $104 million in bonds,

which gave Libya two seats on the Fiat Board, was another manifestation of the growing ties between the two countries, which began
with an accord signed by the Prime Ministers in March 1974.

The *rapprochement* with the USSR in 1972 has also been recorded
in Chapter 13. This resulted in substantial shipments of oil to Russia
in the following two years, but not on a longer-term basis. There have
been significant exports to other East European countries, particularly
Bulgaria and Romania, on a continuing basis, as shown in Table 13.2.
In 1975 Romania and India agreed to enter Libya to conduct joint
exploration activities,[7] but it is still too early to judge what the results
of this will be.

Finally, with the discovery of substantial oil off-shore near the
Tunisian border, the problems of the off-shore boundaries between the
two countries gave rise to an acrimonious dispute which at one time
involved naval frigates in the area. The two governments agreed to
submit the dispute to the International Court of Justice at the Hague
in 1976, after Malta, whose off-shore claims extend into the contested
area, had done so. Meanwhile Libya and Tunisia have agreed to prospect for oil jointly on their Mediterranean continental shelf,[8] but no
developments have been reported up to the time of writing.

Notes

1. Article 2 of the Basic Agreement. This précis is taken from an account
given by Dr Ali A. Attiga, Secretary-General of OAPEC, to the OPEC Seminar
on National Oil Companies held in Vienna, October 1977; the Proceedings were
published by OPEC Information Department. The account is on p. 113 of this
publication.
2. Ibid., p. 115.
3. Ibid., p. 122.
4. *Petroleum Intelligence Weekly*, 15. Dec. 1969.
5. Ibid., 1 June 1970.
6. Ibid., 22 June 1970.
7. Ibid., 23 June 1975.
8. *Petroleum Economist* (November 1976).

15 THE LIBYAN ECONOMY

15.1 The Libyan Currency

In September 1971 the Libyan currency was changed from the pound to the Dinar, and one-thousandth of the Dinar was the dirham. At the same time the new currency was revalued in terms of the US dollar from a par rate of $2.80 to LD1 = $2.90. Subsequently, in February 1972 — after the Smithsonian Agreement and devaluation of the dollar in December 1971 — the Dinar was again revalued to a parity of LD1 = $3.04. This effectively left the IMF gold parity of the Libyan currency unchanged, and revalued in terms of the US dollar by the same amount, 8.57 per cent, as the dollar had been devalued.

The problems of oil company accounts and Government payments arising from changes in the LD/$ exchange rate are described elsewhere (see Chapter 12, section 12.5). In brief, the Government demanded and the oil companies resisted the compilation of fiscal accounts at the old rate, while the Libyan Dinars for tax and royalty payments derived from these accounts had to be bought at the new rates.

The Geneva settlement of February 1972 between oil companies and the OPEC Gulf States, which was finally implemented in a separate Libyan settlement in May backdated to the same effective date — 20 January 1972 — put an end to this dispute. It raised posted prices in dollars by approximately the same amount (8.49 per cent) as the dollar's formal devaluation (8.57 per cent). The oil companies' accounts were henceforth compiled at the new rate, namely $3.04 = LD1, at which the companies also had to purchase Dinars to make their payments to government.

A similar sequence of events took place in 1973, after the dollar was further devalued in February by 11.1 per cent. The Libyan Dinar retained its former gold parity and so was revalued in terms of dollars to $3.378 ($1 = LD 0.296). The second Geneva settlement of June 1973 was adopted by Libya, and this raised posted prices — which were then changing every quarter under the terms of the Tripoli and Geneva I Agreements — by a comparable amount. Subsequent to this time up to the present day the Dinar/dollar rate was unchanged. The pound sterling, to which the Libyan pound had been tied at par until 1967, when Libya was a member of the Sterling Area, was worth about 650 dirhams at the end of 1979.

15.2 Libya's Balance of Payments

The direct and primary contribution to Libya's balance of payments of the oil industry's operations before 1970 was identified as the sum total of the foreign exchange remittances of the oil companies to Libya to pay costs and expenses in Libya and royalties and taxes to the Libyan Government. The State's participation in the operations of the industry began in the summer of 1970 with sales of royalty oil overseas, and thereafter grew rapidly, until by 1976 the National Oil Company owned about 65 per cent of the crude oil produced and exported, excluding its royalty entitlement, and was receiving payment from overseas for the full value of its export sales, whether to third parties or Libyan oil companies.

The contribution of the oil sector to the country's balance of payments in these changing conditions is summarised in Table 15.1. The value of oil exports rose in each year except 1972 and 1975, in spite of falls in volume. In 1974 it doubled on a smaller volume because of the great price rises, but fell back again in 1975 owing to lower unit prices, then more than recovered its 1974 level in 1976 because of greater volume of exports.

The level of imports of oil industry equipment and materials in the years 1970-6 dwindled to about half that of the late 1960s, and this is doubtless a reflection of lower exploration and development activities. The recovery in 1975 follows the fillip given to exploration by the production-sharing deals of 1974 and other measures taken to stimulate these activities — e.g. the arrangement with Oasis in 1974 for three rigs, and the increase in Linoco's drilling activities in conjunction with Saipem.

Line (3)(a) of Table 15.1 shows income from investments in the oil sector, partly estimated by the IMF. This doubtless refers to the profits of oil companies in Libya paid as dividends to parent companies in their home countries. The highest level of these profits was probably in 1968 (see Table 11.1), after the closing of the Suez Canal had given Libyan oil a great competitive advantage in the markets of Europe. They were well sustained in the following three years, and only fell markedly in 1972. In this year Libyan oil had lost its competitive advantage in Europe, after the realignments of posted prices in 1971 had made it more expensive relative to Arabian Gulf oil, at a time of general economic recession.

During the following three years the income from investments of the Libyan oil companies rose to and remained on a modestly higher

Table 15.1: Libyan Balance of Payments — Oil Sector, 1970-6

LD Millions	1970	1971	1972	1973	1974	1975	1976
(1) Exports of petroleum	+853	+961	+809	+1,048	+2,133	+1,845	+2,545
(2) Imports — oil sector	−28	−18	−16	−13	−14	−24	−17
(3) Invisibles — oil sector:							
(a) Income from oil company investment in Libya	−197	−198	−73	−119	−126	−118	−256
(b) Other — net	−95	−61	−50	−58	−109	−78	−76
(4) Direct investment/disinvestment in Libya	+50	+50	− 4	−49	−80	−203	−164
(5) Balance of payments — oil sector	+583	+734	+666	+809	+1,804	+1,422	+2,032
(6) Line (5) as percentage of line (1)	68	76	82	77	85	77	80

Sources: Central Bank of Libyan Arab Republic, *Economic Bulletin* (March/April 1977); IMF, *Balance of Payments Yearbooks*.

level, in spite of the nationalisations. This implies that the per barrel profits of the oil remaining to the companies were substantially higher than previously — the total volumes of exports were lower in these years, as well as the oil companies' owned share of them — and sufficient to make up for the oil they bought back from the nationalised portion of their concessions, on which they made no profit in Libya at all. In 1976 the level of income from investments more than doubled over the 1975 level. This reflects the greater competitiveness of Libyan oil relative to the Gulf after the Government had narrowed the price differentials in successive stages, with the result that exports recovered to the two million b/d level before the end of the year.

The oil company payments overseas (lines (2) and (3) (b)) carry on the series of Table 11.1 (3) of their payments outside Libya for operating costs and expenses. A law of 10 July 1973 imposed control on company payments abroad, but it seems to have had little effect on the level of these payments. The edict, according to the Central Bank,[1] prohibited companies from using their funds to finance projects outside Libya,[2] and required all company commercial transactions and salaries to be paid in Dinars, and overseas payments arising therefrom to be subject to exchange control procedures. This was in conflict with the provisions of the Petroleum Law, which even at that late date was still formally observed.

The direct investment/disinvestment in Libya of the oil sector shown in line (4) (much of it estimated by the IMF) started the period with a net inward movement, which turned to an outflow in 1972 and afterwards. Initially the outward movement consisted mainly of amortisation and depreciation charges — together with some export of movable plant and equipment. The capital consumption recognised in the depreciation charges would take the form of repayment of loans to their parents out of surplus funds banked with the parents, who had financed the investment now being written down. So far as Libya's balance of payments was concerned, consumption of oil company capital was an outward movement on long-term capital account. After nationalisations took place, the figures also include the Libyan Government's compensations for nationalisation, whether in cash or oil, usually made after delays and over a period. If payments were in oil, the value of this will still be included in line (1), but it is offset in the net balance of payments by its deduction in line (4).

The net favourable balance of payments of the oil sector shown in line (5) corresponds at the beginning of the period approximately to the remittances of the oil companies to Libya for royalties, taxes and operations expenses.[3] As Linoco entered more strongly into operations, ownership and sales of oil, payments by oil companies to Libya, together with third-party payments for purchases of oil, rose in relation to total value of exports of oil. The companies still remitted money to pay for operational expenses, royalties and taxes for the parts of their concessions retained. In addition they paid 100 per cent of the export value for the nationalised oil bought back from Linoco. Moreover, Linoco began to make large sales of oil direct to third parties when conditions were favourable.

The figures suggest that from 1971 to 1976 the balance of payments net benefit from oil was on average some 80 per cent of the value of oil exports. In the years 1965-70 it was about 55 per cent. The contrast is, however, over-stated, since in the earlier period the oil was over-valued at posted prices, while much of it in the later period was valued at realised price or acquisition cost. If 15 per cent is deducted from exports valued at posted prices for 1965-70 to approximate to realised prices, the net balance of payments benefit for this period becomes 68 per cent of the realised value of oil exports.

The total balance of payments figures given in Table 15.2 show that the favourable balance of payments of the oil sector was more than adequate to meet rising imports, payments for invisibles, transfers and capital remittances abroad, except in 1973 and 1975. Exports of goods other than oil and gas were negligible throughout the period, oil exports comprising 99.8 per cent of the value of total exports.

In the outcome, Libya's foreign exchange reserves grew substantially during the period, with two setbacks in 1973 and 1975. At the end of 1976 these reserves stood at over LD 1,000 million, having risen from about £L 10 million in 1956, when oil industry operations began in earnest.

15.3 Growth in the National Income

The macro-economic aggregates depicting the Libyan economy's growth from 1971 to 1976 are given in Table 15.3. They show a trebling of the gross domestic product in money terms from LD 1.6 billion in 1971 to LD 5.0 billion in 1976. After deducting from GDP net factor payments abroad, which include oil company payments of emoluments to expatriate staff in their home countries, and of profits to parent companies, the gross national product followed the same trend, rising by over three times from LD 1.4 b in 1971 to LD 4.5 b in 1976.

Table 15.2: Libyan Balance of Payments, 1970-6

LD Millions	1970	1971	1972	1973	1974	1975	1976
(1) Exports	+856	+962	+812	+1,053	+2,135	+1,847	+2,547
(2) Imports	−241	−330	−424	−600	−1,109	−1,310	−1,369
(3) Invisibles (net) and transfers	−345	−322	−276	−387	−464	−509	−648
(4) Current account balance	+270	+310	+112	+66	+562	+28	+530
(5) Government grants	−40	−32	−34	−47	−20	−49	−28
(6) Long-term capital	+50	+46	−14	−152	−125	−461	−379
(7) Short-term capital (including unidentified movements)	−35	−15	+72	−183	+93	+22	+187
(8) Total balance of payments	+245	+309	+136	−316	+510	−460	+310
(9) Gold and foreign exchange assets — year end[a]	576	875	977	666	1,110	696	1,026

Note: a. Central Bank figures which include central and commercial banks. Charges in year-end totals do not tally with changes in balance of payments aggregates owing to exchange rate translations and other factors.
Sources: Central Bank of Libyan Arab Republic, *Economic Bulletin* (March/April 1977); IMF, *Balance of Payments Yearbooks*.

Table 15.3: Libyan Arab Republic — GDP, GNP and National Income, 1971-6, at Current Prices (LD billions ('000 millions))

		1971	1972	1973	1974	1975	1976
(1)	Gross Domestic Product of which:	1.6	1.8	2.2	4.0	3.9	5.0
(2)	Government final consumption expenditure	0.3	0.4	0.5	0.9	1.0	1.1
(3)	Private final consumption expenditure	0.5	0.6	0.7	1.1	1.4	1.5
(4)	Gross fixed capital formation	0.3	0.4	0.7	1.0	1.1	1.3
(5)	Exports, goods and services	0.9	1.0	1.2	2.5	2.1	2.8
(6)	Imports, goods and services	−0.4	−0.6	−0.9	−1.5	−1.7	−1.7
		1.6	1.8	2.2	4.0	3.9	5.0
(7)	Net factor payments abroad	−0.2	−0.3	−0.3	−0.4	−0.4	−0.5
(8)	Gross National Product	1.4	1.5	1.9	3.6	3.5	4.5
(9)	National income at market prices	1.3	1.4	1.8	3.4	3.3	4.4

The nets of items (5), (6) and (7) tie in with the current account balance of payments figures in Table 15.2; payments of factor incomes abroad, although an invisible import, is classified separately in this table as a deduction from GDP to arrive at GNP.
Sources: IMF, *International Financial Statistics*; United Nations, *Monthly Bulletin of Statistics.*

Similar trends are apparent in the disposition of the GDP between Government final consumption expenditure, private final consumption expenditure, and gross fixed capital formation. The doubling of the value of oil exports in 1974 after the great price rises was reflected in an 80 per cent increase in the GDP aggregates, and corresponding rises in government and private consumption expenditure in that and the following year, with a rather smaller boost in fixed capital formation.

Population and price movement figures are given in Table 15.4. The population is estimated to have risen by some 4 per cent a year.[4] The cost of living index for Tripoli — there is no other price index available — was influenced by substantial government subsidies, particularly for food,[5] and by price control. Indeed the price index for foodstuffs fell by 20 per cent between 1970 and 1973 and thereafter rose 28 per cent to 1976. Expenditure on most consumer goods was subject to price trends of imports; with a strong Dinar and fierce competition among overseas suppliers, the upward movement in the prices of imported consumption goods during the whole period — as evidenced by clothing, which was mostly imported — was under 20 per cent. The cost of housing, which doubled between 1970 and 1976 in spite of rent control, comprises 32 per cent of total costs in the index. Transport and communications prices (which contain automotive fuels, supplied after 1970 by the National Oil Company) rose by only 4 per cent.

The *per capita* GNP rose from LD 673 in 1971 to LD 1,731 in 1976 at current prices. If this is deflated by the rise in the cost of living, the rise in *per capita* income between 1971 and 1976 is from LD 673 to LD 1,278 at 1971 prices. Private final consumption on the same basis rose by 160 per cent *per capita* at current prices and 92 per cent at 1971 prices.

15.4 The Domestic Product by Economic Sectors

The main economic activities contributing to the GDP from 1970 to 1976 are given in Table 15.5, and the proportions of the GDP attributable to each activity are recorded in Table 15.6. To these latter have been added comparable figures for the pre-revolutionary years 1965-9, as reported in Table 11.5, p. 221.

The figures give the value of the output of each sector after deducting materials inputs, that is to say the value added by the factors of production in each activity. During the whole of the 12-year period

Table 15.4: GNP, Population and Per Capita Income and Consumption, 1971-6

	1971	1972	1973	1974	1975	1976
(1) GNP, LD '000 millions, current prices	1.4	1.5	1.9	3.6	3.5	4.5
(2) Population de jure,[a] millions	2.08	2.16	2.25	2.35	2.44	2.60[a]
(3) GNP per capita, LD	673	694	844	1,532	1,434	1,731
(4) Cost of Living Index, Tripoli (1971=100)	100	101.6	113.8	119.2	131.6	135.4
(5) GNP per capita at 1971 prices, LD	673	683	742	1,285	1,090	1,278
(6) Private final consumption, LD millions	469	543	703	1,140	1,373	1,497
(7) Private final consumption per capita LD	225	251	312	485	573	587
(8) Private final consumption per capita LD at 1971 prices	225	247	274	407	435	433

Note: a. Sc. of Libyan nationality; the 1976 figure is for total population, including foreigners; it was issued by the Libyan Census and Statistical Dept. as reported in EIU Quarterly Economic Review of Libya, March 1976.

Sources:

(1), (2), (6),   United Nations, Monthly Bulletin of Statistics.

(4)   Central Bank of Libyan Arab Republic, Economic Bulletin (March/April, 1977) (source: Census and Statistical Dept.).

(3)   (1) ÷ (2)

(5)   (3) ÷ (4)

(7)   (6) ÷ (2)

(8)   (7) ÷ (4)

Table 15.5: Libyan Gross Domestic Product by Kind of Economic Activity — 1970-6 (LD millions)

	1970	1971	1972	1973	1974	1975	1976
GDP	1,329	1,627	1,798	2,246	4,092	3,897	5,037
Agriculture	33	33	44	60	65	114	140
Petroleum and other mining and quarrying	814	930	925	1,137	2,389	1,960	2,791
Manufacturing industries	22	25	37	51	75	92	113
Electricity, gas and water	6	7	9	11	12	18	23
Construction	88	117	183	261	402	439	535
Wholesale and retail trade, restaurants and hotels	47	76	96	125	184	246	275
Transport, storage and communications	43	87	100	129	193	254	283
Other	276	352	404	472	772	774	877

The 1970 figures are revisions of those in Table 11.5.
Source: United Nations, *Monthly Bulletin of Statistics*.

Table 15.6: Economic Activities as Percentages of Gross Domestic Product, 1965-76

	1965	1966	1967	1968	1969	1970	1971	1972	1973	1974	1975	1976
GDP	100	100	100	100	100	100	100	100	100	100	100	100
Agriculture and fishing	5.0	4.3	4.0	3.1	3.1	2.5	2.0	2.4	2.7	1.6	2.9	2.8
Petroleum, mining and quarrying	54.1	54.4	53.5	60.7	62.2	61.2	57.2	51.4	50.6	58.4	50.2	55.4
Manufacturing industries	2.5	2.3	2.2	1.9	1.7	1.7	1.5	2.1	2.3	1.8	2.4	2.2
Construction	7.0	7.4	8.7	8.3	7.1	6.6	7.2	10.2	11.6	9.8	11.3	10.6
Electricity and gas	0.3	0.3	0.2	0.3	0.3	0.5	0.5	0.5	0.5	0.3	0.5	0.5
Trade, restaurants and hotels	6.6	6.7	6.4	4.2	4.0	3.5	4.7	5.3	5.6	4.5	6.3	5.5
Transport, storage and communications	3.7	3.9	4.1	3.7	3.3	3.2	5.3	5.6	5.7	4.7	6.5	5.6
Other	20.8	20.7	20.9	17.8	18.3	20.8	21.6	22.5	21.0	18.9	19.9	17.4
	100	100	100	100	100	100	100	100	100	100	100	100

petroleum production supplied more than 50 per cent of the national product. From 1968 to 1970 its contribution rose to over 60 per cent. In these years the higher figures were primarily the result of bigger volumes of oil exports. In 1971 and again in 1974, when oil's share was 57 and 58 per cent respectively, the chief factor in keeping the proportion high was price increase; and in 1976, the 55 per cent figure was contributed to by both higher volume and firm prices.

In the years that petroleum contributed a high proportion to the national product, other activities conversely accounted for a smaller share. Allowing for the influence on the figures of the predominance of petroleum, some trends are identifiable which are not materially altered by abstracting from all figures the influence of petroleum. Agricultural production did not rise as fast as the national product and so its share fell until 1975, when it recovered somewhat. This has been so in spite of lavish aid and crop increases described below (see Chapter 15, section 15.8).

Manufacturing industry has held its share, and has been helped in the later years by production from the gas liquefaction plant, the refinery and, at the end of the period, the starting up of some petro-chemical plant. The activities which have increased relative to the whole during the 1970s have been construction, transport and communications. The share of trade, though fluctuating, accounted for much the same proportion of the national product at the end of the period as it did a decade earlier.

15.5 Money, Banking and Prices

The overseas banks were subjected to majority Libyan control (51 per cent ownership of capital and two-thirds majority on management committees) by decree of November 1969. Subsequent to that time there has been a manifold increase in bank advances to the private sector and almost as large a rise in bank deposits.

Principal determinants of the money supply for the period 1969-76 are given in Table 15.7. The stock of money rose on average 28 per cent a year during these years. Until 1972 foreign assets rose faster than the money supply, but in 1973 foreign exchange reserves fell sharply, while the money supply rose by 25 per cent. The fall in foreign exchange reserves was accompanied by a big drop in Government deposits, by budgetary deficit (see Table 15.8) and by large government capital transfers overseas (see Table 15.9). Even so, the money supply remained more than 100 per cent covered by foreign exchange reserves.

Table 15.7: LAR – Money Supply Determinants, 1969-76

End of Year	1969	1970	1971	1972	1973	1974	1975	1976	Increase (1976) Minus (1969)
LD millions									
Assets of Banking System									
Foreign assets	324	572	878	966	669	1,167	690	993	+ 669
Government securities	–	–	–	–	19	24	30	44	+ 44
Advances to private sector[a]	93	96	108	151	240	448	642	762	+ 669
	417	668	986	1,117	928	1,639	1,362	1,799	+1,382
Liabilities to Banking System									
Money supply[b]	202	241	364	393	491	754	844	1,139	+ 937
Quasi-money[c]	74	80	98	175	297	579	491	552	+ 478
Government deposits	97	280	493	531	356	405	336	355	+ 258
Other (net)	44	67	31	18	–216	–99	–309	–247	– 291
	417	668	986	1,117	928	1,639	1,362	1,799	+1,382
Velocity of money[d]	0.9	0.8	0.6	0.8	1.3	1.1	1.4	1.2	–
Consumer price index (1964 = 100)	134.2	137.3	149.7	152.1	170.4	178.5	197.0	202.5	+ 47.5%

Notes: a. Includes loans for semi-government institutions.
b. Currency in circulation plus demand deposits.
c. Time and savings deposits including margins on letters of credit and guarantees.
d. Total debits to demand deposits divided by average total demand deposits.
Source: Central Bank of LAR, *Economic Bulletin* (March/April 1977).

Table 15.8: LAR Government Revenue and Expenditure, 1970-6
(LD Millions)

	Fiscal Years, April-March			Apr-Dec.	Calendar Years		
	1970/71	1971/72	1972/73	1973	1974	1975	1976
Revenues, oil	469	652	646	613	1,776	1,510	2,220
Non-oil	83	86	108	89	268	247	385
	552	738	754	702	2,044	1,757	2,605
Expenditure, ordinary	288	362	437	310	310	437	500
Development	146	248	397	545	916	1,110	1,300
	434	610	834	855	1,226	1,547	1,800

Sources: 1970-1 — 1972-3: actual expenditure figures supplied by Diwan of
Audit to Central Bank (*Economic Bulletin* (March/April 1977)).
1973-1976: budget figures reported by Central Bank and by EIU,
Quarterly Economic Reviews. The development expenditure figures
refer to the three-year plan (1973-5) and the first year of the five-year
plan (1976-80). When original figures in these plans have been revised,
the last published figure is given.

Table 15.9: Government Unrequited Transfers and Long-Term Capital
Movement Overseas, 1971-6

	1971	1972	1973	1974	1975	1976
Government unrequited transfers US $m	90	102	156	69	164	144
Government long-term capital outflow US $m	10	40	364	179	901	978
Total US $m	100	142	520	248	1,065	1,122
Total LDm	34	47	154	73	315	331

Source: IMF, *International Financial Statistics.*

In 1973 for the first time the Central Bank included, as cover for part
of the currency issue of LD 487 million, treasury bills and government
securities to a value of LD 19 million. Another factor which may have
a bearing on the money supply is hidden in the figures for 'Other (net)'
liabilities in Table 15.7. These had, until 1972, been positive, comprising among other things banks' capital and other liabilities of a long-
term nature. In 1973 this item turned strongly negative, and continued
thus in subsequent years. A negative liability is an asset, but the nature
of the net assets of the banking system thus included is not revealed.
As they have not been classified as lending to the private sector, it

seems reasonable to infer that they are associated with a public sector borrowing requirement.

In 1974, when the favourable balance of payments on oil account more than doubled, foreign exchange reserves recovered, and exceeded the supply of money by a comfortable margin of LD 400 million. The position was, however, again reversed in 1975, when a fall in revenue from oil once more resulted in an unfavourable balance of payments and a marked reduction in foreign exchange reserves. On this occasion the supply of money rose above foreign exchange reserves for the first time, and remained higher through 1976 in spite of recovery in the reserves. The government securities backing for the currency issue was raised to LD 30 million in 1975 and LD 44 million in 1976. A further fall in unclassified net liabilities, which were already negative, by LD 210 million in 1975 implied an increase of this amount in financing by banks other than for the private sector.

The movements in the determinants of the money supply suggest a major change of monetary policy in and after 1973. Hitherto money supply had risen at a slower rate than foreign assets. From 1973 the stock of money continued to rise in the face of falling, then fluctuating, exchange reserves, and this was engendered by large bank credit creation. Advances to the private sector (including semi-government institutions) as a proportion of total money supply averaged 36 per cent in the years 1970-2 and 63 per cent in 1973-6. In addition there was a marked increase from 1973 in velocity of money circulation. The great increases in bank advances in and after 1973, which include loans to semi-government institutions, reflect the greater needs of the State oil sector for bank credit, as much of the oil industry became nationalised and a larger proportion of the industry's operations was financed in Libya.

The consumer price index rose, throughout the post-revolutionary period, at an average of 5.5 per cent a year. The largest increases were in 1973 (12 per cent) and in 1975 (10.4 per cent), when the balance of payments was unfavourable. Throughout this period the plentiful exchange earnings allowed expansionary monetary policies to be pursued without excessive inflationary effects, prices being held in check by price controls and subsidies and, in the market sense, by imports which restrained them to international levels modified by import duties, subsidies and bans. The steep rises in imports up to 1974 are reflected in the increases in quasi-money, much of which corresponded to the margins (usually of 100 per cent) deposited for letters of credit, which thus took the money involved out of circulation.

Throughout the 1960s and 1970s rates of interest were stable, as would be expected of a Moslem country. The Central Bank's rediscount rate was 5 per cent and the rate for secured loans and overdrafts 7 per cent.

15.6　Employment and Unemployment

In the field of employment, it was clear even in the 1960s that indigenous manpower resources were inadequate to match the needs of a rapidly expanding oil industry and economy. The liberal attitude of the authorities to the entry of expatriate staff for management and technological guidance in the oil industry was changed after the revolution, but only sufficiently to restrain rather than to prevent its continuance.

Apart from this, there was willing acceptance of non-Libyans to work throughout the economy, from unskilled labouring to skilled professional and senior administrative work both in the public service and the private sector. People from other Arab countries provided the bulk of such workers – Egyptians, Syrians and Palestinians predominating at the senior levels and Tunisians and Egyptians in unskilled operations.[6]

After conscription of 2-3 years' service was extended to all under the age of thirty in 1976, serious shortages were evident which impeded oil operations, public administration and the fulfilment of planned development.[7] Esso, for instance, in the autumn of 1976 declared *force majeure* on contract sales of oil and gas because its Brega operations had to be shut down for a time after the loss of a significant part of its skilled work-force. The Government itself cut its own sales of Zueitina crude at about the same time, also invoking *force majeure*, and attributing it to 'low production and technical problems'.

With an abundance of foreign exchange resources to purchase overseas goods, technology and skills, and with ambitious development intentions, the greatest constraint on rapid achievement was the limited supply of the one factor of production – labour – without which the other two – capital and land – could not be adequately exploited. Throughout the three decades which are reviewed here, unemployment was negligible.[8]

15.7　Public Finance

The oil revenues were more than adequate to sustain high and growing levels of ordinary and development expenditure throughout the 1970s (see Table 15.8). During the 1960s the annual rises in oil revenues had been caused by the great increases in production at slowly rising per barrel government takes, plus the benefit of the 1968 accelerated tax payments agreement. After 1970, oil production fell, but this was offset in government revenues by rapidly rising per barrel take. In 1974 government revenue from oil rose 166 per cent to LD 1,776 million in face of a fall in oil production of over 30 per cent and, after a setback in 1975, exceeded LD 2 billion in 1976.

Revenue other than from oil also rose — by a multiple of four — from 1970 to 1976. In the early 1960s the greater part of this revenue had consisted of customs duties and stamp taxes; in 1968 a new income tax law was passed which increased the contribution of direct taxes from £L 5 million to, initially, some £L 20 million a year. After the nationalisations of the early 1970s a substantial and growing proportion of revenue was contributed by surpluses in government enterprises, amounting to over LD 100 million a year in 1975 and 1976. In 1976 total government revenues amounted to LD 1,000 a head of the population. After devoting all non-oil revenue to the ordinary budget, the need for contributions from oil for this expenditure diminished in the later years of the decade. Large sums were thus available for, and were spent on, development, as described below. Nevertheless, even after providing for all ordinary and development expenditure there were, except in 1972 and 1973, substantial surpluses. These were partly absorbed by government payments abroad in the forms of gifts, loans and investments, which are recorded in Table 15.9.

15.8 Development Plans and Expenditure

The Revolutionary Government has carried on and, with growing revenues, increased the high levels of development expenditure set in pre-revolutionary times. Distribution of appropriations among the different activities has not altered greatly. Figures of allocations are given in Table 15.10, which carries on the series of Table 11.6, p. 223.

Agriculture received a larger share of these funds than any other single function. Since 1973 a separate heading for 'integrated agricultural development' has been established, to which is devoted the greater part of the agricultural expenditure. In addition to encouragement of existing farmers by grants, credit and susbsidies, there have been many development projects undertaken, including the further

Table 15.10: Libyan Development Plans — Principal Allocations,
1971-80 (LD millions)

	April-March 1971/2	1972/3	3 Years Apr-Dec. 1973-5	5 Years 1976-80	1976 Actual Expenditure
Total appropriations	300	364	2,586	7,170	1,187
of which:					
Agriculture and agrarian)					
reform)	50	52	268	445	105
Integrated agricultural)					
development)			328	781	183
Industry and minerals	32	48	320	1,090	165
Petroleum	22	31	179	648	67
Electricity	n.a.	32	255	543	129
Transport and com-					
munications	40	47	221	·632	78
Education and training	30	40	221	470	81
Housing	40	52	368	794	138
Municipalities/local					
government	n.a.	30	194	553	110
Public health	17	14	66	171	28

Sources: 1971/2: Ministry of Petroleum, *Libyan Oil, 1954-1971*.
Remainder: OPEC, 'Opec Member Country Profile: Socialist People's Libyan
Arab Jamahiriya', *Opec Bulletin Supplement*, vol. X, no. 4, 29 January 1979;
EIU, *Quarterly Economic Reviews*. The Plans are reviewed annually and, since
1973, the development budget has been extended by adding one new year
annually on the 'roll-over' principle. Where figures have been revised the latest
known published figure is used.

enlargement of the Kufra schemes and the beginning of one at Sarir.
These should provide valuable experience in desert agricultural development for use elsewhere in the world, although on purely economic
grounds the likelihood of achieving a return on the investment is
remote.[9] In the 1976-80 five-year development budget, it is planned
to bring a further 700,000 hectares under cultivation.

In view of the large amounts contributed to agriculture in the
development plans, results have been superficially somewhat dis-
appointing, and there has been some criticism of progress and
efficiency.[10] In these years the value added by agriculture has been
unimpressive in comparison with the money devoted to it in the
ordinary and development budgets, even after discounting those funds
spent on 'integrated agricultural development', such as Kufra, results
from which can be expected only in the medium or long term.

Nevertheless some progress has been achieved. The Minister of
Economy claimed, at the end of 1975, that the three-year development

plan 1973-5 had been completed, and that production of wheat and barley, and of meat, had all doubled – the former to 323,000 tonnes in 1975, the latter to 46,000 tonnes.[11] Colonel Qadhafi himself at the General People's Congress of November 1976 announced a harvest of 369,000 tonnes of wheat and barley in 1976 and targets of 440,000 for 1977.[12] A review of Libyan agriculture in early 1976 comments that 'the Libyan Government is in a hurry to effect a green revolution which will at once reoganize, and increase, the productivity of the agricultural sector'.[13]

In manufacturing industry the figures for value added suggest that a major return on the large sums invested in the development budgets is still to come. In the same speech as mentioned above, Colonel Qadhafi stated that 74 industrial enterprises had been founded since the revolution, of which 24 were for food processing, 8 for textiles and 6 for chemicals. The latter include petrochemical plants in the Brega industrial complex.

A report of early 1976[14] on the economic performance of the country described it as an 'erratic progression towards state capitalism'. There were, it stated, no financial constraints on development, but its success was limited by deficiencies in the infrastructure and by shortages of manpower. The limit of physical and administrative capacity to handle more imports had been reached. The ports were congested, and the expulsion of many thousands of foreign workers was debilitating the production process. The prospect of nationalisation of trade discouraged enterprise and private investment, and at that time there was a marked contraction of import orders attributed to these causes. These comments must be balanced against another from the same source[15] in the same year that the three-year development plan, 1973-5, recently completed, had 'achieved a certain success'.

The five-year development plan, 1976-80, was endorsed by the General People's Congress, consisting of 980 members, which was summoned in November 1976. The Congress, whose members were elected by people's committees and professional syndicates, had been established as a body with legislative powers by Colonel Qadhafi on 1 September 1976 – the seventh anniversary of the revolution.

At the same time further changes in constitutional structure, announced in September by Colonel Qadhafi, were endorsed. The Revolutionary Command Council relinquished its authority and the General People's Congress was to appoint Prime Minister and Ministers. The Cabinet was renamed the Secretariat, the Prime Minister Secretary-General and Ministers Secretaries. The driving forces behind government, in which Colonel Qadhafi holds no office of state, were to be the broad masses organised in people's committees and professional syndicates.

Notes

1. *Annual Report*, 1973/4, p. 140.
2. It is difficult to envisage how this could be effective, since once surplus funds of Libyan oil companies have been paid as dividends or repayment of loans to shareholding parent companies, they are outside Libyan jurisdiction.
3. This series continues that of Table 11.1, for total oil company payments in Libya. The figure for 1970 in Table 15.1 of LD 583 million compares with £L569 million for the same year in Table 11.1. The difference is partly explained by the different definitions in the two tables (oil company operations in the one and oil industry in the other) and partly by the difference in sources and timing of records as explained in Chapter 11, note 3, and by subsequent revisions to figures. The same applies to the total balance of payments figures for 1970 in Tables 15.2 and 11.2; in addition translations of currency values have been made at rates of exchange which were subject to variation.
4. A census in 1973, reported in the ILO *Yearbook of Labour Statistics*, gave the following figures of population of LAR as at 31 July 1973:

	Total No.	Active No.	Percentage Active
Male	1,191,846	504,264	42.3
Female	1,057,376	36,910	3.5
	2,249,222	541,174	24.1

5. See Central Bank, *Economic Bulletin* (Oct.-Dec. 1975). Also EIU, *Quarterly Economic Review* (of Libya) (1st Quarter, 1975), where it is stated that the food subsidies programme for 1975 amounted to LD 105m.
6. See EIU, *Quarterly Economic Review* (3rd Quarter, 1976). This reports official figures published as giving a total population of 2.6 million, of which 691,000 were in registered employment. Of these nearly 50 per cent – 337,000 – were residents from other countries, who included 229,000 Arabs, 8,000 Yugoslavs, 6,000 Turks, 3,000 Romanians, 3,000 British and 2,000 each of Italians, Greeks and Americans. At this time disputes with Egypt and Tunisia resulted in the expulsion of many of their nationals, there being in all about 200,000 Egyptians and 50,000 Tunisians in the country. At the same time the Minister for Social Affairs intimated that there were vacancies in the work-force for 250,000 Turks. There was a law promulgated in 1975 which encouraged the immigration of skilled Arab workers.
7. These shortages and the administrative and operations problems arising from them are referred to in the EIU, *Quarterly Economic Review* in almost every issue from no. 2 of 1976 onwards.
8. ILO Geneva, *Year Book of Labour Statistics* (1976), gives the following figures for unemployment:

Year	No.	Year	No.
1967	680	1970	2,580
1968	460	1971	1,340
1969	420	1972	5,310

9. J.A. Allan, 'The Kufra Agricultural Schemes', *The Geographical Journal*, vol. 142 (March 1976), p. 55.

10. E.g. in the Central Bank *Economic Bulletin* (Oct.-Dec. 1975), in which it was reported, among other things, that 15 per cent of cereal and other crops were wasted by being left in the ground, and that production continued to lag behind local demand.

11. EIU, *Quarterly Economic Review* (for Libya) (1st Quarter, 1976).

12. Ibid. (1st Quarter, 1977).

13. Allan, 'Kufra Agricultural Schemes'.

14. EIU, *Quarterly Economic Review* (2nd Quarter, 1976).

15. Ibid. (1st Quarter, 1976).

16 EPILOGUE

In this concluding chapter a summation is attempted of the findings of the preceding work under each of the three aspects of the Libyan oil industry enumerated in its preface — government-company relations, the petroleum markets and the Libyan economy.

16.1 Government — Oil Company Relations

There are a number of perspectives from which to view government — company relations in general, and those in Libya in particular. One is ideologically tinted, and detects in them the rise and fall of the neo-colonialism of the oil companies, and their unsuccessful striving to impose a new era of capitulations on the country whose riches they sought to exploit.

A second view — more political than economic — concentrates on the weapons available to each of the parties in what is seen as an on-going conflict. The companies had a banner rather than weapons — the sanctity of contract under the aegis of international law interpreted by impartial tribunals. Their decisions to embark on huge and irreversible investments could be made only in the reasonable expectation of security of their operations and property from arbitrary intervention and seizure. The host country, however, was well armed. The exercise of sovereignty, together with the principle of changing circumstances enunciated by OPEC in 1968,[1] justified in its eyes the adaptation of the concession contracts to these by new laws and other measures. Supported by the panoply of State power within its boundaries, and by recognition and validation in international councils, sovereignty was bound to prevail over the sacred immutability for fifty years of contracts, the terms of which were fast becoming incongruous with the economic realities of energy needs in the outside world. The home governments of the oil companies, though concerned to protect the interests of their nationals overseas, were no longer willing, if able, to do so by force, both because of their commitment in the United Nations and elsewhere to refrain from intervention in the internal affairs of other countries, and their accountability to electorates sensitive to the dangers of, and already hurt by, involvement overseas.

A third view is one of economic pragmatism. The oil resources of Libya were indisputably the property of the nation before their discovery. The concession contracts defined the price at which the Government was willing to sell the country's oil resources to the world through the medium of the concessionary oil companies. The original bargain was a very unequal one — an inexperienced government treating with sophisticated companies equipped with complete information, as well as the resources of capital and skills without which the oil would never be recovered at all. In the case of Libya the 1955 Law attempted only to define this price as 50 per cent of the oil companies' profits, whatever they might be deemed to be. The 1961 and 1965 Amendments tried to establish it — without the support of most-favoured-nation protection — as 50 per cent of posted prices less operating costs; the posted price being derived from those of other oil-producing countries, with adjustments for different gravity, quality and freights so as to equalise the values of the various oils at a common consuming country destination.

In the 1960s the disputes between Government and companies were largely centred around the interpretation of these legal provisions. With the Law, and respect for the Law, as it then was, it was difficult, if not impossible, for Government views to prevail over the oil companies short of arbitration, which was eschewed by both parties. The companies *de facto* dictated the price received by the nation for the oil they took by their control over posted prices, their superior knowledge of operations and markets, their overwhelming possession of financial and technical resources, and their built-in resistance to changes adverse to themselves, when armed with guaranteed contractual rights not to be touched without their own consent, plus the protection of 'most-favoured-company' treatment.

The collapse of the oil company front in the 1970s, and the part played by Libya's Revolutionary Government in bringing it about, have been described in the text of the book now drawing to its close. The OPEC countries have wrested from the oil companies their control over prices of crude oil, the management decisions on operations and the ownership of much of their investments. Libya no longer has to assail the companies' impregnable stone wall on posted prices, but manages them itself without fear of resistance, as well as tax and royalty rates, company buy-back prices and direct sales to third parties of a significant portion of its oil production. This is done by 'fine-tuning' so as to keep Libyan oil competitive in world markets with that of other OPEC countries at desired levels of production, with the object of maximising the country's oil revenues.

The oil companies have adapted themselves to this way of life and business, and are flourishing as never before. While they were still fighting to the best of their ability losing battles against nationalisation and the relinquishment of price management, in Libya some were already negotiating and concluding production-sharing deals to obtain the ownership of new crude at bare cost of production, in exchange for financing and carrying out exploration, and developing and operating new fields as government agents and contractors. In this way they kept new investment at risk to a minimum, while the Government went some way to counter the menace to the future caused by withering investment in new exploration and development.

The oil companies are still needed by oil-producing countries to perform the downstream operations and to market their oil products throughout the world. The influence of the majors in the markets remains predominant, though somewhat impaired compared with a decade or two ago. It is reasonable to expect that they – together with American independents and European State companies – will continue to be the principal customers of the oil-producing countries, whose national oil companies have only a negligible stake in downstream operations. In addition they still carry out the greater part of the crude oil production operations – 85 per cent of the total in Libya is done by American companies and the remainder jointly by the National Oil Company and European State companies.[2]

Investment for the future gives most cause for concern. The companies virtually stopped new exploration and development in Libya in the early days of the revolution, and have since confined it to the minimum required to safeguard their existing position, apart from the production-sharing ventures already mentioned. These latter require the National Oil Company to finance the State's 85 per cent share of development costs. The financial capability to do so on a large scale is not disputed, backed as it is by the high oil revenues of the present day. The NOC also has its own ventures to finance, and there may well be misgivings about the administrative implementation of forceful oil development programmes. In the most recent 'Transformation Plan' (the word adopted for development budgets) large sums have been allocated to the general heading of 'Industry and Minerals'.[3] The translation of these plans into the provision at the right time of adequate funds for effective exploration and development of new oil resources remains to be seen. The decisions on such expenditure are in the hands of government not solely concerned with oil, as are the oil companies, but with the whole range of possible uses of funds in accordance with changing priorities of political and economic policies. These considerations, in Libya and elsewhere, may put greater constraint on future world oil supplies than those of the prospective physical exhaustion of commercially exploitable oil.

16.2 Libya and Petroleum Markets

In its early years of production — 1962-4 — Libyan oil contributed to a weakening of oil prices in Europe, partly because of price-cutting and other measures taken by two of the Oasis companies — Continental and Marathon — to obtain footholds in the markets. Even so, this influence was no stronger than that of the growing low-priced Russian exports to Europe of that time. Throughout the rest of the decade of the 1960s Libyan oil, because of its cheapness in relation to its quality and nearness to Europe, and as a result of the rapid increases in its exports, probably kept market prices lower than they would otherwise have been. After the closure of Suez in 1967, which completely altered the cost of Arabian Gulf oil delivered in Europe, the increases in Libyan exports had a moderating influence on prices, and certainly helped to bring them down to earlier levels sooner than otherwise would have been expected. But Libyan production was not the only factor in this; the emergence of the very large crude carrier to bring Arabian Gulf oil round Africa also played a significant part.

Conversely, the withdrawal of some Libyan oil by the cut-backs imposed in 1970, together with the closing of Tapline, had the opposite effects. The falling of the axe on short-haul oil sent freights soaring. Independent refiners, insecure of their crude supplies, bid excessively high prices for any crude available, in fear of a dearth which would put them out of business. Their costs were soon reflected in rising product prices, which the integrated companies were not reluctant to follow.

The rises justified the posted price increases, and gave the opportunity for the tax rate increases subsequently imposed. They created new levels of market prices which in effect were irreversible, though subject to mild erosion when crisis conditions faded. This pattern of events has, at the time of writing, been twice repeated — in 1973/4 and 1978/9 — each time with greater intensity.

Libya's influence in stimulating the price movements of the years 1970 and 1971 was paramount. In 1973 and after, when OPEC took the bit between its teeth, Libya was obliged, if not contented, to go along with the other members, but always aiming for the top end of the price rises. Even so, the aggressive nationalisation measures pursued from mid-1973 in Libya set the pace for and provided a powerful stimulant to the expectations and actions which culminated in the quintupling of prices in that year. Thereafter Libya was obliged to moderate its price targets, which at first made its oil uncompetitive with that from the Gulf, in order to bring its flagging production up again to the desired level of 2 million b/d.

These great changes have, ironically enough, resulted in much-enhanced profits for the oil companies. To attribute this phenomenon to once-only stock profits each time crude oil prices rise does not reveal the whole story. In the 1960s a conventional view was that oil company profits were being squeezed between consuming country governments' repression of product prices and producing countries' insatiable tax demands. This was never really the case; the fact that any significant increases in costs of delivered crude oil — such as those of freights in 1956, 1967 and 1970 — more or less immediately found their way into higher product prices in the markets demonstrated even then that there was no effective resistance, governmental or otherwise, to cost-push price enhancement.

Price rises from higher freights, the profits from which accrued mainly to the oil companies, could also be achieved by host governments raising their share of the proceeds of oil company exports. In the 1970s decade this goal has been achieved in an unexpectedly devious way. It was demonstrated by events that there was no effective price resistance by consumers to price increases resulting from supply shortages, in a commodity so price-inelastic and income-elastic as oil. Imposed and contrived cut-backs of crude production — and even anticipation of them — especially of short-haul oil, sparked off price rises which gave full justification in law and the terms of the concession contracts to host governments' demands for higher posted prices from which to derive and increase their oil revenue.

In times of supply shortage and general inflation the gaps between product realisations in the market and crude costs to the companies have invariably widened. Each time prices rise, oil companies with crude oil resources in non-OPEC countries, as well as those fortunate enough to own or have access to crude in the lower-cost OPEC countries, have reaped a rich harvest. They have learned that they do not have to fight the producing country governments to keep down taxes on and prices of crude oil for survival; but rather to strengthen their operating margins and markets as the downstream agents of the OPEC countries.

16.3 The Libyan Economy

A large oil production and export industry may reasonably be expected to bring to a country with a small population such as Libya wealth and prosperity. The macro-economic measures available to assess these expectations confirm their fulfilment. More than adequate foreign exchange resources, a trebling of *per capita* real national income and of personal consumption in face of a fast-growing population, negligible unemployment, a stable currency and comparatively stable prices all demonstrate growing wealth and infer increasing prosperity.

The revenue from oil has placed large resources at the disposal of the State for allocation to the development of agriculture, industry and public works, for economic and social welfare, and for overseas aid and investment. So far as the last category is concerned, the choice has been governed by the ideologies of the decision-makers, and an understandable desire to help other Islamic developing countries, particularly in problems of oil payment after the great price rises of 1973. The influence and prestige of Libya in these areas has increased accordingly.

To economic development in Libya great funds have been allocated and progress made. The returns on agricultural and industrial investment and the net benefits of public-sector capital expenditure can only be modest on average, in view of the limited availability of the factors of production other than capital, namely fertile and well watered land, skilled labour and managerial experience and talent. The last two have been bought in extensively from abroad. That the capital stock and resources of the nation in their broadest meaning have improved and are improving is indisputable.

It is beyond the scope of this book to pass judgement on the intangibles of personal welfare and well-being. Between the 1960s and the 1970s there has been in Libya a transition from a market economy to one which is substantially State-controlled and centrally directed; and from a western style of living to a more directed and corporate type of society — a society governed in both decades by Islamic principles and the spirit of Islamic law.

The new form of governance, mentioned at the end of Chapter 15, came into being in 1977. Colonel Qadhafi claimed that it was a triumphant synthesis of capitalism and Communism, and a perfection of democracy hitherto reached only in ancient Greece. The Libyan Arab Republic was to be known henceforth as the 'Socialist People's Libyan Arab Jamahiriya'.

16.4   Postscript

At the end of the decade of the 1970s, little change in policies, practices and operations is reported from Libya. Oil production has hovered for the three years since 1976 at the 2 million b/d level, in spite of efforts in 1977 and after to boost it to 2.4m b/d or higher. For most of 1979 it has been above 2m b/d, and the Minister of Petroleum has predicted[4] an increase of 100,000 b/d in 1980.

In the second half of 1979 attention has been concentrated by the authorities on increasing exploration and improving production from existing fields. Action has been foreshadowed against operators failing to implement adequate secondary and tertiary oilfield recovery programmes. More significant are plans to terminate sales contracts with existing operators and award them to others who will undertake exploration in new production-sharing ventures. Of these the Minister has stated[4] that more than a dozen are nearly ready to start, involving expenditure of $1billion over the next five years, with companies from Europe, east and west, and from America.

The events of 1978 and 1979 in Iran and elsewhere, which have caused shortages and generally steep rises in oil prices, have resulted in great advantage for Libya. The official price for Zueitina 40° crude was raised in stages to a basic $30/b by the beginning of 1980, with premia and surcharges bringing it to $34.72/b. The price rises have been followed by other OPEC countries, but Libya retains its lead in this respect. Libyan oil, as always, enjoys a price premium because of its high quality and nearness to markets, particularly the USA where, at the time of writing, 40 per cent of its exports are being delivered.

Notes

1. Resolution No. XVI. 90, 25 June 1968, claiming 'reasonable participation' in concession contracts with no provision for it.
2. See Chapter 12, note 48.
3. See Table 15.10, p. 320.
4. *Petroleum Economist*, November 1979.

SELECT BIBLIOGRAPHY AND REFERENCES

Books

Adelman, M.A. *The World Petroleum Market* (Johns Hopkins University Press, Baltimore, 1972)

Allan, J.A. 'Managing Agricultural Resources in Libya: Recent Experience', *Libyan Studies* (London, 1979)

—, 'The Kufra Agricultural Schemes', *The Geographical Journal*, vol. 142 (March 1976)

—, McLachlan, K.S. and Penrose, E.T. *Libya: Agricultural and Economic Development* (Cass, London, 1973)

Arabian Gulf Exploration Company *Petroleum Agreements* (Benghazi, 1973)

de Chazeau, M.G. and Kahn, A.E. *Integration and Competition in the Petroleum Industry* (Yale University Press, New Haven, 1959)

D.B. Eiches, 'Libya' in *A History of Exploration for Petroleum* (American Association of Petroleum Geologists, 1975)

El Fathali, O.I., Palmer, M. and Chaikerian, R. *Political Development and Bureaucracy in Libya* (Lexington Books, Massachusetts, 1978)

Frank, H. *Crude Oil Prices in the Middle East* (Praeger, New York, 1966)

Frankel, P.H. *Essentials of Petroleum* (Chapman and Hall, London, 1969)

Ghanem, S.M. *The Pricing of Libyan Crude Oil* (Adams Publishing House, Malta, 1975)

Hartshorn, J.E. 'From Tripoli to Tehran and Back', *The World Today* (July 1971)

—, *Oil Companies and Governments*, 2nd edn (Faber and Faber, London, 1967)

—, 'Oil Diplomacy: The New Approach', *The World Today* (July 1973)

Ibrahim Hangari, *The Libyan Petroleum Law, 1955, as Amended up to 1965* (Tripoli, 1966)

Jacoby, N.H. *Multinational Oil: A Study in Industrial Dynamics* (Macmillan, London, 1974)

Jenkins, C. *Oil Economists' Handbook* (Applied Science Publishers, London, 1977)

Kubbah, A.A.Q. *Libya – Its Oil Industry and Economic System* (Rihani

Press, Beirut, 1964)

The Libyan General Petroleum Corporation *The Objectives of the Corporation and its Law* (Tripoli, 1968)

Longrigg, S.H. *Oil in the Middle East*, 3rd edn (Oxford University Press, Oxford, 1968)

Madelin, H. *Oil and Politics* (Saxon House/Lexington Books, London, 1975)

Ministry of Petroleum Affairs *Petroleum Development in Libya, 1954 through 1964* (Tripoli, 1965)

Ministry of Petroleum Affairs, Kingdom of Libya, *Libyan Oil, 1954-1967* (Tripoli, 1968)

Ministry of Petroleum, Libyan Arab Republic, *Libyan Oil, 1954-1971* (Tripoli, 1973)

OPEC *Selected Documents of the International Petroleum Industry* (Information Dept., OPEC, Vienna), published for individual OPEC member countries over a number of years; *Libya, pre-1966*, pub. 1977

Al Otaiba, M.S. *OPEC and the Petroleum Industry* (Croom Helm, London, 1975)

Pelt, A. *Libyan Independence and the United Nations* (Yale University Press, New Haven, 1970)

Penrose, E.T. 'The Development of Crisis' in 'The Oil Crisis in Perspective', *Proceedings of the American Academy of Arts and Sciences*, vol. 104, no. 4 (Fall 1975)

—, *The Growth of Firms, Middle East Oil and Other Essays* (Cass, London, 1971)

—, *The Large Firm in Developing Countries* (Allen and Unwin, London, 1968)

Petroleum Commission *Petroleum Development in Libya, 1954 through 1958* (Tripoli, 1959)

Rifai, T. *The Pricing of Crude Oil: Economic and Strategic Guidelines for an International Energy Policy* (Praeger, New York, 1974)

Schurr, S.H. and Holman, P.T. *Middle East Oil and the Western World* (American Elsevier Publishing Co., New York, 1971)

Stocking, G.W. *Middle East Oil* (Vanderbilt University Press, Nashville, Tennessee, 1970)

Tugendhat, C. and Hamilton A. *Oil – the Biggest Business*, rev. edn (Eyre Methuen, London, 1975)

US Federal Trade Commission *The International Petroleum Cartel* (Washington, DC, 1952)

US Senate, *Hearings before the Subcommittee on Multinational Corporations (Church Committee) of the Committee on Foreign*

Relations on Multinational Petroleum Companies and Foreign Policy, 93rd Congress (Washington, DC, 1974)

World Bank Mission *The Economic Development of Libya* (Johns Hopkins University Press, Baltimore, 1960)

Principal References to Annual and Other Publication of an On-going Nature

Central Bank of Libya (previously National Bank of Libya, then Bank of Libya), *Annual Reports, Economic Bulletins* (*c*. quarterly)

Chase Manhattan Bank, New York, *Financial Analysis of a Group of Petroleum Companies*: annual publication

De Golyer and McNaughton, *Twentieth Century Petroleum Statistics*

First National City Bank, New York: monographs, esp. *Oil Prospects and Profits in the Eastern Hemisphere* (1961)

International Monetary Fund (IMF) *International Financial Statistics* (monthly), *Balance of Payments Yearbooks*

Oil and Gas International Yearbooks (Skinner's), London

Oil companies: individually, including Amerada-Hess, BP, Continental, Exxon, Gulf, Marathon, Mobil, Occidental, Royal Dutch/Shell, Socal, Texaco Annual Reports: Financial and Operational Statistical Supplements: Returns and Reports to the New York Securities and Exchange Commission

OPEC, Vienna: Resolutions of the OPEC conferences; *Annual Review and Record*; Proceedings of Seminars; *Annual Statistical Bulletin*; various publications of the Information Department

Principal References to Journals and Periodicals

Arab Oil and Gas Paris (esp. 16 June 1979 issue containing article on 'Oil, Gas and Economic Development in Libya')

Econonomist Intelligence Unit, Quarterly Reviews (Libya, Malta, Tunisia)

Middle East Economic Survey (*MEES*), weekly, Beirut

Oil and Gas Journal and *Oil and Gas International* (later *Petroleum and Petrochemical International*), weekly, Tulsa

Petroleum Economist, formerly *Petroleum Press Service*, monthly, London

Petroleum Intelligence Weekly (*PIW*), New York

Petroleum Review, Institute of Petroleum, monthly, London
Platt's Oilgram News Service and *Platts Oilgram Price Service*, daily,
    New York

INDEX